A Grammar of Christian Faith

A Grammar of Christian Faith

Systematic Explorations in Christian Life and Doctrine

Volume I

JOE R. JONES

ROWMAN & LITTLEFIELD PUBLISHERS, INC.
Lanham • Boulder • New York • Oxford

ROWMAN & LITTLEFIELD PUBLISHERS, INC.

Published in the United States of America
by Rowman & Littlefield Publishers, Inc.
4720 Boston Way, Lanham, Maryland 20706
www.rowmanlittlefield.com

12 Hid's Copse Road
Cumnor Hill, Oxford OX2 9JJ, England

British Library Cataloguing in Publication Information Available

Library of Congress Control Number: 2002104284

ISBN 0-7425-1310-6 (cloth : alk. paper)
ISBN 0-7425-1311-4 (pbk. : alk. paper)

Printed in the United States of America

♾️™ The paper used in this publication meets the minimum requirements of
American National Standard for Information Sciences—Permanence of Paper for
Printed Library Materials, ANSI/NISO Z39.48-1992.

To Sarah

Companion in Adventures of
Faith, Love, and Hope

Contents

Preface   xi
Abbreviations   xvii

Volume I

1. **The Context and Task of Christian Theology**   1
   Language, Grammar, and Understanding   4
   On Clarifying the Concepts of Pragmatics and Practice   14
   Some Basic Theses about Language   17
   Proposals for the Meaning of 'Theology'   19
   A Theological Definition of the Church   25
   The Church's Witness as Summoned to Accountability   30
   The Task of Systematic Theology   35
   Systematic Theology, Dogmatics, and Apologetics   42
   The Dialectic between Church and World   47
   Some Diagnostic Points about the Situation of the North American
      Church and the World Today   53

2. **Revelation and the Knowledge of God**   57
   Biblical Notes   58
   Notes from Traditions   63
   Interlude: Some Diagnostic Notes about Knowings   70
   Epistemology and Confessional Theology   76
   The Grammar of God's Self-Revelation in Jesus Christ   79
   God's Self-Revelation, the Bible, and Human Discourses and
      Practices   86
   The Grammar of Faith as Knowledge of God   88
   Knowledge of God Apart from God's Special Self-Revelations   96
   Jesus Christ and Continuing Revelation in the Church   100
   Further Notes on the Christian Grammar of 'Truth'   101

3. **Sources and Norms of Theology as Dialectical
   Confession and Profession**   111
   Theology and the Presiding Model of the Gospel   111

The Basic Sources of Theology   114
The Bible as the Church's Holy Scripture   121
Church Traditions   131
Grammar and the Development of Doctrine   135
Theology as the Discourse of Dialectical Confession and
    Profession   141

4. The Triune God   **149**
Language about God   153
Patriarchy and 'Father' Language   158
Some Notes from Church History   166
Puzzles in the Contemporary Discussions of Trinity   174
The Grammar of God's Self-Identifications: The Economic Trinity   180
The Grammar of God's Unity, Multiplicity, Relationality,
    and Complexity   189
The Grammar of God as the Triune One Who Loves in Freedom   198
The Grammar of God's Essence and God's Actuality   204
The Grammar of the Immanent Trinity   212
The Grammar of God's Essential Attributes   215
The Grammar of God's Self-Determined Relational Attributes   225
The Grammar of God's Transcendence and Immanence   230

5. God the Creator: Creation, Providence, and Evil   **233**
Orientation to the Doctrine   233
Biblical Notes   241
Basic Elements of the Grammar of God the Creator   244
The Grammar of the Providence of God   259
Further Issues in the Grammar of God's Action in Relation
    to the World   264
The Grammar of Evil and Theodicy   276
Creation Pragmatics   290

6. Human Being as Created and Sinful   **293**
Human Being as Creaturely Being: Creature among Creatures   296
Human Being as Personal Being: Person among Persons   300
Human Being as Spiritual Being: Spirit among Spirits   322
Jesus the True Human Being   336
Preliminary Observations on Human Sin   343
Knowledge of Sin in Jesus Christ   345
The Origin of Sin   352
Exploring the Multiple Shapes and Faces of Sin   356
The Consequences of Sin and Jesus Christ   362

Volume II

7. The Person of Jesus Christ · 365
Orientation to Christology · 365
Some Problems of Faith and History · 370
A Theological/Historical Schematic Narrative of the Actual Jesus · 381
The Grammar of Christological Titles in the New Testament · 385
Notes from Church History · 393
The Grammar of the Identity of the Human Jesus as the
Incarnate God · 402
The Grammar of Jesus' Identity as the Messianic Bearer of the Spirit · 419
Some Further Questions · 422

8. The Work of Jesus Christ · 427
Some Elements of the New Testament Witness · 429
Atonement Issues and the Salvific Work of Jesus · 433
The Grammar of Jesus the Prophet · 435
The Grammar of Jesus the Priest · 443
The Grammar of Jesus the Victor · 458
The Grammar of Jesus' Work and Human Salvation · 473
Narrative and the Rationale of God's Salvific Work · 480

9. The Doctrine of the Holy Spirit · 483
The Trinitarian Context of the Doctrine · 483
The Witness of Scripture · 485
Notes from Tradition · 492
A Constructive Grammar of the Holy Spirit · 495
A Schematic Grammar of Salvation · 503

10. The Christian Life · 511
The Grammar of Just Deserts and Justification by Grace · 513
The Grammar of Faith and the Christian Life · 519
The Grammar of Christian Freedom · 528
The Grammar of Sanctification · 537
The Grammar of Discipleship · 545
The Grammar of the Works and Passions of Agapic Love · 553
The Grammar of Christian Vocation · 588
Summary · 590

11. The Doctrine of the Church · 593
Images of the Church in the New Testament · 596

Notes from Church History   602
Basic Ecclesial Grammar   609
The Ecclesial Grammar of the Practices of the Body of Christ   617
The Nurturing Practices of the Body of Christ   623
The Outreach Practices of the Body of Christ   627
The Administrative Practices of the Body of Christ   634
The Ecclesial Grammar of Unity, Diversity, and Boundaries   645
The Dialectic between Church and World   648

12. Proclamation, Sacraments, and Prayer   **655**
The Grammar of Proclamation   656
The Grammar of 'Sacrament'   658
The Grammar of Baptism   662
The Grammar of the Lord's Supper   670
The Grammar of Prayer   676

13. Christian Hope and Eschatology   **689**
The Grammar of Hope as a General Human Phenomenon   691
The Grammar of Christian Hope as Eschatological Existence   695
The Grammar of Hope and Historic Redemption: Everyday Futurity   697
The Grammar of Hope and Historic Redemption: Works of Love
    and the Kingdom of God   699
Interlude: Is There a Dual Destiny?   709
The Grammar of Hope and Ultimate Redemption: Death and
    Eternal Life   724
The Grammar of Hope and Ultimate Redemption: The End of
    All Things in God's Absolute Future   736

Bibliography   749
Index of Subjects   765
Index of Names   779
Index of Scripture References   783
About the Author   795

Preface

This text arises out of more than four decades of my engagement in theological education, as student, professor, and administrator. Its present shape originates in teaching a yearlong course in systematic theology beginning in 1990 at Christian Theological Seminary in Indianapolis, Indiana. After sojourning for seventeen years in university and seminary administration, I eagerly embraced this opportunity to teach theology again in the classroom. Team-teaching variously with Edward Towne and Clark Williamson, we followed a traditional ordering of topics, which persists into the present text. Initially I began the practice of distributing lecture outline notes for the students, and these grew in detail over the years, culminating in a two-volume text of lectures reproduced by the CTS Bookstore. It is these two volumes that have been extensively revised and transformed into the present text.

These new volumes still bear the marks of being addressed to seminary students who are on their way to being ministers, counselors, administrators, and discerning laypersons in the life of the church of Jesus Christ. It is the church, in its mission of witness to the reality of God, for whom I write. If other theologians find my explorations useful or provocative, that is an added plus. But my intended audience are those in the church who have a searching appetite for understanding and living Christian faith.

All texts have limiting conditions under which they are written and published. Mine is no exception, though I have been generously supported by Rowman & Littlefield in space and time allowances. Yet given necessary limitations of space, I have chosen to use footnotes for two primary purposes: (1) to refer to sources cited or mentioned in the text; and (2) to refer the reader to other books that might be of interest on various topics. Accordingly, I have diminished—but not omitted—the amount of footnote space expended in conversation with other theologians and theological sources. To have carefully documented and critiqued all those with whom I agree and disagree, even on major points, would have exceeded the spatial limits in which these two volumes have been conceived. This does not mean, however, that conversation aplenty is not taking place in the text as it moves through the various theological topics.

None of us can escape the influence of those conversation partners that have 'chosen us' for earnest engagement. As will become evident, in addition to Holy Scripture, I have been chosen to engage in life-giving but wrenching conversations with Søren Kierkegaard, Karl Barth, Paul Tillich, the many faces of so-called linguistic philosophy, the metaphysics and theology of that 'process school' of thought arising from Alfred North Whitehead and Charles Hartshorne, the myriad voices in liberation theology, and the sobering writings of feminist theologies. Augustine, Anselm, and Thomas Aquinas, as well as Martin Luther and John Calvin, have always been at hand to challenge some of my criticisms of tradition and suggest more subtle and faithful patterns of thinking about God and the Gospel of Jesus Christ. These conversation partners have given me more to chew on than I have been able to digest thoroughly. However, I hope that these two volumes exploring the grammar of Christian faith give ample evidence that these partners have indeed been chewed upon.

I was also blessed with professors in seminary and graduate school at Yale who have left their footprints of faith and understanding upon my reflection. In particular, I remain in awe of Julian Hartt's unrivaled intellectual dialecticity, rhetorical power, and theological acuity. His genuine encouragement toward publishing this text has been invigorating. Paul Holmer, for whom I was a teaching assistant for two years, left a hefty imprint of his interest in Kierkegaard, Wittgenstein, and things pertinent to the concreteness of the life of faith. William Christian, Paul Weiss, and Wilfred Sellars impacted significantly the trajectory of my intellectual development. In retrospect I suppose I was rather postmodern in philosophy and theology before that word became a slogan. Hans Frei and George Lindbeck were in the early stages of their teaching and writing and not yet advocates of a 'postliberal' school of theologizing, and I have since profited from their writings.

The reader versed in the theology of the last hundred years will detect the wide-ranging influence of Karl Barth on my theologizing. My doctoral dissertation was on Barth, and his works have never been remote and forgotten as I have struggled to become clearer about the full contours of Christian faith. While I decidedly diverge from Barth at significant points, he remains a constant counselor and agitator in my theologizing. I foreswore early in my teaching endeavors, however, that I would not spend a professorial career explaining, defending, and critiquing Barth. Hence, even now I have not wanted to convert this text into a running conversation with Barth, carefully documenting where I agree and disagree with him. Rather, with Barth looking over my shoulder, I have set out to construct my own comprehensive understanding of the main doctrines of Christian faith. I am hopeful that Barth would not be too displeased.

In 1989 the writings of John Howard Yoder blessedly intruded upon my theological reflection through the urgings of a Mennonite student of mine, Mark Nation. Since that time, Yoder's writings have been a formidable conversation partner, and the footprints of his trenchant theological mind are scattered throughout this text.

As these explorations are now being printed for a larger audience, I have the sinking feeling that, after the arduous process of producing this text, I might just now be getting into a position to do serious theology. Yet holding onto my thoughts until they achieve greater clarity and insight has been a lifelong tendency that has kept me hesitant and unpublished for too long. So, here is the best theologizing I can do at this point in time. I remain aware, however, that God still has 'ineradicable questions' to put to me in the days ahead.

I wish to thank those students over the years who have kept me focused, honest, and forthcoming by their insistent questioning and suggestions. It is a profound gift that so many students have blessed me with their conversations and writings. In particular, in recent years these students have been especially stimulating conversation partners: George Dunn, Mark Nation, Lisa Cressman, Elisabeth Baer, Linda Patrick, Jim Bisch, June Barrow, Jim Mulholland, David Poe, Lana Robyne, Sue Larson, Kent Ellett, Laurie Hearn, Joseph Hogsett, William Landers, and Dorothy Hunter.

Having taught in three theological seminaries, Perkins School of Theology, Phillips University Graduate Seminary, and Christian Theological Seminary, I have been graced with many wonderful colleagues. Special mention must be made of two of those who spent twelve recent years at CTS trying to nudge me into discernment and responsibility. Clark Williamson team-taught systematic theology with me several times, and every audition of his lectures improved my theologizing. J. Gerald Janzen, the most scintillating and insightful biblical theologian I know, kept the biblical texts constantly before me as texts demanding probing theological understanding and conversation.

Janzen's critiques of most of my present chapters, with his soaring imagination, unencumbered passion for theologizing, and relentless wrestling, often revealed and challenged my flat-footed muddlings and summoned me to more subtle and deeper articulations of the faith.

Other beneficent colleagues from the past include Joe Allen, Fred Carney, Bill Babcock, John Deschner, Van Harvey, Schubert Ogden, and Albert Outler from Perkins days; Gene Boring, Fred Craddock, Clark Gilpin, Harold Hatt, and Stuart McLean from Phillips. Special conversations continually arose with Pam Pearson, Ron Anderson, Brian Grant, Bernie Lyon, Ron Allen, Charles Allen, Calvin Porter, and Newell Williams at CTS.

Former students Russell Allanson and Janet Hoover provided enormous preparatory help: Russell by checking all my biblical references to eliminate errors and misuses; Janet by arduously copyediting all of the present chapters. They both made me a more competent author, for which I remain in their debt. Verity Jones and Sarah Jones also maintained long vigils of proofreading, continually pulling me back from the abyss of careless mistakes and ill-advised phraseology. Sarah has also diligently compiled the Scripture index.

For several years Stanley Hauerwas has been reading my lectures and encouraging me to get them into print quickly. It was Stanley who brought the existence of the lectures to the attention of James Langford at Rowman & Littlefield. My thanks go to Stanley and to the generous and supportive judgment of James. In addition, I am indebted to Paul Crow, Jim Duke, Bill Barr, Kathryn Tanner, and Stephen Webb, who have read and assessed large portions of the lecture version and have encouraged publication.

My own family has kept me theologically acute over many years with their vigorous questions, objections, and affections. Daughter Serene has become a marvelous professor and theologian in her own right, tutoring me often in the profounder points of Calvin, Barth, and feminist theology. Daughter Kindy is an indomitable lawyer with a consuming passion for social justice; she cuts to the practical quick of most theological issues. Daughter Verity is a congregational pastor who preaches and writes with theological verve, intelligence, and faithfulness; the sheer magnificence of her pastoral witness and competence keeps me hopeful about the possibilities of ministerial leadership. These daughters, with their grandeur and vitality, keep me humble and grateful.

It is to my life-partner, Sarah, who has generously and patiently enhanced my life over many years, that I dedicate this text. She above all knows intimately the drama of aspirations, frustrations, wounds, sheer doggedness, and unutterable joys that have beckoned this text into its present form. Her encouragement and conviction that this text should be written and published never flagged nor hesitated, and upon that confidence I have repeatedly drawn. It is sheer grace that the embers of almost a half century of sweet companionship and mutual affection still ardently glow and give light and life.

So these acknowledgments merely scratch the surface of the many gifts I have received from others throughout my life and teaching. I have been surrounded unceasingly by a communion of saints. The grace of God has never been an abstraction. Gratitude and joy abound!

I pray that these volumes might be luminous and upbuilding for persons earnest about understanding Christian faith and the Gospel of Jesus Christ.

Joe R. Jones
Anchor Point
Ft. Gibson Lake, Oklahoma

Abbreviations

ABD   *The Anchor Bible Dictionary*. 6 vols. Edited by
David Noel Freedman. New York: Doubleday, 1992.

IDB   *Interpreter's Dictionary of the Bible*. 4 vols. Edited
by George Arthur Buttrick. Nashville, Tenn.:
Abingdon, 1962.

ODCC   *Oxford Dictionary of the Christian Church*. 3d ed.
Edited by R. L. Cross and E. A. Livingston. Oxford:
Oxford University Press, 1997.

TDNT   *Theological Dictionary of the New Testament*. One-
volume abridged edition. Edited by Gerhard Kittel
and Gerhard Friedrichs. Edited and translated by
Geoffrey W. Bromiley. Grand Rapids, Mich.:
Eerdmans, 1985.

Church   Karl Barth, *Church Dogmatics*. 13 vols. Edited by
Dogmatics G. W. Bromiley and T. F. Torrance. Translated by
G. W. Bromiley et al. Edinburgh: T. & T. Clark,
1936–1969. Using Barth's unique system of
designating volumes by reference to Roman
numerals and parts; for example, *Church Dogmatics*,
II/1.

All biblical quotations and reference style, unless otherwise noted,
are from the New Revised Standard Version Bible, copyright 1989,
Division of Christian Education of the National Council of Churches
of Christ in the United States of America.

Chapter One

The Context and Task of Christian Theology

Søren Kierkegaard: *"It always holds true that a person only grasps what he has use for."*[1]

Christians are people of the word and the deed. They are dependent on written Scriptures, they speak and act in the light of those Scriptures, and they are shaped by the life, death, and resurrection of Jesus Christ as the spoken and enacted Word of God. It is a central belief of this text that the Gospel of Jesus Christ is the normative self-revelation of God and as such is disarming and startling good news that convicts, liberates, and redeems human life. When this Gospel of the incarnate love of God for all humans is soundly taught and embraced in the church, then the multiple discourses and practices of the church will bristle with life, vitality, faithfulness, and veracity. This text in systematic theology pivots around the concern to see how the church's identity in the Spirit is constituted by its distinctive words or discourses and deeds or practices.

It is essential for every generation of the church that the people learn how to speak and understand its distinctive Gospel-formed discourses and how to perform its distinctive practices. It is a constant temptation

---

[1] Søren Kierkegaard, *Concluding Unscientific Postscript to Philosophical Fragments,* vol. 1, *Kierkegaard's Writings,* vol. 12, 1, ed. and trans. Howard V. Hong and Edna H. Hong (Princeton, N.J.: Princeton University Press, 1992), 590.

1

and threat to the church that the very language and practices that are intended to shape and give content to its life might fall into disarray and misuse. In the situation of the church in North America, which is the given location of this text in theology, it is especially urgent to face the disarray that threatens the church's life here at the beginning of the third millennium. Churches and individual Christians often find themselves confused about and struggling to discern the distinctive discourses and practices that ought to be forming their life in the world. But the most common misuse of Christian discourse today is the haunting spectre of hypocrisy: when the distinctive words and utterances of the faith are used without relevance to and power over the concrete life of the speakers and hearers. This is Christian discourse as empty talk unrelated to life-shaping and redeeming practices.

I am concerned in this book to be useful to the church as it continues to struggle to become clear about the distinctive content of Christian faith and about how that content is intended to shape human life. In this aim to be useful, I will identify some of those doctrines and those practices that I regard as essential to the faithful performance of Christian witness and life in the world. Our discussion will be designed to proceed in a systematic way about the crucial parameters and content of Christian discourses and practices.

When I use the word 'discourses,' I am simply referring to all those linguistic forms and contents that are in fact used in the life of the church. Singing hymns, reading Scripture, reciting creeds, and saying prayers, for example, are forms of church discourse. Discourse is always an active form of speech; people are doing something when they speak in the multiple forms of Christian discourse. Hence, I am not using the word 'discourse' in that restricted sense of 'discursive theoretical speech.' Yet, it is also true that such theoretical discursive work is an important form of discourse in the church.

This first chapter is about the context and task of systematic theology. We will explore what systematic theology is and is not, what its special task is and is not, and what its defining context of work is and is not. I will argue that systematic theology is a special task of the church and that the church is therefore the proper context for pursuing this task. Two points should be noted here: (1) systematic theology exists in the midst of the *discourses and practices* of the church and therefore is itself an instance of the *enactment* of those discourses and practices; and (2) systematic theology is *reflection* on those discourses and practices, aiming to become responsible for and clear about their faithful form and content. This enactment of systematic theology is a discourse of the church's life and witness, and it properly involves reflecting on what the church is saying and doing in its life. Enactment/reflection and reflection/enactment will be present throughout this text. Hence, it will be a constant theme of our work that we are both enacting and reflecting on the enacting of the church's discourses and practices.

The enactment of systematic theology makes important drafts on our use of language and therefore on our understanding of how language functions. For example, we might request a definition of the word 'theology' and receive a surface reply that it goes back to the Greek words '*theos*,' meaning roughly that which is divine or god, and '*logos*,' meaning roughly that which is word, logic, or doctrine. While this surface definition might get us started in a certain direction, we quickly encounter questions. Which god or divine being? Which word, logic, or doctrine? These questions bring home to us that we are inescapably dealing with *the meanings of words and deeds* as we enact—do or perform—Christian theology.

When we try to clarify some of our key words it becomes quickly apparent that sometimes words get up and walk around on us.[2] Our language can sometimes seem unstable, even mercurial. Often the meanings of some of our key words are opaque and in dispute. This leads some persons to make the pejorative comment that theological disputes are no more than intellectual disputes over words and therefore merely verbal and not substantive. While there is sometimes a measure of truth in such comments, it is nevertheless the case that disputes over the meanings of words in theology are profound disputes about a subject matter that is being discussed and described. These discussions and disputes are not superficial impediments to understanding. Rather, they are themselves the very stuff and media of our understanding, and to use the words wrongly or thoughtlessly might mean missing the subject matter altogether.

I contend that to do Christian theology we must repeatedly strive for clarity about, and responsibility for, the meanings of words and locutions. These are not idle and empty discussions but bear on the very substance of *learning how to speak and perform Christian witness and life.* While there is no perfect dictionary that can be invoked to settle all our disputes and disagreements about Christian discourses and practices, the

---

[2] See Plato, *Euthyphro*, 11, b–c.

doing of systematic theology is one way—and not the only way—to come to an understanding of Christian faith. I will explain and defend the claim that Christian faith is enacted in the faithful performance of its distinctive discourses and practices. Getting clear about Christian faith involves discerning the forms and contents of the distinctive discourses and practices of the faith.

Many of our confusions about theology and Christian faith are rooted in confusions about *how human language functions*. Insofar as we are confused about how human language functions, we might also be confused about how to confront and reflect on the disarray in the discourses and practices of the church today. In preparation for doing Christian systematic theology, I will set forth in the next section a few points about human language, thereby providing some *diagnostic concepts* that I hope will be useful in our further theological discussions. These concepts should empower us to understand why we must refuse to sever Christian discourses from Christian practices. Indeed in this respect, one of the aims of this text is to *teach some aspects of how to speak and enact Christian life and witness faithfully and truthfully*. This speaking and enacting involve learning what I call the *grammar of Christian faith*.

Language, Grammar, and Understanding

By the word 'language' I refer first to the 'natural languages' of large human communal traditions, such as English, German, Spanish, Swahili, etc.[3] However, within such natural languages there are also the languages of particular, more focused communal interests, such as the language of politics, the language of physics. I propose there is something called *Christian language* that can be spoken and used in most of the natural languages.[4]

Essential to human language is the use of both oral and written means, and thus language involves *physical tokens* to get its work done.

---

[3] I am not pursuing here the interesting question of whether language exists among some nonhuman animals. Were we to call such communicative transactions among animals 'language,' we would be trading on their similarity to some features of human language.

[4] In putting it this way, I am denying that Christian language is restricted to any one natural language. To be sure, given the historical character of Christian tradition, Hebrew and koine Greek are essential to the shaping of Christian language in the various natural languages.

These tokens can be sounds, marks, words, even gestures and drawings. But tokens do not *mean* anything or have *sense* until they are put to particular *uses* by human beings. When tokens are put to uses and have meaning or sense, we will call them *signs*. Putting tokens to use as signs involves human intentions and actions and human social practices and conventions. Hence, I offer the following *stipulative* distinctions: '*token*' refers to all the possible media of language; '*locution*' refers to words, utterances, and sentences, whether oral or written; all locutions are also tokens; '*sign*' refers to the meaning and uses locutions have.[5]

Language is a living dynamic process of actions and interactions among speakers and hearers (writers and readers) who are trading on, and sometimes stretching, given social practices and conventions regarding the meaning of the tokens they are using as signs. These actions and transactions of meaning I will call *communicative transactions*: meaning is being conveyed. We cannot invent language completely moment by moment. Much of our intellectual work is involved in clarifying how we and others are using locutions as meaningful signs.[6]

Often when confused about a locution, we are confused about how it is being used: we do not know what the user means. Therefore, it is a good and common practice to ask people: 'how are you using that locution?' But most of the time—contrary to what intellectuals often say—people make good sense and communicate quite well. Whitehead worried over the inherent 'deficiencies' of language insofar as it is repeatedly inadequate and imperfect for human users.[7] But if this were

---

[5] A note about the use of single and double quotes. Single quote marks ['. . . .'] are used to indicate one of three signals. (1) It can signal that we are talking *about* a word or sign, as in the sentence 'The word 'language' is used to refer to the natural languages of persons.' (2) It can signal that we are highlighting a special use of a word or locution, as in 'The actions of 'perichoresis' are crucial to church life.' (3) It can signal that we are talking about the meaning of the sentence itself that is included within the single quotes, as in the two sentences used above. Functions one and two of the single quotes can also be accomplished by use of *italic* type. Double quote marks [" . . . "] are used when I am actually quoting from another text or a person's speech.

[6] Helpful general discussions of meaning and language are: Max Black, *The Labyrinth of Language* (New York: New American Library, 1968); and William P. Alston, *Philosophy of Language* (Englewood Cliffs, N.J.: Prentice-Hall, 1964).

[7] See Alfred North Whitehead, *Essays in Science and Philosophy* (New York: Philosophical Library, 1948), 131–140. This and other passages from

true, we would always be confused or incommunicative or inaccurate in what we say—which is clearly false. What he might have meant is that language often *appears* dense and obscure when put to some important uses—to which I agree, especially in theology.

The Grammar of Language

Since this text is titled *A Grammar of Christian Faith*, it is important to understand how I am using this word 'grammar.' Ludwig Wittgenstein, one of the most creative and influential philosophers of the twentieth century, often used the term 'grammar' to refer to the discernment of how language functions. Philosophy was thought of as *grammatical investigations* into how our language actually functions in particular uses, and he was suspicious that persons such as philosophers were often given to such abstract analyses of locutions that they misconstrued the grammar that clarified how a locution might concretely be used. He further distinguished between the *surface grammar* and the *depth grammar* of our uses of locutions as signs. The surface grammar pertains to the ordinary grammar of the rules of putting different types of words together into intelligible sentences. We are often fooled by surface similarities among sentences in supposing their grammar is the same, thereby losing sight of the depth grammar that is present in the actual use of the sentences in living speech. For example, the sentences 'God is the creator of the world' and 'Gates is the creator of Microsoft' seem like similarly structured declarative sentences; in surface grammar one sentence describes God and the other describes Gates. What is missing in this analysis is the depth grammar that describes the sort of *uses* these locutions might have in concrete human speech, or what I referred to as 'communicative transactions.' When we are bumfuzzled by our language, Wittgenstein recommends that we strive to *describe* the grammar of those locutions that are giving us trouble.[8]

Whitehead expressing similar beliefs about the inadequacy of language are explored with great subtlety by Alice Ambrose, *Essays in Analysis* (New York: Humanities, 1966), 157–181. Of course, one of Whitehead's concerns was the impediment of language to clarity and precision, which leaves us wondering what the paradigms of clarity are.

[8] These themes in Wittgenstein can be traced through Ludwig Wittgenstein, *The Blue and Brown Books* (Oxford: Blackwell, 1958); *Philosophical Investigations*, trans. G. E. M. Anscombe, 2d ed. (Oxford: Blackwell, 1958); *Zettel*, eds. G. E. M. Anscombe and G. H. von Wright, trans. G. E. M. Anscombe (Oxford:

It will be helpful in further understanding the grammatical function-ing of language if I borrow some terms, if not conceptual definitions, from Charles W. Morris.[9] He argues that language functions according to *syntax, semantics,* and *pragmatics.* Using these terms somewhat differ-ently from Morris, I think they will help us better understand what are the multifarious dimensions of discerning the grammar of language in Wittgenstein's sense.

Syntax

The syntax of a language is the structure of relations among locu-tions in their use as signs. Ordinary grammar is about the syntax or rules of combination among the so-called parts of speech, such as, in English, nouns, pronouns, verbs, adverbs, adjectives, conjunctions, prepositions, etc. Ordinary grammar is part of the syntax of language. But the syntax of a language is more than ordinary grammar. The locution 'the ball wrote a song' is well formed by ordinary grammar, but it is nonsensical by syntax, for the term 'ball' does not go with writing a song. We might, of course, wonder whether there is some poetic stretching of language here, but we would need a larger context of use before we could deter-mine that. Further, it is a function of syntax that we *define* signs by using other signs, and we combine signs into utterances or sentences in making sense. Logic is the form of how signs can be related in assertions, impli-cations, inferences, arguments, and distinctions. Hence, there are *rules* that govern the ways in which we can combine signs into sense-making units.

When we say 'rules,' we need not conjure the image that they are all written down somewhere in an encyclopedia of linguistic rules, for many of them are simply rooted in social practices. The *definitions* we find in dictionaries intend to identify the prime socially established *usages* of

---

Blackwell, 1967); *On Certainty,* ed. G. E. M. Anscombe and G. H. von Wright, trans. Denis Paul and G. E. M. Anscombe (Oxford: Blackwell, 1969); *Culture and Value,* ed. G. H. von Wright in collaboration with Heikki Nyman, trans. Peter Winch (Chicago: University of Chicago Press, 1980). Among the many interpretations of Wittgenstein, Norman Malcolm's *Wittgenstein: Nothing Is Hidden* (Oxford: Blackwell, 1986) is especially illuminating and accessible.

[9] See Charles W. Morris, *Foundations of the Theory of Signs,* International Encyclopedia of Unified Science, vol. 1, no. 2 (Chicago: University of Chicago Press, 1938).

words. As the *Oxford Dictionary of the English Language* reminds us, words cannot only be variously used, but they have a history of usage. Syntax is not static and may itself develop over a period of time for any particular community of language users. Syntactics is the study of the combinatory relations among signs in a given language. Syntactical study of the sense-making rules for Christian discourse will be important and often primary in our systematic theologizing.

Semantics

Semantics—as another dimension of the grammar of a language—is the *relations between signs and the objects or subject matters that can be referred to by the signs.* Semantics is about how signs *refer* or are *about something* or *have a referent.* Since there are many different sorts of signs that can be used referentially, we must see that signs can refer differently: e.g., names, concepts, images, metaphors, analogies, models, even sentences and paragraphs, etc. When we are confused, it sometimes helps to discern the *semantic rules* that govern the reference of our signs. But we must remember that not all signs and locutions are used referringly or are about something. Even more important, it is humans who do the *referring* in using signs; the sign simply as a token does not refer just in and of itself. Semantics, then, is about how humans use language referentially in acts of speech.

I should point out that it is often difficult in practice to distinguish the syntax of a locution and its semantics. For example, one way to begin learning the semantics of the Christian use of 'God' is to see how it gets combined with other words and in utterances. And discerning the syntactical combinations for Christians will clarify how the word 'God' might be used referentially. I will contend later that the semantics of 'God' is guided by the syntax of its use in the Bible in such linguistic forms as stories of God's actions, teachings, and commands.

Pragmatics

The pragmatics of a language pertains to the social and personal situations in which language is put to use by human beings. Here we ask what persons are *doing* in their uses of language—what human action or practice is going on here? Accordingly, the pragmatics of signs is connected to human intentions, actions, feelings, interests, agreements, and social practices. We understand signs when we grasp and understand their social and personal settings and uses. This is often called the *context* of the meaning of the signs. Wittgenstein made the helpful suggestion that language *happens meaningfully* only in the midst of human *games* or social practices that have human communal point. When we abstract signs from these games or pragmatic situations, we easily become confused about their meaning. Thus I am using the term 'pragmatics' to refer to the communal or social and personal settings in which humans are doing something when they speak and act. This means that humans are engaged in *communicative actions that are intentional and can be socially identified and described.*[10]

The full functioning of language involves the interworkings of the syntactic, the semantic, and the pragmatic dimensions of language as signs in use. We could not describe the syntax of a language without understanding how that syntax is grounded in social conventions and agreements. There is no syntax to the word 'God' without some given social practices of use. Likewise, semantics is dependent on understanding how people agree to use words and locutions referringly. Hence, the pragmatics of signs can never be ignored in our inquiry into the meaning of signs. It is this dimension of use that is so often neglected in some exercises of intellectual inquiry. In intending to present a grammar of Christian faith, I am proposing to describe some of the essential features of the syntax, semantics, and pragmatics of Christian discourses and practices. So, further uses of the term *grammar* in this text will always mean *depth grammar* and will include trying to remain clear *how Christian discourses have sense-making and life-shaping power for their users.*[11]

Language and Speech Acts

J. L. Austin made some suggestions about the functioning of lan-

---

[10] The renewed interest in *rhetoric* has in view the way in which speakers have *purposes, settings, and audiences* in mind in their speaking. Thus rhetoric can be understood as a dimension of the pragmatics of language.

[11] There are other theologians who have made grammar a central theme of their theologizing. Paul L. Holmer's *The Grammar of Faith* (San Francisco: Harper and Row, 1978) is a sustained inquiry into theological work that has been helpful to me, especially in exhibiting what I am calling the pragmatics of theology. However, I suspect Holmer might regard my interest in doctrines misleading about the grammar for Christian faith.

guage that will help us in our analysis.[12] He emphasized the respects in which the concrete functioning of language involves *speech acts*. Being competent in a language entails knowing how to perform multifarious speech acts of the language. Austin distinguished between what he calls *locutionary acts* and *illocutionary acts*. A locutionary act is simply the act of uttering a locution. Let us take the locution 'Smith is a feminist.' The uttering of this locution—the locutionary act—can involve performing various illocutionary acts. At the syntactic and semantic level we could start asking what this locution might mean, and we could come up with saying it looks like a sentence stating a proposition. Of some identifiable person named Smith it is the case that he/she is a feminist. We might use other words in trying to clarify what the word 'feminist' means. Leaving aside the obvious question of the difficult syntax and semantics of 'feminist,' we need to see that this locution can be used to perform different speech acts. For example, it can be used to commend Smith or it can be used to condemn and stigmatize Smith. In fact, the locution has many possible illocutionary uses.

What might we learn from this analysis of 'Smith is a feminist'? First, the mere fact that the same word is being used does not require that it has the same syntax and semantics in all its uses. The word 'feminist' is like that: it gets up and walks around on us insofar as it is subject to multiple meanings in the hands of folk. We will confront this sort of problem repeatedly in our exploration of the grammar of Christian discourse in that folk often think that the mere presence of the same word implies that there is one and only one definitional meaning of the word as sign. But a closer look will persuade us that there are often many signs being conveyed in the various uses of the same word, even though there might be some significant overlapping of meanings in these different uses of the word. I will often use the practice of *stipulating* how I am using a word when there are other competing and confusing meanings available.

Second, we can see how the life of language is also rooted in human

---

[12] See J. L. Austin, *How to Do Things with Words*, ed. J. O. Urmson (Oxford: Clarendon Press, 1962) and *Philosophical Papers* (Oxford: Clarendon Press, 1961). John R. Searle, *Speech Acts: An Essay in the Philosophy of Language* (Cambridge: Cambridge University Press, 1969) has helpfully explored the implications and applications of Austin's work. Donald D. Evans, *The Logic of Self-Involvement* (London: SCM Press, 1963) is an extensive investigation of the import of Austin's philosophy for religious language, especially as it might pertain to the language of God as Creator.

intentions and actions. It is important in grasping the communicative transaction of the uses of the locution 'Smith is a feminist' to understand the speaker's intention in a particular concrete context of social conventions and practices. Consider that in uttering the locution 'I promise to be there,' one is performing the illocutionary act of *promising*. The speech act of promising is a social practice that has rules and social consequences. When people hear the words 'I promise' being used in an unproblematic social setting, they have a right to hold the person to the promise, to count on the promise being fulfilled. So, for promising there are *pragmatic* conditions that have to be fulfilled. But persons often break promises, and even sometimes persons use the *locutionary forms* of promising—uttering the words 'I promise'—with no intention of authentically making a promise. In response to this we can either say that he broke a promise or that he spoke emptily. Here we can note that these pragmatic conditions for performing the speech act of promising also involve personal conditions of self-involving sincerity and honesty.

The Pragmatics of Speech Acts

We are now prepared to see that most speech acts have their pragmatic conditions of performance: (a) *social* conditions—a requisite social setting in which the speech act can be identified, described, recognized, and thereby understood; and (b) *personal authenticity* conditions—the personal self-involving conditions of intentionality appropriate to a given social context. To perform speech acts involves mastering these pragmatic conditions of meaningful speech.[13]

Similarly, in Christian discourse, I will be contending that the locution 'God is the creator of the world' is not yet fully understood simply by tracking out the syntax and semantics of the locution in Christian community. Such syntax and semantics are, of course, important, and I will expend much effort trying to describe and clarify such matters. But we miss the mark of an adequate understanding if we do not discern the pragmatic conditions of this locution as part of a whole way of life. It is

---

[13] So-called deconstructionists are inclined to argue that the meaning of all human language is reducible to subjective intention. Since such intentions are infinitely variable, it is claimed that there is no stability in language except what we make up along the way. This perspective on language, however, neglects the social and intersubjective character of meaningful speech. But it can alert us to the fact that such social and intersubjective conditions can change over time.

the appreciation of these pragmatic conditions that is often neglected in theological work. The locution gets abstracted from its use in the context of believers sharing a way of life.

So, in Christian discourse there are pragmatic conditions for saying 'I love the Lord with all my heart'—namely, the conditions of being in a community that can identify and recognize the intention to profess love of God and the condition of performing this speech act with personal authenticity. A person cannot say this authentically, according to Christian grammar, without being involved in a whole way of life with, for example, its practices of neighbor love. Hence, as in ordinary language, the successful performance of intelligible speech acts in the Christian community involves mastering the requisite grammar of the signs: knowing their relations to other signs, their referential powers, and their pragmatic conditions.

Much Christian discourse today is stalked by the fact that its apparently standard locutions are often misused by persons who have not mastered the syntactic, semantic, and pragmatic conditions for speaking them meaningfully. So, to learn how to speak Christianly involves learning how to engage authentically in Christian discourses and practices. Contrary to the diagnoses of some theologians, the primary issue for Christian discourse today is not that it needs to be changed, updated, and modernized. Rather, it is that too much of its distinctive grammar has been emptied of its content by misguided, superficial, and distorting uses. Christian discourse is designed to *transform* human life by changing persons to fit the distinctive concepts, beliefs, and practices of the faith, rather than supposing the discourse should be continually changed and updated to fit humans in their worldly dispositions.[14]

To illustrate these points further, consider what Paul says in First Corinthians 12.3: "No one can say Jesus is Lord except by the Holy Spirit." In our time of glib and empty uses of prime Christian words and locutions, we can make Paul's point more telling by rephrasing thus: "No one can say and *mean* 'Jesus is Lord' except by the Holy Spirit." People today might perform the locutionary act of saying 'Jesus is Lord' but say it emptily, never understanding it can only be meant authentically if it involves the speaker in a whole way of life over which Jesus reigns and the Holy Spirit empowers. The pragmatic conditions of authentic per-

---

[14] Holmer has often articulated these points. See especially Paul L. Holmer, *Making Christian Sense* (Philadelphia: Westminster, 1984). With fine subtlety and insight, Robert C. Roberts, in a much neglected book, makes similar points: *Spirituality and Human Emotion* (Grand Rapids, Mich.: Eerdmans, 1982).

formance of this utterance are what need to be recovered and cultivated.

Hence, when we ask what certain words and locutions *mean*, we can be inquiring variously about several dimensions of how language means. There is no one sense even of the word *meaning*. According to the interests of the person asking the question, we could reply simply by offering a syntactic *definition*. But the inquiry might push further into the semantics and pragmatics of the locution. This multiplicity of meanings that are to be understood also shows the multidimensional aspects of human understanding.[15] And the phases of understanding Christian discourse are indeed difficult and demanding. To the readers of this text I would recommend what I call the *existential rule for authentic speech*: 'what would it mean *for me* to say and mean some locution?' That is, what are the requisite social and personal conditions for using that locution meaningfully? This rule can usefully guide anyone exploring the discourses and practices of Christian faith.

This text in theology is concerned to teach the grammar of Christian discourses and practices. We can now see the importance of the concepts of discourse and practice. We have intelligible discourses when there is a community of language users trading on their agreements about the syntax, semantics, and pragmatics of their linguistic activities. Such discourses would be impossible without some intelligible practices of communal agreement and performance.

Emotive Language

It may appear that these concepts of syntax, semantics, and pragmatics as comprising the grammar of a language have left out an important dimension of our human linguistic performances and communications, namely, an *emotive* dimension. It should be obvious that our speech acts themselves can express and convey definite feelings and passions. Indeed such expression and conveyance are often the primary point of a speech act. Further, most of our language performances and interactions have definite emotive undertones and overtones that are important to the full meaning being conveyed. However, these emotive tonalities of language are often idiosyncratic to the speaker and the hearer,

---

[15] This fact should lead us to abjure from supposing there is some all-encompassing *theory of understanding* that applies to all situations in which we understand something.

the writer and reader, and therefore are difficult to identify as the gram-mar of the signs being used. So, for one person the word 'feminist' might conjure feelings of closure, while for another it might conjure feelings of approval and praise. And emotion might vary for the same person from one moment of use to another. Hence, emotion—both in the speaking and in the hearing—is an elemental dimension of the pragmatics of lan-guage. This is especially important to the ways in which Christian dis-course can be understood to convey joy and awe in the Lord, for exam-ple. Indeed, I am claiming *that Christian discourse itself shapes, expresses, and conveys some of the distinctive passions and feelings of Christian faith.*

On Clarifying the Concepts of
Pragmatics and Practice

The word *pragmatics* may be confusing, as it is often associated with that which is 'unprincipled' or unconcerned about 'objective truth.' I hope it is obvious that I do not mean such things in my concept of prag-matics. But I do not want to review here the history of the term and its various conceptualities.[16] Rather I am emphasizing pragmatics as the concrete social and personal setting in which persons are doing some-thing in their speaking—words have meaning in their *uses* by human beings. I have claimed that language functions meaningfully only in these concrete social transactions. I have further claimed that these speakings and doings are *practices* that people learn and perform. Hence, the *concept of practice includes both linguistic practices and nonlinguis-tic practices.* The linguistic practices I have called *discourses or words*

---

[16] It is obvious that I share some of the concerns and insights of that school of philosophy called *pragmatism*, which is commonly associated with C. S. Peirce, William James, and John Dewey. But the conceptual issues are too com-plex for me to explore in this context where I agree and disagree with this or that contention of pragmatism. There is, however, a convergence today between the sort of philosophizing arising from Wittgenstein and Austin and that of the pragmatists. See Richard Rorty, *Consequences of Pragmatism (Essays: 1972–1980)* (Minneapolis: University of Minnesota Press, 1982). Cornel West has stimulated my thinking about discourse and practices in his work; see in particular *Prophetic Fragments* (Grand Rapids, Mich.: Eerdmans, 1988) and *The American Evasion of Philosophy: A Genealogy of Pragmatism* (Madison: Uni-versity of Wisconsin Press, 1989).

and the nonlinguistic practices I have simply called *practices or deeds*. To be sure, nonlinguistic practices depend on discourse for their meaning and standing as social practices.

To clarify the relevant sense of practice, I stipulate that a *practice is a repeatable human action that stands in a communal tradition of identification and description*. Such identifications and descriptions yield an understanding of *practices as types of human actions* that can be repeatedly enacted or performed by the communal members. Insofar as we describe a practice as being repeatable and reduplicable in a variety of times and places, we understand the practice as a type of action. Particular performances of the practice are concrete actions. Hence, *Smith being hospitable to Brown* is itself a concrete, particular action that is an instance of the *practice of hospitality*. We can also note that the same concrete action can be an instance of more than one practice. Smith's being hospitable to Brown can also be a practice of agapic love. So our typologies of actions and practices can involve significant overlap without being confusing. It is this concept of action and practice that I am using to clarify the pragmatic situation of Christian grammar.

It may be helpful to provide a further common distinction between a *supervening action* and its *subsidiary actions*. I stipulate that a supervening action is an action the performance of which requires performing some subsidiary actions. For example, Smith's being hospitable to Brown is a supervening action and practice that requires for its actualization the performance of many subsidiary actions, such as greeting Brown in a friendly manner, speaking warmly to Brown, feeding Brown, etc. The practice of singing praises to God—as a supervening action—involves at least the subsidiary action of singing. And, of course, not all singing is singing praises to God. Using our earlier distinction, we can see that the *illocutionary speech act* of singing praises to God involves the *locutionary act* of singing some words.

Insofar as discourses and practices are human actions and types of actions, as practices they have what I have called *conditions of authenticity*. The performance of the practice must be intentional and therefore performed with the intention of achieving the goal that is imputed to the action in its identification and description by the community. In this sense, then, *most of the characteristic practices—both linguistic and nonlinguistic—of Christian faith require self-involving sincerity for their authenticity*.

We can now understand why there is often a measure of ambiguity that adheres to the performance of Christian practices. An action might be performed in such a way that it *looks like* a practice of faith but which fails to achieve the authenticity of faith. For example, singing hymns is not in every instance a singing of praises to God; they can be sung by rote and without self-involvement. Hence, in all the practices of the church there remains the haunting possibility that actions will be performed that *look like* practices of faith but which fail to achieve or express the self-involving meaning and authenticity intended by the community. Yet it is important to note that the continued existence of the *forms of the practices* in the church, however inauthentically they might from time to time be performed, still promises by their very regularity that they might *become* in the future *practices of genuine faithfulness.* For example, that individuals and congregations regularly engaged in the practice of reading the Bible—however emptily and superficially it may be performed from time to time—is nevertheless a sure sign of the possibility—*carried and kept alive by the practice itself*—of its becoming in the future the faithful practice of reading the Bible *as* the Word of God.

In developing further the concept of the forms of discourse and practice, we can understand that linguistic and nonlinguistic actions might be enacted without the human agent coming thereby to *occupy or inhabit* the forms of discourse and practice as the language and action of faith. Søren Kierkegaard fretted endlessly over what he took to be obvious, namely, that many people in the church in his time used the forms of locutions and practices of the church but were not *'existentially shaped'* by that use. Kierkegaard was clear that the forms of Christian discourses and practices were for the formation of lives of faith. When these forms are used in detachment from—or in the absence of—that self-involving intention and formation, they are being used emptily and without authentic inhabitation.

So how do persons come to occupy and inhabit the discourses and practices of the Christian faith? I claim that—in general—they come to faith through *learning how to speak and practice the faith*, however frail and fragile that might be at any point in time. But I posit that there is no single experiential and pragmatic route that every person of faith *must follow* in coming to be formed by the language of faith and thereby coming to inhabit the discourses and practices of the church. The church is the necessary context for the movement of faith, but the movement itself can only be performed by the individual person over a period of time with the empowerment of the Holy Spirit.[17]

Some Basic Theses about Language

We are now ready to take some of the themes we have been exploring and put them into succinct theses. Hopefully the theses will focus for us just how important language is to our experience and our understanding—indeed, to our lives.

1. *The uses of words and locutions to make sense are embedded in traditions of usage.* We can't speak language without some community of users bound together through social conventions and rules of practice. These communal practices may be stretched, revised, or flouted, but they cannot be completely omitted and still make sense. Note: *making sense* is a communal activity as well as an individual activity.

2. *Language has to be learned and such learning involves learning skills in using words in social settings and communal games.* Mastering signs is learning how to use the requisite words in determinate social settings, to be able to engage in particular social practices. Mastering signs is like learning how to use *tools* for making sense in life, for working intelligibly in one's life in the world.[18] Think, for example, of *learning how to sing praises to God.*

3. *Language provides the structure of our experience, understanding, and perspectives.* We experience the world and have a world in and

---

[17] The concern for *practice*—however vaguely that word may from time to time be used—is widespread in Christian theology today. Many trace their interest in practice to the work of Alasdair MacIntyre: see Alasdair MacIntyre, *After Virtue: Study in Moral Theory* (Notre Dame, Ind.: University of Notre Dame Press, 1981) and *Three Rival Versions of Moral Inquiry: Encyclopedia, Genealogy, and Tradition* (Notre Dame, Ind.: University of Notre Dame Press, 1900). Craig R. Dykstra has written insightfully about practices in *Vision and Character: A Christian Educator's Alternative to Kohlberg* (New York: Paulist, 1981) and in *Growing in the Life of Faith: Education and Christian Practices* (Louisville, Ky.: Geneva Press, 1999). With Dorothy C. Bass, he has also edited a significant series of essays on practices of Christian faith: *Practicing Our Faith: A Way of Life for a Searching People* (San Francisco: Jossey-Bass, 1997).

[18] Throughout his later philosophy Wittgenstein made extensive use of the image of tools to illuminate sometimes obscure ways in which our language makes sense.

through language, through signs, speech acts, and practices. Our *discourses and practices* are how we have a world, or worlds.

4. *In learning particular language networks, we are learning the discourses and practices that comprise having the world in that way.* Think of learning the language of physics: one *sees and understands* the world differently, and one acquires skills in investigating and explaining the world. What we are empowered to see, discern, and describe is dependent on the language we possess.

5. *The limits of our language are in some ways the limits of our understanding and therefore of our world.*

6. *Language is thus a human construct and construal.* It is produced by human interactions, agreements, and social practices. Hence, words do not have eternal and necessary meanings independent of their locations and usages in human communities and traditions.

7. *It is only within some language that we can test our construal of the world; we cannot completely abandon and step outside of all language and look simply at the world.*

8. *Our humanity is shaped by our language and the communities of discourses and practices in which we participate.* Our living discourses and practices shape human self-understanding.

9. *The description of the grammar of language is a description of how human language makes sense in its syntactic, semantic, and pragmatic dimensions.* The *depth grammar* of a particular set of linguistic practices will show how these dimensions of language hang together to make sense. For example, the depth grammar of trinitarian talk will show how embedded that talk is in self-involving, communal practices of identifying, praising, and witnessing to God in the church.

10. *Learning how to experience Christian faith is learning how to construe the world and oneself through the discourses and practices of the church with its peculiar language, its peculiar ways of being-in-the-world and having-a-world.*

To conclude this discussion of language, I remind the reader that I have taken us through these conceptual considerations in order to provide some *diagnostic conceptual tools* for pursuing the task of Christian theologizing. Admittedly, my discussion has been all too succinct to provide ready access to and training in the understanding of language I have been constructing. However, I hope that in the further *use* of these conceptual tools in the course of this text it will become clearer just how the tools will facilitate understanding and help us avoid some pitfalls. At the beginning of this chapter I quoted Kierkegaard: we typically only understand something when we have a use for that understanding. In this sense, I hope further that these theological explorations will prove useful to persons interested in understanding Christian faith.

Proposals for the Meaning of 'Theology'

Since the word 'theology' has been put to many uses in the history of humanity and its various communities and traditions, it is appropriate to look at some *contemporary proposals* for identifying and describing its use.

Theology Happens Wherever the Word 'God' Is Used

One proposal is that theology happens wherever the word *God* or its functional translations in other natural languages is used in human discourse. But why should we suppose that the *word* 'God' has just one uniform and common use or meaning? Our distinction between word and sign should help us see that there are many different *signs* functioning in the myriad uses of the *word* 'God.' This is connected to another common mistake of supposing that the meaning of a word such as 'God' is the *object* to which it seems to refer. It would seem to follow that since we are using the same word, we must be referring to the same object. Then we are inclined to say such things as 'We all know what "God" means, but we might disagree as to how God should be further described.' In talking this way we obscure from ourselves the enormous differences in syntax and semantics of the word 'God.' Instead of these misguided assumptions, it is helpful to ask what are some of the differing semantic and syntactic rules in the various uses of the term 'God' in various communities of language. We get better focus if we ask how 'God' is being used in a particular community of speakers. It is here that we see how useful the distinction between a word and a sign can be to our understanding of some of the confusions that seem to haunt our discourses.

Theology as Religious Search

Another proposal is that *theology happens where there is a religious search for meaning or a human ultimate concern.* Tillich and others suggest something like this.[19] This proposal presupposes some theory of what it means to be *religious,* and this can be as disputatious as the term 'theology.' However, this point can be useful and make some connections to a broad spectrum of human interests. I will construct a Christian conception of 'religion' in the chapter on the doctrine of humanity. But for now, this proposal has some serious shortcomings. Except for sociological theories, a theory of religion is, of course, never neutral about what is 'divine' or 'God.' This means that the concept of divine thus used in the theory either already presupposes Christian usage or it imports a meaning that will skew how 'God' is to be used in Christian discourse. Further, the use of this definition of theology too often yields to the temptation to consider Christian faith a particular instance of the general human phenomenon of religion, which makes the Christian discourse about God depend on the general theory of religion for its meaning and, often, for its credibility. To put it another way, the criteria of the theory of religion become the inescapable criteria for understanding what is essential to Christian faith. To start our discussion of theology in this way could mean that Christian theology is merely one religious discourse among many, without having any decisive leverage on questions of truth.

Theology as an Academic Science

Some other proposals pivot around the belief that *theology happens in the modern academy and is an objective intellectual discipline or science.* Here theology is purported to be an 'objective science,' wherein a science is 'a field of rational inquiry with fairly explicit rules and procedures for describing, explaining, and verifying the behavior of its subject matter.' It is typical that the word 'objective' functions here to assure us both that the discipline is *about something real,* in distinction from mere subjective musings, and that all idiosyncratic personal interests and dispositions of the theologian have been expunged and are immaterial to the methodical working of the science. There are three prominent ways in which theology might be thought of as a science: (1) theology as metaphysics or ontology; (2) theology as historical or phenomenological description; and (3) theology as a science of revelation.

---

[19] See especially Paul Tillich, *Systematic Theology,* vol. 1 (Chicago: University of Chicago Press, 1951), 11–15. Tillich's *Dynamics of Faith* (New York: Harper & Brothers, 1957) can be understood as a study of the concept of faith as ultimate concern.

Theology as Metaphysics

Let us first consider *theology as metaphysics or ontology.* I use these terms more or less interchangeably. Here is a working definition: 'metaphysics is a theory about what basic sorts of things there are and how they are related and to be explained.' It asks what is really real or most basically real. And insofar as it is theological, it proposes that 'God' is a concept that is crucial in identifying the basic sorts of things and explaining their interrelations. Most forms of natural theology are engaged in doing metaphysics. I define a *natural theology* as proposing to advance arguments for truth-claims about God that are not dependent on any privileging of faith or revelation. To execute this task, a natural theology intends to erect or adopt a general metaphysics that will give credibility to belief in its god. Obviously, if Christian theology were primarily this sort of theology or was logically dependent on this theology, then the fundamental rules for semantically identifying God would be provided by this metaphysics. I will question these claims later.

The critical question here is whether it is plausible that there is a rational, neutral, and objective method of inquiry by which this theological game can be launched and sustained. In our day there are deep disagreements about the possibility of metaphysics as a scientific/rational discipline. This is not to deny that it is possible to make metaphysical or ontological claims about what is really real—Christians do this repeatedly in discourses of witness. But the puzzle comes as to whether there is some *rational* or objectively neutral way of settling disagreements about these claims or verifying the claims. I will argue that Christian theology properly understood is not objectively neutral but is passionately self-involving for its practitioners, though this does not deny that it is an orderly and rational exercise.

Theology as Historical Description

Theology as historical or phenomenological description aims to provide a scientific, objective description of religious concepts, beliefs, and practices. The aim is not to describe some entity called 'God' but to describe what people mean when they speak of gods, their particular uses of 'God.' Hence it is a kind of science *about* the religious beliefs, concepts, and practices of some thinkers or some community. These are the *objects* to be described and explained. Anders Nygren and Gustaf Aulén attempted to make theology scientific as the description and explanation of the essential ideas of religion and in particular of Christian religion.[20] But note: *describing* the essential ideas is not the same as *asserting and believing* the ideas. Hence, the sentence 'Christianity believes in a Redeemer God who is incarnate in Jesus' is *about* Christianity and is *not about* God or Jesus. One could have an interest in making this description of Christianity but have no interest whatsoever in believing that the Redeemer God is incarnate in Jesus.

Paul Holmer proffered a distinction that has become almost commonplace today, namely, between the *language of religion* and the *language about religion*.[21] The language of religion is the language being put to use by religious people and is expressive of their religious understanding. The language about religion is quite simply the voluminous language that has grown exponentially in the last two hundred years in which people aim to describe and explain religion or a particular religion. We see this language about religion in the philosophy of religion and in multitudinous historical studies. The grammar of language about religion dominates biblical studies today. The seduction lurking in the scholar's pursuit of such ostensibly scientific studies is that the transition from such *language about* to the *language of*, say, Christian faith is never a matter of accumulating more and more language *about*. It is a transition of deep personal dimensions of change.[22]

So, the proposition 'Israel believed it was elected by Yahweh' is a different proposition than 'Israel was elected by Yahweh.' The speech acts of saying the two different assertions have different grammatical conditions of meaning and truth. The first can be said with personal neutrality, while the second—said in the church or synagogue—requires

[20] See Anders Nygren, *Meaning and Method: Prolegomena to a Scientific Philosophy of Religion and a Scientific Theology,* trans. Philip S. Watson (London: Epworth, 1972) and Gustaf Aulén, *The Faith of the Christian Church,* 2d ed., trans. Eric H. Wahlstrom (Philadelphia: Fortress, 1960).

[21] See Paul L. Holmer, *Theology and the Scientific Study of Religion* (Minneapolis: T. S. Denison, 1961).

[22] In my judgment it has been a common failing of much seminary education for the past fifty years that it has almost exclusively engaged in the communicative transactions of the language *about* Christian faith and its history and sociology. What was left uneducated, except to the extent the student brought it with her, was how to speak and enact the discourses and practices *of* Christian faith. The current concern for *spirituality* arises in the vacuum created by the absence of education in *how* to be a Christian.

passion and self-involvement. *This distinction and its implications are crucial to this whole project of systematic theology.*

However, it cannot be denied that any exercise in Christian theologizing will necessarily often rely on language about Christian discourses and practices that intends to be adequate to its subject matter. When I say my intent is to *describe the grammar of Christian faith*, I am implying that this cannot be done without some sound historical knowledge of the Bible and Christian traditions. But I will explain below why Christian theology cannot be only in the mode of language *about* faith but is also repeatedly in the mode of the language *of* faith.

Most academic study of religion in universities and seminaries today is deeply preoccupied with such descriptive and purportedly *neutral* inquiry and is seldom engaged in the uses Christian people make of the language when they are being faithful. We can make this general observation about the modern academy: it is not particularly hospitable to theology as talk about God. Hence, at least in many universities, whatever passes for 'theology' is some form of *objective* study *about* Christianity and other religions.

Theology as a Science of Revelation

Some theologians also think *theology is a science of revelation.* Thomas Torrance has spent a lifetime making this case.[23] He has compared theology to the natural sciences and argued that both are simply trying to describe their different objects. The object of Christian theology is the revelation of God in Jesus Christ. He thinks he is following the example of Karl Barth in *Church Dogmatics.*[24] I appreciate the basic concern of Torrance and Barth to affirm that the prime subject matter of theology is the God as revealed in Jesus Christ. But the use of the word

---

[23] See especially Thomas F. Torrance, *Theological Science* (London: Oxford University Press, 1969).

[24] Torrance, *Theological Science*, 131, referring to Karl Barth, *Church Dogmatics*, I/1: *The Doctrine of the Word of God*, trans. G. T. Thomson (Edinburgh: T. & T. Clark, 1936). A new translation by G. W. Bromiley of this volume was published in 1975 by T. & T. Clark. For Barth's cautious discussions of theology as 'science,' see *Church Dogmatics*, I/1, 3–24, 275–287 [Bromiley's translation]; I/2, 771–772. All future references to *Church Dogmatics* will be in this abbreviated form of *Church Dogmatics* followed by the identified volume as I/1, etc.

'object' here and the claim to be scientific leave the impression that the revealed object is simply there awaiting our realistic descriptions. Further, in a way that Barth does not, Torrance tends to omit the church as the context in which this peculiar talk of revelation and object make sense.

However, any systematic theology executed in the context of the church will intend to follow an orderly discussion and description of its prime subject matter, which I will affirm is the reality of the triune God. We are not simply 'gassing and guessing' when we speak of God. But neither are we to suppose that systematic theology can verify of itself that its subject matter is simply *there* for us to analyze and describe in some neutral fashion. Barth's tortuous but discerning discussion of 'pure doctrine' is sufficient to make us hesitate—though he does not hesitate—to call theology a 'science.'[25]

Theology as Confessional Church Theology

In differentiation from these proposals about the meaning of 'theology,' I make *the constructive proposal that Christian theology is situated first and foremost in the context of the church.* Hence, it is *church theology.* There are many other possible uses for the term 'theology' and many other possible 'theologies'; I am not disputing this linguistic fact. But I am interested in theology that is appropriate to the church and that *presupposes and serves the church.* In this service to the church, without any independent theory to secure its full truthfulness, Christian theology is *confessional theology.*

The church already exists as concrete historic communities with their distinctive discourses and practices. Christians sing hymns; baptize in the name of the Father, Son, and Holy Spirit; receive Holy Communion; pray; preach; exhort; console; encourage; argue and quarrel; confess sins; judge; tell stories and narratives; read the Bible; assert truth-claims; say creeds; speak to and about God; etc. There is a multitude of practices—both linguistic and nonlinguistic—that constitute the Christian social or communal world.

I contend that Christian theology—as church theology—is a multidimensional practice of the church itself and will be related to the concrete practices of Christian life and witness. While some of our systematic theological exercises will focus on the syntactic and semantic aspects

---

[25] See *Church Dogmatics*, I/2, 743–796.

of the church's elemental grammar, it will everywhere presuppose that the full meaning and intentionality of Christian discourse are inseparable from the pragmatics—the concrete, communal/personal practices—in which Christians live in the church, with the world, and before God. Therefore, in this text, we will be doing church theology in and for the church and therefore also in and for the world.

It should be noted that I am *not* beginning this text with the isolated individual and her search to build *her own theology*. That is, I am not making this individual definitive and paradigmatic for doing theology. I view as troubling and misleading that this practice of beginning here with the individual is widely embraced in church and seminary. I am leery of the picture that each of us is expected *to invent* his or her own *personal theology*. Is Christian faith the endless inventing of our own individual theologies? To be sure, even as we do theology in and for the church, there is an unavoidable sense in which each of us has to lay claim to it as authentically something to embrace.

Church theology does also take place in the academy—and properly so—but primarily in those academies that are related to the church. *But a theology that is presuppositionless and relies on nothing more than some so-called neutral, scientific reason is an intellectual will-o'-the-wisp.*

A Theological Definition of the Church

To make further progress toward understanding what confessional church theology is, we need a theological understanding of the church in order to see how theology arises for Christians in the pragmatic context of the church. Here is a proposed *theological definition of the church*:

> The church is that liberative and redemptive
> community of persons
> called into being
> by the Gospel of Jesus Christ
> through the Holy Spirit
> to witness in word and deed
> to the living triune God
> for the benefit of the world
> to the glory of God.

This definition is *theological* to begin with and will enable us to see where, how, and why Christian theology is essential to the life of the church. The definition is decidedly not a historical or sociological description of the church. As a theological definition, it is proposed as a *normative* definition that will guide our further discussions of the church and its theological work. By beginning with its theological character, and thereby not trying to deduce a theological description from history or sociology, we will be conceptually empowered to enter immediately into further theological discussion. I must admit, however, that this definition is a *proposal* and therefore must admit that there are other theological definitions that might be found in the life of the church. I am simply signaling here that we are entering into that wider theological discussion.

While this definition will be elaborated throughout this text and at greater length in the chapter on the church, it is important to our enterprise to identify diagnostically some of its decisive concepts. First, it affirms that the church is a concrete, historic *community of persons*. As a community the church is a socially interrelated world of distinctive discourses and practices. The New Testament refers to this community of persons as an *ekklesia*—an assembly or gathering of persons summoned together by Jesus Christ, and a *koinonia*—a communion or fellowship among persons and with God. The sense of community includes both community as local and community as a community of local communities.

The church is a *liberative and redemptive community of persons*. By characterizing the church in this way, I am declaring the importance of *salvation*, or soteriological, concerns in the life of the church. In particular the persons of the community have been *liberated* from the domination of sin and its consequences and are engaged in practices of participating in God's *redemptive* work in the world. Hence, the church is both liberated and redeemed by God and summoned to be an agent of God's liberative and redemptive work for the world. In ways that will become clearer as we proceed, describing the church as liberative and redemptive does not preclude describing the church as comprised of sinners, albeit sinners forgiven by God.

This liberative and redemptive character of the church is given further definition when we say that it is a *community called into existence by the Gospel of Jesus Christ*. The church is summoned by the Gospel of Jesus Christ. In putting it this way, I am denying that the church is a community of persons coming together simply out of common but yet-to-be-defined interests. At the heart of the church is the Gospel, which

requires the church always to remain clear and decisive about who calls
it into life. Hence, Jesus Christ is the Lord of the church, and the Gospel
of Jesus Christ is the defining self-revelation of God.

This *summary of the Gospel* shows the centrality of the Gospel for
the church:

The Gospel of Jesus Christ is the Good News
that the God of Israel, the Creator of all creatures,
has in freedom and love become incarnate
in the life, death, and resurrection of Jesus of Nazareth
to enact and reveal God's gracious reconciliation
of humanity to Godself, and
through the Holy Spirit calls and empowers human beings
to participate in God's liberative and redemptive work by
acknowledging God's gracious forgiveness in Jesus,
repenting of human sin,
receiving the gift of freedom, and
embracing authentic community by
loving the neighbor and the enemy,
caring for the whole creation, and
hoping for the final triumph of God's grace
as the triune Ultimate Companion of all creatures.

In later discussions I will refer to this summation of the Gospel as the
Presiding Model of the Gospel and the *material norm* of the church's
theological activity.

The definition of the church accents that the *Holy Spirit*, as the dynamic Spirit of God, empowers persons to say yes to God's work in
Christ and moves within them to form authentic communities of love and
peace. As should be obvious from the statement of the Gospel, we are
moving into decidedly trinitarian terrain as we talk of the God of Israel,
God's eternal Son, and the Holy Spirit.

The church is called to *witness in word and deed* to the living triune
God. I am here identifying the *raison d'être* of the church. Witnessing in
word and deed to God is the *mission* of the church in the most comprehensive sense. Such witness is (a) a witness in word: the church speaks!
and (b) a witness in deed: the church performs actions in the world!
Word and deed are inseparable: word separated from deed is hypocritical, vain, deadly, and a lie; and deed separated from word loses its de-

fining context, intentionality, and luminosity. Word and deed in witness are emphasized in saying that *the church as witness to God is constituted by and exists in its distinctive discourses and practices.*

The church witnesses to the *living triune God.* The particular and peculiar witness of the church is to the triune God who is Father, Son, and Holy Spirit. It is this God who self-communicates Godself in a history of disclosive acts in the life of Israel, in the life, death, and resurrection of Jesus of Nazareth, and in the Holy Spirit's redeeming and renewing life. In God's relation to the world, God is Creator, Reconciler, and Redeemer of the world. As will become clear as we proceed, the doctrine of the Trinity is a necessary implication of the Gospel of Jesus Christ. In the absence of or the neglect of this triune self-identification of God, the church's discourses and practices fall into profound disarray and disorientation.

It must be underscored that all the discourses and practices of the church are to be construed as witnessing to God. This witnessing to God is the most elemental sense of the word 'theological.' It means that the church is first and last oriented toward God in all that it says and does. In all its rich variety, *witnessing to God is the most elemental and primary sense of theological language and theologizing which are definitive of the kind of community the church is.* It is an oxymoron—contradictory, nonsensical, and absurd—to say any community could be the church of Jesus Christ and not be theological. Of course, it is possible that the theology evident in the witness of any particular church community is, by standards we will discuss, inadequate or illusory or heretical theology.

The claim here is that the Gospel-called church is, through the Holy Spirit, given a *defining mission of witness in word and deed to the living triune God.* All that is intrinsic to the church being truly the church of Jesus Christ can be understood as implied in this comprehensive mission of witness. We can now ask the question: what kind of witness in word and deed is this? What are the various discourses and practices of such witness? Very briefly, I propose that *the church witnesses to God in three interrelated spheres of discourses and practices*:

   a. *Nurture*: worship, education, communal care;
   b. *Outreach*: evangelism, prophecy, works of love for justice and peace, vocation;
   c. *Administering nurture and outreach.*

The definition affirms that *the church teleologically exists in witness for the benefit of the world.* God is indeed the Creator of the whole world and has created the world in love. And God has been engaged in liberative and redemptive work in the world on behalf of the world since the beginning of human history. Consistent with that work of God is the emphasis now on the contemporary world that God loves with an unfathomably rich graciousness and intends to redeem. We must say decisively *that the church does not exist for itself—it finds itself and fulfills its calling truly when it exists for the world.* When this teleological ordering of the church is neglected, then we have the church turned in upon itself and thereby simply existing for itself alone. Any refusal to be for the benefit of the world flagrantly manifests the church's sin. Another way of affirming this being-for-the-world is to say that the church is commanded to love the neighbor and the enemy in all that it does.

The *benefit* that the church brings to the world in its witness is that the world might be *transformed by the Gospel of Jesus Christ* and know and live in the light of the reconciliation of Christ and live toward the redemption and fulfillment of the Spirit in the eternal life of the triune God. Such a transforming benefit involves summoning humans to conform their lives to the love of God, to form themselves into communities of mutual love, and in so doing to transform those forms of life in the world that are against God and human good. God created humans for flourishing and has come in Jesus Christ through the Spirit to bring transforming flourishing to humanity in the midst of their penchant for sinning and rebelling against God and thereby rebelling against their own proper flourishing.

It must finally be insisted *that in all that the church does in witness it lives from and to the glory of God. God's glory* is the beginning of all things and that toward which all things move—the real telos of the church and the world. And the church knows in the Gospel of Jesus Christ that the glory of God includes the wondrous and liberative glory of humanity, the glory of the world. [Jn 17.22–24] God's glory is not a selfish and exclusive glory, but it is distinctively God's glory in a way that is unique and fundamental. Whenever the church forgets its orientation to the glory of God, it typically falls into glorifying some other god or idol as the source and purpose of its existence.

I recapitulate *that in all these ways the church is a liberative and redemptive community.* As liberative, it is itself liberated from the destiny determining power of sin, and in its witness it is engaged in liberating work for the world. As redemptive, its liberation is toward redeeming life as the good gift from God and as that which will finally be fully redeemed in God's future with the world.

The Church's Witness as Summoned to Accountability

Faith Seeking Understanding

Having firmly established that the church is defined by a mission of witness to the living triune God, we will now explore how that witness becomes accountable to God. Precisely as the discourses and practices of witness, the community of the church is a *community of faith*. In line with the great traditions of the church, I claim that intrinsic to faith itself is the inescapable quest for further understanding of the God in whom faith believes and trusts and to whom it is called to witness. Hence, all aspects of the witness of the church involve *faith seeking understanding* [*fides quaerens intellectum*].

This locution—*fides quaerens intellectum*—is generally associated with St. Anselm of Canterbury who wrote in the eleventh century three influential books: *Proslogion, Monologion,* and *Cur Deus Homo*.[26] He also used the expression *credo ut intelligam*—I believe in order to under-stand—which meant that faith itself leads to and is a precondition of the sort of understanding of God that Christian faith teaches. In what I call the *route of faith*, every person who comes to faith along some route of experiences, believings, and passions starts with some *understanding* de-rived from an encounter with some aspect of Christian discourses and practices. To be sure, such nascent understanding might be finally wide of the mark of truth, but it provides some traction for getting launched on the route of faith as the quest for further understanding.

It will be helpful if we use a distinction from church tradition be-tween faith as *fides qua creditur*—the act or activity of the subject who believes or has faith—and faith as *fides quae creditur*—the object or what is believed. The locution 'the faith of the church' can refer either to

---

[26] For an informative discussion of the methodology of Anselm in these books, as applications of *credo ut intelligam* and *fides quaerens intelligam*, and of the interpretations of other scholars of this methodology, see John McIntyre, *St. Anselm and His Critics: A Re-Interpretation of Cur Deus Homo* (Edinburgh: Oliver and Boyd, 1954), 1–55. Karl Barth credits his study of Anselm for pro-viding fresh understanding to his own theologizing: Karl Barth, *Anselm: Fides Quaerens Intellectum*, trans. Ian W. Robertson (London: SCM Press, 1960). To be sure, what understanding—*intelligam*—finally comes to is a complex ques-tion. It at least meant coming to understand the syntactical and semantical grammar of Christian talk about God. It is clear, however, that Anselm knew such grammar was rooted in the pragmatic life of the church.

the subject or to the object. When we say faith seeks understanding, we are affirming that the subject who believes is intrinsically moved to understand more adequately what is believed. This movement of faith is not something imposed from without but arises naturally from the activity of believing, or of having faith. This distinction between the subject who believes and the object or content that is believed should be understood as applying both to the individual believer and to the church as a communal subject.[27]

Looking at this seeking in the situation of the believer, the seeking is at heart a quest to know God more fully and intimately. But the quest cannot be fully and honestly pursued without raising questions: to quest is to question, to inquire, and to seek answers. Hence, the questing believer asks questions, confesses doubts and confusions, and aims to seek those in the church who might give guidance. Questioning, then, should not be understood as an instrument of the devil but can be the *instrument of the Spirit* leading the quester to greater and deeper understanding.

What do we mean by the *understanding* which faith seeks? What is the understanding the church and all the persons of the church seek? We must be cautious here because the word 'understanding' has many interrelated uses in the life of the church. It is related to such concepts as knowing God, knowing self, being wise, being competent in speaking and acting the faith, discerning the Spirit, and much more. Christian understanding is so multifaceted because living the Christian life and witnessing to God are complex activities. But the church has repeatedly confessed that in all that we seek we will never be able to *comprehend God*. We might *know* God, but we can never put God among the items of our world by placing God in a class of objects in the world.[28] God is not a manageable object. But this incomprehensibility of God is not an invitation to premature resignation in understanding God; in fact the confession of God's incomprehensibility might be a sure sign that one is beginning to understand something of God and oneself. The concept of God's

---

[27] In the next chapter a fuller discussion of the grammar of the Christian understanding of faith will be provided.

[28] See Thomas Aquinas, *Summa Theologiae,* part I, q. 3, art. 5, which affirms that *"Deus non est in genere,"* which means that God is not a member of a class of beings with other members. God is not in a class of any sort. See St. Thomas Aquinas, *Summa Theologiae,* vol. 2, *Existence and the Nature of God (Ia. 2–11),* ed. and trans. Timothy McDermott (New York: Blackfriars and McGraw-Hill, 1964), 34–37.

incomprehensibility, then, is itself part of the grammar of 'God' in Christian discourse.

I propose that the understanding faith seeks is understanding how to construe the world as God's and how to identify and pray to God, how to be faithful and competent in witness to God, and how to love the neighbor. This emphasis on *how* cannot be separated from understanding the *what*, or content, of faith; they go hand in hand. This *understanding how* is what the discourses and practices of the church are intended to nurture. It is to become proficient in the grammar of the faith, which may not always mean being able to explain the grammar to others. But increasing proficiency in the grammar of faith means proficiency in understanding self and God and the potential to explain the grammar to others. The very witnessing of the church for the benefit of the world entails teaching the world how to understand the Gospel of Jesus Christ and its transformative good news. The *what* and the *how* of this witnessing are subject to questioning and the quest for deeper understanding. Keeping the what and the how continually interrelated and interdependent is one of the reasons for emphasizing that the grammar of the church involves syntax, semantics, *and pragmatics*. Thus, the sort of inquiry that faith pursues must be seen as multifaceted, and we must be wary of reducing faith's understanding to just one facet.

Questioned by the World and by God

It is also the case that the witness of the church is *questioned by the world*. Precisely because the church's witness is finally for the benefit of the world, the church must take seriously the questions put to it by the many faces and forms of the world in which it exists. Further, because Christians are first persons in some larger social world, that world and its discourses and practices are already in the person who comes to faith. She already has the world's questions in her mind and heart. It may well be the case that the witness of the church and the Christian never fully satisfies the questions and concerns of the world. Nevertheless, the church is still summoned to enable the world to understand the most fundamental and authentic Christian convictions, passions, and actions. In all of its witness, the church aims at being luminous truth for the world, even if it is not this on the world's own terms.

But more decisive than the questioning of the world, *the witness of the church is questioned by God*. Just as it is intrinsic to faith to be open to God and to question and be questioned, so too the church is open to

God and questioned by God. At the heart of the Christian witness is its recognition that faith lives only by virtue of the fact that God has spoken to us in Jesus Christ by the Holy Spirit. This revealed grace of God in Jesus Christ through the Holy Spirit summons us to acknowledge our sin and to accept God's forgiveness of sin. Hence, it is God who summons the church to critique its own witness so that it does not fall into profound idolatry or error about the Life of God and the Gospel of Jesus Christ. It is God who reminds the church of the threat of sin to distort the church's witness.

Because of its particular understanding of God, in the depths of the church's heart and mind it knows it is *questioned by God and summoned to accountability for its witness in word and deed.* This questioning by God is *ineradicable*—it is never fully and completely answered once and for all in the historic life of the church. Hence, we must confess that God puts ineradicable questions to the church's witness. It is in response to these questions that the church is summoned by God to give an account of its witness and therefore to engage in the theological critique of that witness.[29]

The Ineradicable Questions

These are the ineradicable questions that intrinsically confront the church's witness:

a. *The Central Ineradicable Question* is:
    Whether the church in its actual contemporary witness is:
    1. adequate and faithful to the Gospel of Jesus Christ, and
    2. luminous, truthful, and transformative for the world?

b. This question leads to *Ineradicable Foundational Questions*:
    1. What do we mean when we say what we say in witness? [We need an account of the meaning and content of present witness.]
    2. What do we intend when we do what we do?
    [We need an account of the present characteristic practices of the church. Note: both *saying* and *doing* are *concrete practices* of

---

[29] See Barth, *Church Dogmatics*, I/1, 11: "Dogmatics is the self-examination of the Christian Church in respect of the content of its distinctive talk [*Rede*] about God."

the church.]

3. With what right or authority do we say and do what we say and do?

[We need an account of the norms and criteria for judging the church's present witness.]

4. What should we say and do in actual witness that is:

a. adequate and faithful to the Gospel of Jesus Christ, and

b. luminous, truthful, and transformative for the world?

[We need a paradigmatic ruling and summary of the distinctive and essential convictions and practices of authentic and faithful Christian witness.]

Because of these ineradicable questions God puts to the church, these *Diagnostic Questions* are inescapable for every generation of the church:

a.   What is the Gospel of Jesus Christ?

b.   Who is the God to whom we witness and who in freedom and love self-communicates to humans, and who calls and summons the church to accountability?

c.   Who are we humans—in the church and beyond the church—and what is our destiny?

d.   What are we humans called to do and become in the light of the Gospel of Jesus Christ? [the ethics of grace]

These questions of accountability to God are *ineradicable* in the sense that neither the church nor the Christian can ever finally and completely answer these questions. This is because: (a) the God whom the church worships and to whom it witnesses is not under the control of the church, but lives freely and lovingly in relationship with the world and the church, and is therefore an *unfathomable but self-communicating mystery;* (b) it is intrinsic to faith that it quests continually for an understanding of God that is truthful and adequate; (c) the church itself can never fully and completely remove itself from the sin-corrupted world in which it lives; (d) the church and the Christian are ineradicably fallible; and (e) the world in which the church exists and to which it witnesses is always a world in the midst of both radical and slow change, however much it is also true that there are constancies and continuities among the various worlds of human history.

Theology as Enactment of and Reflection on Witness

The probing of these questions in the life of the church is quite simply the quest to illuminate the faithful and truthful depth grammar of Christian witness and life. This quest involves both *enacting the witness* and *reflecting on the witness*. Both the enacting and the reflecting are theological activities and involve theologizing. *Theologizing is simply that multifaceted reflective process by which the church pursues responsible understanding of the Gospel and the reality of God by constructing and critiquing its own living witness.* Theologizing and theological discourse are not merely options that the church may or may not choose to pursue: they are part of the *esse*, the essence, of the church, and are that without which no empirical group is the church, whatever else it might claim about itself. The church theologizes, for example, when it enacts its worship and reflects on its adequacy to the Gospel, when it celebrates the sacraments and reflects on the meaning of the sacraments, when it performs marriages and funerals, when it prays, and when it hands on and teaches the faith.

This theologizing is a complex *communal and individual process* and is not best thought of as a once-and-for-all completed system. The church is continually reworking, rethinking, evolving, testing, questioning, revising, reappropriating its distinctive discourses and practices. This theologizing unceasingly intends: (a) to be grounded in the biblical witness and the past witnesses of the church; (b) to be in critical and responsible conversation with these past witnesses; and (c) to construct faithfully and truthfully the present and future witness of the church.

Therefore, *doing theology is not something that is the preserve of so-called professional theologians. All the churches—indeed all Christians—are called to do theology and to be theologians.*

The Task of Systematic Theology

Systematic theology is a special task and practice that arises in the context of the church's theological critique and construction of its witness to the reality of the triune God in its multifaceted and multiformed discourses and practices. It can be performed by any Christian who seeks preparation in the reflective work of witness. Phases of its work can be performed in part or piecemeal or in essays. The performance of the task of systematic theologizing is in the service of the church's own ongoing construction and critique of its witness. However, in calling it a 'special task and practice,' I am reminding us that theology and theologizing already preexist in the life of the church, and we are not to suppose that the only 'serious theology' is systematic theology. But I do insist that serious and deliberate construction and critique of the church's witness will necessarily lead to doing systematic theologizing, whether one calls it that or not.

Systematic theology is that disciplined practice that aims to provide a critical, constructive, and comprehensive account of the basic doctrines of Christian faith insofar as they are:

a.   adequate and faithful to the Gospel of Jesus Christ, and

b.   luminous, truthful, and transformative for the world.

Systematic Theology and Doctrine

Systematic theology aims to identify, explain, and assert the basic doctrines of Christian faith. What, then, is a *doctrine*? All church traditions have agreed that Christian faith involves *teachings, convictions, and beliefs* that claim to be true about God, human life, and the world. But they have disagreed about the following: (a) what is a doctrine or dogma; (b) the ecclesial status of a doctrine; and (c) who or what process decides what the doctrines are.

I propose here that we understand *doctrines functionally: doctrines are those pivotal or focal convictions that structure the interconnections within the church's discourses and practices and that can be identified by topics and themes deemed essential to the church's life.* So, it is possible that a particular church tradition might functionally have doctrines without calling them 'doctrines.'[30]

Doctrines, thus, intend to state the truth about their subject matter: those topics and themes which are deemed essential to Christian witness and life. While questions of truth and falsehood are notoriously difficult to decide, the church's witness would wither away if it gave up the claim to be speaking the truth about God, humanity, and the world. But the church has in its Protestant variants repeatedly tried to discern what doctrines were *essential* to the church and what are *nonessential,* however

---

[30] Eschewing doctrines seems to be the case with such Free Church, anti-creedal traditions as the Disciples of Christ. But it is quite clear that the various versions of Disciples of Christ have their own essential and formative teachings.

important they might also be. Unfortunately, these distinctions of doctrines were mostly tied to the criterion of whether the doctrine was necessary for belief *in order to be saved*. I regard the discriminating of the essential and nonessential doctrines on the basis of their epistemic necessity for salvation as having had a notoriously negative and misleading effect on the understanding of the nature and use of doctrines.[31]

The explication of doctrines also involves elucidating the basic *grammar* that structures the church's discourses and practices. Hence, the identification and explications of doctrines involve: (a) elucidating the *syntax rules* of conceptual *implication* and *interpretation*; (b) elucidating the *semantic rules* for identifying the subject matters of faith, for excluding other subjects, and for making sound *truth-claims* about its subject matters; and (c) elucidating the *pragmatic rules* for how the convictions *shape and form* the concrete lives—the concrete convictions, actions, practices, and passions—of the Christian believer and the church community.

In sum, systematic theology works with doctrines so far as they: (a) assert the elemental convictions—truth-claims—of the church; (b) elucidate the grammar which those convictions embody; and (c) shape the life and witness of the church. Therefore, it is false to reduce the functions of doctrine to only one of these indispensable functions, as, for example, George Lindbeck does by distinguishing and separating doctrine as truth-claim from doctrine as rule of discourse.[32]

Accordingly, systematic theology both *describes* and *asserts* the doctrines. Insofar as it is merely descriptive, the theological effort might be performed other than as an activity of faith; to this extent the theo-

---

[31] At a later point in the text I will propose more helpful ways of interrelating faith, knowledge, and the several meanings of salvation. The point to be emphasized now is that the testing of doctrine according to what one *must believe in order to be saved* has skewed honesty in the church about having doctrines and has made it sound as though *our believing* is what saves us.

[32] See George A. Lindbeck, *The Nature of Doctrine: Religion and Theology in a Postliberal Age* (Philadelphia: Westminster, 1984), especially 71–108. This is a discerning book that has been influential in contemporary theology and can be read with great profit. As came to be recognized in contemporary analytic philosophy, the same locution can be used now in one context as an assertion and then in another context as a rule of use. Think of the locution 'Jesus is Lord.' Is that making a truth-claim about Jesus or is it answering the question of who is the Lord of the church and the Christian? Or can these be easily separated?

logical discourse is *about* the grammar of the doctrines. Insofar as it is assertive of the doctrines, the theological effort itself has the pragmatic conditions of being performed in the obedience of faith; to this extent the discourse is itself part of the *assertorial witness of faith.*

Thus doctrines are essential to the capacity of the church to have an integral life of coherent and consistent discourses and practices that can concretely shape and form the life of the church and its witness. Disarray in doctrine—as disarray in the fundamental convictions that structure the church's life and witness—is damaging to the power of the church's actual discourses and practices to form human life. Hence, agreement in doctrine should never be construed as merely an intellectual or verbal affair: it has to do with the vital heart of the *formation and performance of Christian life and witness.*

Some of the focal doctrinal topics of this systematic effort are: (1) Revelation and the Knowledge of God; (2) Triune God; (3) God the Creator; (4) Humanity as Created and as Sinful; (5) Person and Work of Jesus Christ [Christology]; (6) Holy Spirit; (7) Christian Life; (8) Church [Ecclesiology]; (9) Eschatology. I have made no consistent attempt to identify exactly what part of a discussion of a doctrinal topic is the doctrine as such and what part is the elaboration and explanation of the doctrine. In most cases, this is a conceptually difficult distinction to make, though an ecclesial body might make such a distinction. The Roman Catholic tradition has been much more confident in identifying specific wording as the dogma or doctrine as such, while permitting discussion of its elaborated meanings.[33]

Systematic Theology as a Systematic Task

Systematic theology is a critical task insofar as it critiques—analyzes, diagnoses, and assesses—the witnesses of the church, in the past and in the present, according to their conformity to the Gospel of Jesus Christ. It is here that the sources and norms of theology have to be identified as the tools by which the past and present witnesses are as-

---

[33] In addition to Lindbeck, important contemporary discussions of the concept of doctrine are: Wolfhart Pannenberg, *Systematic Theology,* vol. 1, trans. Geoffrey W. Bromiley (Grand Rapids, Mich.: Eerdmans, 1991), 1–61; and from a Roman Catholic perspective, Karl Rahner, "Dogma," *Encyclopedia of Theology: The Concise Sacramentum Mundi,* ed. Karl Rahner (New York: Seabury, 1975), 352–370, and Karl Rahner, *Theological Investigations,* vol. 1, trans. with introduction by Cornelius Ernst (Baltimore, Md.: Helicon Press, 1961), 39–78.

sessed. I have argued that the Gospel of Jesus Christ is such a critical norm for the church's theologizing. Such critical assessment is never a completed task, which is in part affirmed in the ineradicable questions. As a critical task, it is a rational exercise in and for the church.[34]

Systematic theology is a constructive task insofar as it intends to construct the witness of the church for today and tomorrow on the basis of the past witness of the church in Scripture and tradition. It is not a simple repetition of the past witness, for it intends to check that past witness for its faithful and truthful conformity with the Gospel of Jesus Christ. Further, it intends to address a truthful, luminous, and transformative witness for the contemporary world in which it lives. As constructive, systematic theology is not *reinventive*, though it can properly be *revisionary*. The construction undertakes to revise the past witness when it is determined that such witness misphrases, misleads, or misrepresents the Gospel.

Systematic theology is a comprehensive and holistic task insofar as it intends to understand and articulate the faith of the church in its wholeness and unity as *one faith*. Practically it aims to bring together basic doctrines into a framework that is systematic and comprehensive of the basic topics and themes of Christian witness. In this search for comprehensiveness, systematic theology intends to omit no doctrinal subject matter that is constitutive of the church's witness in its discourses and practices. As should be obvious, such efforts at comprehensiveness will variously be more or less detailed and elaborate.

Systematic theology is a systematic task insofar as it intends to be an *orderly, coherent, and consistent* elaboration of the doctrines of the faith. This is the primary sense of 'system' in its performance. As orderly, it follows some identifiable and methodical order of presentation and explanation. It does not seem essential to the faith that there is only *one* permissible order. As coherent, it asks whether the doctrines hang together in such a way that they are interconnected and mutually complementary. As consistent, it asks whether the doctrines are without self-contradiction. According to this sense of *systematic*, there are two inappropriate meanings of 'system': (a) as a set of doctrines derived deductively from one or two fundamental principles; and (b) as a set of axioms deductively interrelated. The pursuit of such orderliness, coherence, and

---

[34] In chapter three the issues of norms and sources will be explored and elaborated.

consistency marks this theological effort as rational.

Systematic theology is a task of mapping the discourses and practices of the church. Insofar as systematic theology aims to provide a map, it is more nearly the large-scale sort we would find on a map of the interstate highway system in the United States. It is a useful map that shows us how to identify and travel to major locations and places of interest. But it does not contain all the myriad details a microscopic-scale map has about state and county roads, city streets, and other less prominent locations and routes. We can think of the whole complex of actual discourses and practices of the church as the more detailed mapping of the daily life of the church, while systematic theology aims to map only the macroscopic doctrines, interconnections among doctrines, and their bearing on the general practices of the church's life. Sermons and essays are the sort of microscopic mapping that concretely shows us the route of being Christian in particular times and places, elaborating with illuminating power the landscape of the church in its locale.

Systematic Theology Inquires about Orthodoxy and Heresy

In the light of the church's past practices of slaughtering, persecuting, and mistreating presumed 'heretics,' the modern Protestant churches have virtually dismissed questions of orthodoxy and heresy. Historically this practical dismissal was virtually necessary, but theologically this dismissal has been debilitating for the church's witness and self-understanding. How can the church's witness have any integrity if just anything is permitted to occupy and define its witness? It has had the effect of *privatizing faith* as simply our *individual preferences,* without regard for the historic teachings of the church or for the church as the community in which one learns the faith.

I am contending that functionally every church and every systematic theological effort must confront the following questions:

    a. Questions of orthodoxy and orthopraxis: what must *always* be said and done in the church's witness;

    b. Questions of heresy and heretical praxis: what must *never* be said and done in the church's witness; and

    c. Questions of permissible and nonschismatic disagreement and diversity.

Aside from the questions of 'who decides?' and 'by what procedures does the church decide?,' I would propose the following as a place to start: The church must always say 'Jesus Christ is the self-revelation of

God' and must never deny that Jesus is Lord of the church. The church must always love the neighbor and renounce violence and must never enact violence against heretics and other 'enemies.'

The doctrines of the church—as stated in locutions and connected by implication and interpretation to other locutions—are always *reformable*. While it is a virtual tautology that truth is irreformable, *our statements of the truth* in the church are subject to fallible interpretations as the church moves through various social worlds and historic epochs. The locutions of doctrines must always receive explication in terms of their syntax—their logical and interpreted connections to other locutions, their semantics—their capacity to refer truthfully to their referents, and their pragmatics—their capacity to form and shape the lives and understanding of the faithful. For example, the locution 'Jesus is the Son of God' is virtually meaningless without understanding the uses it has been put to in some community of language users. And herein we come up against the historical fact that the locution itself has been subject to various uses and interpretations. It has had various syntactical interpretations and implications with other signs. For example, some say '*Son of God* means no more than a spirit-inspired prophet,' while others say '*Son of God* means that Jesus is of the very essence of God.' It has had various semantic rules. For example, some say 'Jesus is the one born of the Virgin Mary,' while others say 'Jesus was one who taught like a cynic philosopher.' It has had differing pragmatic conditions. For example, some say 'Jesus is my Savior from sin,' while others say 'Jesus shows us how to do what is right.'[35] Because of this undeniable linguistic situation in the history of the church, we must admit *that the locutions of the doctrines of the church are always reformable and never infallible or inerrant.* This is consistent with our earlier point that God puts ineradicable questions to the church in every age of its life of witness.

Systematic theology intends to make a normative proposal concerning the basic beliefs and practices of Christian witness. Insofar as systematic theology intends to state the truth of Christian faith, it seeks that which is normative for Christian belief and practice. It seeks to identify, describe, explain, and assert what it takes to be the truthful content of the doctrines of the faith. To this extent it seeks to state a *normative grammar for the church*, knowing all along that there are in the church some

---

[35] These examples show how intertwined syntax and semantics are in actual speech.

competing grammars. A particular systematic effort certainly must engage and argue with other grammars, even if it cannot of itself finally
settle the issues. Yet a systematic theology is only a *proposal to the
church.* It seeks the church's acceptance and implementation. Here we
can identify the paradox of systematic theology: it seeks to state the
truth, yet it cannot finally vouch for itself, and it is always fallible and reformable. Thus, systematic theology is always treading a path toward
orthodoxy and in differentiation from heresy, yet swimming valiantly in
the sea of the permissible and the disputable.

Systematic Theology and Other Theological Disciplines

*Systematic theology is integrally related to other disciplines in the
large process of theological reflection in the church,* such as: (a) biblical
theology, which engages the ineradicable questions and the biblical witnesses; (b) historical theology, which engages the ineradicable questions
and the historical traditions of the church's witnesses; and (c) practical
theology, which engages the ineradicable questions concretely in the ecclesial practices of the church. These are best thought of as inseparable,
though distinguishable, phases in the practices of the church's theological life. These distinctions are not intrinsic to the life of the church, but
arise primarily in the church's organized curricular efforts to educate
leadership for the church. But it should be noted that these are *theological disciplines,* and therefore are concerned with the ineradicable questions of the church's witness in the past, present, and future.

Systematic Theology, Dogmatics, and Apologetics

The Priority of Dogmatics

Systematic theology must deal with the issues concerning dogmatics
and apologetics. I raise this question: is systematic theology one or the
other of these theological exercises or both? By *dogmatics* I refer to that
concern to clarify the distinctive content of Christian faith *for the church*
itself, so that the church can be clear about what it believes and why in
its witness to the world. But in light of our stated concern to witness to
the world in luminous and transformative ways, we can discern the real
temptation to develop the distinctive content of Christian faith in a way
that does not communicate luminously and transformatively for the

world.

By *apologetics* I refer to that concern of the church to *make a case* for its witness to the world in order to *persuade the world.* But in light of our stated concern to be adequate and faithful to the Gospel of Jesus Christ, we can discern the temptation to adopt assumptions, as shared in common with the world, which might distort the Gospel.

To be sure, in the performance of dogmatics, the witness of the church will intend to show the world *why* it ought to believe the Gospel, precisely insofar as the dogmatics involves the stating of reasons for why the church believes as it does. In terms of current discussion, the dogmatics of the church is surely *public theology* as well: it intends to be a discourse that addresses the world about the reality of the triune God.[36] The temptation of apologetics is to start with the world, with its various assumptions, predispositions, and epistemologies, and then attempt to make a case on those terms for why the world should believe the Gospel. The issue here between dogmatics and apologetics is how does the church show the *credibility* of its witness, and *credible* on what grounds for what *public.* I have already affirmed that the church's witness makes truth-claims about God and much more; but how are these truth-claims justified and justified for whom?[37]

While I contend that *the dogmatic moment should have a priority on the work of systematic theology, the apologetic moment cannot be completely omitted.* Yet if systematic theology started primarily with the apologetic moment, then it would be inclined to adopt only those concepts and beliefs that could be persuasive for the world *on the world's terms.* But this might render null and void the ways in which the Gospel of Jesus Christ questions the assumptions of our worlds. As I will argue in the next section, there is a *dialectic between church and world* that can easily be skewed if systematic theology were primarily aimed at con-

---

[36] The various claims in American Christianity for a 'public theology' are odd in the extreme, as though Christianity ever intended to be a 'private theology' just for believers. If it were such a theology, then the church could not execute its mission of witnessing to the world. To witness to the world means to be a public theology. The hidden premise in some of this talk, however, is that to be public means necessarily to be convincing to a 'reasonable person.' But what does it mean across the board of our contemporary discourses and practices to be a reasonable person?

[37] These issues will be explored in a greater detail in the next chapter on revelation and the knowledge of God.

vincing the world of the truth of its witness to God on the world's own terms.

Types of Apologetic Persuasion

There are appropriate apologetic moves in systematic theological reflection and witness if we think of *apologetics as Christian persuasion of the world.* But we need to distinguish *two types of such persuasion.*

First, there is the *apologetics of clear interpretation and explanation* of what Christian faith truly is and how it bears on and illuminates human life. The world is often quite confused or illiterate about what Christian faith fundamentally is and claims. Such clarifications, which have the world in mind and try to address the misunderstandings and objections of the world, often just of themselves persuade. The church must repeatedly be astounded at questions and objections of the world that are rooted in fundamental misunderstanding of just what the church is claiming and enacting. Acute theological conceptual work can often rebut and dismantle putative objections to Christian faith. But it is unwise to expect that all such objections might be rebutted, for it remains possible that a person might understand accurately the syntax and the semantics of Christian beliefs, but still refuse to find them credible and pragmatic for her life. But the apologetic interpretation, with a world in view, can show how Christian faith shapes and forms concrete human living and understanding, thus showing *how Christians make sense out of life in that world.* It will be a contention of mine throughout this text to demonstrate the *sense-making power of Christian discourses and practices in the concrete daily experiences of believers.*

Second, there is the *apologetics of epistemic justification* in which the concern is to justify the truth-claims of the church to the satisfaction of the world or some segment of the world. There are two possibilities of such apologetic work: (a) noncircular epistemic justification and (b) circular epistemic justification. The *noncircular justification* of Christian beliefs aims, *without assuming basic Christian beliefs and concepts,* to rationally justify the truth of Christian beliefs or at least some basic Christian beliefs. This is the lure of much natural theology. It has been kept functionally alive in the Roman Catholic tradition of employing a general philosophical epistemology to justify those propositions that are the presuppositions of faith, the so-called *preambula fide*.[38] In my judgment, such theologizing actually is intrinsic to systematic theology and should never be understood as standing on its own independent of the revelation of God in Jesus Christ. Transcendental reasoning is not necessarily the pursuit of a metaphysics rationally defensible apart from Christian belief, but it can be employed in the explication of the presuppositions and implications of God's self-revelation. When the preoccupation with the metaphysics of an independent fundamental theology takes over the controls of the explication of Christian faith, then it threatens to subvert the church's elemental conviction that God has uniquely revealed Godself in the history of Israel and in Jesus Christ.[39]

The appetite for the apologetics of epistemic noncircular justification has waned in the last half century. We seldom read attempts to 'prove' the existence of God. Whatever such attempts were in the past, they were already presupposing the world of Christian discourse or they were naïvely confident in some presumed power of natural, neutral, objective reason to mount compelling arguments to all rational persons. Consider, for example, the so-called ontological argument first made famous by Anselm. Rather than being a noncircular argument proving the existence of God, it is more nearly the logical unfolding of what I call the syntax and semantics of the Christian concept of God: for Christian theology, given who we think God is, it is true that God necessarily exists. While such reasoning shows the logic of the Christian concept of God, it does not independently 'prove' that God exists. Few nonbelievers will be persuaded by this reasoning as such.[40]

---

[38] See entries on "Fundamental Theology," "Theology," and "Transcendental Theology" in Rahner, *Encyclopedia of Theology*. One of the controversial concerns about Rahner's project is whether he thinks the transcendental reasoning of fundamental theology requires a metaphysics or ontology that stands on its own independent of Christian discourse or is simply the internal unfolding of how Christian discourse makes sense. For example, is the belief that human being is by nature 'open' to the being of God a belief that is defensible without recourse to Christian discourse, or is it simply the view of the nature of human being that is intrinsic to Christian discourse as such? I will argue in the doctrine of humanity that this is a Christian construal of human nature that itself presupposes that God is Creator, Reconciler, and Redeemer of humanity.

[39] I will return to this theme in the discussion later of so-called natural knowledge of God.

[40] For interesting collections of text dealing with the ontological argument see: John H. Hick and Arthur C. McGill, eds., *The Many-Faced Argument* (New

Circular justification, on the other hand, is an exercise that touches, *in a large circular movement,* many of the world's own beliefs and yet does not rely on them to found and ground the basic truth of Christian beliefs.[41] Without claiming that basic Christian beliefs must be grounded in the world's own truth-claiming discourses if they are to be responsible, this justification seeks to show that the faith is compatible and consistent with many of the beliefs of the world and that the faith can make coherent sense of these many beliefs. This exercise in epistemic justification is close to the interpretative sort of apologetics, and is quite plausible for Christian theological reflection.

While the interest in the apologetics of epistemic noncircular justification has faded,[42] the preoccupation with *hermeneutics* in the last seventy-five years can be seen as concerned to practice the apologetics of interpretation and can support the apologetics of circular epistemic justification.

In concluding this section, I admit that this text in systematic theology will tilt more in the direction of dogmatics than in the direction of apologetics. Unless the church becomes clear about its own basic grammar, its various apologetic exercises carry the risk of dissolving the centrality of the Gospel of Jesus Christ in the interest of persuading some world of the truth of Christian faith. Further, the full exercise of the apologetic impulse is exceedingly complex and can hardly be accomplished in the limits of this text. But apologetics will always be haunted by the question of toward which world—or which segment or audience in the world—is the apology aimed. The intellectual elite? Who are they? The indifferent and morally complacent? Who are they? These questions lead us into the next section to discuss what I call the dialectic between church and world.

York: Macmillan, 1967) and Alvin Plantinga, ed., with introduction by Richard Taylor, *The Ontological Argument* (Garden City: Anchor Books, 1965). For a spirited defense of the argument within the context of process metaphysics, see Charles Hartshorne, *Anselm's Discovery: A Re-Examination of the Ontological Proof for God's Existence* (LaSalle, Ill.: Open Court, 1965).

[41] In calling this a large circle of justification, I intend to refute the charge that it is a 'vicious circularity' in which the conclusion of an argument is already deductively contained in the premises. The network of Christian beliefs is a complex network that is interconnected, but it is not deduced from some basic first principles.

[42] In some circles of classical and process theisms and in some practices of Roman Catholic theology, the enthusiasm for such apologetics is still strong.

The Dialectic between Church and World

In the previous discussions I have had occasion to use the word 'world' in various connections. It is now appropriate to analyze some differentiated meanings of this word. I have emphasized that the church exists for the benefit of the world. This claim posits some differentiation between church and world. This difference between church and world is conveyed in the dictum that the church is *in* the world but not *of* the world.[43] This points us toward a tension that exists at many levels in the life of the church. I am referring to these many levels or dimensions of tension between the church and the world as the dialectic between the church and the world. The term *dialectic* refers *to the dynamic interaction and penultimately irreducible tension between the church and the world.*

To explain this dialectic, it is necessary to understand *three different but interrelated meanings of the word 'world' in the church's discourse*:
  a. the world as the cosmos of creatures created by God;[44]
  b. the world as any human culture/society with its structures, relations and relationships, powers, values, discourses, practices, and traditions;[45]
  c. the world as any human culture/society infected and skewed by human sin.[46]

From these distinctions we can conclude that there are many different cultural/social worlds in which the church has existed in the past and present. The church has existed in the Roman empire in the second century and in Paris, France, Paris, Texas, and Rio de Janeiro, Brazil, in the twentieth century, for example. Further, because every culture/society has its own distinctive structures, relations and relationships, powers, values, meanings, languages, and traditions, we can understand that there are many different *dimensions, spheres, and characteristics* of the particular cultural/social world in which the church exists. These include such complexes, for example, as government, politics, economics, education, arts, communications, and ethos. We cannot reduce a culture/society to just one dimension or sphere. Hence, we need to be able

---

[43] See 2 Cor 10.3–5; Jn 17.14–18.

[44] See Jn 1.1–4, 9–10; 21.25; Acts 17.24; Rom 1.20; Phil 2.15.

[45] See Mt 4.8; Lk 12.30; Mk 8.36. For the purposes of this discussion I will use 'culture,' 'society,' and 'social world' interchangeably, unless otherwise stipulated. For other purposes we might pursue a distinction.

[46] See Jn 12.31; 16.11; Rom 5.12; 1 Cor 1.21; Gal 4.9.

to differentiate among the various worlds themselves and among the different dimensions and spheres that comprise any one world. When we use 'world' in a large social sense as, for example, in talking about the 'the American world,' we recognize that there are within that world a host of 'subcultures/societies.' In our discussion of language I argued that these more focused social units often have their own distinctive discourses and practices that differentiate them from the larger social world in which they exist. Hence, we must be wary of using 'world' too simplistically, even though the differentiated concepts are important to the sort of theologizing I am proposing and doing.[47]

As a liberative and redemptive community of persons, the church is always some cosmologically, historically, and geographically locatable empirical group of persons *in the world* in all three senses of 'world.' It is in the world as that cosmos of creatures created by God. It is in the world as some specific historical and geographical social location. It is in the world as infected by sin, which also infects the church. Yet it is also the case that in all three senses, *the world is in the church.* The church can never simply remove itself from its social locations. Hence, we must not forget, given these senses of being in the world and the world being in the church, *that the church is always an "earthen vessel" ever in need of grace, renewal, and reform.* [2 Cor 4.7 (RSV)]

However, as a *community comprised of distinct discourses and practices,* the church itself is always a particular culture/society—or *subculture*—within some larger culture/society/world. The church has its distinct *identity and differentiation* from the larger social world precisely in and through these discourses and practices. It is in these theological discourses and practices that the church itself diagnostically and constructively *construes* the world as: (a) created by God; (b) socially arranged in complex ways; (c) skewed by human sin; and yet also (d) the object of God's sovereign, gracious intention to redeem and fulfill.

---

[47] See Kathryn Tanner, *Theories of Culture: A New Agenda for Theology* (Minneapolis: Fortress, 1997), 1–119 for a discerning discussion of the differences in the theories of culture that have influenced theological reflection. Tanner also has her own proposals concerning the uses and the limits of concepts of culture in theological analysis and construction. Clifford Geertz's *The Interpretation of Cultures* (New York: Basic Books, 1973) usefully explores the role of language in the formation and unity of a culture. His work has been influential in that contemporary movement of theology called 'postliberal,' a term employed by George Lindbeck to describe his theological perspective. See Lindbeck, *The Nature of Doctrine.*

Hence, theologically the church defines itself and the world by way of the Gospel of Jesus Christ and must not succumb to the temptation of being defined and placed by the world on the world's own terms.

A Multidimensional Dialectic

The dialectic of the church's relation to the world must be multidimensional, discerning, and discriminating on the basis of the Gospel of Jesus Christ. H. Richard Niebuhr's influential typology of church and world relations in *Christ and Culture* can be misleading without further awareness of the different dimensions and spheres of culture.[48] Substituting 'church' for 'Christ,' we have Niebuhr analyzing five different types of church/world relations:

a. Church *against* Culture
b. Church *of* Culture
c. Church *above* Culture
d. Church and Culture in *Paradox*
e. Church the *Transformer* of Culture.

John Howard Yoder has convincingly argued that Niebuhr's understanding of culture is too 'monolithic.'[49] Culture or world is not just one phenomenon; it is many. So, the church might be against culture in one sphere, while quite accommodating to culture in another sphere. But this typology, especially a, c, d, and e, can be helpful if seen as a delineation of actual possibilities of the church's complex multidimensional relations to the world, in all three senses of 'world.' I do affirm that these possibilities are brought together under the unified mission of the church to

---

[48] H. Richard Niebuhr, *Christ and Culture* (New York: Harper & Brothers, 1951).

[49] See "How H. Richard Niebuhr Reasoned: A Critique of *Christ and Culture*" in Glen Stassen, D. M. Yeager, and John Howard Yoder, *Authentic Transformation: A New Vision of Christ and Culture* (Nashville, Tenn.: Abingdon, 1996), 31–90. Yoder's works have been especially helpful in understanding and analyzing what I am calling the dialectic between church and world. See John Howard Yoder, *The Priestly Kingdom: Social Ethics as Gospel* (Notre Dame, Ind.: University of Notre Dame Press, 1984); *The Royal Priesthood: Essays Ecclesiological and Ecumenical*, ed. with introduction by Michael G. Cartwright, with foreword by Richard J. Mouw (Grand Rapids, Mich.: Eerdmans, 1994); and *For the Nations: Essays Evangelical and Public* (Grand Rapids, Mich.: Eerdmans, 1997).

witness to and participate in God's *transforming and redeeming* work for the world.

We can affirm, therefore, that the church is not *opposed* to everything in every human cultural/social world in particular or in principle. Yet the church is engaged in prophetic critique of much of the cultural/social worlds insofar as they are skewed by human sin and destructive of human flourishing. But this critique and opposition must be multidimensional, discerning, and discriminating. The church may be in critique of a particular government or governmental policy without being against civil government in principle. In summary form we can say that *the critique and opposition to a world skewed by sin are the nonviolent practices of the Gospel in which the church seeks God's peace and justice for the world through works of love.* In this critique of and opposition to the world, the church intends to convey and embody an *alternative way of living in the world.* In this respect the church can be *countercultural.* Yet even when opposed to the world in some dimension—as countercultural—the church is basically *for-the-world* as that reality on behalf of which it exists in mission. But this being-for-the-world arises from the call of the Gospel and is not grounded in the world's own discourses and practices.

The Perils and the Promises of the Dialectic

As I have said, there is an *incessant dialectic* between the church and the world in which it exists and which is the object of its mission of witness. I have said that the word '*dialectic*' refers to the dynamic interaction and penultimately irreducible tension between the church and the world. Let us look now at some reasons for the dialectic.

First, the church itself is inevitably influenced and concretely shaped by the world in which it exists. It is influenced by language, historical memory, institutional practices, power structures, values, traditions, and other things. This inescapable influence poses the following *perils*: (a) that the church will itself be no more than a *mirror image* of the world in which it exists; (b) that the church will have no distinct Gospel-identity in differentiation from other communities in that world; and (c) that the church's 'gospel' will become no more than what the world endorses and defines on the world's own terms of self-understanding and its preferred modes of truth, morality, salvation, and hope. When these perils happen, the church ceases to be a countercultural community that can exist with its own integrity and yet exist for the benefit of the world. That this has often happened in the history of the church is beyond dispute.

Second, the church properly and vigorously cultivates its own distinct discourses and practices in order to capacitate the church's witness as adequate and faithful to the Gospel of Jesus Christ. This salutary cultivation, however, can pose the following *perils*: (a) that the church's distinctness will so devolve into *separation* and *withdrawal* from the world that it will have no effective witness *for* the world and thereby will defeat its own purpose and mission; and (b) that the church may *seem* to be adequate and faithful to the Gospel in its witness but is not luminous, truthful, and transformative of the particular world in which it exists. Thus when the church becomes countercultural in a separation or withdrawal model, it can easily neglect its call to *witness* to its contemporary world.

Third, the church intends its witness to be luminous, truthful, and transformative for the contemporary world in which it exists. However laudatory this intention might be, it is difficult to execute faithfully, and thus poses the following *perils*: (a) that its witness may not be so luminous, truthful, and transformative because it is a witness that was created for another and different cultural world than the one in which it now actually exists; (b) that the church may not concretely understand and diagnose adequately the particular world in which it exists and thereby its witness might miss the mark; and (c) that the church in a particular exercise of theologizing might speak to one subculture to the exclusion of other subcultures.

All three of these perils can be multiplied exponentially when we see that there are also the subcultures within every large social world that are especially attractive to or repugnant to any particular exercise of the church's witness. The legitimate impulses of apologetics are repeatedly imperiled.

This penultimate dialectic between church and world poses some ongoing diagnostic questions and issues for the Church: (a) How does the church exists *in* and *for* the world without being *of* the world? (b) How does the church know the world truly, including knowing how the world is structured and actually organized? (c) What are the various self-understandings (or, rationalized discourses) of the world in its various dimensions and spheres? (d) How does the church dialogue and converse with the world, including speaking a language that is both distinctive and persuasively understandable? (e) What are the distinguishing features of the Christian's actions and life in the world, which include the shape of

Christian ethics? (f) How does the church remain mindful of the fact that it is witnessing to various social worlds and subcultures all the time?

The dialectic and these questions and issues will be with us throughout this systematic theology project. Short of the eschaton, *there is no final, once-and-for-all resolution and cessation of the dialectic between the church and the world so far as the church is always in the world, the world is always in the church, and the church exists for the transformative redemption of the world.*

Some aspects of this dialectic can be positively construed as a *dialogue or conversation* with the world: (a) to listen to the world, to know the world's own self-understandings, maybe better than the world knows itself; (b) to listen to the world characterize the church and its Gospel; and (c) to speak to the world, to address the world, to challenge the world, to answer the questions and critiques of the world, and to be 'good news' to the world. The conversations with the world must of necessity be fluid and multidimensional. I do not believe there is some strict 'method' of 'correlation' between church and world, such as Tillich advocates.[50] Rather, the conversation is more *ad hoc* and changing in its concrete expressions as time moves in the church and in the world.[51] But in engaging in these conversations with the world, the church intends to be witnessing to the living triune God for the salvific benefit of the world.

---

[50] See Tillich, *Systematic Theology*, vol. 1, 34–68. See Francis Schüssler Fiorenza, "Systematic Theology: Tasks and Methods" in Francis Schüssler Fiorenza and John P. Galvin, eds., *Systematic Theology: Roman Catholic Perspectives*, vol. 1 (Minneapolis: Fortress, 1991), 1–85, especially 55–65 on the method of correlation. David Tracy has been searching for a method of correlation in *Blessed Rage for Order* (New York: Seabury, 1975) and *The Analogical Imagination* (New York: Crossroads, 1981). It strikes me that Tracy's learned exercises have a particular intellectual culture in mind and that he never elides the perils of the dialectical and therefore unsystematic character of the church/world multiple relationships.

[51] Hans Frei insightfully developed this occasional and *ad hoc* character of theologizing in his *Types of Christian Theology*, ed. George Hunsinger and William C. Placher (New Haven, Conn.: Yale University Press, 1992), 70–92.

Some Diagnostic Points about the Situation of the North American Church and the World Today

In light of the preceding discussion of church and world, it might be helpful if I identify some of those *worldly* conditions that are in the forefront of this systematic theological effort.

The situation in the empirical church in North America confronts us with the following daunting infelicities: There is real disagreement in the church about the authority for belief and action, especially concerning biblical authority. There is no empirical consensus about what the Gospel is, and therefore, no consensus about who God is, about what we mean when we say 'God.' There are urgent questions about the adequacy of past and present practices of the empirical churches. Much of the language of the past seems dead, empty, confusing, hypocritical, and just plain false to some persons in the church and in the world. And yet it also seems that few folk in the empirical churches understand distinctive Christian concepts, beliefs, and practices, and most live actual lives primarily shaped by the larger social worlds. The empirical church itself seems dominated by the reigning cultural powers, and the critiques of this domination often seem driven simply by ideological opposition to these cultural powers. The church can no longer assume the situation of 'Christendom' in which it had a privileged position in relation to the dominant powers of the world. Christendom is dead!

Nevertheless, there is a restless quest in many churches for a more vibrant and meaningful life of witness. There is as well, though it may have some different sources, an acknowledgment of an ecumenical togetherness across denominational lines.

The situation in the world confronts us with the following challenges: The world is massively *pluralistic* and *accessible*. There is a plurality of cultures, religions, political perspectives and goals, economic conditions and classes, moral practices, racial and ethnic and national traditions. This plurality is accessible, being vividly and unavoidably evident and present in the communicative transactions of the world. Hence, there are *worlds* instead of just one world, and it is impossible to find *one world* to which to witness. This poses the question of which worlds we will address and with whom we will converse.

There is also the new, irrepressible rising consciousness of the historic oppression of women by the world and by the church. From many sides there is the critique of the manifest and subtle forms of patriarchy in world and church. This is the quest for new, nonpatriarchal forms of practice and belief in all phases of human life.

There are the irrepressible calls for economic and political justice by poor, oppressed people. This is the discovery of and the finding of 'voice' by the poor. Closely related is the quest for racial and ethnic identity, recognition, dignity, and equality. But here we confront the widespread and overwhelming devastations wrought by racial and ethnic conflicts and oppressions in the last century in our contemporary world. How do we honor ethnic and racial identity and the quest for economic justice without violence and rivalry?

The environmental crisis sounds a new call for understanding and relating positively and morally to the nonhuman and cosmic environment in which we live. Clearly if this cosmic environment is God's world, then somehow it requires humanity's concerted efforts at sound ecological practices. Without dramatic interventions this crisis will continue to worsen and endanger creaturely prospects for life.

We cannot forget the situation of being *post-Holocaust*, of having witnessed the horrible destruction of Jewish life by demonic forces and powers hiding under the rubrics of 'civilization' and 'Christianity.' The history of Christian anti-Jewish practice and belief is unavoidably pressing upon our critique of the church's witness.[52]

There is also the intellectual theory that we are in a *postmodern* era. This is the conviction that the Enlightenment confidence in the power and reach of neutral, objective, and disinterested *reason* to understand and transform the world is an illusion. Postmodernism contends that there is no *neutral standpoint* unaffected by human interests, values, perspectives, and political location and power. Human interests, emanating from socio/political locations, affect all aspects of the human enterprise of beliefs and actions. This is the loss of confidence that there is something called *ontological reason*, which is a depositum of 'truths' and which can solve and resolve important human disagreements about what is real and what is morally right and universal. Rather, reason is itself always *reasoning* in some context and location of human interests and

---

[52] I am indebted to my colleague and friend Clark M. Williamson for educating me in the far-reaching issues of the Holocaust and relations among Christians and Jews. See Clark M. Williamson, *Guest in the House of Israel: Post-Holocaust Church Theology* (Louisville, Ky.: Westminster/John Knox, 1993). See as well how these concerns with post-Holocaust theology shape his fine systematic theology: *A Christian Theology: Way of Blessing, Way of Life* (St. Louis: Chalice, 1999).

investments.

Hence the task of Christian theologizing is to critique and construct the Christian church's witness to the triune God for the benefit of this contemporary world or worlds.

The defining context is the church.

The larger contexts are microscopic and macroscopic in relation to the worlds in which the church lives, thinks, and acts and for whom the church exists in witness to the triune God.

Chapter Two

Revelation and the Knowledge of God

We now ask *foundational questions* of Christian faith. The answer to the question 'how is God known?' will affect every other doctrine of Christian faith. All the doctrines have to do with God. Hence, we ask the following: (a) what do we mean when we say 'God is known'? (b) what do we mean by 'God'? (c) what do we mean by 'know'? and (d) with what right (or reason) do we say 'God is known'? We must remember that disputes over how to answer these questions are serious *grammatical* disputes over what we mean in Christian faith.

In the definition of the church offered earlier, I emphasized that the church is 'called into being by the Gospel of Jesus Christ.' To explain and elaborate this *call* is to invoke some understanding of revelation. I am claiming that the call is God's self-revelation in Jesus Christ. This is the *Gospel* and here we *know* God and derive our most basic right to speak of God. This self-revelation of God in Jesus Christ is the *foundation upon* and the *center around* which everything in Christian witness builds and pivots.

By way of contrast, we can note the range of other possible 'calls' that might be identified as foundational for the church and its witness: the law of Moses, the prophetic tradition, nature, human longing, general human religiousness, the quest for ultimate rational explanation, the various causes of social justice, the liberation of the oppressed, women's experience, ethnic experience, etc. If we were to identify one of these calls as the foundation and center of the church's being and witness, then we would be identifying what the church should regard as its definitive revelation of God. How one identifies the basic call of the church will determine how one talks about all the other dimensions of Christian witness.

The purpose of this chapter is to elucidate a doctrine of revelation and the knowledge of God. Or, in the language we have been developing, I will elucidate the Christian grammar of revelation and knowledge of God.

Biblical Notes

We must not forget that the language of the Bible is human language, comprised of particular traditions of human usage. In our English language today, there are many terms or words that function as *epistemic concepts*: know, believe, see, perceive, cognize, recognize, apprehend, comprehend, understand, discern, judge, notice, construe, insight, etc. So too there are many such functions of Hebrew and Greek words that were adopted by Israel and the apostolic church and put to special uses. This is also the case with words used as *revelational concepts*: reveal, uncover, unveil, make known, manifest, show forth, speaking, commanding, telling, etc.

Old Testament Notes

The most commanding image of God in the OT is *God speaking*: God speaking to persons, God commanding persons, instructing persons. God speaks to Adam, to Noah, to Abraham, and to many others. It is decisive for the OT that *God names or self-identifies Godself as Yahweh*—tells Moses and Israel who he is [Ex 3.13–15].[1] All such speakings, self-identifyings, and commandings are *actions performed by God at God's own initiative and under God's own power*. It is never suggested that persons discover God or come upon God or find God out in such wise that God is made into a locatable creaturely or worldly object. Hence, God is not like a creature and is not an object in the world like creatures are. Yet the language used to talk about God's speaking is lan-

---

[1] As will be apparent in a later discussion of patriarchy and language about God, I will embrace many of the critiques of exclusively male pronouns for God. However, when discussing how the OT speaks of God, I will employ its characteristic male pronouns.

guage that is analogous to human speaking. This analogical talk will persist throughout the OT, even though God is not a human person in any worldly sense of that term. Yet, following the analogy, the OT will employ vividly the language of human personal traits and actions in characterizing God's speakings and actions and attitudes.

In correlation to God's speakings and actions, it is regularly asserted in the OT that persons know God, hear God speaking, understand God's actions. To the extent, then, that God addresses people, it is implied that God is *informing* the recipients of his reality, character, and will. God's character variously is holy, righteous, almighty, merciful, steadfast love, wrathful, faithful in promises, and in declaring his will, God is directing people how to live in covenant with God and with one another. But such knowledge and understanding of God is always *relational* to God as the One who is encountering persons. That is, persons know God only in relationship to God, in which obedience to God is always the preferred relationship. Such knowing is never detached and theoretical but always self-involving and engaging for the knower. Consistent with the analogy of God's speaking to human speaking, knowing God is like knowing another person, though now the other person is not a bodily present human being.

The essential revelational theme of the OT, then, is that persons know God because God has made Godself known. It is by God's action that persons know God, encounter God, talk with God, hear God speak. God's making Godself known is often by way of using creaturely agents to speak and do God's word and action. For example, God speaks through the prophets and messengers/angels. God is mainly known, thus, through interactions and encounters with persons in creaturely history. God meets people in their lives in time and reveals his character and will. It is not a prominent theme in the OT that God is known through nature or through inferences from nature, though it is readily affirmed that God created the nonhuman order.[2]

Though God is known by humans, God remains hidden and elusive, for God's ways are not simply the ways of human beings.[3] Even as God is known and encountered by humans, God's ways and God's understanding are *unsearchable* or *unfathomable*.[4] The church will later formulate this unfathomableness of God as God's incomprehensibility; God

---

[2] See Pss 19.1–6; 29; cf. also Rom 1.19–20; Acts 14.15–17; 17.24ff.
[3] See Isa 40.28; 55.8–9; Ps 145.3.
[4] See Job 5.9; 9.10; Ps 147.4–5; see also Rom 11.33.

does not fit any of our human words and concepts perfectly.[5]

In looking back over the OT from the perspective of what God had done in Jesus Christ, it becomes clear in the NT that the communicative transactions of God with and in the history of Israel form an overarching narrative of the works of God in creating the world and communicating with the first human beings; calling the patriarchs; giving Moses and Israel God's own name, Yahweh; giving Israel Torah; and speaking to Israel through the prophets. This narrative of God's communicative transactions comes to illuminate and be illuminated by Jesus Christ as God's incarnate communicative transaction with Israel and the whole world.

New Testament Notes

The following terms are often used in the NT: *apokalypto*: to reveal, uncover, unveil; *apokalypsis*: revelation; *phaneroo*: to make manifest, reveal, show; *phaneros*: manifestation, revelation; *ginosko, epiginosko,* and *gnosis*: to know; *pistis*: faith, the essential way for knowing God.[6]

It is everywhere presupposed in the NT that God is the God of Israel and that God has a history of communicative interactions with the people of Israel and has spoken through Torah and the prophets. There are explicit NT references to God speaking in the history of Israel: Matthew 15.4; Mark 12.26; Luke 11.49; First Corinthians 6.16; Hebrews 1.1.

The heart of the NT is that the God of Israel has revealed Godself decisively in the life, death, and resurrection of Jesus of Nazareth. See especially:

Matthew 11.27: All things have been handed over to me by

---

[5] For a succinct discussion of revelation in the OT see Brevard S. Childs, *Old Testament Theology in a Canonical Context* (Philadelphia: Fortress, 1985), 20–62. A useful survey is provided in René Latourelle, *Theology of Revelation* (Staten Island: Alba House, 1966), 21–44. It should be apparent that my brief account of revelational concepts in the OT is not making the claim that the whole of the OT itself is revelation or that concepts of revelation exhaust ways in which the OT talks of God.

[6] See the entries on these terms in Gerhard Kittel and Gerhard Friedrich, eds., *Theological Dictionary of the New Testament,* translated and abridged in one volume by Geoffrey W. Bromiley (Grand Rapids, Mich.: Eerdmans, 1985). Hereafter this volume will be referred to as *TDNT*. See as well the entries on these terms in George Arthur Buttrick, ed., *The Interpreter's Dictionary of the Bible,* 4 vols. (Nashville, Tenn.: Abingdon, 1962), hereafter referred to as *IDB*. Latourelle, *Theology of Revelation*, 45–81 is discerning and accessible.

my Father; and no one knows [*epiginosko*] the Son except the Father, and no one knows the Father except the Son and anyone to whom the Son chooses to reveal [*apokalypto*] him.[7]

Luke 2.32: [Jesus is] a light for revelation [*apokalypsis*] to the Gentiles and for glory to your people Israel.

John 1.1ff: In the beginning was the Word [*logos*], and the Word was with God, and the Word was God. . . . All things came into being through him. . . . The true light, which enlightens [viz. throws light on] everyone, was coming into the world. He was in the world . . . yet the world did not know [*ginosko*] him. He came to what was his own, and his own people did not accept him. . . . And the Word became flesh and lived among us, and we have seen his glory, the glory as of a father's only son, full of grace and truth. . . . No one has ever seen [*horao*] God. It is God the only Son . . . who has made him known [*exegeomai*].

Hebrews 1.1–3: Long ago God spoke to our ancestors in many and various ways by the prophets, but in these last days he has spoken to us by a Son, whom he appointed heir of all things, through whom he also created the worlds. He is the reflection of God's glory and the exact imprint of God's very being, and he sustains all things by his powerful word.

Colossians 2.2–3: So that they may have all the riches of assured understanding and have the knowledge [*epignosis*] of God's mystery [*musterion*], that is, Christ himself, in whom are hidden all the treasures of wisdom [*sophia*] and knowledge [*gnosis*].[8]

Ephesians 1.8–10: With all wisdom and insight [God] has made known [*gnorizo*] to us the mystery of his will, according to his good pleasure that he set forth in Christ, as a plan for the fullness of time. . . .[9]

Paul is quite clear that he "received [the gospel] through a revelation [*apokalypsis*] of Jesus Christ," which is also a revelation by God.[10] Such revelation is not of "human origin." And Paul takes it quite for

---

[7] See also Lk 10.22; Jn 1.18; 14.7; 1 Jn 5.20.

[8] See also Col 1.25–26.

[9] See also Eph 3.3–9 and Rom 16.25–27.

[10] Gal 1.11–12, 15–16; see also Eph 3.1–4; 2 Cor 12.1, 7.

granted that others receive revelations from God.[11]

What God has done and made known in the life, death, and resurrection of Jesus Christ is to be witnessed, proclaimed, for it is good news [gospel: *euangelion*] to all people. This good news is a message [*kerygma*] which can be spoken to others and received in faith. Again it is evident in the NT that this gospel message is informative of God and human salvation.

> 1 John 1.1ff: We declare to you what was from the beginning, what we have heard, what we have seen with our eyes, what we have looked at and touched with our hands, concerning the Word of life—this life was revealed [*phaneroo*], and we have seen [*horao*] it and testify [*martyreo*] to it, and declare to you the eternal life that was with the Father and was revealed to us . . . and truly our fellowship is with the Father and his Son Jesus Christ. . . . This is the message we have heard from him and proclaim to you, that God is light. . . .
>
> Romans 1.16–17: For I am not ashamed of the Gospel; it is the power of salvation to everyone who has faith. . . . For in [the Gospel] the righteousness of God is revealed through faith for faith.

Those who hear and respond to the Gospel of Jesus Christ are empowered by the Spirit and live by faith.

> John 14.26: But the Advocate [*paracletos*], the Holy Spirit, whom the Father will send in my name, will teach you everything, and remind you of all that I have said to you.
>
> 1 Corinthians 2.10: These things God has revealed to us through the Spirit.
>
> Ephesians 3.5: This mystery was not made known to humankind, as it has now been revealed to his holy apostles and prophets by the Spirit.

The Gospel of Jesus Christ, as the manifest wisdom and knowledge of God, is in contrast to the wisdom and knowledge of the world.

> For the message about the cross is foolishness to those who are perishing, but to us who are being saved it is the power of God. . . . Has not God made foolish the wisdom of the world?

---

[11] 1 Cor 14.6, 26, 30; Phil 3.15.

> For since, in the wisdom of God, the world did not know God through wisdom, God decided, through the foolishness of our proclamation [*kerygma*] to save those who believe. . . . we proclaim Christ crucified, a stumbling block to the Jews and foolishness to Gentiles, but to those who are the called, both Jews and Greeks, Christ the power of God and the wisdom of God. For God's foolishness is wiser than human wisdom, and God's weakness is stronger than human strength.[12]

To know God in Christ is to live in faith through grace: it is a way of life. As in the OT, to know God in Christ is a personal, relational knowing, involving the heart and actions of obedience.[13]

While Jesus Christ is the disclosure of that mystery of God's purposes from the beginning, the follower of Jesus looks forward to that day when Jesus and the Father will be even more perfectly and fully revealed: "as you wait for the revealing of our Lord Jesus Christ."[14]

We can focus this brief examination by underscoring that the NT witness is knit together around the belief that Jesus Christ—his life, death, and resurrection—was the central new divine self-manifestation. Jesus Christ is the Gospel and the message to which the church is called to witness. There is no grammar of revelation in the NT that does not pivot around Jesus Christ and the discipleship of faith in which Christ is known and obeyed in faith. Such knowing and obeying, however, are empowered by the Holy Spirit.

Notes from Traditions

The Theme of Informative Revelation

Precisely because it was a common belief of the early church that Jesus Christ's life, death, and resurrection were a decisive self-manifestation of the God of Israel, it became important to collect and edit the written testimonies to Jesus Christ. Hence we have the process of the church deciding on a *canon of writings* that would ground, found, and

---

[12] 1 Cor 1.18ff.

[13] Rom 10.9–10.

[14] 1 Cor 1.7; see also Rom 8.18; Col 3.4; 2 Thess 1.7; 1 Pet 1.7, 13; 4.13; 1 Jn 2.28; 3.2.

rule the ongoing witness of the church. This canon, which included not only the new writings about Jesus but the Hebrew Scriptures, was regarded as authoritative witnesses to the reality of God. Hence, the church inherited from Israel the belief that God was uniquely active and self-revealing in the history of Israel and now extended that belief to God's unique self-revealing in Jesus Christ and the witness of the early church. The God of this canon was thus a God who not only created the world but also was repeatedly active in the world, giving direction and knowledge of his will and the destiny of the world. Crucial, then, to this sense of revelation is that God has provided a decisive *narrative* of the economy of God's activity in and with the world. This revealed knowledge was not something persons could have discovered on their own by various methods of philosophical reflection and introspection apart from the overarching narrative of the canon.

The various ecumenical councils and creeds of the church were typically brought into being as defensive measures to ward off misunderstandings of the Gospel and therewith to settle issues not directly settled in Scripture. It is thus interesting to note that there were no divisive disagreements about the authority and status of the canonical Scripture as being a revelatory witness to God's salvific work in Israel and in Jesus Christ and the apostolic church. It was assumed that Scripture embodied informative knowledge of God derived from God's self-revelations. I call this elemental set of beliefs *'The Model of Informative Revelation.'*[15] Consider the grammatical structure of this model:

a. that God has *enacted communicative transactions*[16] with the people of Israel, especially through the Torah and the prophets, and with Jesus Christ and his apostles;

b. that some of these communicative transactions were *informative* about God, humanity, and the world;

c. that God's communicative transactions were decisively enacted and culminated in the life, death, and resurrection of Jesus Christ, the Son of God and the Word of God, as the good news about the *salvation* of human beings;

d. that the life, death, and resurrection of Jesus Christ were the *en-*

---

[15] An earlier version of this model was developed, elaborated, and explored in Joe R. Jones, "Karl Barth and Informative Revelation: A Conceptual Analysis" (Ph.D. diss., Yale University, 1970).

[16] A communicative transaction of God includes God's speakings, commandings, conveyances, and historical actions that have God as the agent doing the communicating to some recipients.

acted self-communication of God;
e.   that those who have received these communicative transactions were therewith put by God in a *privileged position to know* what God has communicated;
f.   that some of those communicative transactions have been *truthfully recorded* in the Old and New Testaments by some of those who were in a privileged position to know what God had communicated;
g.   that in order to know what God has communicated, those who are not in a privileged position to know, for whatever reasons, are *dependent* upon the *authoritative witness* of those who were in a privileged position to know;
h.   that *all humans* need to know what God has communicated for their own salvation;
i.   that the heart of the biblical witness is the self-communicative transactions of God in the life, death, and resurrection of Jesus Christ as the enacted *incarnational narrative* of God.[17]

Because this model was so taken for granted right through the Reformation—which did not challenge the model as such—the following practices emerged in the life of the post-apostolic church:
a.   the Bible was the principal authority and source for the church's knowledge about God's communicative transactions in the history of Israel and in the life, death, and resurrection of Jesus Christ;
b.   the Bible was interpreted as at least containing informative truth-claims that must be interpreted appropriately in order to understand what God had revealed for humanity's salvation;[18]
c.   the church's own authority for its witness to God was grounded in God's self-revelation as recorded in the Bible;
d.   hence, the church in its witness regularly adduced propositions as truth-claims about God, humanity, and the world based on

---

[17] I appropriate the felicitous phrase 'incarnational narrative' from C. Stephen Evans, *The Historical Christ and the Jesus of Faith: The Incarnational Narrative as History* (Oxford: Clarendon Press, 1996).

[18] It should be noted that the model did not require that the Bible was simply a set of truth-claims in all of its sentences, and the model did permit an appreciation of various literary figures in the biblical text. This is not yet the biblical inerrancy and infallibility of the later church, but it veers in that direction.

God's own revelation.[19]

With the rise of the Enlightenment, the model comes under increasing critique. It was asked whether all Scripture is making truth-claims, or whether something else is going on in its various modes of language. It was asked whether the putative truth-claims of Scripture were in fact true. It was asked whether there were any extra-biblical criteria and evidence that could confirm that any, some, or all Scriptural statements are true. In these ways the Bible became subject to the same epistemic criteria that seemed to be applied to other pieces of ancient literature, which is the rise of so-called biblical criticism. Precisely in this way the Enlightenment came to deny that any of the biblical writers were in a privileged position to know what God had communicated in Israel and Jesus Christ.

Nineteenth- and twentieth-century theology became preoccupied with reworking the doctrine of revelation in the light of the apparent collapse of the model. A prominent theme of the middle half of the twentieth century in Protestant theology was to say that the Bible *witnesses* to God's revelation but is *not identical* with that revelation, and that God's revelation is *self-revelation*—God imparting Godself to recipients—and not the depositing of *revealed propositions*.[20] But this only raised the question of the relation between the self-revelation of God and the discourses of the church. Do such discourses make truth-claims about God on the basis of God's self-revelation? The so-called *fundamentalism* of the twentieth century can be understood as an attempt to preserve a remnant of the model of informative revelation by insisting on the truth-claiming *inerrancy* of the Scripture. So-called *liberal theology* can be understood as emphasizing that Scripture is basically illustrative stories of moral and religious truths that can be verified on grounds independent of the Scripture itself. Hence, it is clear that in such liberal theology the

---

[19] That there were revealed truth-claims does not mean that the Bible did no more than provide intellectual knowledge. The truth-claims were practically important for the shaping of the lives of the individual Christian and the church, which at least included their faithful appropriation of the knowledge of God.

[20] This view is most often associated with Karl Barth and Emil Brunner, and in lesser ways with Rudolf Bultmann. For an accessible discussion of this prominent theme see John Baillie, *The Idea of Revelation in Recent Thought* (New York: Columbia University Press, 1956).

model of informative revelation is virtually eradicated.[21]

General and Special Revelation/Knowledge

A continuing theme of much tradition and even in contemporary theology is the distinction between general revelation or knowledge and special revelation or knowledge. As an epistemic concept, the term 'revelation' seems to emphasize the respects in which God is the *agent* of the revealed knowledge, whereas the term 'knowledge' emphasizes the *cognitive result*, whether or not it is brought about by God's action. This distinction becomes immaterial to the extent to which both general and special knowledge of God are considered as brought about, in some sense, by God's revealing activity.[22]

General revelation refers to those places or dimensions in general human experience in which God either is known or can be known. The word 'general' means either that which is simply universal in all humans or in principle available to all humans. *Special revelation* refers to those particular revelatory actions of God directed to particular recipients at particular moments or occasions in human history.

General Revelation

General revelation claims that all humans either do know God or can know God. On the one hand, such general revelation is sometimes characterized as immediate or intuitive or noninferential knowledge of God.

---

[21] Hans W. Frei, *The Eclipse of Biblical Narrative: A Study in Eighteenth and Nineteenth Century Hermeneutics* (New Haven, Conn.: Yale University Press, 1974) traces clearly the decline of the biblical narrative in the hands of the developing liberal tradition in such wise that the *realistic narrative* of the Bible is reduced to the illustrations of theological and moral matters that the reader already has means to confirm on her own. Unfortunately, to my lights, Frei leaves the relation between 'realistic narrative' and 'truth-claims' vague and unclear.

[22] It is one of the distinctive insights of Karl Rahner to put both general and special knowledge of God in the concept of gracious divine self-communications. This significantly redraws the distinction between nature and grace, since there is no nature that is not already graced. See especially Karl Rahner, *Hearers of the Word*, trans. Michael Richards (New York: Herder & Herder, 1969) and *Foundations of Christian Faith: An Introduction to the Idea of Christianity*, trans. William V. Dych (New York: Seabury, 1978), 1–89.

This seems to be what John Cobb and David Griffin have in mind by "prethematized awareness" of God[23] or what Rahner means by "unthematic knowledge"[24] or what Schleiermacher means by "the feeling of absolute dependence."[25] On the other hand, this immediate knowledge of God can be contrasted to that general knowledge that can be called inferential or acquired knowledge insofar as it is not immediately available to all humans. Such knowledge is claimed to be available in general to human reason, experience, and reflection. This is the typical locus of so-called natural theology, which is that attempt to demonstrate certain truths about God without assuming any beliefs based on special revelation.[26]

Two qualifiers are usually made about such general knowledge of God. First, that such knowledge is often confused, clouded, and rendered opaque by human sin. Second, that such knowledge is not 'saving'—it is insufficient and incomplete. Hence, general revelation was not considered sufficient for full saving knowledge of God, and such salvific knowledge is what is given by God's special revelations. There are truths of revelation that exceed the competence of human reason alone.

One of the *strengths of these views* of general revelation is that they seem to make loose sense of the conviction that all humans are sufficiently aware of deity that they are responsible for their sinful rebellion against God. In Romans 1.18–21, Paul says:

> Ever since the creation of the world [God's] eternal power and divine nature, invisible though they are, have been understood and seen through the things he has made. So they are without excuse; for though they knew God, they did not honor him as God or give thanks to him but they became futile in their thinking, and their senseless minds were darkened.

The interpretation of this passage has had a tortuous history right up to our present time.

However, there are formidable *problems with these views* of general

---

[23] John B. Cobb Jr., and David Ray Griffin, *Process Theology: An Introductory Exposition* (Philadephia: Westminster, 1976), 30–40.

[24] Rahner, *Foundations*, 20–22.

[25] Friedrich Schleiermacher, *The Christian Faith*, ed. and trans. H. R. Mackintosh and J. S. Stewart (Edinburgh: T. & T. Clark, 1928), 12–18.

[26] This acquired knowledge of God, in distinction from God's special revelation, is clearly enunciated by Thomas Aquinas, *Summa Contra Gentiles*, I, 3–8 and *Summa Theologiae,* Ia. I, 1–8.

revelation. For one thing it is very difficult to formulate clearly what this universal knowledge is. Further, when formulated, it looks suspiciously like something we Christians *read into* the general human situation *from the perspective of faith* rather than something *read off* the general situation.[27] That is, it looks like the sort of conviction that is appropriate from the perspective of faith, but is not readily intelligible or credible apart from faith. And if it is not intelligible apart from faith, then it is obscure in just what sense all humans *know* God or *can know* God.

An even more serious problem emerges when the general knowledge of God is so formulated on grounds independent of God's special revelation in Israel and in Jesus Christ, that it is tempted to become the normative and foundational grounding of the understanding of God. When this happens, it easily claims to provide the basic rules or foundation of God-talk, of what can and cannot be said of God even with regard to special revelation. That is, this so-called general revelation or knowledge becomes the *controlling semantic rules* for identifying and describing God. This is especially the case with philosophically formulated *natural theology* and has had deleterious consequences for Christian theology in the form of *classical theism*, in various forms of Platonism, and in contemporary process theology or *neoclassical theism*. Thus, from this perspective of general knowledge one tends to see special revelation as an *example of* or further *elaboration of* what is available in general revelation and knowledge.

Special Revelation

Special Revelation is primarily used to refer to the economy of God's speaking, acting, and revealing—which can be called *special*

---

[27] See the devastating critique of immediate knowledge of God by Wayne Proudfoot, *Religious Experience* (Berkeley: University of California Press, 1985). While Proudfoot is skeptical of all claims to know God, his basic point is that characterizations of and appeals to immediate knowledge of God, such as Schleiermacher proposes, are unintelligible apart from the language of the religion itself. Hence, one cannot appeal to the experience itself as confirmation of the truth of the religious discourse. I am sympathetic with this analysis insofar as I think the language at our disposal already structures what we think we are experiencing. An extraordinary effort to blunt Proudfoot's strictures is undertaken by William P. Alston, *Perceiving God: The Epistemology of Religious Experience* (Ithaca, N.Y.: Cornell University Press, 1991).

communicative transactions of God—in the salvation history of Israel, Jesus Christ, and the calling of the church. It is at least questionable whether the church has consistently tried to allow this special revelation to set the basic or foundational rules for its talk and understanding of God and thereby also to allow it to be the critical principle for understanding general revelation. Some forms of natural theology have repeatedly provided foundational grounding for the church's theology and witness and its characterizations of God's special revelations.

I will focus on the biblical incarnational narrative of God's special revelation in Jesus Christ as the *particular* in terms of which the *general* might be further characterized and the history of Israel understood. Hence, I will construct a *doctrine of revelation* aimed at the *grammar* of Christian witness to the reality of God and how this *God is self-identified in specific acts of self-revelation*. From this distinctive faith perspective, I will also construct a grammar of the *original grace* of the Spirit of God that constitutes all persons being created by God.[28]

Interlude: Some Diagnostic Notes about Knowings

Most persons learn quite well how to use a variety of words in the family of uses about knowing: know, believe, see, see as, perceive, guess, discern, judge, notice, recognize, construe, be acquainted with, apprehend, comprehend, convinced, certain, credible, insight, etc. But we often get confused when we are asked to give an account of how we are using

---

[28] See Latourelle, *Theology of Revelation* for a discerning discussion of the traditions of the Roman Catholic Church. Avery Dulles, *Models of Revelation,* 2d ed. (New York: Doubleday, 1992) is an interesting discussion of varying emphases in the possible grammars of revelation.

On the Protestant side, the elongated discussions of God's self-revelation by Karl Barth in *Church Dogmatics*, I/1, I/2, II/1 have been heavily influential for the twentieth century. Paul Tillich, *Systematic Theology*, vol. 1 (Chicago: University of Chicago Press, 1951) develops an existential concept of revelation. H. Richard Niebuhr's *The Meaning of Revelation* (New York: Macmillan, 1955) attempts to straddle Barth and Troeltsch with insightful results. Interesting recent efforts are: Ronald F. Thiemann, *Revelation and Theology: The Gospel as Narrated Promise* (Notre Dame, Ind.: University of Notre Dame Press, 1985); Gabriel Fackre, *The Doctrine of Revelation: A Narrative Interpretation* (Grand Rapids, Mich.: Eerdmans, 1997); Nicholas Wolterstorff, *Divine Discourse: Philosophical Reflections on the Claim That God Speaks* (Cambridge: Cambridge University Press, 1995).

some of these words. In this section I will make a few remarks on topics that are quite complex and which have consumed many forests of trees trying to put it all in order.

First, what is *epistemology*? The term derives from the Greek term *episteme*, which is one of several Greek terms that are translated as 'knowledge.' Let us stipulate that *epistemology is that area of philosophy which attempts to provide an account of what sorts of objects can be known and how they can be known,* and therewith to establish both the *foundations* and the *limits of human knowledge.* This project has preoccupied much modern philosophy since Descartes, reaching monumental proportions in Kant's philosophy in the late eighteenth century. Basically Kant said our knowledge is limited to sensible objects in space and time and all attempts to know the supersensible or nonsensible are bound to end in futile and unresolvable controversies. In effect, he was saying concepts of God, the soul, and the world, for example, may be useful in various ways, but they are not concepts that can refer to something we can know. These objects transcend human knowing. For Kant it is morally useful to believe in God, and there is even an argument that helps, but we cannot know God or know that God exists.

But these projects of epistemology always start by taking some purported knowing as paradigmatic of all knowing and then seek to limit knowing to that paradigm. Many such projects have assumed that the most basic sort of knowings are matters about which we are *absolutely certain and have indubitable judgments.* If we cannot find some basic point of knowing that is absolutely certain, then all our knowledge claims seem unfounded or without foundations. They would seem more like guesses. Solipsism—the belief that we can never get outside ourselves to know anything for certain beyond ourselves—and skepticism—there is no knowledge claim that cannot be doubted—have always thrived on human vulnerability to doubt. Since Wittgenstein, the interest in writing an epistemology that settles all these questions has waned dramatically.

What is loosely called 'postmodernism' eschews the project of finding that *absolutely certain foundation* upon which we can erect our knowledge and be assured that we truly know *reality as it is.* In this sense *postmodernism is anti-foundationalist*: apart from the various practices of human communities there are no absolutely certain and indubitable truths and knowledge that guarantee that we have stated what is really the case. Such postmodern philosophers are more nearly content to look at the various contexts and practices in relation to which people use epistemic language and how it works in making sense in those contexts.[29] A typical concern in philosophy is reflection on when and how, or under what conditions, are beliefs *justified*.

All epistemic claims are dependent on language for their intelligibility. The notion of an isolated knower who knows without any language is an intellectual illusion. Further, all epistemic claims are dependent on the discourses and practices of a community of persons as providing the basic context in terms of which epistemic claims make sense. It is in such communal discourses and practices that such terms as 'rational,' 'objective,' 'knowledge,' 'belief,' 'fact,' and 'truth' have their location and sense-making power. There is no translinguistic context in which these terms have their 'true and universal' meanings.

It does not follow from these judgments that we can never know *reality truly*. It just means that all claims to know reality are claims that depend on communal discourses and practices for their intelligibility. Hence, any *reality* that we might claim to know is a reality that is known only under these linguistic conditions. This does render suspect claims to know reality that are utterly unaffected and unshaped by human discourses and practices. Further, it does not follow that all our claims to know are 'mere human constructions' and therefore 'fictions.' If all reality claims are therefore fictions, then the word 'fiction' here has been rendered meaningless, for its typical contexts of meaning involve a contrast between fiction and nonfiction. If all is fiction, then 'nonfiction' has been rendered meaningless. We really do not know what we are saying if we say—as some deconstructivists say—that all knowledge claims are mere fictions of human construction. But these considerations do mean that we cannot just step outside of all language—all human discourses and practices—and just look at reality and compare our language to the

---

[29] From varying positions see the following discussions of the practices of rationality and belief formation and sense-making in Stanley Cavell, *The Claim of Reason: Wittgenstein, Skepticism, Morality, and Tragedy* (Oxford: Clarendon Press, 1979); Stephen Toulmin, *Human Understanding* (Oxford: Clarendon Press, 1972); Richard Rorty, *Philosophy and the Mirror of Nature* (Princeton, N.J.: Princeton University Press, 1979); Richard J. Bernstein, *Beyond Objectivism and Relativism: Science, Hermeneutics, and Praxis* (Philadelphia: University of Pennsylvania Press, 1985). See also Nicholas Wolterstorff, *Reason within the Bounds of Religion*, 2d ed. (Grand Rapids, Mich.: Eerdmans, 1984) for a critique of classical foundationalism and for constructive proposals concerning theory formation and critique. Except for Rorty, none of the above authors applies the term 'postmodern' to his work.

reality as such.

Epistemic concepts can be clustered around *various models of what knowing is*. One cluster is those terms that emphasize what I will call *direct experience*: see, perceive, experience, apprehend, intuit, recognize, encounter. Another cluster is those terms that emphasize what I will call *judgment*: believing, judging, justified belief, truth-claim, proposition, statement. Yet another cluster is those that emphasize what I will call *understanding*: understand, comprehend, discern, insight, theory. I do not think there are any sharp delineations here, but claims to know variously emphasize the direct presentation of the object known to the knower or the justified belief/judgment about the object or the understanding and comprehending of the object. Clearly the meaning of the term 'object' is simply corollary to the term 'subject' as that about which the subject knows something. I contend that none of these models of knowing functions intelligibly apart from the concrete discourses and practices of human society.

Many epistemic claims will involve *making statements*, which are then the bearers of a discussion as to the statement's—or proposition's—truth. In the specified contexts it is appropriate to ask what one has to go on in making a statement, which is a request for some type of justification or argument that will provide warrants or evidence or reasons for belief. Evidence, reasons, warrants, and justifications may vary greatly in their clarity and applicability from one context to another.

Most epistemic claims are related to the *purposes at hand* in some discursive context. Given the purposes at hand in one context we might have no reason to doubt or question Fred's statement that he had four eggs for breakfast. But if Fred were a suspect in a murder and we are the detectives trying to ascertain his guilt, then it might be very important to find evidence that might corroborate what he says. Hence, contextual *trust* plays a role in our epistemic claims. That is, some claims and assumptions—some practices—must remain in place and not under doubt if we are to make headway in discussing particular claims to the truth.

We must not confuse certainty with knowing. Certainty is basically a psychological state, not so much an epistemic state. As a psychological state it can be occasioned by any number of different factors of human consciousness. And as a psychological phenomenon it can often be induced to doubt, and yet other times it seems invulnerable to doubt and argument. In the hands of a skilled interrogator most of us are vulnerable to having our certainties destabilized and doubt produced in us. But it is not a helpful practice to suppose that we only know that about which we are absolutely certain and which is therefore invulnerable to doubt. We should give up the search for absolutely certain and indubitable foundations upon which claims to know can be built. It is this search that misleads us into believing that we know reality only if we have some indubitable statements.

What is deemed *credible* or *plausible* is also context dependent. So we should ask in our epistemic searches and discussions: (a) credible for whom? (b) credible in what context? and (c) credible under what assumptions? If we are practicing the methods of inquiry of scientific biology, then we have some guidelines about how credibility is conferred on beliefs, hypotheses, and large theories. It is not uncommon that something is credible to one learned intellectual and not to another. This should warn us against supposing there are some universal norms or criteria for what is credible and plausible.

There are also the loose-fitting practices of credibility that function in most societies about what is valuable or important to human life. It should be clear that many basic Christian beliefs and practices are really quite *incredible* to much of the world's discourses and practices about what is important and what is finally real. It should also be obvious by now that there is no *neutral rationality* from which credibility and incredibility can be indubitably and absolutely conferred in any and all contexts.

The *sorts of objects* that people claim to know and the *positions* from which they know vary widely. Getting into a position to know something about the stars will involve exposing oneself to studying astronomical texts. Which texts? Those of newspaper astrologers? Rather the texts recommended to you as substantial, reliable, and accredited by some reference point or recognized authority.

Day in and day out all of us rely practically on *authorities*: persons or texts we *take* to be accredited and reliable. We *trust* the authority relative to some subject matter. None of the practices of making epistemic claims can escape completely the function of trust in authorities. Such authorities can at any point be questioned and doubted, but not all authorities all the time. Think of how we confer authority on persons called 'scientists.' Think of how we in the church trust in the basic credibility of the biblical witness to the reality of God's self-revelations, even though such claims are incredible to many other persons. Think of how church persons presume their pastor is an authoritative interpreter of the Bible and Christian faith. But, of course, on any particular occasion one can pause and examine reasons for trusting in an authority.

Basic Perspectives or Worldviews

Human beings typically have *basic perspectives which orient them to their world and in terms of which they have a world.* Such basic perspectives can also be called 'worldviews.' Basic perspectives are structured by *fundamental convictions* about the world: convictions making truth-claims about what comprises 'reality' and what is truly valuable and important in human life. Basic perspectives are rooted in communal traditions of discourse and practice and are constituted by communal construals of the world.[30] These fundamental convictions are not as subject to debate and refutation as the knowings and beliefs formed on the basis of the convictions. It is from these perspectives that people make *construals* about themselves and the world.[31]

When persons are prepared to become reflective about their basic perspectives, it is apt to ask them about the *route* by virtue of which they came to embrace the perspective on the world they do occupy. A 'route' is that experiential and existential path a person travels in her life that brings her to occupy a basic perspective. People may occupy the same basic perspective but have traveled different routes in getting there, and they may travel different routes in giving up the perspective.

While it is suspect that there is something called *universal reason*, which purports to be the position any reasonable person would occupy in whatever context, it is still the case that it is important for humans in a variety of situations to aim at stating what is in fact the case in the world. There is then a *common sense realism* in most of our talk about the world, including Christian talk: we are intending to state what is the case factually or to state what is true about God, humanity, and the world. If we gave up that intention it would drastically alter the form of life of Christian faith. What has passed from the scene, however, is the convic-

---

[30] This is not to deny that within a basic perspective there might be genuine differences among individuals who share the perspective. But when the basic convictions themselves begin to differ dramatically or there arises fundamental doubt about the convictions, there might well be a transitioning out of the perspective.

[31] For an engaging discussion very close to the one given here, see James William McClendon Jr., and James M. Smith, *Convictions: Defusing Religious Relativism*, rev. ed. (Valley Forge, Pa.: Trinity, 1994).

tion that there is some neutral perspective that is rational, universal, and objective and can bestow absolute certainty on such reality claims.

When considering how we know anything, we can distinguish the following:

a.   the statement a person utters in the speech act of making an epistemic claim (a truth-claim of some sort);

b.   the social context of discourses and practices in which the statement functions;

c.   the arguments or justification which might be provided in that context to support the claim;

d.   the purposes at hand in the uttering of the claim;

e.   the basic perspective in which the claim occurs.

When puzzled about how an epistemic term is being used, ask the existential rule for authentic speech: what would it mean *for me* to use that term? What would I be claiming?

Epistemology and Confessional Theology

We will now explore how these previous epistemological considerations might apply to Christian faith. *Christian faith is at least a basic perspective—a basic set of convictions and construals about God, humanity, and the world.* As such, then, it is not so much Christian faith that needs to find its place in the modern or postmodern world, but that Christian faith itself becomes the perspective in which these worlds find their place.[32] How these placings work out is complex and multifaceted, as I have suggested in the earlier discussion of the dialectic between church and world. What is lacking, therefore, is any appeal to a neutral, objective, and rational standpoint outside the faith that can be used either to argue the truth of faith's fundamental convictions or to argue the exhaustive falsification of faith's claims. Even the epistemic distinctions we have made above do not of themselves establish the credibility or the truth of Christian faith.

It should also be noted that in using this concept of basic perspective and fundamental convictions, I am not relinquishing the ineradicable

---

[32] I share here the theological conviction of Karl Barth that the modern world is to find its place in the biblical world of God's interactions with Israel and Jesus Christ. George Lindbeck makes this point compellingly in *The Nature of Doctrine: Religion and Theology in a Postliberal Age* (Philadelphia: Westminster, 1984), 112–135.

character of God's questioning the church. There might indeed be some adjusting in such convictions from time to time. But I am contending that *crucial to the Christian perspective is the basic conviction that God, who created all things, has communicated Godself to the world in the life, death, and resurrection of Jesus Christ as that is conveyed in the incarnational narrative of the NT.* While there may be multiple reasons for holding this conviction, there is none that is decisive independent of the narrative itself and its interpretation in the discourses of the church. We should not expect, therefore, that there will be some *theory of revelation* that will garner objective credibility for all so-called *reasonable persons.*

Talk of God's self-revelation is Christian talk about how we think our basic perspective and convictions are grounded in God's self-communication with the world as witnessed in the Bible and the church. We must remember that the grammar of God's self-revelation arises in the language of the church as the language of faith, and that this grammar structures the language of witness to God that is the mission of the church. This language of witness, which we are concerned to describe and enact, is what pivots around the biblical narrative of the life, death, and resurrection of Jesus of Nazareth. If these events enacted in and by Jesus of Nazareth were not decisive for understanding God and human destiny, then there would be no reason for speaking of God's self-revelation.

Inasmuch as there is no neutral/rational set of convictions from which the claim of revelation can be corroborated and warranted, there is no simple argument that can be followed that will get people into a position of Christian faith. In light of these considerations I contend that Christian theology—as church theology—is basically *confessional theology.* It is theology that arises from the self-revelation of God in Jesus Christ and is rooted in faith's communal response to that revelation.

Yet explicit in the Christian perspective is the claim that *its basic convictions do make sense out of human life in the world.* This *sense-making power* of Christian theologizing in discourses and practices shows itself in how we understand ourselves, others, and the world; in how we interact with the world; and in how we witness to the world. It is this sense-making power that confers plausibility on the Christian witness.

I want now to introduce the concept of *faith routes,* by which I mean those *life routes* of persons that are comprised of events, encounters, experiences, decisions, actions, desires, passions, and much more. *A faith route is such a life route by way of which a person comes into Christian faith and sustains such faith.* Such faith routes are infinitely various from person to person, and there is no neat way of putting them into an orderly path of development. Such routes are littered with trustings, decisions, doubting, hesitations, fears, reasonings, listenings to others and reading books such as the Bible, participating in some measure in the concrete discourses and practices of the church, convictions lost and convictions gained, accepting and rejecting arguments. To come to faith is to begin to *inhabit* the discourses and practices of the church as that which gives shape and form to one's life.

This concept of faith routes should help us understand that, as with the grammar of other dimensions of life, *the grammar of Christian faith is finally* ad hominem: *addressed to the person,* soliciting and requiring basic life-decisions. It is deciding to adopt a whole way and form of life, with its convictions and construals, its moral imperatives, and its passionate commitments. This *ad hominem* character comes to expression in typical Christian ways as the person trusting in God, being set free from sin, being empowered to believe what might otherwise seem dubious, being empowered by the Spirit to love deeply and passionately, and being resonate with a hope that does not depend simply on how things go in the world.

Given then the *ad hominem* character of Christian witness and the variety of *faith routes* persons might travel in coming to faith, we can see how important *narrative and story* are to a person's sense of integral becoming and self-identity. These are the stories of where we have been, how we have traveled and made sense or failed to make sense of our life and where we are going. *Coming to faith is coming to understand one's own life narrative within the incarnational narrative of Jesus Christ.*

In saying that God reveals Godself, makes disclosures of Godself to human beings, Christian grammar is drawing heavily on the analogy to human ways of disclosing self and of hiding self. In disclosing oneself to another we are taking concrete steps to put the other person in a position to know us more adequately. Similarly, Christians claim that God has disclosed Godself in Jesus Christ and therewith has put human beings into a position to know God more adequately.

Having faith involves learning how to construe the world as God's world. Hence, the *knowledge of God that comes from God's self-revelation* is:

    a.   a construal of the language of faith, of the language of biblical and church traditions;

b. a set of convictions that make truth-claims about God and the world;

c. personal knowledge that involves the whole life of the knower: her passions and actions, indeed a whole way of life or form of life;

d. like knowing another person: in faith one encounters God and becomes acquainted with God, learns how to identify and characterize God, and learns how to praise God and be obedient and pray to God.

The deployment of revelation language will thus involve all three clusters of epistemic claims: (a) direct experiences or encounters with God; (b) beliefs about God's self-identifications and human destiny; and (c) understanding the ways of God with the world and the church.

The Grammar of God's Self-Revelation in Jesus Christ

The confession that the church speaks because God has first spoken and revealed Godself is fundamental to Christian witness and self-understanding. The content of this confession, which is the normative, foundational pivot point of Christian theology, is that *God is definitively self-revealed in the life, death, and resurrection of Jesus Christ.*

By *definitive self-revelation* I mean that criterion in terms of which all other claims to 'revelation' and 'knowledge of God' are to be judged. It is also called *final revelation* in Tillich.[33] If God is not decisively known here, then Christian faith is rootless. To deny this normative and definitive claim is to confess some other norm as definitive for Christian faith and therefore some other 'calling' as essential to the church. But 'definitive' *does not mean* that the church can exhaustively conceptualize and comprehend the fullness of God's actuality. God's self-revelation in Jesus Christ does not authorize the church to put God or Jesus Christ into some pre-established classifying category of 'divine self-revelations.'

Throughout these systematic explorations I will use the locutions 'revelation,' 'self-revelation,' 'self-communication,' and 'communicative transaction' interchangeably as ways of talking about God's revelatory activities. Included in such are the various events of God's speaking to persons, God speaking through some creature, God encountering some

---

[33] Tillich, *Systematic Theology*, vol. 1, 157–159.

creature and being present to the creature, and God's acting upon or within some creaturely actualities and/or events.

Revelation, Jesus Christ, and Israel

God's self-revelation in Jesus Christ presupposes, authenticates, and transforms the understanding of God's communicative transactions in the history of Israel. Jesus Christ cannot be abstracted from God's revealings in the history of Israel. The *particularity* of God's self-revelation in the Jew Jesus of Nazareth is bound to the *particularity* of God's election of and life with Israel. For the church, these particularities are intertwined. God reveals Godself in electing and liberating Israel from slavery in Egypt, in giving Torah to Israel, and in speaking through Israel's prophets and writings. The God revealed in Jesus Christ is the God of Israel and Israel's God. Jesus Christ is unintelligible if severed from his Jewishness and the history of God's activity in Israel.

We can epistemically affirm this by saying that the God Christians know in Jesus Christ is the God who has already revealed Godself in the life of Israel. We will refer to this as *God's self-identification as Yahweh: the One who will be who he will be.*[34] It is this God of Israel who is the Creator of the whole world and becomes known in the apostolic church as the divine *Father of Jesus Christ.*

Yet in Jesus Christ the God of Israel does something *new* and is identified concretely with the life, work, death, and resurrection of Jesus of Nazareth. *For the church this self-identification of God becomes a new point of departure and a definitive self-revelation of God.* This involves an *authentication and transformation* in how one understands *God* and *Israel.* Here there is *continuity* and *discontinuity.* It is continuously the God of Israel acting, which is authenticated in Jesus, and discontinuously the God of Israel now doing this new thing in Jesus of Nazareth, which is transformative of how we are to understand God.

That there is discontinuity in Jesus Christ and in the calling of the church does *not* mean that God has *rejected* Jews who do not acknowledge God's self-revelation in Jesus Christ. Israel remains God's specially elected people; God's covenant is not broken or cancelled by God. Israel's election by God was never and is not now dependent on their virtues as a people, but is the election of the *free grace of God.* Hence, neither Israel nor the church deserves God's gracious presence nor can

---

[34] Ex 3.13–15.

either control God's presence.

God is for Israel in Jesus Christ—even as God in Jesus Christ is for all humanity. Christian grammar must *deny* that God in Jesus Christ is *just for Gentiles.* Jesus Christ was the self-revealing presence of God for Paul the Pharisee and for all the Jewish disciples of Jesus. If God in Jesus Christ were just for the Gentiles and Judaism itself remains undisturbed, then Paul made a *conceptual mistake* in accepting Jesus as his own Lord and Savior.[35] Hence, just as it is proper to say that *Jesus Christ is Israel's gift to the Gentiles,* so too it is proper to say that *Jesus Christ is God's gift to Israel.* Note: this does not say 'Jesus Christ is the church's gift to Israel.'[36]

Jesus Christ *fulfills* God's work in Israel and *extends* it beyond Israel. *Fulfill* does not mean that God's work in Israel was *empty. Fulfill* means 'brings to focus and completion,' similar to the meaning of Jeremiah that a *new covenant* will be "written on their hearts [Jer 31.31–34]." Jesus Christ picks up on and illuminates the Jewish theme that Israel is to be a "light to the nations [Isa 49.6]." But the accent is on what God does in and for Israel and the world in Jesus Christ, not on what Israel or the church does.

The church does not *supersede* Israel in the sense of rendering God's covenant with Israel null and void. Even today the church can be reminded by the existence of Jewish people that God's presence is always a free and inscrutable presence that is not under the control of the church.[37]

---

[35] Gal 2.19–20.

[36] It is troubling that, in these times of great advances in mutual understanding between Christians and Jews and the sturdy critique of historical Christian anti-Jewish discourses and practices, it is sometimes proposed that Judaism is for Jews and Christianity is for Gentiles. Such a proposal has the logical and practical effect of wiping out the NT witness as a conceptual mistake insofar as it is a witness by Jews to Jesus being their Messiah and Savior. Clearly, it is a different matter to say Judaism is comprised of Jews and Christianity is comprised of Christians, for such is simply tautologous.

[37] See my discussion of this and other issues in my essay "Jewish and Christian Theology on Election, Covenant, Messiah, and the Future" in *The Church and the Jewish People*, ed. Clark M. Williamson (St. Louis, Mo.: Christian Board of Publication, 1994), 51–58. See the welcome recent critique of Christian attitudes and theology by Jewish theologians and philosophers, with responses by Christian theologians: *Christianity in Jewish Terms*, ed. Tikva Frymer-Kensky et al. (Boulder, Colo.: Westview Press, 2000).

The Bible, the Holy Scripture for Christians of both the Old and New Testaments, is a long narrative of God's actions and workings in creation, in Israel's life, in the life of the Jewish Jesus, and in the life of the early church; *and* it is a narrative of the actions and discourses of Israel, of Jesus, and of the early church. The church would be unfaithful if it did not read the Old Testament from the perspective of what God has done in Jesus Christ. It is the revelation of God in Jesus of Nazareth that authenticates that the God of Israel is indeed the God active in Jesus and the calling of the church. Of course, the church can and should also read the OT from the perspective of the persons and times in which it was written. But the church would also be unfaithful if it did not read the New Testament from rootage in the Old Testament. Hence, the Old Testament is the *church's book*, however much it is also *Tanakh* or *Jewish Scriptures* or *Hebrew Scriptures*. But in calling it *Old* Testament the church does not mean that it is something cancelled, but it is old as something historically and theologically antecedent and essential to the *new*.[38]

God's Self-Revelation in the Life and Destiny of Jesus Christ

God's self-revelation in Jesus Christ is in the personal life and destiny of Jesus of Nazareth, and the language describing God's self-revelation is inextricably analogous to the language of human personal self-disclosure. It is God who is at work in the fully human life, death, and resurrection of Jesus of Nazareth. It is because God is decisively known in Jesus that his personal life and destiny are the incarnation of God, the very speaking forth of God's Word in human space and time. *The life, death, and resurrection of Jesus are the performative speaking forth of God's character, purposes, and salvific love and their concrete enactment.* Jesus is the concrete speech-act of God.

I will later describe this performative enactment of God in Jesus

---

[38] As controversial as it may seem to some, I will nevertheless persist in using the locution 'Old Testament' for three reasons: (1) to affirm with the apostolic church that the OT is Christian Scripture; (2) to repudiate Marcion, who thought the OT was an alien and cancelled testament to an alien god; and (3) to refuse to fall into the conceptual trap of supposing that since the OT is really the Hebrew Bible, it should never be interpreted from the perspective of Jesus Christ as a Christian Scripture. The locutions 'First Testament' and 'Second Testament' are not without value, but their blandness obscures the decisiveness of Jesus Christ for the church.

Christ as the salvific work Jesus does as *Prophet*—the one who proclaims and enacts the kingdom of God; as *Priest*—the one who is crucified for the sins of the world; and as *Victor*—the one who is raised from the dead and vindicated as the true Lord over human history and destiny. As this Prophet, this Priest, and this Victor, Jesus Christ is that historical communicative transaction that discloses the very actuality of God. In the life and work of Jesus the church confesses that it apprehends the free and loving grace of the God of Israel taking up the human plight in sin and reconciling humanity to God's own life.

God's Revelation as Self-Revelation

That God's revelation in Israel and in Jesus Christ is *self-revelation* means:[39]

   a. God is the *subject* who reveals. Negation: that God is ever the predicate or property of some other entity.
   b. God is the *agent* who reveals. Negation: that revelation is ever something *done to* God by some other agent. Hence, we are not to understand the work of the prophet as an autonomous agent doing something to reveal God. Whatever the prophet does to reveal God is done under the prior agency and empowerment of God.
   c. God is *free* to reveal Godself. Revelation is always God's *decision* to reveal Godself. As free revelation it is the revelation of God's *grace*. Negation: that self-revelation is necessary to God for God to be God.
   d. God is the primary *object* or *content* that is revealed. Hence, it is called *self*-communication or *self*-revelation. Negation: that some propositions or some texts are the primary content of revelation.
   e. God is *truly* who God is in God's self-revelation. God's self-revelation is truly a revelation of the *actuality* of God. Negation: that revelation is not truly who God is, but only a partial *appearance behind which the true God is* and who could be significantly other than what the revelation discloses. I will affirm this

---

[39] This succinct grammar of self-revelation is indebted to the grand theology of revelation in the work of Karl Barth. See especially *Church Dogmatics*, I/1; I/2; II/1.

further by saying that God's being or actuality is revealed in God's acts.

f. God *self-identifies* Godself in self-revelation. To know God paradigmatically is to know God in God's own self-revelations. Negation: that God can be adequately identified independently of God's own self-identifications, self-communications.

God's Self-Revelation Is God's Objectified Presence in a Creaturely Actuality

Jesus of Nazareth is the primary and definitive creaturely self-objectification of God. But many creaturely objects may be used by God to convey Godself: for example, human language and words, historical events and sequences, persons, nonperson objects. I will call these creaturely objects the *media* of God's self-objectification. But we must say that God *uses* the media, yet God is never the predicate or property of the media. This is affirmed in saying that God is the prime agent in revealing Godself in this mediated presence. The point here is that God presents Godself in and through the creaturely reality that is present to the recipient of the communicative transaction.

Hence, insofar as God self-objectifies Godself in a creaturely actuality, the creaturely object both *reveals* God and *veils* God. It reveals God to the extent God communicates Godself through the creaturely object, and it veils God precisely because God is not simply the creaturely object as such in its creatureliness. By itself, the creaturely object has no power to reveal God.[40] Hence, two errors or misunderstandings are always possible: (1) some persons will apprehend only the creaturely object—in this sense the creaturely object hides or veils God; and (2) some persons will repudiate the creaturely objectification and will yearn to apprehend God independently of any creaturely object. Therefore, we have one important negation: that God's self-objectification is a simple presence as a creaturely object. And we have posed an important question: if God's self-revelation involves creaturely mediation, is it ever the case that God

---

[40] Jesus is, of course, that creature that is directly identified as the eternal Son of God, but even this does not cancel the fact that simply as a human being, Jesus is present to others in ways that also veil God. Many contemporaries of Jesus obviously perceived him as a human without also perceiving him as the self-revelation of God. The veiling and unveiling of God in self-revelation through creaturely actualities are paradigmatically given in Jesus of Nazareth.

is known by humans *immediately and without creaturely mediation?*[41]

God's Self-Revelation as Salvific Event
through Faith by the Holy Spirit

God's self-revelation, as God's self-communicating presence, is al-ways an event or a happening involving God and some human recipient or recipients. It is an event of God encountering some human recipient. In using this event language, which is strongly biblical, I am denying that God's revelation is ever a static *datum.* God's self-revelation is made into such a datum every time it is identified with a given text or state-ment or object as such and thereby with its simple givenness as a crea-turely object. Further, in affirming that revelation is always an event of divine self-communication, we are acknowledging it as a freely given action of God.

The event of God's self-revelation encloses the human recipient. *The Holy Spirit is that power that moves the recipient to know God in God's self-objectifications.* Without the movement of the Holy Spirit persons could not apprehend God's self-communicating presence. Because the action of God's self-revelation does so enclose the recipient and thereby fulfills itself in the recipient, this interior movement of the recipient by the Spirit is essential to the whole event of self-revelation.

God's self-revelation can only be known and received in faith. It is human faith, empowered by the Holy Spirit, that apprehends God in the encounter with the creaturely media God is using to convey Godself. Hence, God's revelation is not as such available to disinterested and de-tached reason. Disinterested reason can look at the creaturely objectifi-cations, but the self-revelation is always an event of personal self-disclosure to persons in faith. And it is the Spirit that empowers faith to

---

[41] The question of immediate or unmediated revelatory presence is a diffi-cult grammatical issue, the semantics of which are important. If all one means by 'immediate presence' is *direct presence to some recipient*, then surely we could acknowledge such divine communicative transactions. But if we mean by 'immediate' that nothing creaturely mediates the presence, then it seems to ex-clude all those factors that seem to be necessary to ever knowing God, such as human langauge, expectations, social traditions that condition the human recipi-ent. See, however, Alston, *Perceiving God,* for a sustained argument for the in-telligibility of direct experience of God, which he calls "Christian Mystical Per-ception of God."

experience the mediating creaturely object *as* the revelation of God. Many people experienced the man Jesus of Nazareth in ordinary perceptual and social forms without experiencing him as the definitive self-revelation of God. It is to the *eyes of faith* that Jesus appears as the self-communicating presence of God, but we should not fall into the conceptual trap of supposing that human faith is a preexisting condition necessary for receiving revelation. Rather, it the divine action that creates faith in the event of God's self-disclosure.

God's self-communication is essentially a salvific event. God's self-revelation is the presence of God's gracious and salvific love for the recipient, which heals and liberates the recipient. God's self-revelation is more than a simple epistemic event: it is a salvific event for the recipient-knower, who is thereby empowered to a new way of life. God begins to heal the encumbrances and wounds of sin.

God's Self-Revelation, the Bible, and Human Discourses and Practices

God's self-revelation is always received and understood by humans through their traditions of discourse and practice, however much it may also *transform* those. God's revelation only becomes intelligible to humans through its reception in and through human language. This is another way of understanding the mediated character of God's revelation. Calvin refers to this as God's condescension and accommodation to the finitude of human language and knowing.[42]

Because God's communicative transactions in Israel and in Jesus Christ are historically particular, their availability to later generations in time requires traditions of witness to such revelations. Hence, God's self-revelations in Israel and in Jesus Christ are available to later generations indispensably through the witness of the Bible and the witness of the church. The Bible itself is a 'deputized sign' of God's past self-revelations and is about persons and events that are deputized signs as well. *Deputized signs are those creaturely media of God's self-communication in the special salvation history of Israel and of Jesus Christ and the calling of the apostolic church in the Spirit.* I use the word 'deputized' in order to make clear their *givenness and chosenness* as media of God's self-revelation in Israel and Jesus Christ and in a way that

---

[42] Among many references, see John Calvin, *Institutes of the Christian Religion*, 1.5.1; 2.11.13; 2.16.2; 3.18.9.

cannot be certified by general human experience. That is, general human experience could never have expected that God would have to or choose to communicate with the world through Israel and the Jew Jesus of Nazareth. God *freely elects* these deputized signs to be the media of God's self-communications to the world.

Insofar as the biblical deputized signs are primary for the later church, we may say that *narrative* is the primary linguistic form in which God's revelation is given and received: the narrative of God's self-communicating acts in Israel, in Jesus of Nazareth, and in the calling of the apostolic church. This is the narrative of the economy of God's interactive work with, within, and upon the world of Israel and the church. In affirming that Jesus Christ is the definitive self-revelation of God, I am affirming the *centrality of the incarnational narrative of Jesus Christ in the NT as the centerpiece of the biblical narrative.*

God's Self-Revelation and the Ineradicable Regulative Provisos of Its Grammar

In light of the grammar of the preceding theses about God's self-revelation, we can identify *two provisos or rules that govern the grammar of Christian talk of revelation*:

a. The *Ultimacy Proviso* rules that only God can reveal God.
b. The *Penultimacy Proviso* rules that God has chosen or deputized some definite signs in the history of Israel and of Jesus Christ as the special media of God's self-revealing activity.

The Ultimacy Proviso is empty and abstract without the Penultimacy Proviso. The Penultimacy Proviso is unfaithful and idolatrous without the Ultimacy Proviso. *The dialectic between these two provisos is essential to and formative of Christian discourse about God's self-revelation.*

God's Self-Revelation, Trinity, and the Witness of the Church

The full unfolding of who God is in God's self-revelation necessarily involves the development of the doctrine of the Trinity as the doctrine of the triune self-identification of God in:

a. electing and covenanting with Israel;
b. incarnating in Jesus of Nazareth;
c. moving persons by the Spirit to respond in faith.

In the chapter on the doctrine of God, the doctrine of the Trinity will be fully developed and elaborated.

I have already affirmed that the church is called into being to witness to the reality of the triune God, and we are now to understand that this witness is grounded in and empowered by God's historic communicative transactions in Israel and in Jesus Christ and the calling of the apostolic church. Yet the church's witness and theology are not as such God's self-revelation, but are *witnesses* to God's triune Life. But the shape and content of the church's witness are dependent on the deputized signs of the biblical witness. As witness to God, however, the church's discourses and practices may also be used from time to time by God's Spirit to mediate God's presence in the living moment. Hence, the witness of the church in word and deed, as creaturely objects and media, may *become* the self-revealing and self-communicating presence of God to some recipients.

God's Self-Revelation and God's Word

Insofar as God's revelation is God's self-communication—God's giving of Godself to the human recipient in the Spirit-empowered event of faith—we can say *that all of God's revelations are God's self-speaking, are God's Word*. The events of God's speaking forth are events of God's performative speech-acts. *Jesus Christ, as God's historically enacted speech-act, is God's definitive Word [logos]*. Hence, in the grammar that has been developed there is no need to juxtapose God's self-speaking to God's communicative transactions in historical events. Wherever God reveals Godself, there is the Word of God being communicated.

The Grammar of Faith as Knowledge of God

In the previous section I developed the concept that God's self-revelation is paradigmatically an event of self-communicating presence through some creaturely media to a recipient who receives the communication in faith through the Spirit. Hence, the paradigm of knowing God is faith's knowledge. We will now develop further the grammar of faith as knowledge of God.

In the NT and in church traditions the term 'faith' [*pistis* in NT] has a family of uses.[43] It can be used to refer to the total existence and life of the believer as well as to particular dimensions of that believing life. Here we will sort through the grammar of some of these interrelated uses in the hope of showing how the talk of faith hangs together. We must resist the temptation to look for a single definition of faith that will apply to all uses of the word 'faith' either in the Bible or in the discourses of the church. We may distinguish between the many *routes of faith*—as those phenomena of individual paths of experiences, encounters, and decisions of persons—from the *structure of faith* that is common to the many routes. Here we are mainly concerned with the structure of faith as knowledge of God.

Faith as Gracious Gift of the Spirit

Whatever the route of faith might be, faith is always to be understood *first* as a gracious gift of the Spirit.[44] As gift, then, faith is never to be regarded as a human achievement about which boasting and pride are appropriate. Faith is made possible by God's gracious self-revelation, self-communication in Jesus Christ through the Spirit. Faith is not some possibility of humanity's apart from the divine self-communication. That is, faith is not an autonomous possibility which any human being possesses and which she can actualize on her own. Faith is not some state or condition into which we can will ourselves on our own, independent of the empowerment of the Spirit. Put another way, faith as knowledge of God is impossible without the movement of the Spirit of God.[45] This emphasis on faith as a gift of the Spirit will continually remind us that faith is not a form of works righteousness under the disposing of the believer. But as will be seen below, faith as gift does not preclude another sense of faith as decision and action.

---

[43] For discussion of biblical senses of faith, see *TDNT*, 849–857 and *IDB*, 2: 222–234.

[44] Eph 2.8; 1 Cor 12.9.

[45] We could say that faith is a *conferred possibility*, as distinct from a possibility inherently possessed by humans. The differences between Barth and Rahner occur, however, as to whether the conferred possibility is graciously conferred in creation or graciously conferred in the event of God's self-communication. Both would agree that faith cannot be realized without the power of the Spirit.

Faith as Orientation of Heart to God

Comprehensively, faith is a basic orientation of the whole person to God. As such an orientation it involves the person's *heart*: orients her identifying and defining passions and attendant convictions, construals, emotions, and actions. The person's heart is her spirit, and faith involves a new heart and spirit.[46] This is the qualitative *how* of a person's life that gives it focus and shape and direction, which was emphasized by Kierkegaard. Faith involves the whole person, the whole self—not just some part of the self. We must resist efforts to reduce faith to just one aspect of human life. As an orientation, faith is a *basic perspective* with a set of basic convictions about who God is and what human life is truly about.

Faith as Grateful Acknowledgment

Faith is an act of acknowledgment and an affection of gratitude. It is in its first moment an *acknowledgment* of God's prior graciousness in Jesus Christ and gratitude for that grace and forgiveness. This, of course, involves acknowledging too that one is a sinner forgiven by grace. Here the word 'acknowledgment' means the same as 'recognition': it is the recognition of a reality that precedes and brings about the acknowledgment. Closely tied to this acknowledgment, as the proper emotive dimension of acknowledgment, is gratitude for that salvific grace. This gratitude to God is thus an essential emotion of faith, which I am calling *doxological gratitude.* Faith happens in the emotive dimensions of praise and thanksgiving for that which faith has not created but merely receives and thus acknowledges. As such, faith is a confession of the self of having been rescued by the gracious presence of God's self-communicating life.

Faith as Epistemic

Faith is epistemic: a knowing, believing, and construing. As epistemic, I am claiming that faith comes to be in the encounter with the self-communicating life of God through some creaturely media, but typically

---

[46] See the associating of heart and spirit in Rom 2.29; 5.5; 1 Cor 1.22; 2 Cor 1.21–22; Gal 4.6. In the OT see especially Ezek 11.17, 19–20; 36.26–28. I develop this concept of heart further in chapter six on the doctrine of humanity.

through the discourses and practices of the church's witness. The grammar of the epistemic dimensions of faith, however, requires that we understand the appropriateness of faith as knowledge in all three of the previously identified clusters of epistemic terms: faith as the *apprehension* of God in a direct encounter with God; faith as the *beliefs* or judgments or convictions about God; faith as *understanding* the grammar of Christian faith.

In the first sense of faith as knowledge, *faith arises in the direct but mediated apprehension of God in and through the discourses and practices of the church.* This knowing is existential and personal, and it is to know God as personal presence, to know 'someone,' to know a *thou*. This personal knowing of a personal God is profoundly self-involving for the believer. Bearing in mind a sufficiently rich and complex understanding of the reach of the church's discourses and practices, we can understand faith as arising and being sustained by the episodic encounters with God's self-communicating presence in the many places of the church's life. These episodic events of encounter with God can happen, for example, in worship, prayer, reading Scripture, hearing the proclaimed word, enriching conversations within the church, serving the neighbor, and even in studying systematic theology! Yet it must be remembered that God is not an object that can be apprehended in so-called neutral 'objectivity' and personal detachment.

God is known as God gives Godself to be known, and this means that it is a knowing someone or a thou as *characterized and identified* in some way. Without the characterization, the identifying references, there would be little reason to claim any apprehension of God. Hence, in knowing God existentially and personally one also *believes something about God.*[47] This is the second dimension of faith as knowledge of God. Of course, I am claiming that central to this characterization and identification of God is encountering God in the work of Jesus Christ. And it is this identification that leads to the trinitarian identification of God.

In believing something about God, faith can also be seen as a responsive *construal* of the reality of God, the world, humanity, and oneself. As a construal of God's reality, faith has convictions as to who God is, how God is to be characterized, and how God acts. In distinction from the ways in which other social worlds construe the world and human life, faith construes the world as God's creation, construes enemies as neigh-

---

[47] See Rom 10.8–10.

bors, construes oneself and other persons as forgiven and justified.

Hence, faith as belief always has some content of belief. It is not only the *faith which believes* (*fides qua creditur*) but the *faith which is believed* (*fides quae creditur*), not only the *act of believing* but also *content believed.*[48] As *fides quae*, the faith is embodied in *doctrinal convictions* that are essential to Christian self-understanding and understanding of God. This believing of faith is given and constructed in the church's distinctive discourses and practices of witness. When the church's *actual* discourses of witness are confused and/or obscure and/or misleading, then it is difficult for Christian understanding to thrive and flourish among the people.[49]

Faith as understanding, the third epistemic dimension of the grammar of faith as knowledge of God, is that deepening understanding of knowing God by way of knowing one's way around in the discourses and practices of the church and construing all things before God. It includes knowing how to think about God both concretely and abstractly, how to think about oneself and the world in increasingly discerning ways. It especially includes the capacity to reason about God and life, to be able to make and follow arguments. The temptation of epistemic understanding is to become detached from the faith as the concrete, practical apprehension of God. When the practical and the abstract are kept intertwined, we have *faith as wisdom*.

Faith as Trust in God

Faith is *fiducia* or trust in God. At its heart, to trust in God is to trust one's whole life and self-understanding to the sustaining presence of God. It is to trust in the fidelity of God to God's own self-communications in Israel and in Jesus Christ. It is to trust that God is as God has shown Godself to be in these patterned constancies of God's salvific life with the world through Israel and Jesus Christ. This trust is created by the encounter with God in direct but mediated apprehension of God. But to trust in God is also to know who God is and to live life as a gift from God. *Fiducia* is *faith in* God's living actuality as Creator, Reconciler, and Redeemer. The focus of such trust is *faith in Jesus Christ as the Lord and Savior of the world*.

While we can grammatically distinguish between *belief about God*

---

[48] Faith as content can be seen in Acts 6.7; Gal 1.23; Eph 4.5; 1 Tim 4.1, 6.
[49] See 1 Tim 1.3–8; Eph 4.14.

and *trust in God*, we should never separate them or suppose that either can be authentic without the other. How can one *trust in* God if one does not know who God is and therefore believes something about God? How can one truly *believe something about* God if one does not trust in God? Whatever such so-called believing about God might mean, there is no authentic belief about God that is not trust in God. Knowing God truly is inconceivable apart from trust. But faith as trust is not some vague or ambiguous trust in a cipher of what is presumably at the depths of things.

Faith as Knowledge of Self

Faith as knowledge of God necessarily involves knowing oneself before God. As Calvin has argued, it is impossible to know God truly without knowing oneself, and it is impossible to know oneself truly without knowing God.[50] To know God in faith is to know the love of God in Jesus Christ as love for oneself, who is now grasped as a sinner forgiven by the grace of God. Apart from faith's knowledge of God, the self is repeatedly inclined to misconstrue her situation in the world, and especially inclined to trust in objects and creaturely powers that cannot finally bestow life and fulfillment. Further, we do not truly know God if we regard ourselves as unloved and unredeemable and doomed to despair. Hence, to know God is to know how God is disposed in Christ toward oneself.

Faith as Trust in Christian Witness

Faith involves trust in the fidelity and truthfulness of Christian witnesses. While the quest for understanding is intrinsic to faith, it is always deeply dependent on the trustworthy testimony of other Christians both in its articulation and communal confirmation. Hence, our trust in God is impossible without trust in the fidelity and truthfulness of some aspects of the Christian witness to God in discourses and practices. How could we trust in God if we trusted in no item of the church's discourses and practices as being truthful representations of and witnesses to God's self-revelation? Remember, we do not know God apart from creaturely media. God becomes an object for faith in and through the discourses and practices of the church as these are empowered by and used by the Holy

---

[50] John Calvin, *Institutes of the Christian Religion*, I.1.1–3.

Spirit.

If we refuse to construe the Bible as a narrative whose sole purpose is to convey stories that illustrate eternal truths about God and humanity, but truths which can be confirmed independent of the biblical testimony, then the importance of trust in the testimony of others becomes apparent. Not only do we trust the biblical narrative to be a faithful witness to God, but we trust various testimonies in the history of the church as to who God is and how God is to be known in Jesus Christ. This means that there are no noncircular arguments that could ever confirm the Bible as a trustworthy narrative of God's communicative transactions with the world.

Yet in saying this about trust in the communal witness of the church, I do not deny that the knowings of faith—as expressed in convictions and construals—are always *subject to the scrutiny of the church's communal activities of theological self-criticism.* Any particular item of the church's discourses and practices is subject to the ineradicable questioning of the church's witness which God requires of the church. Hence, while the church's witness is fallible and corrigible, it is not without abiding doctrinal convictions. Hence the knowledge of faith is that of a participant in a community of vigorous, self-critical discourse. It is the process of the community of faith being led by the Holy Spirit to discern the communications of the Spirit.

Faith as Intentional Action and Knowing-How

Faith involves *decisions and actions*, and in that sense faith is intentional action. But as decision, faith is *responsive* to the divine encounter and summons. God's summons is always *ad hominem*: directed to the concrete human person. It is a real, concrete human decision to believe, to do, to feel, and to be in a certain way. A faith that did not dispose one to particular sorts of actions and the actual enactment of those actions is not faith in the Christian sense. In addition to the fact that faith itself is repeatedly a decision and action of the person in which she is embraced by God's loving presence and embraces that presence, the grammar of faith requires faith to issue in the works or practices of love.

Insofar as faith is decision and intentional action, *faith is as much a knowing-how* as it is knowing-who, knowing-that, and knowing-what: knowing how to live within the distinctive discourses and practices of the faith; knowing how to love and praise God, to give thanks to God, to pray to God, to witness lovingly to God for others. This is why faith, as an orientation of the heart and mind, is always pragmatic in its life-determining and life-shaping ways. In this sense, faith's knowings are also *practical knowings*. Without the concrete practices—whatever else may be the shape of a person's route—it is not yet the coming-to-be of faith in God. This practical knowing of faith is *faith as wisdom*.

Faith as Relationship with the Triune God

In all the above dimensions, faith is fundamentally a relationship with God. It is an intentional relationship with the structure of these enumerated attributes. As relationship, it is a *form of life*, a way of life. This is faith as life-in-the-Spirit of Jesus Christ.[51] It will be the commanding theme of our description of the grammar of the Christian life to characterize it as the life of yes-saying to the grace of God in Jesus Christ.

There is one encompassing *negation*: that knowledge of God is ever authentically achieved in disinterested, detached theoretical inquiry and judgment. Such detached and disinterested inquiry and argument might approach something called 'beliefs about God.' But knowledge of God is at heart faith's knowledge and involves passionate commitment to God's way and kingdom. This does not mean that faith's knowing of God occurs without rational and responsible inquiry and insight. But it is always reason in the service of faith's responsible understanding. This is not to deny that for some person such disinterested and detached inquiry might become the route by which she comes to faith. Probing around and disinterestedly examining the testimonies of the tradition, for example, can be intriguing and worthwhile in its own right. And such may become the occasion for an encounter with the self-communicating life of God. But the coming-to-faith is itself the dissolution of the disinterest and detachment by doxological gratitude and the passion of commitment and conviction.

This means that the language of God's self-revelation is the language of faith. According to the grammar of this language, it is impossible to say and mean: 'God revealed Godself in Jesus Christ, but I don't believe it.' The language about God's self-revelation is intrinsically the self-involving language of faith.

---

[51] See Gal 2.19–20; Rom 8.2, 9–11.

Knowledge of God Apart from
God's Special Self-Revelations

Having now developed a doctrine of God's self-revelation in Israel and in Jesus Christ, we can return to the question mentioned earlier in our discussion of so-called general revelation. It is the question of whether God is known, either by revelation or by rational construction, apart from God's special self-revelations. But I will confront the question from the perspective of God's self-revelation in Jesus Christ. I make no pretense that what I say can be *read off* human actuality as such, given the multiple respects in which our apprehension and understanding of actuality are so language dependent. Rather, the question is, how is Christian theology to construct an understanding of claims to know God apart from God's special self-revelations?

The Endowment of the Original Grace of God

Insofar as God's self-revelation in Israel affirms that God is the Creator of all things and that human being is especially created in the image of God, there is reason to affirm further that the Spirit of God graciously constitutes humans for relationship with God and summons them into life with God and with the created neighbor. We can call this the *endowment of the original grace of God for every human being.* While there may be *signals* of this endowment in human experience and history, this belief about the endowment is neither an empirical generalization nor an ontological deduction from an independent ontology. It is a conviction rooted in the self-identifications of God in Israel and in Jesus Christ.[52]

Hence, because we believe that God's creative Spirit gives life to all humans and constitutes them human, the Christian construal of human being requires that in some sense of *knowing*, God can be known apart from God's economy of self-revelation in Israel, Jesus Christ, and the

---

[52] This expresses my agreement and disagreement with Rahner: God's original grace is constitutive for human being, but this concept is only adequately known in Jesus Christ. It is in Jesus Christ and from reflection on him that light is thrown on such endowment and on the sin by which it has been encumbered. Drop out the conviction about Jesus Christ and the epistemic status of Rahner's "transcendental supernatural" becomes suspicious. I develop this concept of original endowment of grace further in chapter six in the section on 'created humanity as spiritual being.'

church. But this *knowing* is ephemeral, transient, confused, incomplete, and difficult to state, especially in a form that would be universally acceptable or recognizable. We are confronted here with the *mystery* that human being, created by the Spirit and summoned to life before God, finds inevitable ways of suppressing and repudiating such knowledge. Therefore, both its ephemeral character and its distortion and subjugation by human sin argue that such original endowment cannot itself serve as the *foundation* for Christian theology. Rather than such odd knowings being able to throw light on Jesus Christ, Jesus Christ throws light on the original constitution of human being and its endowed summons to life with God.[53] Therefore, we can affirm that while human being is not simply closed off to God, the Spirit of God is still at work in the world in a variety of ways. The extent to which such work of the Spirit rises to knowledge of God is to be determined by the congruence of such claims with the revelation of God in Jesus Christ.

The Restless Signals of the Original Endowment

We are now authorized to reflect further on the implications of Augustine's rightfully influential utterance: "O God our hearts are restless until they find their rest in thee."[54] As God's creatures it makes Christian sense to say that all humans are created to have relationship with the Creator and that apart from such relationship the creature is incomplete and unfulfilled, or *restless*.[55] I am claiming that Jesus Christ gives us a *map* to these ephemeral but significant experiences and knowings of persons. In this sense, then, *Jesus Christ and the triune Actuality of God is the horizon for understanding humanity as restless and longing for God.* These knowings can be seen as rooted in the general human situation in which the following types of questions are inevitably asked, however fleetingly:

What is the point or purpose of life?
What is the good and how can I realize it?
What are the limits of human life?
What does it mean to die?

---

[53] These points are explicated further in chapter six: Humanity as Created Being and as Sinful Being.
[54] *Confessions*, bk I, ch. 1.
[55] See also Acts 17.23: "to an unknown God."

Why do people suffer?
Whence evil and so much violence and hate?
What is ultimately real and what is only illusion and fraud?
What is justice and can it be realized in the human world?
For what can humans hope?
What is truth?

These *types of questions express a deep human need to make sense out of life.* Christian theology can interpret these questions and longings as *signals* of God's disturbing and solicitous presence in all human life, in life that has been created by God. In Jesus Christ the church confesses that it sees a definitive self-revelation of God as the creating, reconciling, and redeeming Lover of all humans, and this revelation *throws light on* these generic human questions as signals of a deep and profoundly human longing and questing for the reality of God.

In this context of understanding, some apologetic and proclamatory work of Christian witness can be undertaken, even if such is not foundational for the whole structure of that witness. Tillich is right that the church can and must address these questions and longings. Barth is right that Christian theology cannot be founded and erected upon these questions and that the Gospel *transforms* these questions and says something that is not simply presupposed in the questions.

Revelation and Other Religions

We can now briefly confront the related questions as to whether God is known in other religions. It must be admitted, however, that there is no neutral theory of what counts as a religion, and that most such theories either are so loose as to be unhelpful and confusing or so laden with some theological convictions as to already beg the present question. An example of this latter position is the proposal that all religions are basically about a common ultimacy, though the ultimacy is variously conceived. The pretense here is the claim to rise above all the religions and to characterize them according to some putative common core. This pretense has the following conceptual dilemmas, however. It seems to presuppose that the various religions cannot interpret themselves adequately within their own doctrines and must have the transcendental perspective in order to understand themselves more truly and more profoundly. It also glosses over what seem to be significant incompatibilities among the religions. For example, it does not seem to be the case both that Jesus

Christ is the definitive self-revelation of God and that the Koran is the definitive guide to how to live before God. Further, attempts to interpret each religion as though each is equally grounded in self-communications of God are conceptually obfuscating. Oddly enough, some proposals also render the concerns about *idolatry* null and void, since the forms and practices of all religions are apparently on equal footing.

Obviously such discussions among the religions and about the religions are a minefield of semantic looseness and imprecision. There are, however, good reasons to encourage understanding among religious traditions. Significant comparative work can be had by exploring how a religion addresses the generic questions posed above. But it is clear that Christians should not pretend to converse and speak from some position *above* Christian faith; they should speak honestly as Christians *from* the Christian perspective. But from that perspective, this affirmation is crucial: all the people of the other traditions of religion are our brothers and sisters, created by God, loved by God, and ultimately redeemed by God. They are this whether they share the Christian convictions or not. Such respect for others, then, is not dependent on shared theological beliefs nor on the agnostic belief that somehow we are all just '*gassing and guessing*' and nobody really knows what is what.[56] Hence, without supposing that all religions know the divine or God or the ultimate in their differing ways, we enter into the discussion firm in who we know God to be and convinced that this triune God is alive and at work throughout the world. We simply do not know how to identify such work, however, without reference to Jesus Christ; but it is also true that we have not exhaustively understood Jesus Christ and how he is the *Logos* of the whole world.[57] We, therefore, must listen well to our brothers and sisters.

---

[56] This latter point seems to be the basis for the widespread sense of 'liberal tolerance' in the United States.

[57] In chapter six I develop further a Christian theology of human religion. Among many possibilities currently available for the discussion of interreligious dialogue, this collection of essays is useful: *Christian Uniqueness Reconsidered: The Myth of a Pluralistic Theology of Religions*, ed. Gavin D'Costa (Maryknoll, N.Y.: Orbis, 1990). Holding views that I have criticized above, see John Hick and Paul F. Knitter, eds., *The Myth of Christian Uniqueness* (Maryknoll, N.Y.: Orbis, 1987). Over the years I have found the careful analytic and insightful work of William A. Christian Sr., illuminating, even when I find myself disagreeing with him. See his *Meaning and Truth in Religion* (Princeton, N.J.: Princeton University Press, 1964); *Oppositions of Religious Doctrines: A Study*

Jesus Christ and Continuing Revelation in the Church

The God who calls the church into life is the One who is self-communicating to human beings. God does not cease self-communicating with the close of the NT canon. In fact all persons who come to faith in whatever era come to faith through the movement and empowerment of the Holy Spirit. And the church prays continually for the guidance of the Spirit as it faces the exigencies of its concrete life. So, the church and the individual Christian live by and from the self-communicating life of the triune God.

If God is continually communicating with the church, then in what sense is Jesus Christ the *definitive revelation of God*? Jesus Christ is the definitive revelation in the sense that he is *norm* or *criterion* by which all other real and purported self-revelations of God are understood. The *more* that God continues to communicate to the church in its historic life is not a more that could *contradict or subvert* this definitive self-revelation.[58] This is why the church says that in the Spirit the risen Jesus Christ lives in and for the church through the ages. But that Jesus Christ is the definitive revelation of God does not mean—as I have said earlier—that the church has exhaustively understood this revelation. Therefore, in the traditions of the church there might be such a development of understanding that Jesus Christ might become even more richly and complexly grasped.

These living self-communications of God in the witness of the church are sometimes called *derivative revelations* or *dependent revelations*. They never stand on their own, but always in the light of Jesus Christ. It is the mission of the church to witness to God in the hope that God will from time to time *use* that witness—however fragmentary, broken, and inadequate it might be—as the medium of God's gracious and redeeming presence. The witness of the church is its *confession and profession* of its knowledge of God given in God's self-revelations in Is-

---

in the Logic of Dialogue among Religions (New York: Herder & Herder, 1972); *Doctrines of Religious Communities: A Philosophical Study* (New Haven, Conn.: Yale University Press, 1987).

[58] Note how clearly this sentence is a grammatical sentence. Any subversion of the place of God's definitive revelation in Jesus Christ would simply be tantamount to claiming another revelation as definitive.

rael, in Jesus Christ, and in the apostolic church, and this knowledge is given and confirmed and unfolded in the ongoing traditions and life of the church.

The Dialectic between God's Revelatory Presence and the Church's Witness

There is thus an irreducible dialectic between the eventful self-communicating presence of God to some recipient or recipients in the life of the church and the continuing, creaturely, fallible witness of the church in its discourses and practices. The church witnesses to God in discourses and practices that it regards as warranted and authorized by God's self-revelations in Israel, in Jesus Christ, and in the apostolic church, as these are witnessed to in the Bible. But the church's witness *cannot finally defend* and *verify* its own discourse about God by any worldly criteria. It speaks under the authorization of the *penultimacy proviso* as it had received that proviso in its own life. It speaks also under the *ultimacy proviso*, which it learned from the witness of Scripture, knowing that there is no *place or position* from which it can *demonstrate* God's actuality to the world or from which it can *control* God's *self-communicating presence* to persons. But the church witnesses to God under the promise that God will indeed confer God's salvific presence in the midst of the church's discourses and practices.

But the church can explain its discourses and practices and present the world with the *rationale* of its witness. That the world or anyone in the world will ever *encounter* the self-communicating and salvific presence of God is something at the disposing of God and is beyond the simple control of the church and its witness and of all of its particular witnesses!

Further Notes on the Christian Grammar of 'Truth'

Consider these passages from Scripture:

> Isaiah 45.19: I the Lord speak the truth.
> Jeremiah 9.5: and no one speaks the truth.
> 1 Kings 10.6: The report was true which I heard in my own

> land.
> Jeremiah 10.10: the Lord is the true God; he is the living God.
> Mark 5.33: and told him the whole truth.
> Luke 1.4: so that you may know the truth concerning the things about which you have been instructed.
> John 1.14: Word ... dwelt among us, full of grace and truth.
> John 8.32: and you will know the truth and the truth will make you free.
> John 14.6: I am the way, the truth, and the life.
> John 18.38: And Pilate said to him, 'What is truth?'
> Acts 26.25: I am speaking sober truth.
> Romans 9.1: I am speaking the truth in Christ, I am not lying.
> 1 John 1.6: we lie and do not live according to the truth.
> 1 John 1.8: is a liar and the truth is not in him.
> 1 John 3.18: let us not love in word . . . but in deed and in truth.

Obviously, these are English translations of Hebrew and Greek words, and we could inspect each of these passages in the original language and penetrate further into the meaning of the passage. But we will not find one common core of meaning to the words that are translated as 'true' and 'truth.' And we would not find one common core if we were to inspect the meanings of these terms in English; they have many uses, some interrelated and some quite distinct in their grammar. So, without supposing that there is one core meaning in all these uses, I propose to consider some of these uses in order to see how there might be a Christian grammar of truth.

Various Senses of Truth

Some of these passages are about truth relative to: (a) divine speech and human speech; (b) human life and action; and (c) Jesus Christ and God. Relative to these realities, there are these implicit contrasts in the functioning of the terms 'true' and 'truth'—contrasts between *true and false,* between *truth and the lie,* between what we might call *the true or authentic* and *the inauthentic.* Relative to these contrasts, using concepts previously developed, we can have:

a. true and false locutionary statements;
b. true and false illocutionary speech acts;
c. illocutionary speech acts that are not only false but also a lie;
d. patterns of living that are either true and authentic or false and inauthentic;

e. the relation between one's words and one's deeds can either be true and authentic or a lie and inauthentic.

'Being true' can therefore be a property of: (a) a statement; (b) a speech act; (c) a pattern of life; or (d) a particular person's life.

Truth, Meaning, and Reference

With regard to human speech, some of these passages seem to express what might be called a 'common sense realism': a human locutionary statement is true if and only if what it says is in fact the case. A semantic definition of truth states this nicely: the locutionary statement 'the cat is on the mat' is true if and only if the cat is on the mat. This precipitates a tedious discussion of 'facts.' We might say 'facts are what true statements state.' Yet there seems to be an ambiguity between 'a fact is what is *stated*' and 'a fact is what is stated *about.*' So, are facts what true statements are about or are facts what true statements state? Or, is the fact *in* the language or *in* the world? In a common sense way, we want to say facts are what true statements state and when statements are true, they are *about*—refer to—the facts in the world.[59]

Discourse that claims to be true is discourse that makes some claim *about* something else, most often about that which is the case in the world. So we will stipulate that locutions that make truth-claims can be called *judgments, statements, propositions.*[60] About those locutions that

---

[59] There is indeed much here that begs for further analysis. The fact/truth discussion is significantly explored in the essays by J. L. Austin and Peter Strawson in *Truth*, ed. George Pitcher (Englewood Cliffs, N.J.: Prentice-Hall, 1964). My sympathies are more nearly with the views presented by Austin on the issue of some version of a correspondence theory of truth. But I do not understand the correspondence between statement and the world to be anything more than conventional correlations. Hence, we should not think of the correspondence as *depicting* or *picturing* or *representing* the facts in the world. There is no mirror here. I had these considerations in mind when I said earlier that semantics is not the name for one simple way of referring to and describing what we think is the case. Semantical relations are various, but they are rooted in human agreements and interactions.

[60] I will use the term 'locutionary statement' to mean the respects in which a statement might have meaning independent of any particular utterance by a particular person. That is, 'Smith is a feminist' has some meaning, whether or not it is spoken by a particular person. But this sense for a statement does not adequately attend to the respects in which the locutionary statement has meaning in

seem to be making truth-claims, we can ask: 'what does the locution *mean*?' This is a request to clarify and explain what is being claimed by the statement. We cannot *determine* whether the claim is true or false unless we know *what* is being claimed. Much of the time we explain the meaning of a locution by explaining syntactically and semantically the various constituent *terms* of the *locution*.

Hence, in 'Fred deliberately fisolexed Priscilla,' we can ask what the terms mean. It *looks like* a truth-claim, but unless we know what 'fisolexed' means and how it is being used, we cannot determine whether there is a claim being made, and if there is, we cannot determine whether it is true or false without knowing the semantic rules of the use of the term 'fisolexed.' And we can ask: 'which Fred?' 'which Priscilla?' We certainly could not assess whether it is true if we did not know which Fred is being named. We need here 'identifying references' for Fred and for Priscilla. Hence, understanding what a locutionary statement *means* always precedes deciding whether it is true or false. It turns out that the above utterance is not a truth-claim because no meaning can be found for 'fisolexed'; it is a piece of nonsense I invented.

The most difficult part of assessing truth-claims is learning *how to determine* whether a claim is true or false. It is here that the important epistemological questions and disputes arise. These are questions both of (a) under what conditions is the truth-claim true, and (b) under what conditions is one justified in asserting the truth-claim? These are not the same 'truth conditions.' I might make a true statement without having any justification for asserting it. I might say 'the governor is home with the flu today' without having any justifying warrant for saying that, when in fact she is home with the flu. In learning language contextually, we learn mostly how to tell such matters. In learning the language of biological science you learn how to judge truth and falsehood according to the 'scientific' procedures and practices in that field of discourse.

---

an illocutionary speech-act by a particular person. In this latter event we can grasp more clearly the contextual grammar of the locution as put to a particular use. Hence, speech-act pragmatics will, in the Christian context, caution us against becoming too focused on a locutionary statement abstracted from the uses Christians might concretely make of the locution in their speech-acts, in their concrete discourses and practices.

Complexities of Christian Discourse
on Meaning and Truth

In Christian discourse questions of meaning/reference and truth are difficult and odd when it comes to assessment. This is partly due to such discourse being dependent for its full meaning/reference and truth on the particular practices that comprise the church and the Christian life. That is, *such discourse can seldom be fully understood simply as an abstract locutionary piece of language independent of the practices in which it makes sense.* However, because Christians believe the whole world should believe and adopt their particular convictions and practices, it is imperative that the church undertake to explain its discourse and truth-claims as clearly as it can to the world.

So, let us take the locutionary statement: "Jesus Christ died for our sins [1 Cor 15.3]." The Christian will need to explain what the terms mean and to what they refer. Who is Jesus Christ? In what sense 'died'? What are 'sins'? How did he die for our sins? There is no doubt that much neutral analysis and explanation can take place that does not presuppose any commitment by the explainer to the claims of Christian faith. But we cannot fully execute the explanations of these concepts without ascertaining what illocutionary acts might be performed in saying this locution and what the communal context of those performances is. What are Christians doing when they utter this locution? And *why* should someone believe this? What is *involved* in believing this? Or, why might anyone *say* this? In other words, we can do some explanation of terms, but we will finally have to attend to the possible illocutionary acts that might be performed in the context of Christian discourses and practices.

If we take a broad view of the NT, we can see that it is dealing with just these questions all the time in its witness. But in considering these questions, the biblical witnesses are always inviting and challenging the hearers to see themselves in a new way and enter into a new situation. They never encourage detached neutrality and disinterested objectivity, even though they make it clear that it is true that Jesus Christ died for our sins, indeed died "for the sins of the whole world [1 Jn 2.2]." But no one could truly or authentically believe this about Jesus without believing something about herself as a sinner before God and believing a host of other claims about God and humanity.

So, when someone asks what this utterance means and why she should believe it, there is no simple direct, neutral *argument* that is going to get her into a position to understand it and believe it to be true. Of course, it is always possible that any particular hearer of these witnesses will say 'that is all nonsense to me.' The depth grammar of this sort of discourse cannot be fully plumbed without these *existential, self-involving, practical* dimensions. Hence, we cannot quite fully get into the Christian claims simply by looking abstractly at the syntactic and semantic dimensions. We need also a sense for the pragmatics of the discourse.

So, the illocutionary *speech-act* in someone's mouth and life of 'Jesus Christ died for our sins' is *true*,

if and only if Jesus Christ died for our sins, and

if and only if the speaker means it faithfully, and

if and only if it goes with a whole way of life.

These are the *truth-conditions* for this *kind* of speech-act. Hence, Christian discourse has meaning/reference and truth conditions that draw deeply on the individual speakers. And this shows why this discourse can so easily be *misused* or said so emptily that it is a *lie*.

In putting the matter this way, it should be noted that I am *not saying* that the speaker's *believing* of the locution *makes it true* that Jesus Christ died for our sins. Rather, Jesus either did or did not die for our sins, in some straightforward common sense realism. But there is no authentic *asserting* of this 'fact' independent of the self-involvement of the speaker in a whole way of life. Put the odd semantics and pragmatics of this even more bluntly: it is *grammatically impossible*—in the relevant sense—to authentically *believe* this locution without pragmatic self-involvement. Put another way, it is impossible to *say and mean* 'Jesus Christ died for our sins, but I do not believe it.'

But, it might be asked, how do we determine whether Jesus Christ did in fact die for our sins? Can that be determined by some noncircular, objective, and rational argument that does not presuppose faith and which might indeed be the rational ground for having faith? Christian talk of revelation is a way of saying why Christians believe they are *authorized* to make such claims as 'Jesus Christ died for our sins.' It is the Jesus-story as God's salvific story, as witnessed in Scripture and church, that authorizes the truth-claims of the church's discourse. I affirmed these points in the previous discussion in this chapter by saying that the locutionary statement "Jesus Christ died for our sins" is an assertion of the discourse of Christian faith.

So, *the uses of 'truth' in Christian discourse pertain at least to*: (a) language used referentially; (b) language used self-involvedly; and (c) the concrete lives of the users and speakers, all in the communal context of the church. Showing the deep grammar of Christian discourse and its primary claims is a matter of showing *how* the language *means* in syntax, semantics, and pragmatics. And in systematic theology this involves not only speaking *about* Christian discourse but also *using and speaking* the discourse and, where relevant, *asserting the truth-claims*.

Assessing Christian Truth-Claims

How then are the primary Christian convictions, as truth-claims, to be assessed? We are asking at least two different questions here: (1) by virtue of what arguments are the primary convictions or doctrines of Christian faith identified, described, and justified *for the church*? (2) by virtue of what arguments are the primary convictions or doctrines vindicated or confirmed as true *before the world*? The first question is internal to the life of the church and will be answered in a complex process of whether the identified convictions are in fact fruitful and faithful to the Gospel of Jesus Christ for the church. The second question looks like an invitation to move away from the assumptions of Christian discourse to some independent or neutral frame of reference and to proceed therefrom to adduce noncircular arguments for the justification of the various truth-claims of the church. I have previously argued that such a strategy is ill-conceived.[61]

The more appropriate response to the question of assessing the truth-claims of Christian faith is to engage in the following practices for the world: (a) describe accurately and clearly just what the primary convictions of the faith are and what the rationale is for their status as doctrinal convictions; (b) describe further the grammar of the convictions used in the church, showing what sort of form of life they go with and thus make possible; and (c) with respect to various particular beliefs, show how they do or do not depend upon or confirm some of the beliefs of the world.

I will be claiming that *contemporary learning* is a source of theological understanding in many aspects of Christian beliefs and prac-

---

[61] Of course, as I have argued earlier, the world is in the church and those of us in the church are always in quest of deeper understanding of the discourses and practices of the church. Hence, we cannot always tell the difference between arguing for a belief or concept simply within the church and arguing for such simply because our world within us prompts us to such arguing and discerning.

tices.[62] For example, some of my proposals concerning language and grammar are not peculiar to Christian faith. There will be many such beliefs that we will legitimately gather from the world. Further, we might strive to show why some beliefs and theories that seem antithetical to faith might be interpreted within Christian theological concepts, e.g., showing why acceptance of *a* theory of evolution need not be inconsistent with Christian beliefs.

But all these descriptions and related arguments are subject to the assumption of a detached and disinterested attitude toward Christian beliefs and way of life, and the overcoming of this detachment is never finally a function of further argument. Rather, it is a matter of self-involving and passionate decisions and construals and episodic encounters with the self-communicating Life of the triune God. It is to be hoped that a non-Christian reading this text might develop an understanding of what the basic grammar of Christian faith is in its various convictions and practices and its totally consuming and passionate way of life. But there are no cheap entries into this way of life: it demands a person's whole life and is never part-time.

There is, therefore, no *one way* in which all the truth-claims of the church's living discourses can be assessed. While much of the faith is grounded in God's self-revelation, it is not the case that all beliefs of the church are so grounded. Certainly such beliefs must be consistent with or noncontradictory of God's self-revelation. But Christians use lots of truth-claims from other domains and practices of life in the service of their own construal of the world. Some of these claims have less difficult truth-conditions, for example, 'that humans often inflict great harm on one another.' And it is also the case that Christians are often disputing among themselves about some of their claims and are regularly revising some of the claims of past traditions. Christians are not infallible in their speech and truth-claiming.

Today there are two great perils stalking the church's discourse. First, there is the peril that many in the empirical communities called 'church' by the world are quite ignorant and/or neglectful of the peculiar conditions for speaking the Christian faith, and thus their speech is empty, false, a lie, and misleading for the world. Second, there is the peril that so-called neutral, secular *reason* will be thought of as the *only way* in which the truth-claims of the church can be honestly assessed.

---

[62] See the discussion of sources and norms of Christian theology in chapter three.

Speaking and Living the Truth

Some Christians use Christian discourse with astonishing skill, dexterity, truthfulness, and spiritual power, but cannot themselves *explain* the grammar well or clearly. We should listen and observe them speaking and living, and even if we don't follow or agree with their explicit explanations of meaning, we might learn from them how to *say and mean* Christian speech-acts. *Christian education is fundamentally and only about learning how to speak, act, and live Christianly and truthfully.* Becoming aware of the grammar sometimes helps. But remember, studying the explicit grammar of the English language does not always guarantee that one can speak grammatically. Similarly, studying the rules of logic does not always make one logical in speech and reasoning. Pastor-teachers of the faith, however, are almost completely enfeebled if they do not know their way around in the deep grammar of Christian discourse and life and know how to convey that to the people. Hopefully, the *teachers of the faith* for this generation of *Christianly illiterate* people in the empirical churches will be skilled in showing the grammar of Christian existence by *being able to explain it, describe it, speak it, assert it, and by being able to live it.*

The deepest form of truth in Christian discourses and practices is a life in intentional conformity to the triune Life of God: a life that performs authentic speech-acts and enacts works and passions of love for God's kingdom. This is to embody the truth of Jesus Christ.

This follows from Jesus being "the way, the truth, and the life" [Jn 14.6].

Chapter Three

Sources and Norms of Theology as Dialectical Confession and Profession

Theology and the Presiding Model of the Gospel

Let us review the meanings of the terms 'theology' and 'theological.' I have claimed that all the discourses and practices of the church are *theological* insofar as they first and last intend to witness to the reality of the triune God. The performances of the many aspects of this witness in the nurturing, outreach, and administrative discourses and practices of the church are ineradicably summoned by God to accountability for that witness. Just as faith necessarily and intrinsically seeks understanding, so too this summons of God requires the church to seek responsible understanding of God's Gospel by reflecting on and assessing its own witness. This *enacting-of-witness* and *reflecting-on-witness*, as *theological practices*, are essential to the life of the church and the life of the individual Christian.

Systematic theology is a special task of the church that aims to provide a critical, constructive, and comprehensive account of the basic doctrines of Christian faith. So, the discourses and practices of the church comprise a much larger circle of *theological witness* than systematic theology as such, but this larger circle too requires accountable and responsible reflection and assessment. Of both this larger circle of the theological witness of the church and the special task of systematic theology, we can ask about the *sources and norms* by which they are performed and assessed.

Gospel as Material Norm

As I have claimed, in the performing of Christian witness and in doing
systematic theology we are confronted with the *Ineradicable Question* of
whether our total witness and our doctrines are: (a) adequate and faithful
to the Gospel of Jesus Christ, and (b) luminous, truthful, and transformative for the world. We cannot respond to the Ineradicable Question without formulating some understanding of the Gospel of Jesus Christ.[1] This
formulation of the Gospel will then function as the *material norm* for the
theological construction and assessment of the church's witness. It will
be by virtue of that witness's conformity to the material norm that we
will assess it for adequacy and faithfulness. I call this material norm the
Presiding Model of the Gospel. It will preside over and norm our construction and assessment of the church's witness and its doctrines.

Some of the church's deepest disagreements are rooted in differences
in formulating what the Gospel of God fundamentally is as the salvific
good news of who God is and what God has done for human salvation.
*One such critical issue is whether Jesus Christ is merely the bearer of
the Gospel or is himself constitutive of the Gospel.* If he is merely the
bearer of the Gospel, then the Gospel can be formulated without reference to his life, death, and resurrection. If he is constitutive of the Gospel, then the Gospel cannot be formulated without reference to his life,
death, and resurrection.

At the heart of my systematic theological effort is the *elemental conviction that Jesus Christ is the essence of the Gospel.* I stated this in the
chapter on God's definitive self-revelation in Jesus Christ. It would be
incoherent to claim that Jesus Christ is the definitive self-revelation of
God and to claim that the Gospel can be stated without reference to him.
I propose the following *Presiding Model of the Gospel*:

> The Gospel of Jesus Christ is the Good News
> that the God of Israel, the Creator of all creatures,
> has in freedom and love become incarnate

---

[1] The church and the student of theology should find the question 'what is
the Gospel?' to be a most edifying and diagnostically illuminating inquiry. This
question will focus the mind on just what is at the heart of Christian faith and
witness. In so doing it will flush out possible pretenders that have been illegiti-
mately functioning as material norms for the church's witness.

in the life, death, and resurrection of Jesus of Nazareth
to enact and reveal God's gracious reconciliation
of humanity to Godself, and
through the Holy Spirit calls and empowers human beings
to participate in God's liberative and redemptive work by
acknowledging God's gracious forgiveness in Jesus,
repenting of human sin,
receiving the gift of freedom,
embracing authentic community by
loving the neighbor and the enemy,
caring for the whole creation, and
hoping for the final triumph of God's grace
as the triune Ultimate Companion of all creatures.

Shorter form:
The triune God has in freedom and love acted in Jesus Christ to save humanity and the world from its self-enacted but false and hopeless destiny.

The presiding model of the Gospel—as material norm—will preside over the use of the sources for theological construction. In stating what one takes to be the Gospel, it is implicit, as with Paul, that the Gospel of Jesus Christ is one and not many. [Gal 1.6–9] Hence, in stating the Gospel I am intending it for the whole church and not as an idiosyncratic personal preference. Obviously, no statement of the Gospel is infallible and preserved from the contingencies of historical and geographic location. What differences in wording there might appear from time to time might be regarded as resolvable issues soliciting further conversation and dialogue. But I am not claiming that all the important doctrines of the church must be contained in the statement of the Gospel, though it will be a useful criterion for assessing the essentials and nonessentials in various doctrinal elaborations.

However, the presiding model of the Gospel as material norm is not the ultimate norm of the church's theological construction and witness. *The ultimate norm of the church's witness and doctrines is the living actuality of God's free and loving self-communicating presence.* It is this actual self-communicating presence which confers real truth and power on the church's witness. But the actuality of God's presence, as ultimate norm, is not under the control of the church and its theology; it is always

the free and loving event of God's self-disclosure. The church can witness to this eventful presence, but *God's self-communicating presence is
not itself a norm that the church can of itself apply.* Here we must recall
the dialectic between the Ultimacy Proviso and the Penultimacy Proviso:
only God can reveal God, and God has deputized the biblical witness as
the penultimate witness to God's life and truth.

This helps us to understand theologically the differentiated meanings
of *authority* in the church's witness. God is certainly the supreme
authority for the church's witness. God has revealed Godself in historical
self-communications to Israel, in the life, death, and resurrection of Jesus
Christ, and in the life of the apostolic church. The Bible, as witness to
God's distinctively self-communicating life, is the penultimate authority
for the church's witness. But the Bible always needs interpretation and
application by the church, which has happened in the living traditions of
the church. Yet this interpretation and application of the Bible by the
church always requires the empowerment and guidance of the Holy
Spirit.

The Basic Sources of Theology

By *sources* I mean those *texts, artifacts, and traditions of discourse and
practice upon which the construction of Christian doctrines and the
larger theological witness of the church can draw.*

I am proposing that there are *Four Basic Sources* for theology, listed
here in order of their importance and normative priority:

a. Holy Scripture
b. Church Traditions
c. Contemporary Learning
d. Past and Present Human Cultures

There is a constant dialectic between these basic sources and the presiding model. The presiding model of the Gospel, as material norm, is itself formulated out of reflection on the sources themselves, especially
Scripture and traditions. We could not state the Gospel without these
sources. Yet the model is formulated in order to guide the use of the
sources and keep us clear as to why just these sources are so important
for the church's witness and how they are to be used. And the model as
material norm empowers us to test the sources and our uses of them for

the adequacy and faithfulness of their witnesses. Yet the presiding model is itself subject to being tested by appeal to the sources, especially Scripture and tradition. A material norm that massively conflicted with the main trajectories of the biblical witness could not function as a material norm for the church. Some model of the Gospel—as a statement of what is at the heart of Christian faith—is presupposed in any and every form of the church's witness. The task is to expose these presupposed models to the scrutiny and assessment of the church's theological reflection.

About Experience

Much tradition and the Methodist Quadrilateral identify four sources, which are also in some sense norms, for the formation of Christian doctrine and witness: (a) Scripture; (b) Church tradition; (c) reason; (d) experience.[2] The Quadtrilateral is clearly different from my four basic sources. I have reservations about calling experience and reason *sources* of theology. We will now look at those reservations and my reformulation of some of the issues.

It seems clear that the practical import of calling experience a source is to indicate that a person's own experience is bound to play some role in the formation of her theological judgments and witness. And how can that be denied? I tried to take account of this in the concept of *individual experiential routes of faith*. But it is still not clear just what it means to call everyone's individual experience a normative source of the *church's faith and witness*. Experience is also sometimes taken to be the collective experience of the church, but then it is not clear what the distinction is between experience and tradition.

I have concerns about calling experience a source. First, the word 'experience' is itself so multiple and complex in its uses that it can easily mislead us into supposing that we are talking about a *common core meaning* in all those uses. This misleads us into supposing that experi-

---

[2] See the clarifying discussion of these matters of the Methodist Quadrilateral in Albert Outler, "The Wesleyan Quadrilateral in John Wesley," in *The Wesleyan Heritage: Essays of Albert D. Outler*, ed. Thomas C. Oden and Leicester R. Longdon (Grand Rapids, Mich.: Zondervan, 1991), 22–37. An excellent discussion of the quadrilateral is also provided by Randy L. Maddox, *Responsible Grace: John Welsey's Practical Theology* (Nashville, Tenn.: Abingdon, 1994), 36–47.

ence is a *something* that can easily be identified and described. But the
word 'experience' typically is syntactically connected with 'of.' Thus the
locution *the experience of* can receive an infinite variety of possible objects. In most contexts of meaning we do not become confused by this
flexible variety of objects, and we get along quite well talking about *my
experience of*, for example, last year's long, dark, and cold winter. But
when we ask for some common meaning to all these possible objects, we
get confused and lost, until someone tells us that there is a *theory of experience* that will help. An overarching theory of experience is as much
an intellectual dead-end as an overarching theory of understanding.

Second, when we make experience a source as such, it is not clear
what we are invoking—my experience? Fred's experience? the church's
experience? Further, some ways of construing experience threaten to
make experience the *only source and the only norm*; experience will then
swallow all the other sources. In this way we would have the *experience
of* reading Scripture when we read and interpret Scripture. But this *experience of* is not itself a *something* over and beyond the actual reading and
interpreting activities. Along this path, our encounters with all the other
sources could be understood as simply more *experiences*, and thus all we
would have would be experience as the only source and norm for Christian theology.

Third, sometimes experience is construed as something quite independent of language and social practices, which I questioned in the earlier discussion of language. This moves us in the direction of finally supposing that all experience is essentially private and inexpressible, which
is a seedbed for the perennial concerns of skepticism.[3] These considerations also point us to the syntactical fact that most of the uses of *experience of* presuppose a *subject* who has the experience. This is the *person-
relative* character of experience, and it gives force to such Christian locutions as, for example, 'Paul's experience of the grace and forgiveness
of God.' The depth grammar of this locution will show the dependence
of such an experience on a community of discourse and practice that can
recognize, identify, and characterize such an experience of grace and

---

[3] One of the more successful arguments of Wittgenstein was against the
philosophical proposal that it is possible to have a private language that is in
principle cognitively primitive and basic and thus prior to the learning of a public, social language. See Ludwig Wittgenstein, *Philosophical Investigations*, 2d
ed., trans. G. E. M. Anscombe (Oxford: Blackwell, 1958), *passim*. Norman Mal-
com, *Wittgenstein: Nothing Is Hidden* (Oxford: Blackwell, 1986), 154–181, is
especially helpful.

forgiveness. It is this grammatical fact that can prevent experience talk from sliding into a morass of infinitely relativized *subjectivity*. When we bear in mind the difference between (a) experiencing Jesus *as* a person proclaiming interesting thoughts and (b) experiencing Jesus *as* the Son of God, we begin to understand the importance of the *construal power of language in our experiences*. This is the difference between 'experiencing X' and 'experiencing X as G.'

In making this argument about the uses of the word 'experience,' I am not suggesting that we omit it from our vocabulary. We cannot get along without it, and if it does not mislead us, its infinite flexibility is a conceptual advantage. One helpful use is the way in which we speak of people having had different experiences and thus one person having some cognitive data that another person might not. Not everyone has had the experience of being the pastor of a congregation or being a county sheriff or being homeless and forsaken or being racially discriminated against, and so on *ad infinitum*. There are many differences in our life routes.

Rather than making experience either a source or norm, I propose that we follow Tillich here and say that experience is itself *ubiquitous* and is the inescapable *medium* of all theological reflection and witness.[4] In this ubiquitous sense, then, everything we think, say, and do in theological reflection is in multifaceted ways experiential and self-involving. But as ubiquitous, experience is not a 'something' which is itself a source of theological judgment. It is the inescapable medium for the making of theological judgments.

About Reason and Imagination

The term 'reason' seems as subject to a variety of uses as the term 'experience.' In theological discourse the term *reason* is often used to refer to one of the following: (a) the processes of reasoning; (b) the results of contemporary learning; or (c) truths about God that claim to be established without recourse to revelation. Following some postmodern philosophical reflections I discussed earlier in my epistemological notes, I do not think we can regard reason as an *independent something*—like the Enlightenment ideal of disinterested, neutral, and objective rea-

---

[4] See Paul Tillich, *Systematic Theology*, vol. 1 (Chicago: University of Chicago Press, 1951), 40–46.

son—which is a field of truth just by itself. In that earlier discussion I claimed that terms like *rational, objective,* and *factual* are context dependent.

I propose that we think of reason as *reasoning*—we argue, critique, analyze, explain, infer, interpret, make a case, point out contradictions and fallacious arguments, etc.—but always in some given social context and tradition of discourse and practices. These are the *practices* the performance of which we call *rational.* Hence, the church within its own theological life and in its dialectic with the world is always engaged in *reasonings*, even if there is no such thing as an overarching reason-in-itself and by-itself. In my identification of contemporary learning as a source for theological judgments, I have accommodated some of these uses in calling reason a source.

Without the intellectual power of reasoning, theologizing in the church would be impossible. In addition to the ordinary ways in which we reason in the church, there are *two formal rational norms* in theology. (1) *Consistency*: are the beliefs and actions free of self-contradiction? It is the very nature of self-contradiction that it cancels out the truth-claims that are deemed inconsistent with each other. This does not rule out the use of metaphors and paradoxes and a sense for mystery in our theologizing, but it does challenge the notion that we would know what we mean if we were to affirm a literal self-contradiction. (2) *Coherence*: do the beliefs and actions cohere together in such a way that they are interconnected and mutually complementary? These rational norms could also be called indispensable rules of syntax and semantics if the church is to be appropriately meaningful and intelligible—and not self-defeating—in its discourses and practices of witness.

Consider also *imagination* as that human power to work with images, narratives, and metaphors to represent objects, events, and situations in a depicting or pictorial way. Typically the semantics of imagination and images involves spatial or pictorial representation of the referent.[5] Think of how important imagination is to the construction and use of narrative—of being able to envisage the events represented by the narrative and to see the point of the narrative. Much of the *luminous* and *transformative* witness of the church in its outreach to the world will involve the evocative power of imagination. But we should be leery of separating

---

[5] Many people think they have not grasped the meaning of linguistic terms until they can somehow mentally 'picture' what the terms are about. While this sense of picturing may be important for some terms and for some persons some of the time, it is a misleading notion of how we understand signs.

imagination sharply from reasoning. While not reducible to reasoning, imagination trades on reason, stretching reason and understanding.

Theologizing cannot be done apart from experience, reasoning, and imagination, but these are not in and of themselves sources of theological judgment and affirmation. If experience is the ubiquitous medium of theology, then reasoning and imagination are the indispensable *tools* of theology's use of the sources.

Contemporary Learning

This source is wide and fluid in content. One of the reasons for calling it 'learning' rather than 'knowledge' is because it is so subject to change. What was yesterday's 'knowledge' can become tomorrow's falsehood. So much of this learning is itself contingent and largely empirical in character. For something to claim us as *learning*, it must be embedded in communal practices of (a) disciplined inquiry and investigation, (b) procedures of discussion and argument, and (c) criteria of judgment about a subject matter. Such learning includes the natural sciences as well as the social sciences and humanities. And the so-called facts and truths of such learning are also quite fluid and revisable, and the practices of identifying such facts and truths are embedded in concrete social traditions and discourses.

The desire to inquire and to discover the truth is part of the intrinsic human quest to know and understand the world, which is a God-given capacity and needs to be celebrated and not feared. This does not mean, however, that any particular putative truth-claim arising in these disciplines has the authority of absolute truth for theology. There is no simple way in which theology *must use* this learning. Hence, there is no abstract, in-principled way of specifying exactly how any piece of contemporary learning should shape some particular aspect of theological discourse. Caution here is warranted because there are many more claims to truth in the learning disciplines of the postmodern world than should appropriately command the assent of the Christian. A continuing conceptual problem is whether any of the claims of these disciplines of learning are shaped by *basic perspectives* that are inimical to theological truth-claims and the Christian perspective. I disagree with those theological positions that presume either that Christian theology can never in principle disagree with contemporary learning or that Christian theology must always refuse to appropriate such learning for its own critical and constructive work. But the church's witness would be incapacitated and unintelligible without wide-ranging appropriation of contemporary learning. The church lives in this world with its variegated forms and practices of learning, and its witness cannot ignore the learning or presume it is all irrelevant to faith.

Barth does not recognize such learning as a source for theological understanding and formulation. Yet in point of practice such learning is repeatedly employed in his elaboration and explanation of the basic doctrines of the faith. Such employment has been described by others as more or less *ad hoc* and subject to the overriding norm of the biblical witness.[6] However, I think it is appropriate to identify such learning as among the legitimate sources of theological reflection. Having affirmed that, I also insist that such learning is ruled by the material norm in determining its availability for theological appropriation. In practice this means that Christian theology does not first have to search for some worldly basic perspective or metaphysics or general epistemology in relation to which the claims of the faith will be framed, interpreted, and authorized.

This brings us to the question of the status of *philosophy* in relation to Christian theology. Whatever we might mean by 'philosophy,' it is clear that I count it among contemporary learning. I will not pursue here any definition of philosophy, except to note that defining philosophy is traditionally understood as a philosophical question. While I have freely appropriated much philosophical learning from the philosophy of language, logic, metaphysics, analyses of epistemic and agential concepts, and a host of other philosophical studies, I do not propose that Christian theology must find its grounding in some philosophical metaphysics or epistemology. And I eschew Tillich's attempt to *correlate* theology and philosophy in some systematic fashion. His proposal presupposes definitions of both theology and philosophy that are systematically unacceptable to my project of construing Christian theology.[7] Training in philosophy and the history of philosophy can certainly be a desideratum for the systematic theologian, but it is not necessary to the performance of the task of theology.

---

[6] Actually Barth does not raise the question of sources of theological reflection but simply argues that, in effect, Scripture and tradition are the only informative sources for theology.

[7] See Tillich, *Systematic Theology*, vol. 1, 3–70, but especially 18–27 and 59–65.

Past and Present Human Cultures

This is a capacious source of theological understanding, and it includes all the ways in which cultures or social worlds, with their structures, relations and relationships, powers, values, meanings, languages, traditions of practices, and artifacts, shape our experience and lives. I am also concerned here to emphasize the ways in which cultures express meanings in their artistic productions such as sculpture, drawings, painting, music, architecture, and poetic and narrative literature. We need to remember that, both as promise and as threat, the church inescapably uses the learning and milieu of its social worlds in order to live and witness to those worlds. While human culture as a source may not play an extraordinarily large role in the execution of the task of systematic theology, it should play a multidimensionally richer role in the church's larger witness to the world. This is especially the case in the church's practices of preaching and educating.

The Bible as the Church's Holy Scripture

The Bible is the *church's book* and as such is *constitutive* of the church's living *textuality*, of its distinctive discourses and practices in which it has its decisive identity and mission of witness. The church is peculiarly that community that is constituted by the *practice* of reading the Bible *as Holy Scripture*—of listening to and interpreting the scriptures as specially deputized for the upbuilding of the church. As so textually constituted, the church *confesses* that it is confronted with God's self-revelations in Israel and in Jesus Christ *in* the witness of the Bible. It should be clear, then, that the grammar of the words *Holy Scripture* in the context of the church is that it has authoritative status and is crucial to the church's own witness and self-understanding.[8]

---

[8] This point is nicely made by David H. Kelsey, *The Uses of Scripture in Recent Theology* (Philadelphia: Fortress, 1975), 89. Kelsey's book is a useful survey of some ways in which the Bible is used by some theologians in the construction of their theologies. The odd thing about Kelsey's book, however, is that it is written in the mode of neutral analysis of concepts and their possible deployment, but he never proffers a theological proposal or judgment of his own. A more recent useful study with a purpose similar to Kelsey's is John Goldingay, *Models for Scripture* (Grand Rapids, Mich.: Eerdmans, 1994).

Apart from this confessional starting point, there is no noncircular argument that can secure the judgment that the Bible is a witness to God's self-revelation. This is not to deny that there are arguments about what it means to say the Bible is a witness to God's self-communications. But the church's confession about the Bible is a *theological (or faith) judgment*, not a conclusion available to the modern disciplines of history or philosophy. Whether and in what sense the Bible is a witness to God's self-revelation is a *theological question*, not a historical question. This further means that the Bible is not revered by the church because it has been independently corroborated by the discipline of history as historically reliable about past events. This is not to deny that historical judgments are important to the biblical witness and to the church's interpretation of the biblical witness.

The church trusts the Bible because it witnesses to the Gospel of Jesus Christ. Jesus Christ—as the definitive self-revelation of God—is also the definitive Word of God. With Luther I affirm that this speaking or self-communicating of God in Jesus Christ, as the definitive Word of God in human history, is the *primary theme* of the Bible for the church.[9] Hence, it is not the case that we trust the Bible and *therefore* trust the Gospel of Jesus Christ. This sort of reasoning—which has been all too common in church history—would be *bibliolatry*. To put this point sharply, independent of hearing the witness to the Gospel of Jesus Christ, the church has no compelling interest in the Bible as important for the church's life and witness.

The Bible as the Primitive Narrative of God's Self-Revelations

Primitive means: (a) the historically closest witness *we have* to God's historic acts of revelation[10] and (b) the theologically irreducible and irreplaceable witness. As *narrative*, the biblical witness identifies and characterizes God in and through God's self-communicating interactions with Israel and the church. It is not *only* narrative, but the narrative forms the connecting context of God's self-revelations. Hence, the Bible

---

[9] For Luther, the Bible is the *cradle* or *manger* which holds Christ. See Philip S. Watson, *Let God Be God: An Interpretation of the Theology of Martin Luther* (Philadelphia: Muhlenberg Press, 1947), 148–152; 178, footnotes 4–9. In saying this, I am not saying that the whole of the biblical narrative is simply about Christ, but that the trajectory of Christ and human sin and salvation is the decisive theme of the Bible for the church.

[10] See 1 Pet 5.1; Jn 19.35; 21.24; 1 Jn 1.1–2.

is the story of God's salvific and self-communicating interactions with Israel and in Jesus and with the apostolic church. The Bible—as witness to the historical economy of God's communicative transactions with Israel and the world—is a narrative collection of deputized signs. And as I have already affirmed, it is the *incarnational narrative of Jesus Christ that is at the heart of the biblical narrative.*

While the term 'narrative' is much bandied about these days, and without opting for some general theory of how narrative presumably functions in all human understanding, the use of the term here specifies the account of the historical particularity of God's dealings with Israel and in Jesus Christ. Insofar as God has chosen to identify Godself in such a particular history and in such particular ways, a narrative is simply an account of those self-identifying communicative transactions of God in human history. Further, the narrative will devolve into nonhistorical myth if it is not the case that the God being identified is a God who creates the world and who acts within, upon, and with the world in its time and space in the particularity of Israel and especially in the particularity of Jesus Christ.[11]

The Bible as Deputized but Human Witness

The Bible as text is only a witness to God's self-revelation; it is not identical with that revelation. God's self-communicating life is not a property of the Bible, though it is for the church a property of the Bible to be the primitive witness to God's self-revelations. But in a derivative sense the Bible is or can become the Word of God to later generations and traditions insofar as they encounter the Word of God in its witness. Yet for succeeding generations, the Bible is the *indispensable witness* to God's self-revelations. The only real Gospel the church knows is known

---

[11] Hans W. Frei has given special prominence to narrative as a distinctive Christian category; see Hans W. Frei, *The Eclipse of Biblical Narrative: A Study in Eighteenth and Nineteenth Century Hermeneutics* (New Haven, Conn.: Yale University Press, 1974) and *Theology and Narrative: Selected Essays*, ed. George Hunsinger and William C. Placher (Oxford: Oxford University Press, 1993). See the essays which pivot around Frei's concerns with biblical narrative in Garrett Green, ed., *Scriptural Authority and Narrative Interpretation* (Philadelphia: Fortress, 1987). For a set of essays on narrative in theology see Stanley Hauerwas and L. Gregory Jones, eds., *Why Narrative? Readings in Narrative Theology* (Grand Rapids, Mich.: Eerdmans, 1989).

through the witness of the Bible. The church cannot step outside of the Bible or dispense with it and find some other *real Gospel* or real revelation. To pretend to do so is to pretend that there might be some other revelation or basic truth or semantics of 'God' that is definitive of the church's understanding and witness. This stepping outside the Bible to find an authoritative gospel in general human reason and experience or in a general philosophical anthropology or metaphysics has been a serious temptation for the church in the last two centuries.

The Bible as witness and deputized sign is: (a) multiple faces and polyphonic voices; (b) different languages, grammars, accents, and emphases; (c) expressive of Israel's and the early church's basic faith convictions; and (d) written by finite and fallible humans in their particular historical situations, languages, and perspectives as responses to God's action. We must avoid a falsely *docetized* Bible, i.e., a Bible shorn of its finitely human traits as witness. It is such a docetized Bible that has been the temptation of the modern forms of Fundamentalism with their insistence on the whole of the Bible being a set of truth-claims in all of its sentences. The church should have no theological interest in regarding the Bible as *inerrant* in the totality of its sentences. It is this humanly fallible creaturely medium that God has condescended to use to convey Godself.

Even if we do not affirm a docetized, inerrant Bible, the church does confess that the Bible—as primitive witness to God's self-revelation—is *inspired* by the Holy Spirit. 'Inspired' does not mean inerrant and infallible in every respect. But *inspired* does mean *deputized by God*. The Bible could not be the witness to God it is without the movement of the Holy Spirit guiding and empowering the Scriptural writers. But God's inspiration does not *displace* the human authors. Further, when the church speaks of the inspiration of Holy Scripture it affirms with Calvin that God accommodates God's self-communications to humans in and through the human language of Scripture. While I am denying that the grammar of Scriptural authority requires the Bible to be inerrant and infallible in every respect, this doctrine of inspiration I am advocating does affirm that the biblical narrative is a trustworthy testimony to God's self-revelations and the human situation before God. These inspired words of witness are given by God for the upbuilding of the faith of the church in its witness to God for the benefit of the world.[12]

---

[12] See 2 Tim 3.16–17; even though it refers primarily to the Old Testament, it nevertheless properly identifies the prime point of the church's use of the Bible as a whole.

The Bible as Canon for the Listening Church

As historically and theologically primitive and indispensable, the Bible is canon for the church. *Canon* means 'rule' or 'measure': the church rules or measures its life and witness by the witness of the Bible. I accept the Protestant Bible of the Old and New Testaments as the canon.[13] As canon the Bible pragmatically forms the life of the church. The church is therefore always the *listening church*, listening to Holy Scripture for the Gospel of Jesus Christ. As so listening, the church is normed in its witness by the biblical witness. As so listening, the church—in its multiple practices of using Scripture—engages in those practices with the expectation that it will hear the Word of God addressed to it in the church's own situation.

The listening church is both *freed* (liberated) and *bound* (normed) by the Bible. It is freed because it hears the Gospel of God's free grace in Jesus Christ that sets humans free from the determination and destiny of sin.[14] It is bound because the Bible is the indispensable source and therefore norm of hearing this Gospel.

The Gospel and Interpreting the Bible

Any reading or listening to the Bible has some *presuppositions*. I contend there is no presuppositionless, traditionless reading of the Bible.[15] The biblical testimony lives in the church, is received by the

---

[13] While not identifying the Apocrypha as Scripture, I am not denying its usefulness in understanding the intertestamental period. It is interesting to note, however, that even in the Roman Catholic Church, which accepts the Apocrypha as canon, there is no evidence that it has been used to launch any doctrines that are not already present in the Protestant canon.

[14] See 1 Cor 3.17; Gal 5.1.

[15] Much of the controversy in the church about the status of the Bible is over what presuppositions are to be brought to bear on the interpretation of the Bible. There is a vast difference between (a) presupposing that the Bible is Holy Scripture and therefore an authoritative witness to God's self-revelations and (b) presupposing that the Bible is an ancient text that must be tested for its historical accuracy and for its meaningfulness by the standards of the contemporary world. James Barr, *The Bible in the Modern World* (New York: Harper and Row, 1973), tracks how the Bible has been interpreted in the so-called modern world. Barr would not share the presuppositions of the Gospel with which I am approaching the Bible.

church, and is interpreted by the church. It is an enormous presupposition that the church reads the Bible as the primitive witness to God's self-revelations in Israel and in Jesus Christ and in the apostolic church. But having affirmed that, we must also maintain that the Bible is *not* just a contentless *cipher* awaiting our presupposed readings. The Bible's witness is not reducible to our presuppositions in reading—the Bible has the capacity to resist our reductions. Nevertheless, *the church's basic presupposition in reading the Bible is that it expects to hear the Word of God in the primitive witness to God's self-revelation in Jesus Christ.*

As the listening church, the church cannot avoid *some presiding model of the Gospel.* Such a model or material norm is the real but reformable norm for reading the Bible. Such a model can also be corrected by new readings of the Bible. From the perspective of some presiding model of the Gospel, the church necessarily *thematizes and prioritizes* some passages, concepts, images, and convictions as more *theologically fundamental* than others.[16] Hence, we employ the ancient rule that Scripture interprets Scripture. In this respect it is true that the model of the Gospel functions as a *canon within the canon*, though not an absolute canon that cannot be questioned by further readings of the Bible itself. By emphasizing that the church trusts the biblical witness to God because of its witness to Jesus Christ, I refuse to regard the Bible as a collection of miscellaneous truth-claims that have binding authority over the church. The peril of Fundamentalism is just this bondage to the assumption that whatever truth-claims might be present at any point in the Bible are therefore authoritative for the church in all times and contexts. This assumption loses sight of the theologically basic conviction that the church regards the Bible from the perspective of its witness to Jesus Christ. Further, by reading the Bible through the lens of the Gospel, we can admit more readily that some trajectories in the Bible's witness are in tension with the Gospel itself. Therefore, through the priority of the model one does not have to give the same weight to every passage and can therefore critique and dismantle unfettered patriarchalism, relative indifference to slavery, and subordination of women, as examples.[17]

---

[16] I am under the impression that my use of the model of the Gospel functions similarly to the concept of a *discrimen* identified by Kelsey, *Uses of Scripture*, 160 ff. Kelsey acknowledges his dependence on Robert Clyde Johnson, *Authority in Protestant Theology* (Philadelphia: Westminster, 1959) for this concept.

[17] It should be noted now that when I do get around to critiquing such matters as patriarchy, it will not be from the perspective of its unacceptability to a

Thus Scripture can be the basis for a *critique* of Scripture. It is for this reason that the authority of Scripture is not to be located in the presumed truthfulness of the wide range of miscellaneous statements it makes about all sorts of matters.

As the listening church interpreting Scripture, the church should at least listen: (a) to the original voice of a passage; (b) to the redacted voice (where applicable); (c) to the canonical voice; (d) to the voice of its witness to the self-revealing transactions of the God of Israel in Jesus Christ; and (e) to the witness for the church today.

The rules constructed in the doctrine of revelation can be a guide to interpreting the Bible. Hence, the Bible should not be construed as: (a) simply a complete set of incorrigibly true or inerrant revealed propositions about God and everything else [Fundamentalism], or (b) simply pictorial and narrative *illustrations* of eternal truths we can know on other grounds [simple Liberalism].

Aside from the modest rules of interpretation I have assembled in this section and in the chapter on knowledge and revelation, it is unnecessary and misleading to seek to develop a *general hermeneutics* in order to *understand* Scripture.[18] Since there is no encompassing theory of understanding—the word 'understanding' does not name one sort of thing in all of its uses—so too there is no general hermeneutics that describes what it is to understand a biblical text, or any text for that matter. This is not to deny that it is appropriate in a variety of contexts and with various intentions to accuse someone of *misunderstanding* a biblical text; but

---

postmodern feminism. Rather, it will be from the perspective of its incompatibility with the Gospel and the biblical theme of the *imago dei*. This is not to deny that such postmodern feminism might be an effective prompt to the church that it does not have to regard the Bible as authoritative for the church in every aspect of its variegated witness.

[18] As is well known, Friedrich Schleiermacher in the early nineteenth century made proposals for a general hermeneutic for understanding *religious texts*; see F. D. E. Schleiermacher, *Hermeneutics: The Handwritten Manuscripts*, ed. Heinz Kimmerle, trans. James Duke and Jack Forstman (Missoula, Mont.: Scholars Press, 1977). The trajectory of this concern for hermeneutics continues into the twentieth century in the prominent stress on existential hermeneutics by Rudolf Bultmann and in the ambitious program of Hans-Georg Gadamer, *Truth and Method*, 2d rev. ed., trans. Joel Weinsheimer and Donald G. Marshall (New York: Crossroad, 1990). I do not deny that there are some gems here and there in these texts and concerns, but the general project is itself an intellectual dead end and profoundly misleading.

such an accusation is simply an invitation to explore what the misunderstanding might be. I do not suppose that a general hermeneutical theory
will help in that exploration.

The interpretation of the Bible is properly a *community activity*—something the people of the church do together and never simply
the private interpretations of assorted individuals. This is why individuals
are encouraged to read the Bible as members of a community of faith.
Christians need one another to learn *how* to read and listen to the Bible as
God's Word. The Protestant traditions have been much too sanguine
about the usefulness of reading Scripture in individual isolation from the
community of faith. Such individual readings are never without presuppositions, and often the readings are demonic and harmful. At least
within the church these presuppositions can be exposed to critical scrutiny. In making this point, I am not saying that interpretation should be
left to the so-called experts, which seems to exclude most laity.

The church's listening to the Bible cannot be isolated from contemporary learning and culture, though these other sources can never vali-
date the Bible *as* the Word of God. Historical studies can greatly enhance
the church's understanding of Scriptural passages, but they cannot tell
the church what is the Word of God in those passages for the church.

The church cannot remove and dissolve the dialectical tension between (a) listening to the Bible as the Word of God—hermeneutics of
generosity—and (b) listening to the Bible as only a fallible, human
word—hermeneutics of suspicion. However, if the hermeneutics of suspicion predominates, it will subvert the church's capacity to be the listening church, canonically ruled and normed by the Bible.

The church confesses that the Bible can only be read or heard as a
witness of the self-revelation of God insofar as the Holy Spirit moves
persons to so hear it. The church—for whom the Bible is Holy Scripture
and Word of God—prays for the illumination of the Spirit in its interpretation of the Bible.

In sum, then, *the Bible as Holy Scripture is both norm and source for
systematic theology.* It is norm as the historically and theological primitive narrative of God's communicative transactions in Israel and definitively in Jesus of Nazareth. But it never properly functions as norm apart
from some model of the Gospel to identify for the church what its witness is most fundamentally about and why the church should regard it as
a normative witness. We must not forget that the ineradicable question to
the church also pertains to the church's uses of Scripture. Further, the
Bible is a multiple source for theological concepts, for practices, and for

guidance of the Christian life.

Scripture and Traditions

Since I have mentioned how the interpretation of Scripture always has some presuppositions and how the interpretation of Scripture is properly a communal activity of the church, it is obvious that Scripture itself lives in the church in and through traditions of use and interpretation. The Reformation emphasis on *sola scriptura*, implying that Scripture alone was all that was necessary for the life of the church, now seems misguided.[19] Further, the concept of Scripture as *norma non normata*—norm not further normed by another norm—can mislead us about the actual and unavoidable practices of the church prior to and since the Reformation. The relation between Scripture and tradition is more dialectical than these slogans indicate. Insofar as the church is continually confronted with the ineradicable question of what is the Gospel that founds and directs the church, it—the church as living tradition—must formulate some understanding of the Gospel which will then guide its use of Scripture. Of course, this statement of the Gospel will itself be tested with how fruitfully it is derived from Scripture and makes sense out of the Scriptural witness.

Furthermore, the Holy Scripture of the Old and New Testaments is itself a product of traditions in Israel's life and of the earliest traditions of the church. These early church traditions wrote the books of the New Testament, and succeeding church traditions determined what would count as Scripture and canon for the church. These previous traditions, now codified by decisions of the church, are normative for the later traditions. Much of the life of church traditions is shaped by Scripture and the interpretation of Scripture. A tradition inescapably says what Scripture means *for that tradition*.[20] The church in a tradition represents to itself and to the world what it thinks the Scripture means. And this saying and interpreting is a source of judgment and renewal within the lives of the church traditions.

---

[19] To be sure, the Reformation use of this locution was aimed primarily at a developed range of practices in the Roman tradition, and for the Reformers the appeal to Scripture was only the most viable recourse.

[20] This thought is interestingly developed by Kathryn Tanner, "Theology and the Plain Sense," in Garrett Green, ed., *Scriptural Authority and Narrative Interpretation* (Philadelphia: Fortress, 1987), 59–78.

So, the traditions within Scripture and after Scripture are processes of handing on and interpreting and reinterpreting what God has done, is doing, and will do. The Jahwist text itself gets transformed when placed in the interpretive context of the Priestly writers—reinterpretation is well under way. The post-biblical traditions of the church are themselves processes of interpretation and reinterpretation, and there is doctrinal development in the traditions of the church. In the light of these considerations, we cannot posit the Scripture as something that arose external to the traditions of the church and therefore can be used as a nontradition norm for the traditions of the church. Rather, the New Testament is itself a product of the traditions of the early church, but its normativity for the church includes precisely this early traditioning of the coming-to-be of the church of Jesus Christ.

In short, the following process of interpretation and reinterpretation prevails in Scripture and traditions: the Old Testament traditions are processes of interpretation and reinterpretation in Israel; the New Testament traditions are processes of interpreting and reinterpreting Jesus in the light of the OT and the OT in the light of Jesus; and later church traditions are processes of interpreting and reinterpreting Scripture as the living Word of God for the church in its continuing life of witness.

So, should we say that tradition has priority over the Bible, both as the creator of the Bible and the prime interpreter of the Bible? This is a tempting claim, but it is misleading about the meaning of 'Scripture' and 'tradition' as these have been discussed. I claim here that the Scriptures of the Old and New Testaments are the *primitive narrative witnesses* and canonical traditions for the church. These canonical traditions, as Scripture, have normative priority over the later traditions of the church. Further, in affirming that the later traditions of the church are the listening church, I have confirmed the priority of Scripture over the later traditions. If we ask the further question of whether it is better to say the canonical Scripture imposed itself on the church or to say the church imposed its decision of canonicity on the previous traditions, I choose to say the *Scripture—by its very inspired and effective testimony to the triune God—imposed itself on the church.*

Church Traditions

In the NT, *paradosis* can mean both 'handed over' and 'handed on.'[21] The Latin word *traditio* means 'handing on' both as: (a) the *process* of handing on, and (b) the *content* which is handed on. Both dimensions of tradition are important and should not be sharply separated.

The primary bearers of the content of any tradition—whether the church or some other social institution—are its distinctive discourses and practices. It is in these that traditions are constituted as distinct processes of handing on and as distinct contents of understanding and construal. Traditions connect persons to a *past* and provide material for present *self-identity*. We remember *through* traditions of memory. Every Christian *experience* and every interpretation of Scripture is *within* some received tradition. Hence, the past we receive through traditions is always an *interpreted past*: a past that is received in and through the tradition's discourses and practices. The church loses its identity when it forgets the biblical call of the Gospel *and* the traditions through which it hears that call in the present. Tradition is thus indispensable to the church that claims to have received historical self-revelations of God in the history of Israel and of Jesus Christ and of the apostolic church.

Church Traditions and Tradition

Church or Christian traditions are inclusively the processes and the contents that hand on Christian witness and understanding through *stories, narratives, texts, testimonies, concepts, images, beliefs and doctrines, rules, experiences, practices, creeds and confessions, persons, and institutions.*[22] But any honest reading of the history of Christianity leads us to the conclusion that *there are traditions, not just one tradition.*

---

[21] See 1 Cor 11.23; 2 Thess 3.6.

[22] Until recently, the Roman Catholic tradition has persistently done more theological reflection on tradition than have Protestants. But the tendency in the Roman tradition has been to strongly identify tradition with the magisterial teachings and dogmas. See the new wrestling between Scripture and tradition in *Dei Verbum* [Dogmatic Constitution on Divine Revelation] in Walter M. Abbott, ed., *The Documents of Vatican II*, with notes and comments by Catholic, Protestant, and Orthodox authorities, trans. Joseph Gallagher (New York: Guild Press, 1966), 111–128. See also Joseph Rupert Geiselmann, *The Meaning of Tradition* (New York: Herder and Herder, 1966).

Hence, this question must be posed: is there real unity in the midst of the differences and disunity of the historic and geographic traditions? Is there one catholic faith everywhere and always believed and taught [*ubique, semper, ab omnibus*]?[23] While I am impressed with the differences in traditions of Christian witness, it must be admitted that every tradition of whatever historical and geographical location had to identify what it determined to be the essential beliefs and practices of Christian faith.[24] In this sense, then, a form of *consensual orthodoxy* has functioned in all the traditions, even though it may not be exactly the same in every tradition.

Even acknowledging the plurality present in Christian traditions, I give priority to the so-called *ecumenical tradition* expressed in ecumenical creeds and somewhat traceable—if not too detailed—throughout the history of the churches. It is this trajectory of tradition that strides out of the NT into the early church theologians—through Nicaea, Constantinople, and Chalcedon; through Augustine, Anselm, and Thomas Aquinas; through Luther, Calvin, and the Free Church traditions; sorting through Kierkegaard and into the twentieth century in Barth, the ecumenical movement, and Vatican II—that has been influential for me.

Any proposed grammar of the church's witness is itself a search for that grammar that is judged to be normative for the primary traditions of the church. Even the proposals for revision of tradition intend to retrieve—even if *redefining*—what is essential to Christian faith and practice. Precisely because tradition is always a product of the *church/world dialectic* in the historical process, I do deny there is a *pure* church tradition, simply internal to the church and unaffected by any historically locatable social world. We must avoid a false docetization of some aspect of tradition as pure and infallible and beyond the scope of the ineradica-

---

[23] This understanding of tradition arose in the attempt by the church to define an 'orthodox' view of the faith. For an insightful discussion of these criteria of the orthodox tradition, see Jaroslav Pelikan, *The Christian Tradition: A History of the Development of Doctrine*, vol. 1: *The Emergence of the Catholic Tradition (100–600)* (Chicago: University of Chicago Press, 1971), 333–339. It is interesting to note that the concept of *consensus*, albeit the consensus of the bishops, was critically necessary to the rise of catholic orthodoxy.

[24] The search for the distinction between the essentials of the faith and nonessentials has been a functional dynamic of the church's historical traditions. The Protestant Reformation and the rise of the liberal traditions in the nineteenth century represent serious efforts to *revise* the previous tradition in determining what beliefs and practices should count as essential to the faith.

ble questions I have postulated as necessary for the church's theological witness. Standing firmly in my Protestant heritage, I remain suspect of any 'infallible magisterium' untainted by the world.[25]

Encountering and Assessing Traditions

How and *what* the church *said*—taught, preached, and witnessed—and *did*—enacted and practiced—in the past traditions are important for the church's witness today. The traditions are important at least because the present itself has been influenced by the past witness, whether this is acknowledged or not.[26] The traditions are important because we need to learn deliberately and reflectively from the past witness of the church in order that our own witness might be more faithful to the reality of God. We may critique traditions but we cannot leap over them to the Bible, and we ignore them only at the peril of misunderstanding the fullness of the Gospel of Jesus Christ. It should also be clear that the traditions themselves cannot escape the application of the ineradicable question.

To learn reflectively from past traditions, we must ask what the church in its traditions taught:

    a.   *must always* be said and done in Christian witness—questions of *orthodoxy* and *orthopraxis*;

    b.   *must never* be said and done in Christian witness—questions of *heresy*;

    c.   is *permissible* of nonschismatic difference, dispute, and dis-

---

[25] The negation here is not against any sort of *magisterium* but against an *infallible magisterium* as found in the Roman tradition. In fact, the Protestant tradition in which I stand can well give more attention to the conception and practice of a truly functional magisterium or teaching office of the church. The peril of infallible doctrine and infallible magisterium is that we the church are seldom able to see clearly just how much we might be influenced in our pronouncements by factors other than revelation. In the spirit of the necessity of the church to interpret Scripture, I can affirm that the church itself should believe that God will finally preserve the church from irremediable and fundamental error—though short-term errors might abound.

[26] For example, the early Disciples of Christ tradition eschewed creeds and fled to the NT, assuming it could step over previous church traditions, but little realizing how deeply its reading of the NT was influenced by Nicaea and Chalcedon.

agreement.

And these questions must be pursued in relation to the larger historical contexts in which the church professed its witness and lived its life.

Other *diagnostic questions* to ask the traditions are:

a. What are the professed beliefs about the essence of the Christian Gospel? What is the rationale of those beliefs?

b. What doctrines, including ethical teachings, are regarded as essential to Christian faith? How are these doctrines related to the identified Gospel?

c. How do these professed doctrines relate to the actual practices of the church and to the lives of concrete Christian people?

d. Do we hear or discern the Gospel in those beliefs and practices?

e. How was Scripture read and interpreted? What authority did it have?

f. How does the world in which the traditions exist shape the church's construal of Christian life?

g. What was the self-understanding of the church in its particular social worlds?

h. How do the traditions critique the church's present witness?

The raising of these questions leads to these *types of possible critiques of traditions*. First, it might be claimed that the professed essential doctrines obscure or distort the Gospel. For example, the early church's adoption of the rule of God's impassibility and simplicity made it difficult to talk aptly of Incarnation and finally of the Trinity. Second, it might be claimed that the professed beliefs and actual practices are inconsistent with the Gospel. For example, unfettered patriarchalism and androcentrism, racism, anti-Jewishness, neglect of the poor and the marginal, and service to the idols of the world seem now to be inconsistent with our formulation of the Gospel of Jesus Christ. Third, it might be claimed that the professed beliefs *and* actual practices are incoherent and inconsistent with each other. For example, the common professed belief that the love of neighbor is a divine command is inconsistent with the actual practice of neglecting the poor and hating the enemy in concrete Christian living. This is the problem of hypocrisy and the lie—the charge of much liberation theology. Fourth, it might be claimed that some of the professed beliefs and practices are not luminous, truthful, transformative of their world or of this contemporary world. The process of so analyzing and critiquing the traditions involves *excavating the grammars* of their discourses and practices.

The traditions as received are always subject to reform,

reformulation, renewal, and re-visioning in the light of the Gospel and the imperative to communicate with the contemporary world. This receipt and re-visioning are necessary to the life of the church. *Traditionalism*—the unwillingness to disagree with tradition—can unduly bind the church's witness today. *Revisionism* undisciplined can subject the church's witness to the 'fads and whims' of worldly times. There is an irremovable dialectic of dependence and revision between the contemporary church and the traditions of the past.[27]

Grammar and the Development of Doctrine

Consider now these central theses from the previous discussions. Christian faith is constituted as a textual faith by its peculiar discourses and practices. The Holy Scriptures are the authoritative or canonical texts grounding Christian witness, because they are the primal and primitive witness to God's self-revealing interactions with Israel and the apostolic church. The traditions of the church hand on Scripture and interpret Scripture, saying what Scripture *really means*, and Scripture norms the traditions' life. Within the witnesses of Scripture and traditions there are narratives, themes, and doctrinal convictions about God and human destiny, and there are grammatical rules for the shaping of the Christian life and witness. Systematic theology is the elucidation of the deep grammar of the church's witness to the triune God, understanding 'witness' to encompass both word and deed, discourses and practices. Through the centuries there have been sharp disagreements as to what the *true grammar* of the church ought to be, and today there appear to be *many grammars* of profound differences. And there appear to be some differences in grammar among the generations of church traditions. So, it appears that every effort to state *the* grammar of the faith is itself a historically and geographically limited and locatable critical and constructive attempt to give a coherent, consistent, and comprehensive interpretation of Christian faith and witness.

What are we to make of this situation of differing grammars and dif-

---

[27] Pastors have a special obligation to know and understand the traditions of their 'denomination' *and* of their particular congregation! No one should pastor a congregation without first asking about and analyzing that congregation's tradition as a witnessing community. The questions mentioned above can be used to diagnose the tradition and present situation of a congregation.

fering doctrinal convictions? Is all that Christian witness needs to believe and do 'contained' in the Bible? Is it possible for the doctrines of the church to *develop* over the centuries, such that some earlier doctrines are reshaped and some new elaborations of doctrine are appropriate and necessary for the church's witness? How are we to distinguish between those doctrines that are essential to the faith in all times and places and those doctrines that are important but need not be shared by all traditions? These are serious questions for the church's systematic theological efforts.

We will explore in this section the possibility of distinguishing between *levels of grammar* in the context of the theological problem of the development of doctrine. Hopefully, this will help us at least understand how some beliefs and practices are so basic that they are essential to the faith in any historical epoch or geographical location, and how some beliefs and practices are quite contingent and nonessential and therefore reformable.

Discerning Levels of Grammar

As I have mentioned previously, Wittgenstein made a helpful but imprecise distinction between 'depth grammar' and 'surface grammar.' Surface grammar is that rather superficial way we are misled by appearances of similarity between locutions. For example, when we think 'the ball is red' and 'Jesus is divine' are two declarative sentences that predicate something of their different subjects—without noting anything about how these locutions function in concrete human discourses—we are on the verge of being misled on the differing meanings of the two sentences. Depth grammar, then, is that concrete, contextual functioning of language in which we discern how the language is working for real human speakers. I have tried to keep us mindful of the *depth* side to grammar and language by reminding us that grammar involves syntax, semantics, *and* pragmatics. So, we might draw attention to similarities at the level of syntax that become more or less irrelevant at the level of pragmatics because the *uses* of the locutions are so dramatically different, as in the two sentences mentioned above about a ball and Jesus. When I use the term 'grammar,' I am typically not worried about a distinction between depth and surface grammar because I am covering both in my continual reference to syntax, semantics, and pragmatics as the dimensions of meaning that comprise grammar as rules of sense-making.

Wittgenstein's distinction does, however, *suggest* another distinction that can be helpful to understanding the grammar of Christian discourse and practice, namely, a difference among *levels of grammar*. At its deepest level the discourses and practices of the faith are framed in form and content around the most basic beliefs and the most basic practices. However, as the larger witness of the church at any point in time, including the early church, is engaged in communicative transactions of witness to its contemporary social world, there are beliefs and practices that are stimulated by and shaped by those transactions. For example, I think I can share in the deep grammar of the post-apostolic church without supposing that its developing practice and beliefs about ordaining only women to the priesthood are essential to that deep grammar. Rather, it is peculiarly something that arises out of transactions within the patriarchal traditions of Israel and the Hellenistic/Roman world. But clearly this practice developed and sustained itself throughout many succeeding generations of church life, only coming under serious theological critique in the nineteenth century. Were we unable to critique tradition and to declare this practice nonessential to church life, then we would be stuck with defending a practice that seems nonessential to the Gospel of Jesus Christ, perhaps even inconsistent with it.

I propose that at its deepest level Christian discourse should only change very slowly, and there should be great continuity in grammar. But the closer we get to the surface of the discourse's interaction in witness to a particular social world, the more we move into those matters about which change might be theologically warranted. In other words, the church/world dialectic will itself produce differing levels of grammatical form and content of varying seriousness to the church's faith and practice. Further, I do propose that genuine improvement in grammar and understanding can occur through the tradition, since the Scripture does not itself answer all the questions that legitimately arise in the church's task of witnessing to the world.

An Example of Deep Grammar
and Doctrinal Development: Jesus Is Divine

As an example of deep grammar, consider that at the heart of the NT is the widespread discourse and practice of worshipping and adoring Jesus, as seen in the various titles ascribed to him, but especially in the uses of 'Lord' or *kyrios*.[28] It is this deep practice of regarding Jesus as a non-idolatrous object of worship—expressed in the common confession that Jesus is Lord and Savior—that led to the question the post-apostolic church had to clarify: in what sense is Jesus divine, if at all? For some Jews such talk was semantically impossible because it seemed to say a creature was divine.[29] And for some good Platonists—e.g., Arius—the divine as such could never be identified with a changing, suffering finite creature. Arius explicitly invoked a common church rule that God is un-changing—or more precisely, God is *immutable* and *impassible*—and concluded that Jesus was not divine because Jesus was obviously a man who changed, suffered, and died in time.

Without directly challenging this theological semantic rule about immutability and impassibility, the church decided at Nicaea that Jesus was as fully divine as the Father/Creator. However, it later had to argue that the eternal Son as such did not suffer, while the human Jesus did. I contend that the church at Nicaea made the right decision that Jesus is divine Savior and non-idolatrously worshipable, but that it erred in not repudiating the semantic rule that God is immutable and impassible. The result was that the church continued to worship Jesus and give thanks for his salvific work on humanity's behalf and to talk of Jesus being God in-carnate, but it was haunted by a semantic rule that, in my judgment, ren-dered this practice unintelligible. I will argue later that the understanding of the triune God will require considerable reworking and reconstruing the nature of God and God's attributes, which increases clarity and intel-ligibility in the development of the church's doctrine of God.[30]

So, at the depths of Christian grammar is the pragmatic affirmation that Jesus is worshipable, salvific, and divine. That deep grammar should not change. What might change and develop is how this is connected syntactically and semantically to articulating what it means to be 'di-vine.' I will argue that we need to drop the impassibility rule in order better to understand the way in which God is a 'complex subject who in freedom and love can become incarnate in Jesus without ceasing to be Creator.' I argue that this *revised grammar* conceptually empowers the

---

[28] See Phil 2.9; Acts 2.36; 10.36; Rom 9.10; 14.9–11; 1 Cor 8.6; 12.3.

[29] In these matters concerning God, syntax and semantics are tightly inter-woven.

[30] Of course, the creed of Nicaea does not itself state or require that God is in all respects immutable and impassible. In fact, it seems to me that creed re-quires that one give up the immutability and impassibility rule in order to clarify how God can become human.

church to understand and articulate the deep grammar of the Gospel of Jesus Christ more clearly. Nevertheless, the grammar gets more complicated in how both the oneness and the threeness of God are articulated, and here it seems to me there is room for disagreement and complexity that may not be as deep for the church as the confession that Jesus is Lord and Savior.

Other Examples of Development

Consider another example. While biblical patriarchy might have some internal rules that help control and diminish it, it is still undeniably there in the grammar of both testaments. But I will propose that the grammar of patriarchy—when played out just on its own—runs into sharp conflict with the grammar of Incarnation and human justification in the cross of Christ, which are also clearly present in the NT. And I will argue that the cross of the Incarnate Son of God is a *deeper grammar* to the church's faith than the grammar of patriarchy. Hence, patriarchy is more nearly something historically contextual in Israel, the ancient world, and elsewhere but is not essential to the Gospel at its deepest level. Patriarchy is closer to the *surface* of the church's interaction with social worlds.

Further, once we have achieved a semantic and syntactic grammar that accommodates God becoming incarnate in Jesus, and once we muscularly grasp God's concrete involvement in the cross and death of Jesus and therewith in the merciful action of atonement, we will have to challenge a common assumption of the NT and much of the church that there is an ultimate *dual* destiny among humans. In other words, I will argue that there is no deep grammatical requirement that there must be an ultimate dual destiny among humans. This doctrinal argument could not be advanced if the NT and the tradition could not be materially normed by the presiding model of the Gospel that I have articulated. Hence, the Gospel itself sometimes requires a stringent critique of *some* trajectories in Scripture and tradition.

Doctrinal Development, Revision, and Church Unity

The distinction about levels of grammar and the examples invoked should help us see how there might be doctrinal development that does not threaten the unity and identity of the church over the centuries and in different cultures. The grammar of the church is rooted in Israel and in the coming of Jesus and the response of people to his life, death, and resurrection, as these are now canonized in the discourses of the OT and NT. If we do not have to defend a fundamentalist view that every sentence of the NT is inerrant, we can probe more deeply for the continuities in grammar of the various witnesses of the NT. We do not have to be misled by some surface dissimilarities and seeming disagreements. And we do not have to suppose that all issues of Christian witness were resolved in the NT or can be resolved by simple citation of the NT. Arius cited the NT, as did Athanasius. But we can see how the church's ongoing witness, rooted in Scripture as it should be, must inevitably confront issues that emerge historically in its own struggle to be accountable to God for its witness to its contemporary world.

The NT does not explicitly *contain* a doctrine of the Trinity, but it does in its deep grammar lead directly into the sort of affirmations about God that trinitarian language intends to hold together and illuminate. Further, a major strand or theme of the NT is that humans are saved by the grace of God, but the church will struggle over how to affirm this in relation to talking about human decisions and human destiny. The church was stalked in these ongoing quests for consistency by the unexamined rule that ultimate destiny must be dual—a destiny for the saved and a destiny for the damned. I will make revising proposals that distinguish among three different meanings of 'salvation,' arguing that questions of salvation bear differently on dual destiny at each level.

These are some ways in which my project on the grammar of the church will be proposing the need to stay with the deepest convictions and to trace more discerningly just how those deep convictions themselves require some *revisions and developments in doctrine.* It is helpful to understand that not every dispute over grammar is at the same level of seriousness for the church. Not every disagreement is a matter of orthodoxy or heresy. There is a wide range of *permissible* differences: differences closer to the surface of the ongoing witness of the church. Many of these differences can be traced to the unavoidable and important interaction of the church's witness to its various historical and geographical social worlds.[31]

---

[31] John Henry Newman's rightfully important treatise of 1878: *An Essay on the Development of Christian Doctrine* (New York: Image Books, 1960) is still haunted by the need to have incorrigible and infallible doctrine. But he is forthrightly on target on the doctrinal inadequacy of the Protestant appeal to *sola scriptura* without a functioning magisterium. See also, on the development of

Theology as the Discourse of Dialectical
Confession and Profession

Theology—as the discourse of dialectical confession and profession—starts with the communal confessional acknowledgment of God's definitive self-revelation in Jesus Christ as the Gospel to the whole world and then moves to the profession of this Gospel in the midst of irremovable dialectical dynamics in its witness to the contemporary world. The discourse of the church in its witness is always theological, that is, it is always intending to say who God is, what God's Gospel in Jesus Christ means, and how the Gospel bears on human life. Systematic theology is the particular task of the church aimed at providing a coherent and consistent diagnostic critique and construction of the identifying shape of the church's proper witness in word and deed for its world. The discourses of the church's witness and the discourse of the systematic critique and construction of the church's witness are the discourses of dialectical confession and profession. My task in this section is to explain the meaning of the concepts of *dialectical, confession,* and *profession.*

I have emphasized from the beginning of these explorations that witnessing to the reality of the triune God is the defining mission of the church. I am claiming that the NT church was defined and structured by its summons by Jesus Christ to witness to the reality of God's merciful love for the benefit of the world. In the NT we find various uses of the forms of *homologein*: (a) to acknowledge or bear witness [Lk 12.8; Mt 10.32]; (b) to confess in faith [Rom 10.9–10]; (c) an act of confession or witness [2 Cor 9.13; 1 Tim 6.12–13]. We also have the many NT uses of *marturia*: to witness, to testify, to give testimony. Note the root here of *martyr.* There are also the many forms of *kerysso*: to announce, to proclaim.

In post-Reformation times, various Protestant traditions had *confessions,* which were public declarations of their common faith: for example, The Augsburg Confession, The Westminster Confession, and in the

---

doctrine, Karl Rahner, *Theological Investigations,* vol. 1, trans. Cornelius Ernst (Baltimore: Helicon Press, 1961), 1–78, and vol. 4, trans. Kevin Smyth (New York: Seabury, 1974), 3–35.

last century, The Barmen Declaration.[32] The word 'confession' is used more recently—and this is closer to my use—by those theologies that emphasize the priority of the communal context of the confession of Christ as the foundational starting point or *given* for theological reflection.[33]

Christian Theology as Confessional

To explain the relevant meaning of Christian theology as confessional theology, the following points must be emphasized. First, Christian theology is a *communal* confession: of and by the church, and constitutive for the church's own self-identity and understanding. It is first the community's discourse and self-identity, and then derivatively, the discourse of the individual person.

Second, the church confesses the encounter with the *givenness and priority* of God's self-revelation in the Gospel of Jesus Christ which calls the church into being and life. As I have argued earlier, such confession begins with *acknowledgment and gratitude*. The givenness of God's self-revelation and call solicits and empowers acknowledgment and gratitude. We confessionally acknowledge the transforming encounter with God's gracious presence in Jesus Christ. This acknowledgment is a being *claimed, called, addressed, saved,* as distinct from a *having discovered,*

---

[32] For the texts of these confession, see John H. Leith, ed., *Creeds of the Church: A Reader in Christian Doctrine from the Bible to the Present,* 3d ed. (Louisville, Ky.: John Knox Press, 1982).

[33] In the twentieth century the single most influential recovery of confessional theology was the theology of Karl Barth; see especially *Church Dogmatics,* 1/2, 822–843, but the theme is present throughout his dogmatics. H. Richard Niebuhr gave a profound elaboration of confessional theology in *The Meaning of Revelation* (New York: Macmillan, 1941). Hans Frei carried matters in related directions, emphasizing 'narrative theology'; see especially Frei's posthumous publications: *Types of Christian Theology,* ed. George Hunsinger and William C. Placher (New Haven, Conn.: Yale University Press,1992), and *Theology and Narrative.* George Lindbeck's *The Nature of Doctrine: Religion and Theology in a Postliberal Age* (Philadelphia: Westminster, 1984), is in my judgment an important variation on confessional theology's themes. William C. Placher, *Unapologetic Theology: A Christian Voice in a Pluralistic Conversation* (Louisville, Ky.: Westminster/John Knox, 1989) is a fine discussion of a confessional perspective. See also the recent discussion: Timothy R. Phillips and Dennis L. Okholm, eds., *The Nature of Confession: Evangelicals and Postliberals in Conversation* (Downers Grove, Ill.: InterVarsity Press, 1996).

concluded, come upon. Acknowledgment and gratitude are not first products of argument or conclusions of reasoning.

Third, the confession can be said to be grounded in a *new point of departure.* The acknowledged encounter with God's self-revelation is the foundation *from which* the confessional interpretation and profession moves, not *to which.* The confession provides the starting point that makes sense of—gives perspective to—one's understanding of God, humanity, and world. Hence, *epistemically* it is confessed that no neutral or transcendental or general epistemological theory or rules can certify or verify God's self-revelation in Jesus Christ. Whatever such a theory could certify as *knowledge* or as *deity* would be a deity that it knows on its own terms and as its own possibility. Instead, confessional theology argues that a *new epistemic situation* is created by the actuality of God's self-revelation. Epistemically the church in its confession can only embrace the revelation and in a large circular way interpret that revelation for itself and for the world. To this extent, confessional theology does not acknowledge the possibility that the Gospel can be justified as true from a neutral or transcendental theory: *no noncircular justification.* Further, with Kierkegaard I affirm that confessional theology, with its new point of departure, always bears the possibility of *offense* for persons for whom the Gospel is unacceptable and existentially indigestible.[34]

Fourth, it is a communal confession within a *tradition of discourses and practices with their characteristic doctrines.* My theological project, as I have mentioned previously, could be said to stand within that tradition coming out of the NT which strides through the great ecumenical councils of Nicaea, Constantinople, and Chalcedon; through Augustine, Anselm, Aquinas, Luther, Calvin, Kierkegaard, Barth, twentieth-century ecumenism, and the Free Church Disciples of Christ tradition.

Fifth, it is *public* confession and profession: by the church *for* the church and the world and thus always *before* the world. The publicness of confessional theology shows itself in the engagement of its witness with the world. It is the world before whom the church witnesses, and in

---

[34] Kierkegaard's supple and trenchant analysis of the distinction between the situation of Socratic recollection and epistemic sufficiency and the situation of the disciple who is put into a position to believe by God's incarnate life in history speaks to this meaning of a new point of departure. See Søren Kierkegaard, *Philosophical Fragments/Johannes Climacus, Kierkegaard's Writings,* vol. 7, ed. and trans. with introduction and notes by Howard V. Hong and Edna H. Hong (Princeton, N.J.: Princeton University Press, 1985).

its *professing* it intends the persuasive teaching of the church's faith. To publically profess the faith means to proclaim and teach the faith to the world. Professing the faith, however, does not imply that the witness of the church seeks to be grounded by the social world to which it witnesses.[35]

Sixth, having made these prior points, we can now affirm that the communal confession is also *personal*. Confessional theology is both 'we confess' and 'I confess.' Even though confessional theology does not start with the individual person's quest to build her own personal theology, it finally must also be authentically the person's confession. Such confession as human activity is *self-involving*: (a) an act of commitment of the whole person; (b) an act of self-identification and self-understanding; (c) an act of passionate belief; and (d) an act of faith in the reality of the triune God. There is no neutral, disinterested confession and profession. Hence, these considerations underline the respects in which Christian faith is *ad hominem* in its deepest character.

Seventh, confessional theology is always a *practice of the works of love and hope*. Where the wider pragmatics of love and hope are not alive and concrete, there is no true confessional theology. Hence, confessional theology could never counsel a separation between theology and ethics. *Confessional theology is ethics, and Christian ethics is confessional theology.* A nontheological Christian ethics is an oxymoron, as is a nonethical confessional theology.

Confessional Theology as Dialectical

In claiming that confessional theology is dialectical, there are several meanings of '*dialectical*' that must be identified:
a. as dialogue and conversation, questioning and answering, arguing, reasoning, and explaining;
b. as the intellectual power of discriminating and differentiating among concepts, images, beliefs, and judgments and of discern-

---

[35] I have been intrigued by the theological project of Douglas John Hall deploying a distinction between confession and profession. However, it is apparent that I put these activities in a different order. I am arguing that confession precedes profession. See Douglas John Hall, *Thinking the Faith: Christian Theology in a North American Context* (Minneapolis: Augsburg, 1989); *Professing the Faith: Christian Theology in a North American Context* (Minneapolis: Augsburg, 1993); *Confessing the Faith: Christian Theology in a North American Context* (Minneapolis: Augsburg, 1996).

ing connections;

c.   as the existential power of choosing to become a self or community constituted in a certain decisive way;

d.   as the dynamic tension between two poles which are not reducible to each other or to a higher synthesis.

All four senses of dialectical are present in confessional theology. In the first sense, confessional theology is dialectical as the readiness to dialogue and converse within the church and with the world, to question and be questioned, to argue, interpret, and explain: to be public professing theology. In these respects confessional theology engages in reasoning about and explaining the faith to the church and the world.

In the second sense, confessional theology is dialectical as the intellectual task of keeping the confession and witness of the church discriminately stated and differentiated from misleading and counterfeit substitutes and of seeing the coherent connections. In these respects, theology must be conceptually astute and clarifying in both its assertions and its negations.[36]

In the third sense, confessional theology is the existential self-involvement of making public confession and having one's life and the church's life constituted by the grace of the self-communicating presence of God in Jesus Christ through the Spirit. In this respect, Christian theology is acutely aware that its witness is finally *ad hominem*—directed to the individual person and inviting life-changing decisions.[37]

In the fourth sense, confessional theology is dialectical in that it cannot eliminate faithfully the tensions between some irreducible poles within which the church witnesses and does theology. It is to these irreducible structural conditions of authentic witness that we now turn.[38]

---

[36] Christopher Morse has discerningly carried through the task of theology by identifying what Christian faith *disbelieves* or negates in his *Not Every Spirit: A Dogmatics of Christian Disbelief* (Valley Forge, Pa.: Trinity Press, 1994).

[37] It is this dialectic that Kierkegaard sustains throughout his writings, but see especially *Concluding Unscientific Postscript to Philosophical Fragments*, vol. 1, *Kierkegaard's Writings*, vol. 12,1, ed. and trans. with introduction and notes by Howard V. Hong and Edna H. Hong (Princeton, N.J.: Princeton University Press, 1992), 361–616. I am persuaded that Kierkegaard was exceptionally competent in all of four senses of dialectical.

[38] In putting these matters these ways, it should be obvious how much my use of dialectical differs from Hegel's claim to hold the differences or oppositions together in a higher conceptual unity.

The Dialectical Poles in Confessional Theology

The dialectical poles and tensions within the discourse of confessional theology include the following:

There is *the dialectic between the Ultimacy Proviso and the Penultimacy Proviso.* The Ultimacy Proviso stipulates that only God can reveal God and the Penultimacy Proviso stipulates that God has deputized signs of God's presence in the history of Israel and in Jesus Christ and the apostolic church. These two provisos cannot be collapsed into each other, and each is misunderstood without the other. It is central to confessional theology that it knows it cannot control God's self-communicating presence and that it trusts God's presence has been faithfully made known in the narrative witness of Holy Scripture.

There is *the dialectic between God's self-revelation and the human response in discourses and practices.* God's self-revelation empowers the human response, but the human response can never bring forward and control God's presence. The response cannot ultimately authenticate itself; it can only be authenticated by God. The response can only *penultimately* explain itself by reference to the biblical and traditional testimonies and sound theological reasoning. Simply by itself, the human response is *corrigible* and questioned by God and the world.

There is *the dialectic between the Presiding Model of the Gospel and biblical witness.* The model is the *material norm* for interpreting the Bible, and the Bible tests the adequacy of the model. There is a similar dialectic between the presiding model and the other sources of theological construction. Hence, this dialectic resists the notion that there is to be achieved a perfect and infallible statement of the Gospel.

There is *the dialectic between the Bible as the Word of God and the Bible as fallible, human, limited word.* Our interpretations and witness cannot elide this dialectic and reduce it to calculable and formulaic proportions. This bespeaks the fruitlessness of a general hermeneutics for the interpretation of the Bible.

There is *the dialectic between contemporary witness and tradition.* Our witness is dependent on the trajectories of the tradition, but also capacitated by tradition to revise and re-vision its witness for our contemporary world. This dialectic requires us to resist unreformable traditionalism and capricious revisionism.

The dialectic between church and world has been explored earlier as we affirmed that confessional theology serves the church's witness to the world. Even as the church exists *for the world*, it is also *differentiated from the world*, all the while existing *in the world*. Within this dialectic the church is subject to continuing perils in which it might erase the dialectic by becoming merely a mirror image of the world or by becoming too separated from the world or by becoming unconcerned about its contemporary world. There is no final cessation of this dialectic short of the eschaton.

All of the above dialectics can be seen in *the dialectic between the imperative to witness in truth to the world and the corrigible, penultimate, preliminary but proleptic character of our witness*. We cannot control God's authenticating and self-evidencing presence but we witness under the *promise* that God will not leave us to our own devices. Hence, confessional theology relinquishes the illusory promise of worldly epistemology or metaphysics that there will finally be an irrefutable argument that will demonstrate to all reasonable persons the truth of the Christian Gospel.

We can also mention *the dialectic between 'we confess' and 'I confess,'* although it is not necessarily an irreducible dialectic. Sometimes we experience a tension between what the church should properly confess, and what the individual can honestly confess for herself. This tension is, of course, often reducible. And confessional theology, as church theology, intends the elimination of this dialectic, even though it acknowledges that the tension is real and compelling for various persons within the church.

Dialectical Confessional Theology and Other Theologies

Dialectical Confessional Theology, by reference to these irreducible structural tensions in Christian witness, can be distinguished from some other forms of theology. It is distinct from *Undialectical Confessionalism*, which does not acknowledge the tensions between God's revelation and human response and witness, and between the Ultimacy and Penultimacy Provisos. It tends to claim that revelation is undialectically given, negotiated, secured, and stated as revealed, incorrigible propositional truths. This undialectical theology is present in some forms of Fundamentalism and Roman Catholic traditionalism.

Dialectical confessional theology is also distinct from *Undialectical Rationalism* in which there is no tension between revelation and response because the only revelation that can be credited is one certified by *rea-*

son. It tends to believe in a disinterested, universal reason that is the sole arbiter of any truth-claim, including Christian witness. Charles Hartshorne and Hegel at least, and maybe Schubert Ogden, can be considered such undialectical rational theologians.

Finally, dialectical confessional theology is distinct from *Dialectical Rationalism* which acknowledges revelation, but is confident that some aspects of revelation and its presuppositions can be certified by reason in a noncircular justification. It is of various opinions about the dialecticity of God's self-revelation. This theological type is present in some forms of conservative, classical theism and in some forms of revisionist Catholic theology, such as Rahner and Tracy.

To conclude this section on the dialectics of confessional theology, let us draw together the points. Confessional theology is necessarily dialectical—in the respects indicated above—in its witness to the world, both in its confessing point of departure and its professing practices of teaching and preaching and enacting its witness to the triune God. Hence, such theologizing does not lack rationality, publicness, connectedness to the world in which it is witnessing.

The theology student will hear echoes in this section of that tradition of German theology in the first half of the twentieth century that was called 'dialectical theology.' At one time or another, Karl Barth, Paul Tillich, Friedrich Gogarten, and Rudolf Bultmann were included under this rubric.[39] However, the concept had a tortuous history, and I will not try here to examine the nuances of its uses by these theologians and others. I can affirm that I have been influenced by this tradition of theologizing, but I do not want to impose my interpretation of 'dialectical confessional theology' on any of them, nor do I want to claim my interpretation is simply a derivation from them.

---

[39] See *The Beginnings of Dialectic Theology*, vol. 1, ed. James M. Robinson, trans. Keith R. Crim and Louis De Grazia (Richmond: John Knox, 1968) for an interesting selection of writings from this earlier period.

Chapter Four

The Triune God

From the previous discussion of language and grammar we recall that the word 'God'—and its rough equivalents in other natural languages—has many uses. In doing Christian theology we are not trying to describe or be accountable for all these other uses and meanings. Rather, *our task in Christian systematic theology is to ask what do we—and what should we—mean when we say 'God' in the discourses and practices of the church?* We will explore how to use the word 'God' in distinctively Christian ways, which is to say that we will see how 'God' functions as a sign in Christian discourse. We will inquire into the right or authority with which we so use the word. To determine the right usage of 'God,' we must also determine what are the misleading and counterfeit substitutes that threaten right and appropriate usage. The whole of systematic theology is an answer to these questions, and it will show the full range and richness of Christian usage and understanding.

Using the conceptuality developed earlier, I am asking about the *grammar* of the Christian use of 'God.' I am concerned about the basic sense-making rules of Christian discourse about God. As such a concern, I will be interested in the syntax of 'God'—the relation of the word 'God' as sign to other signs, and in the semantics of 'God'—the rules of reference, and the pragmatics—the practices and form of life in which the sign has its proper location and meaning.

The doctrine of God was already before us in our previous discussion of revelation and the knowledge of God. The critical and normative function of the doctrine of revelation is to specify the *defining and normative identifying references to God.* It is in terms of the identifying ref-

149

erences rooted in God's own self-revelation, self-identification, self-communication, self-objectification that we develop what we mean when we speak of the Christian God. In everyday language, an *identifying reference* is a sign which enables us to pick out or identify or refer to a particular subject, which differentiates that particular subject from others. For example, 'Joe Jones is the one who is the youngest son of Idabel Augusta Seitz Jones and Dick Sterling Jones' is sufficient to pick a particular Joe Jones out from other particulars; it is an identifying reference. In this chapter I am arguing that there are three critical identifying references in terms of which the church properly picks out and identifies who God is from among other possible realities or candidates. Hence, these identifying references are the fundamental *semantic rules* that structure Christian discourse about God.[1]

In terms of the authoritative biblical narrative testimony to God's self-communicative interactions and the ecumenical traditions of the church, I am claiming that *there are three normative identifying references as to who God is:*

1. God is the One who elected, liberated, and covenanted with Israel and is thereby the One who is the sovereign Creator of all things.
2. God is the One who is singularly incarnate in and thereby definitively self-revealed in the life, death, and resurrection of Jesus of Nazareth.
3. God is the One who empowers the church into being and moves within creaturely life to draw all creatures into a redemptive future.

These identifying references are themselves tied to the biblical narrative, and that narrative provides the connecting context in which to lo-

---

[1] For a discussion of 'identifying references' in ordinary language see Peter F. Strawson, *Logico–Linguistic Papers* (London: Methuen, 1971), 74–95. Robert W. Jenson also uses the locution 'identifying reference' in developing his doctrine of the Trinity. I have been helped by his discussion, but I phrase the critical references quite differently from his, and I do not understand God as an event in the way in which he does. See Jenson's *The Triune Identity* (Philadephia: Fortress, 1982) and "The Triune God" in *Christian Dogmatics*, vol. 1, ed. Carl E. Braaten and Robert W. Jenson (Philadelphia: Fortress, 1984), 79–181. His recent *Systematic Theology*, vol. 1, *The Triune God* (New York: Oxford University Press, 1997) carries his elaboration further.

cate and identify the self-revelations of God. The claim is that the doctrine of the Trinity is essential to giving an account of these foundational identifying references, thereby showing who the God is whom Christians worship and obey. I do not claim that the doctrine is explicitly in the New Testament. But the trajectory of its basic elements of the doctrine is in the NT. The *doctrine* of the Trinity is simply that set of rules and concepts proposed for the right understanding of the self-revealing God witnessed to in the Bible.

I must emphasize that christological conviction is essential to the development of trinitarian doctrine. Without the conviction that God is singularly and uniquely incarnate in the life, death, and resurrection of the Jewish Jesus of Nazareth, there would be no occasion for developing the doctrine. Everything pivots around the issue of the *divinity* of Jesus Christ. If Jesus Christ is not *essential* to the identification of who God is, then the doctrine of Trinity is unnecessary. Hence, those theologians and traditions that have denied the divinity of Jesus Christ are also anti-trinitarian.

It is a central implication of the doctrine of Jesus Christ as the definitive self-revelation of God that this Jesus Christ tells us most decisively and normatively who God is. Throughout this systematic theological effort, it is maintained that God is not adequately identified and characterized apart from Jesus Christ—*that the question of who Jesus Christ is must affect, transform, and restructure who we think God is.* In the same vein, it is the revelation of God in Jesus Christ that itself calls for further clarification as to who the God of Israel is.

Important Negations

Starting with these three identifying references *negates* the following alternatives. First, it negates the claim that the basic identification of who God is will be provided by a logically independent metaphysics, ontology, or natural theology, such as that of classical theism, process theism, or metaphysical idealism. Consider briefly what is called 'classical theism.' There it is argued that God can be rationally identified independent of revelation as the one who is simple, infinite, immutable, impassible, the first cause of all nondivine beings. These very rules—as *semantic rules*—govern the grammar of everything else we say about God, which make it obscure how this God could be incarnate in a human being. Furthermore, these rules stand on their own quite independent of the narrative history of God's interaction with the world.

Second, the triune identification negates the claim that the basic identification of who God is will be provided by natural or universal religious experience. If such were to give us the basic understanding of God, then Jesus could be understood as a splendid example of knowing God but could not be understood as the unsurpassable incarnation of God. In this sense then, it would be impossible for Jesus to be the definitive self-revelation of God.

Third, the triune identification of God *negates the claim that God is essentially ineffable and indescribable*, because it implies that God has *not spoken God's own Word* in human history. If ineffability is basic to the grammar of 'God,' then it is obscure how any talk of God might get launched or how there would be any discriminating criteria for talking about God. Silence would seem to be the only appropriate practice. While I do claim the God we know in Jesus Christ is and remains an *incomprehensible mystery*, I do not mean by that concept that God is ineffable. Rather, I mean that our language about God, including our identifying references, is human language and can never quite talk about God as one would talk about an object in the world. Hence, I do not see how it can be claimed that God is both ineffable and self-revealing, but I do claim that God is both mystery and self-revealing. Even as self-revealing, God is not under the control of human language, including its semantic rules. Yet if there were no semantic rules at all, except negative rules, then it is unclear how even the negative rules could be derived and legitimated.

In negating these alternative grammars of God, I do not deny that the explication of the Christian understanding of God might employ some metaphysical or ontological concepts, rules, or theories. But their employment is *subservient* to the foundational identifying references. If the co-opted concepts and theories do not empower intelligible and nondistorting interpretations of the biblical testimony to God's self-communications, then they should be rejected. But it is admitted here that, properly construed, the doctrine of the triune God has nothing to do with any metaphysical speculations about the necessity of three-in-oneness or the dialectical unity of the World Spirit or the unity of subject and object.

Language about God

All language about God is human language, bound to human traditions, practices, conventions, and intentions. The language in which we *receive and represent* God's self-revelations as intelligible and definite is just this human language. This is God's *accommodation* in human signs to us.[2] And this language is always limited dialectically and in content as to how well and precisely God can be spoken of. We must always remember the *Ultimacy and Penultimacy Provisos,* which stand over the whole of Christian discourse about and to God and the resulting dialecticity that prevails in that discourse.

The main traditions of the church have generally been clear that God cannot be put in a category and thereby defined and comprehended. To define something is to put it in a *class* of things; God is not in a class—*deus est non in genere.*[3] In this sense then God cannot be spoken of in *univocal concepts*, that is, in concepts that mean exactly the same in their application to God and to creatures. Hence, there is an irreducible *mystery of God* that cannot be captured in our language, which we can call the rule of the incomprehensibility of God. Even in God's self-revelations God does not cease being mystery to human beings and their language. Yet, if God cannot be identified and described in univocal concepts, how then are we to talk about God?

Analogy of Being

The so-called *analogia entis*—analogy of being—provided the basic rules for God-talk for much of the tradition that was under the influence of classical theism.[4] The first such rule is the *rule of negation:* we must

---

[2] See John Calvin, *Institutes of the Christian Religion*, I,17,13; II,11,13, ed. John T. McNeill, trans. Ford Lewis Battles (Philadelphia: Westminster, 1960).

[3] See Thomas Aquinas, *Summa Theologiae,* part I, q. 3, art. 5 in *Summa Theologiae,* vol. 2, *Existence and the Nature of God (Ia. 2–11),* ed. and trans. Timothy McDermott (New York: McGraw-Hill, 1964), 34–37.

[4] *Analogia Entis* is generally associated with Thomas Aquinas, though it is widely debated just how much of a *doctrine* of analogy can be found in Thomas. Interesting discussions of analogy in Thomas are Ralph M. McInerny, *The Logic of Analogy: An Interpretation of St. Thomas* (The Hague: Martinus Nijhoff, 1961); Hampus Lyttkens, *The Analogy between God and the World: An Investigation of Its Background and Interpretation of Its Use by Thomas of Aquino*

explicitly negate those traits which cannot apply to God. We have already moved in this direction when we said that God cannot be conceived as a member of a class of objects like creaturely objects. Therefore, we must say that God is *not finite* like a creature is, and thus is *infinite*. 'Infinite' does not render any positive trait of God; it simply negates *finitude* and any other trait that might make God finite and limited. The infinite God is unlimited. Other similar negative attributes of God are: (a) that God is *simple*—not composed of parts, and in this sense, God is not a quantity that can be divided; (b) that God is *immutable*—not subject to change in any respect; and (c) that God is *impassible*—not subject to being affected or having *pathos*. As I will argue below, these particular negations have had a devastating effect on the Christian doctrine of God through the ages.

The rule of negation does not give us any further conceptual determination of God. If God were to be thought of only in these negations or as *ineffable* and indescribable, then all we could do is *negate* traits—God is *not this and not that*. This rule of negation by itself would be only *apophatic theology*. This is the temptation of some Christian mystics. However, if these negations are the only rules of God-talk, then God is simply an unknown X that utterly transcends the world. Paradoxically, if negation is all that we have, then by virtue of what semantic rule would we even know to deny all positive traits of God? Obviously, the main traditions of the church did not want to delimit God-talk to this extent. What other rules might be helpful?

The *rule of eminence* states that God is the highest or most perfect of some value or trait that we discern in the world. For example, Christians agree that God is good, and if this is to have any meaning, then God is the greatest or most perfect good. But this rule does not sufficiently differentiate God from finite creatures. Here we turn to the *rule of anal-*

(Uppsala: A-B. Lundequistska Bokhandeln, 1953); George P. Klubertanz, *St. Thomas Aquinas on Analogy: A Textual and Systematic Synthesis* (Chicago: Loyola University Press, 1960). The significantly dissenting opinions of David B. Burrell, *Analogy and Philosophical Language* (New Haven, Conn.: Yale University Press, 1973) and *Aquinas: God and Action* (Notre Dame, Ind.: Notre Dame University Press, 1979) and Victor Preller, *Divine Science and the Science of God: A Reformulation of Thomas Aquinas* (Princeton, N.J.: Princeton University Press, 1967) need also to be considered. While I am more in sympathy with the philosophical orientation and concerns of Burrell and Preller, I am suspicious of their interpretations of Aquinas. I will proffer here a rather traditional interpretation in this analysis of analogy of being.

ogy—the working together of the rules of negation and of eminence enables us to say some things positively about God, albeit *analogically*. 'God is good' is an analogical predication of God in that 'good' is proportional to God's preeminent actuality analogous to how good is proportional to, e.g., Socrates. But when a sign is used analogically about God on the basis of its meaning as applied to a creature, then there will always be a sense in which the analogy does not 'fit' God. Hence, analogy helps us to say some things meaningfully, but there are genuine semantic limits to its use in Christian discourse. This point relates to the earlier point about God's incomprehensibility: an analogical concept of God does not put God in a class concept and it is that which delimits the analogical concept's use in implications and explanation.

We can now make a distinction between the *meaning* of an analogical concept and the *justification* of the application of the analogy to God. What *rationale* or *warrant* justifies the application to God? The theory of *analogia entis* is the ontological theory that the finite beings of the world bear an analogy to God, who is *esse ipsum*, act-of-being-itself, and is the *cause* of all finite beings. It provides the rationale for supposing some analogies do obtain between God and creatures. Here this theory invokes the ontological rule—the effect is *like* the cause. So, from the world of creatures—insofar as they are like their divine cause—we can infer some analogies about God. This is grounding God-talk in a natural theology of questionable dimensions.

But the question of why we should suppose any analogy or metaphor can be applied to God—that would be a semantic 'rule of reference' or a 'rule of description'—is a very difficult question for those who suppose we *invent* metaphors which are socially useful. It is not simply the question of what the analogy or metaphor *means*, but what *justification* or *warrant* is there for supposing it applies to God in some truthful way?

Metaphor

The word 'metaphor' has become the great genie of theological conceptuality in the last decades.[5] Metaphors are essential to the biblical nar-

---

[5] Sallie McFague in *Metaphorical Theology: Models of God in Religious Language* (Philadelphia: Fortress, 1982) and *Models of God: Theology for an Ecological, Nuclear Age* (Philadelphia: Fortress, 1987) musters a case for saying that all religious language is metaphorical, but in the course of saying this the concept of metaphor gets up and walks around on us. It is as though all language

rative and to much Christian talk about God. While it is difficult to provide a uniformly convincing definition of 'metaphor,' I will stipulate that
a metaphor obtains when a sign with a clear syntax and semantics in one
context is used in another context in which it does not literally fit—that
same syntax and semantics do not fully apply. When a sign or locution
functions as a metaphor, we have some straining in the appropriate semantic interpretation of its use and in the syntactic implications we can
make with it. It might appear that in the Bible such terms as 'Father' and
'Lamb of God' are being used metaphorically. The term 'Father' seems
to have quite clear applications in our ordinary discourse. But when 'Father' is applied to God, the semantics becomes more strained: we cannot
infer that God is a sexual something. With some signs used metaphorically, we can restate them in literal language without loss of meaning,
but not with all metaphors. And many signs—which may have originally
been metaphorical—have become nonmetaphorical through a regulariza-
tion of use in syntax and semantics. This is true, for example, in the uses
of the word 'heart.' Much of the language of theology is analogical and
metaphorical, and our tracing of the syntax, semantic, and pragmatic dimensions of their use is intended to show how and to what extent they
have meaning and reference.[6]

Analogy of Faith

I propose that we follow what has been called in Protestant circles
the *analogia fidei*—analogy of faith. Here the claim is that the rules of
God-talk are derived from and justified by reference to the language of
the Bible as witness to God's self-revealing activities. This is still human
language, but focused by what I have called their character as *deputized
signs*. As deputized by God, the biblical language is the witness of *faith*
to be received and understood by *faith*. And as pointed out in the Ultimacy and Penultimacy Provisos, God is never under the control of our
language, but God has pointed to these definite biblical discourses as
deputized by God's self-revelation. Their being deputized is the *rationale*
for their use to speak of God. But even following the *analogia fidei*, we
still have to sort through the deputized signs for those that make most

---

is somehow metaphorical as well. Part of the conceptual problem here is that
McFague does not attend carefully to what Wittgenstein calls 'family of uses' of
the same word or locution.

[6] For a subtle and helpful discussion of metaphor, see Janice Martin
Soskice, *Metaphor and Religious Language* (Oxford: Clarendon Press, 1985).

consistent sense with what we discern is the Gospel of Jesus Christ. Jesus Christ—as the definitive self-revelation of God—is a principle of critique of some biblical signs that do not appear consistent with the Gospel.

Our language about God is always in concepts, images, metaphors, and analogies that can never exhaust the plenitude and mystery of the divine life. There is always some sense in which our language does not exactly *fit* the divine life. By invoking this Protestant rule of the analogy of faith, I am intending to emphasize the extent to which it provides a *rationale* for why any signs and locutions might be said to refer to God. Insofar as 'analogy' is not a precise concept in this tradition, and easily slides to include metaphor, image, simile and allegory, it is used here in such wise as to include the various ways in which any sign can be said to be about God, to refer to God, or to describe God and God's actions. Thus *analogia fidei, in our use, is a general semantic rule of reference.* It states clearly that there are definite limitations in our capacity to track out the semantics of our talk of God. We will not be able to track out and identify God and characterize God in the same ways in which we identify and characterize physical objects in space and time. Our semantics of God are always adequate *only to a certain extent.* We must avoid the peril of supposing our linguistic signs about God are of the same univocal meanings we might use about creatures.

Discussions of analogy have been notoriously confusing, especially in contemporary works. Both *analogia entis* and *analogia fidei* agree that some analogy does obtain between some creatures and God. The decisive difference between the two sets of rules is their differing rationales or warrants and therewith their differing assumptions about how God can be fundamentally identified. *Analogia entis* pretends to sit on its own bottom and justify from there how some of the biblical language might apply to God, who has already been identified as First Cause, Simple, Infinite, Immutable, and Impassible. *Analogia fidei*—in my use—states that the basic language about God has been selected by God in the testimonies of the Old and New Testaments. Hence, *analogia fidei* is basically a rationale and rule derived from the grammar of God's self-revelation.

Patriarchy and 'Father' Language

Pursuing further issues concerning the language of theology, this section will explore some of the concerns raised by what can generally be called *feminist theology*—which intends to be a Christian theology that makes the liberation of women from their multiple oppressions in the church and the world its main critical principle.[7] If some aspect of Christian discourse and practice continues to support the oppression of women and thereby deny the full humanity of women, then that is sufficient reason to call it into question as legitimate theology. There are some differences in *how* this critical principle is applied in identifying the sorts of language and practice that are deemed oppressive to women. I will be dealing throughout this systematic effort with many of the concerns of feminist theology, but in this section we will look at some issues pertaining to patriarchy and the use of father language in the church's discourse about God.

Patriarchy

I define patriarchy as that system of social organization in which the male is understood as superior to the female and as the natural head of the family, clan, and larger social order.[8] The male head or 'father' thus has priority and privilege over females and other males. It involves the systemic subordination of women to men. Such social organization is presupposed in much biblical testimony and in much of the historical discourses and practices of the church. While patriarchy is not everywhere the same nemesis for women, and there are signals of critique of patriarchy in the Bible and in some church traditions, the overwhelming effect of patriarchy is that women have not been practically empowered to the same fulfillment as males in life before God and in the discourses

---

[7] This basic theme binds together many different projects of feminist theology, however much they may also differ in execution and judgment. For a clear statement of this principle, see Rosemary Radford Ruether, *Sexism and God-Talk: Toward a Feminist Theology* (Boston: Beacon, 1983), 18–20. For a more recent and constructive understanding of the feminist project in Christian theology, see Serene Jones, *Feminist Theory and Christian Theology: Cartographies of Grace* (Minneapolis: Fortress, 2000), especially 1–21.

[8] See the succinct description of "Patriarchy" by Rosemary Radford Ruether in *Dictionary of Feminist Theologies*, ed. Letty M. Russell and J. Shannon Clarkson (Louisville, Ky.: Westminster John Knox, 1996), 205–207.

and practices of the church and of the world. But, however much this may be true of the biblical and church traditions, it is a historical mistake to suppose that patriarchy is something peculiar to the biblical traditions; patriarchy has been present throughout most previous cultures and traditions.

We must attend to two basic Christian beliefs in order to grasp why patriarchy must be critiqued. First, there is the belief that male and female are both created in the image of God [Gen 1.27]. Second, the christological belief that the male and female creatures God created are the ones who have been taken up equally in the reconciling work of Jesus Christ and that in him there is "no longer male and female; for . . . all are one in Christ Jesus [Gal 3.28]." In the light of these two compelling beliefs, and much more, I contend that patriarchal oppression of women, with its discourses and practices, must be dismantled in the church and the world. If neither maleness nor femaleness has any priority in receiving and participating in the reconciling work of Jesus Christ, then how can the church support practices that systemically subordinate women to men in any respect? While there may be other practical social reasons why some persons might be subordinate functionally to others, there is no theological rationale for in-principled subordination of female to male, either as a doctrine of creation or as a doctrine of reconciliation and redemption, including ecclesiology.

While these points demand further elaboration and defense, which they will receive throughout this systematic project, it is essential to the well-being of the contemporary life of the church and its witness that it ferret out the myriad ways in which patriarchy infects and distorts its language and life. This ferreting out and critiquing are essential as well to systematic theology as it assesses the past and present witness of the church and offers constructive proposals of what the church should say and do in conformity to the Gospel. While much of what needs critiquing is obvious and accessible, some of these issues are often so deep and pervasive and sometimes opaque that it is not always clear exactly how to proceed.

Biblical Uses of 'Father'

While the use of 'father' terms to speak of divinity is not peculiar to the Bible or Christianity, most father images in other traditions trade heavily on male sexual functions. And they are seldom used as a term of *caring* and affection.

In the OT 'father' is used to refer to God only about eleven times. In distinction from the NT, it is not used as a term of personal address and affection. It is never used to refer to male sexual functions, as though these would apply to God. Rather, in the OT it is a fundamental rule that sexuality is something that applies to human beings but never applies to God. It is humanity that is male and female, but not God, for "God is not a human being [Num 23.19]." Hence, even though the OT throughout uses male pronouns in reference to God and in other ways draws heavily on the patriarchal matrix, the 'maleness' of God is not a sexual maleness in differentiation from female sexuality. While they are few and far between, the OT does use some female images—basically mothering images—to describe God's action and care:

> Deuteronomy 32.18: you forgot the God who gave you birth.
> Isaiah 42.14: now I shall cry out like a woman in labor, I will gasp and pant.
> Isaiah 49.15: Can a woman forget her nursing child, or show no compassion for the child in her womb? Even these may forget, yet I will not forget you.
> Isaiah 66.13: As a mother comforts her child, so I will comfort you.

In the NT 'father' [*pater*] is used more than 260 times to refer to God. It is used by Jesus more than 170 times in the Gospels as a term of personal address and reference to the God of Israel. 'Father' is the central name given by Jesus to the God of Israel: 'my Father,' 'your Father,' 'our Father.' Some case can be made for saying Jesus also used *abba* as a term of special intimacy, roughly translated as 'papa.'[9] As in the OT, 'Father' in reference to God is never used to suggest male sexual functions, as something peculiarly male in distinction from the female. It is never used in deliberate contrast to the mother or female, as though to suggest superiority. And it is never used as invidious comparison to the female or mother. However, male pronouns are used throughout the NT in reference to God.

---

[9] Mk 14.36. See also Rom 8.15; Gal 4.6. It is hotly disputed in NT scholarship whether *abba* is unique to Jesus. This issue does, however, seem minor in relation to the larger question of whether Jesus did use 'Father' repeatedly as a word of personal address to the God of Israel. And this use seems to me beyond serious doubt.

The NT picture of God as Father is that God cares, forgives, looks after, goes in search of God's children. The father/child relationship is accentuated between God and humans. Even the Father as the sovereign Creator is One who seeks out the creature for the creature's own good. But note also "Father of lies" in John 8.44, which suggests that 'father'—as a term—is not always a term of positive praise. And note the critique of human fathers in Matthew 23.9: "And call no one father on earth, for you have one Father—the one in heaven."[10]

In saying these things about father language in the NT, I do not mean to deny that patriarchal grammar emerges often in the NT regarding female subordination to males. However, there is no evidence that Jesus related to women according to the norms of patriarchal relationships, and in fact, he should be understood as bringing such relationships implicitly under critique.

On Using Male and Female Images of God

Most of the traditions of the church have emphasized male pronouns in speaking of God. But much of the tradition has always confessed that God is neither male nor female in any defining sense. God is beyond gender, except in the situation of Jesus in which God becomes a particular human male. Yet much of the tradition uses arguments based on God's Fatherhood and Jesus' undeniable maleness to justify an only male priesthood. When these are combined with persistent practices of subordinating women to men, we can understand how the constant and exclusive use of male images and male pronouns in speaking of God might reinforce these subordinating patriarchal practices. And *in our time*, with the rising feminist consciousness of both women and men, there is the distinct sense that unreserved and exclusive use of male terms to refer to God suggests that God is simply male to the exclusion of women from being 'in the image of God.'

Clearly there are warrants in Christian discourse for using feminine images in speaking of God. Aside from images of 'mothering' and 'giving birth,' however, it is not clear that there are traits that are *essentially*

---

[10] Elizabeth Schüssler Fiorenza, *In Memory of Her: A Feminist Theological Reconstruction of Christian Origins* (New York: Crossroad, 1988), 151, interprets this passage as showing that Jesus calls God Father precisely to deprive all patriarchal fathers of their dominating status, as a gesture of radical egalitarianism.

and distinctively female. Contemporary feminist theory is especially wary of designating peculiarly female traits for fear such will be used to categorize women unfairly. In the same sense, are there traits that are essentially and distinctively male? Is it essential to women—in contrast to men—to be nurturing? gentle? patient? kind? affective? We should distinguish between those traits that are distinctive to the female as such and those traits that are historically constructed as the *gender roles of women.*[11]

Matters become more complicated when we are asked to dismantle so-called *hierarchical* images of God. But what are such images? Is this no more than the bad image of a bully god who selfishly dominates all creatures? This image we can thankfully do without, though the prime warrant is that it contradicts the God we know in Jesus Christ. But if anti-hierarchical means that God is in no way superior in power and characteristics to human beings, then the dismantling of God's hierarchy has gone too far. Clearly it is essential to Christian theology that God is superior to and sovereign Creator of the world of creatures, even though this God becomes a human being and dies on a cross for the salvation of the world. We will spend much effort on down the way trying to sort out the differences between inappropriate hierarchies of God and appropriate, necessary ones.

Some tough questions remain: Is 'Father' like a proper name, such as 'Fred,' and is therefore by biblical warrant simply the 'name of God'? If 'Father' is not just the proper name of God and if there is nothing essentially male in calling God 'Father,' then can we just substitute 'Mother' at any point for 'Father' without loss of meaning? If God is essentially personal or a person in an analogical sense, then how can God be neither male nor female? Mustn't we use personal pronouns of God, because God is surely not an impersonal 'it'? If we do use personal pronouns, how can we exclude the use of 'she' as well as 'he'?

Some Interim Suggestions

No particular word should be thought of as having an eternal and necessary meaning independent of actual human usage. Yet I will repeat-

---

[11] For an interesting, if finally ambiguous, discussion of these issues, see Elizabeth A. Johnson, *She Who Is: The Mystery of God in Feminist Theological Discourse* (New York: Crossroad, 1992), 17–57. Serene Jones, *Feminist Theory and Christian Theology*, has an exceedingly interesting and subtle examination of various feminist theories of 'women's nature.'

edly argue that there are some critical Christian concepts that must be retained and carefully explicated even in the face of massive misunderstanding in the larger culture. But I am largely unpersuaded that exclusive use of 'he' and 'Father' in reference to God is theologically justified in our time and in faithfulness to the Gospel of Jesus Christ. Below, however, I will make a case for the retention of Father language internal to trinitarian discourse. Here are some tentative suggestions to the Christian and the church in the interim until our linguistic situation becomes clearer and we see our way out of some impasses. In making these suggestions, it must be remembered that human language itself is a human construction and it develops over time in traditions of usage.

1. Let us give away nothing to patriarchy as such and its infection of theological discourse. But be prudent, not arrogant and defiant, in helping the church come to grips with this complex and profound shift in sensitivity, understanding, and language.

2. 'Father' should not be used as the exclusive way of referring to God. Such exclusive referrings—as I will argue below—actually undermines the real trinitarian character of God, supposing that God is *really* the Father alone. Further, God can be called 'Mother.'

3. Male pronouns should be avoided as the *exclusive* way of speaking of God in personal terms. Try saying 'Godself' and just repeating 'God' when 'He' seems tempting. Try to deprive the language of its *apparent* maleness by refusing to say 'He/Him' exclusively.

4. But why not use female pronouns to refer to God at least some of the time? Try it, especially when speaking of God as the One Living Subject. But often this will only confound the church, though maybe someday it will not confound any longer. But never say the barbarism 'He or She' when referring to God. It crudely suggests that God is either or both male and female, but we just don't know which.

5. Do not suppose that every 'male' image of God is *ipso facto* bad and demeaning to women, and do not suppose that every 'female' image is *ipso facto* good and appropriate to God.

6. Even if there is nothing that is essentially female, except birthing and mothering, try to use traits from the historical experience of women to characterize God's life and relationships. Let stories about women be used as parables and images of God and God's profoundly rich interactive life with the world.

7. Absolutely resist male exclusivism in referring to the human as such or to the human in general.

8. Do all things to the glory of God, which includes the upbuilding of God's female and male creatures, who are both created in the image of God.

Father and the Trinity

But having made these recommendations, I want now to argue *that the sign 'Father' cannot be deleted from trinitarian talk.* The reasons are several. The most compelling reason is that this 'name' was the principle name used by Jesus for the God of Israel. It is from this usage that Jesus is then referred to as 'Son.' Jesus is the Son of his divine Father who is the God of Israel and the Creator of the world. Hence, without sexualizing God being Jesus' Father, the NT shows us how the word 'Father' should be used in reference to God. Further, since this Jesus goes to the cross in doing the will of the Father and the Father raises this Jesus from the dead, we really do not have a mere 'patriarchal metaphor.' Something cosmic is taking place in Jesus' death and resurrection that is dismantling all forms of human domination and oppression, including patriarchy.

In the NT use, 'Father' is more like a proper name and is not reducible to a common noun for a class of traits. Therefore, we should never argue that fatherhood as such—or as a humanly constructed role—is naturally fitting for God. *We speak of the God as Father only because that is the way Jesus and the NT talk.* This is the *deputized* character of the name. This sort of emphasis subverts all arguments that want to say fatherhood is naturally fitting to God.[12]

The primary issue here is how we are to refer to the first person of the Trinity. It is not the issue of whether female images or 'she' can be used of God; they can in some contexts and for some purposes. In speaking of the Trinity, I do not propose that we should substitute 'Mother' for 'Father' when referring to the *first person* of the Trinity. In

---

[12] The highly provocative and useful collection of essays in *Speaking the Christian God: The Holy Trinity and the Challenge of Feminism*, ed. Alvin F. Kimel Jr. (Grand Rapids, Mich.: Eerdmans, 1992) can be read with advantage. However, it seems to me that too often some of the arguments bespeak an attachment to Father language that is suspect and harmful to the adequate witness to the triune God today. Yet, there are important critiques in some of these essays that are on the mark against some feminist attacks on language about God. In this whole section I am sorting through the ways in which I both agree and disagree with some of these essays.

my judgment, Catherine Mowry LaCugna gets into serious confusion by repeatedly substituting 'God' for 'Father' when speaking of the first person of the Trinity.[13] But this only reinforces the tendency to think that the first person is alone the real God. And contra the Orthodox tradition, the tendency to posit the Father as the source and cause of the other persons of the Trinity is understandable but finally misleading and subordinationist.

While preserving 'Father' for the first person of the Trinity, we must eschew all arguments that would invoke a male understanding of this term in order to justify an exclusively male priesthood or to argue for some superiority of male over female.

I can recommend the following for liturgy and theology: *"The Father, Son, and Holy Spirit, One God, Mother of us all."* I see no problem in referring to the Living Person-Subject who exists in three modes or persons as 'Mother.'[14] It can appropriately capture the mothering characteristics of the Trinity in its multiple interactions with the world.

In sum, the issue is not whether God the triune Subject can be referred to as Mother or She, for I have conceded that. The issue is whether the first person of the Trinity should be so referred to. Here I must insist *that the locution 'Father, Son, and Holy Spirit' is the primary triune name for God.* We must be wary, therefore, and not be trapped into *exclusively* using nonpersonal terms like 'Creator, Redeemer, and Sustainer' to refer to God's triune life. These do describe real relationships and activities of God, but their exclusive use tends to blot out the personal dimensions of God's activity in Israel and in the historical person of Jesus of Nazareth. Further, we need 'Father, Son, and Holy Spirit' as terms referring to the persons of the Trinity in their inner-trinitarian relationships, especially, as I shall argue below, when we talk about the Primordial Trinity *before* the creation of the world and in characterizing the reconciling work of Jesus the Son in relation to the Father, to whom he is

---

[13] Catherine Mowry LaCugna, *God for Us: The Trinity and Christian Life* (San Francisco: Harper, 1991).

[14] This suggested phrasing I owe first to William C. Placher, *Narratives of a Vulnerable God: Christ, Theology, and Scripture* (Louisville, Ky.: Westminster John Knox, 1994), 61. But unknown to me at the time of reading Placher, this formula had been in use for some time by the Riverside Church in New York. For a discussion of this use at Riverside, see Ruth Duck, *Gender and the Name of God: The Trinitarian Baptismal Formula* (New York: Pilgrim, 1991), 163–166.

obedient.

In any case, when referring to the threefold activities of God, I prefer *Creator, Reconciler, and Redeemer*, and this usage will be systematically followed in these systematic explorations.[15] While I can grant that such terms as 'Reconciler,' 'Redeemer,' 'Sustainer,' and 'Savior' have a measure of fluidity in their biblical and traditional uses, there is no reason why we might not strive for a measure of consistency in our systematic theological uses. While Christ is certainly Redeemer, it seems to me that the Spirit is also Redeemer, and that more so than merely Sustainer. Christ's work is salvific mainly in the sense of reconciling humanity and God, while the Spirit is salvific mainly in the sense of the continuing redemption of humanity and the world.

Some Notes from Church History

The concrete priority of practice with regard to the trinitarian doctrine is illustrated in the practice of baptizing "in the name of the Father and of the Son and of the Holy Spirit [Mt 28.19]." This is one of the earliest practices of the church and gave impetus to trinitarian thinking. And behind this practice was the practice of worshipping Jesus as Lord and Savior and Word and Wisdom of God as well as praying to Jesus. These liturgical practices forced the clarification of theological issues implicit in the language of the practices.

The controversy with Marcion kept clear that the God of Israel depicted in the Hebrew Scriptures is the same God Christians know in Jesus Christ through the Spirit. Marcion did see, though quite inadequately, that what God does in Jesus Christ is a new thing for God. But he drew exactly the wrong conclusion from this, namely, that the loving God revealed in Jesus was a different God than the creating, electing, and judging God of the Hebrew Scriptures. Yet without the development of trinitarian language, the claims of Marcion would continue to haunt the church's discourse about who God truly is.[16]

---

[15] This usage is implicitly proposed by Karl Barth.

[16] On Marcion, see Jaroslav Pelikan, *The Christian Tradition: A History of the Development of Doctrine*, vol. 1, *The Emergence of the Catholic Tradition (100–600)* (Chicago: University of Chicago Press, 1971), 71–81.

The Nicene Creed of 325

The controversies that brought about and followed from the Council at Nicaea can be understood as the church's search for adequate grammar of who God is. Arius was the radical monotheist who thought—on biblical and philosophical grounds—that it was *impossible* for the transcendent and unchanging—immutable and impassible—God, who is a simple One, to either *become* a human being or have the same reality as a human being. Arius was, however, studiously realistic about Jesus the Son suffering and being crucified, but could not identify that reality of Jesus with the reality of God. Therefore, Jesus is the highest of creatures, but still *only* a creature, yet oddly a diminution of divinity. Athanasius went around Arius and argued on soteriological grounds that if Jesus is not of the same reality as the transcendent Father/Creator, then our transient, fleshy, creaturely life has not been *assumed* by God and is not thereby *saved by God* from such finitude and transience and death. The Council was on the side of Athanasius on the divine reality of Jesus, but left virtually intact the rule that God is in all respects immutable and impassible, which continued to create problems of intelligibility as to how such a God could become incarnate in a human being and it threatened the intelligibility of the relation between the divine and the human in Jesus.[17]

Consider the Nicene text:

> We believe in one God, the Father All Governing [*pantokratora*], creator [*poiteten*] of all things visible and invisible; And in one Lord Jesus Christ, the Son of God, begotten of the Father as only begotten, that is, from the essence [reality or substance] of the Father [*ek tes ousias tou patros*], God from God, Light from Light, true God from true God, begotten not created, of the same essence as the Father [*homoousion to patri*], through whom all things came into being, both in heaven and in earth; Who for us men and for our salvation came down and

---

[17] For a wide-ranging discussion of the Arian Controversy, see R. P. C. Hanson, *The Search for the Christian Doctrine of God: The Arian Controversy, 318–381* (Edinburgh: T. & T. Clark, 1988). For helpful treatments of the development of trinitarian doctrine during the patristic era, see Pelikan, *The Emergence of the Catholic Tradition;* J. N. D. Kelly, *Early Christian Doctrines*, rev. ed. (San Francisco: Harper, 1978); Aloys Grillmeier, *Christ in Christian Tradition: From the Apostolic Age to Chalcedon (451)*, trans. J. S. Bowden (New York: Sheed & Ward, 1965).

was incarnate, becoming human [*enanthropesanta*]. He suffered and the third day he rose, and ascended into the heavens.
And he will come to judge both the living and the dead. And
we believe in the Holy Spirit.[18]

The critical theological points of the Nicene text are: (a) Jesus is of
one essence or substance [*ousia*] with the Father; (b) it made a distinction
between 'begotten' and being 'created'; (c) Jesus Christ was incarnate—became human—for humanity's salvation; and (d) the Holy Spirit
is mentioned, but not explicitly said to be of one substance with the Father and the Son. Before full trinitarian conceptualization can be
achieved, however, the *difference* between the Father and the Son will
have to be explained. So, Nicaea precipitates the further discussion of
how God is both one and three.

How God Is One and Three

After Nicaea a tenuous consensus began to emerge in both the East
and the West about how to identify the oneness of God and the threeness
of God. The Greek trinitarian formula in the East is *"one being [ousia]
of God in three hypostases [hypostaseis]."* This formula was mainly articulated in the fourth century by the Cappadocians: Basil of Caesarea,
Gregory of Nyssa, and Gregory of Nazianzus. They made an important
distinction between *ousia* and *hypostasis*, which had in previous discussions been used roughly interchangeably. The *ousia* of God is the common essence of the three hypostases. The essence is what constitutes God
as God. There is one essence, and this essence or *ousia* is called the
'Godhead.' The Father, Son, and Holy Spirit are three hypostases [also
called *prosopon*, which has the same meaning as *persona* in the West]
and are three individual subjects who have the one common essence. The
hypostases are *constituted* also by their inner-trinitarian *relationships* to
one another: the Father is only the Father as the Father who begats the
Son and as the one who spirates the Spirit. Here there is a strong sense
for the constitutive relationality of the Father, the Son, and the Holy
Spirit. This relationality was further elaborated as the *perichoresis* or interanimation of the hypostases; they interpenetrate one another and act
together. Yet they tended to say the Father was in some sense the *source*
of the other two hypostases, which to this day is an understanding com-

---

[18] See John H. Leith, ed., *Creeds of the Church*, 3d ed. (Louisville, Ky.:
John Knox, 1982), 28–31.

mon to the Eastern Orthodox tradition.

Hence, in this tradition 'God' [*theos*] can be used to refer to: (a) the common essence or Godhead, which is a logical subject, but not an ontological subject; (b) the Father from whom the other hypostases are begotten and spirated; (c) each hypostasis individually, who are equally divine and are the ontological subjects of which the essence can be predicated; and (d) the Trinity as a whole, which is not as such another ontological subject.[19] If we now ask how the three hypostases are one, we have two interrelated answers: they are one in essence or *ousia* and they are one in their perichoretic interactions and relationalities.

These concepts are the basis for what today is called the 'social Trinity.' The Cappadocian formulation has the conceptual advantage of identifying the respects in which the hypostases are different and therefore making sense out of the NT narrative of the enacted relationships between the Father and the Son. There is also conceptual strength in recognizing that the Godhead is a logical subject of which predications can be made but is not itself another ontological subject like the three hypostases. Yet, in thinking the three hypostases are three instances of the essence, they seem to me to flirt with *tritheism*, in which there are three individual instances of the one common essence, or three gods.

The Latin trinitarian formula in the West is *"one substance [substantia] of God in three persons [personae]."* This formulation is first clearly articulated by Tertullian in the early third century and fully developed by Augustine in the early fifth century. The Latin word *substantia* did the same sort of work as both *ousia* and *hypostasis* did in referring to the basic reality of something. Without differentiating between that basic reality as essence or *ousia* and as subject-agent or *hypostasis* as in the East, the use of *substantia* tended to hold both of these together without differentiation. There is, therefore, a heavy accent on the oneness of God, tending to regard the *substantia* as itself the ontological subject. *Persona* was understood in the sense of the mask or role which actors wear and play; their roles are their personae. Hence, the personae of the

---

[19] This analysis of the Cappodocian formulation is dependent on the analysis of Cornelius Plantinga Jr., in three essays: "Gregory of Nyssa and the Social Analogy of Trinity," *The Thomist*, 50 (1986), 325–352; "The Threeness/Oneness Problem of the Trinity," *Calvin Theological Journal*, 23 (1988), 37–53; "Social Trinity and Tritheism," in *Trinity, Incarnation, and Atonement*, ed. Ronald J. Feenstra and Cornelius Plantinga Jr. (Notre Dame, Ind.: University of Notre Dame Press, 1989), 21–47.

Trinity are the Father, Son, and Holy Spirit. Though the persons of the Trinity are distinct, they seem to be overwhelmed by the unity of the substance. For contemporary discussion the following question arises: does *persona* mean the same as our modern sense of *person* as a center of consciousness, intentionality, will, and agency? Are there three individual centers of consciousness and willing in God?[20]

Three Basic Trinitarian Heresies

While the church was developing a rough consensus as to what constitutes orthodoxy, so too there developed a consensus as to what constitutes heresy. In the patristic period the church came to identify three basic trinitarian heresies.

Modalism is truly difficult to identify precisely because the term was and is multiply used. In its distilled meaning it referred to that theology in which the distinctions among the persons were obliterated and the singular oneness of God was central. From that common core of meaning, it could further say the persons were only successively temporary manifestations of a more real God who transcends the world and remains untouched by the manifestations. Or it could affirm in realistic language that the one God became human and suffered on the cross—a form of what was called *Patripassianism*. In either form, modalism denies that the distinctions among the persons are real distinctions *within* God. In some sense, then, the manifestations of the Father, the Son, and the Holy Spirit are transient realities mediating between the utterly transcendent and simple One and the world of finite creatures. Though we do not have his texts as such, Sabellius is generally thought of as the main representative; thus modalism is also called Sabellianism.[21]

Subordinationism denied that the Father, Son, and Spirit are equally God, and tended to think of the Father as the real God. It traded heavily on the NT sense that the Father *sends* the Son and the Son is *obedient* to

[20] I claim no independent learning about the eastern and western formulations, but have been helped by the discerning discussions by Colin Gunton, *The Promise of Trinitarian Theology* (Edinburgh: T. & T. Clark, 1991), especially 31–57; Jenson, *The Triune Identity*, especially 57–159; LaCugna, *God for Us*, especially 21–109.

[21] See H. E. W. Turner's entries on "Modalism," "Mode of Being," "Trinity," and "Tritheism" in *A Dictionary of Christian Theology*, ed. Alan Richardson (Philadelphia: Westminster, 1969). See also Pelikan, *Emergence of the Catholic Tradition*, 177–179.

the Father, interpreting this to mean that the Son was not quite divine in the same way as the Father. This idea takes the *functional* subordination expressed in the NT as an *ontological* subordination. Subordinationism remains one of the great temptations of the church, and wherever it works itself into systematic expression we have a *unitarian* understanding of God. The real target of the subordinationist is the divinity of Jesus Christ.

Tritheism maintains that there are really three gods, who may have a common essence but are nevertheless three different subjects or agents. One essence with three *instances*. While tritheism is easy to conceptualize, it is—as a historical fear of the church—very difficult to find real proponents. As I have said above, I think the Cappadocians veered in this direction, but they had enough other qualifiers in their theory that they were not thought of as tritheists. The background of tritheistic fears is the polytheism of the Greco/Roman worlds. Tritheism emerges as a threat when the differences among the persons are conceived as too discrete.[22]

Beyond the Patristic Age

As we move out of the patristic period into the Middle Ages—when the church's institutional character became even more defined—we find the common practice of distinguishing between theology as *theologia* [*De Deo Uno*], which deals with the essential reality and oneness of God, and theology as *oikonomia* [*De Deo Trino*], which deals with the Trinity of God. It was, then, the case that *theologia* could be largely practiced on the basis of grammar rules derived from that form of natural theology I have called 'classical theism,' which understood God to be essentially simple, infinite, immutable, impassible, and *esse ipsum* in which essence and existence are identical. All this could be said about God without reference to God as triune. This distinction between *theologia* and *oikonomia* had the practical effect of allowing the philosophical theism to determine what is basically permissible and intelligible in trinitarian reflection.[23]

---

[22] Plantinga's attempt to describe the threat of tritheism as a polytheism of diminishing divinities, with special reference to Arius, does not seem plausible to me. Tritheism of that sort is simply the heresy of subordinationism. See Plantinga, "Social Trinity and Tritheism."

[23] See LaCugna, *God for Us*, especially 142–180, on Aquinas's theology for a fine discussion of how this came about. It is amazing, however, that the delete-

In the Reformation, Calvin and Luther restored the primacy of the biblical narrative about the reality of God, both emphasizing the Incarnation as central, with Luther even saying the death of Christ went to the heart of God. But neither Luther nor Calvin made trinitarian thinking as such the focus of their theologies. And both Luther and Calvin were haunted by the continuing notion of the 'hidden God' who lurked behind the biblical economy of revelation as *potentia absoluta*: the mysterious God of absolute and unconditioned power.[24]

During the 'Enlightenment' of the eighteenth century some forms of *Deism* came to the fore, affirming that God was the transcendent creator and moral governor of the world but did not interact with the world. Since God does not interact with the world, Deism reduced Jesus to—at best—a moral teacher and example. Deists were fundamentally unitarians.

In the early nineteenth century, G. W. F. Hegel reacted against the deistic god and its anti-incarnational theology, and constructed the first full-blown modern Protestant doctrine of the triune God. For all its other shortcomings and obfuscations, Hegel's theology of metaphysical idealism emphasized that in God there is complexity, otherness, movement, change, suffering, and a capacity for existing in the otherness of the creaturely world. God is the absolute dialectical Spirit [*Geist*] who posits the world in otherness, becomes concrete in the otherness of the world, and successively moves the world to reconciled unity with Godself. Hegel and his successors had trouble with the singular particularity of Jesus and with the freedom of God and made it a requirement that God needs the world in order to be God.[25]

---

rious effects of the grammar of simplicity, immutability, and impassibility go unnoticed and uncriticized in her discussion. If Aquinas had been more attentive to the economic narrative of the life of God with the world, he might not have fallen into sanctioning these attributes of God. It is no wonder that Aquinas and much medieval theology became preoccupied with the eternal and internal relations of the persons of the Trinity, since the grammar of simplicity and impassibility made it well nigh impossible to theologize about the economic Trinity.

[24] See the excellent discussion of Luther on the hiddenness of God by John Dillenberger, *God Hidden and God Revealed* (Philadelphia: Muhlenberg, 1953).

[25] See Georg Wilhelm Friedrich Hegel, *Lectures on the Philosophy of Religion*, one–volume ed., *The Lectures of 1827* , ed. Peter C Hodgson, trans. R. F. Brown, P. C. Hodgson, J. M. Stewart, with the assistance of H. S. Harris (Berkeley: University of California Press, 1988), especially 417–489. Karl Barth's analysis and assessment of Hegel is justly famous. See Karl Barth, *Protestant Theology in the Nineteenth Century: Its Background and History* (Valley Forge,

The twentieth century has seen the emergence of four theological trajectories in the doctrine of God. First, there is the stupendous achievement of Karl Barth in his massive *Church Dogmatics*. From his inspiration, trinitarian and christological theories received substantively new life. Second, there is the surprising achievement of Karl Rahner and Bernard Lonergan in Roman Catholic theology that prepared the way for Vatican II. Rahner in particular has stimulated new recoveries of trinitarian concepts. Third, there is the rise of the process theism of Alfred North Whitehead and Charles Hartshorne. Process theism is a new form of natural theology, arguing that God is the chief exemplification of the metaphysical categories necessary to explain all of reality. It emphasizes the capacity of God to change, to suffer empathetically with the world and to have an interactive history with the world.[26] Fourth, there is the emergence in the last half of the century of one of the most fruitful periods of trinitarian theologizing in the history of the church, with Jürgen Moltmann, Wolfhart Pannenberg, Robert W. Jenson, and Eberhard Jüngel as important players.[27]

My systematic project pivots around significant arguments with both

---

Pa.: Judson, 1973), 384–421. Cyril O'Regan's *The Heterodox Hegel* (Albany, N.Y.: SUNY Press, 1994) is an arresting study of the deep trinitarian concerns of Hegel.

[26] See John B. Cobb Jr., and David Ray Griffin, *Process Theology: An Introductory Exposition* (Philadelphia: Westminster, 1976); John B. Cobb, Jr., *A Christian Natural Theology* (Philadelphia: Westminster, 1965); Schubert M. Ogden, *The Reality of God and Other Essays* (New York: Harper & Row, 1960); Marjorie Hewitt Suchocki, *God, Christ, and Church: A Practical Guide to Process Theology*, new rev. ed. (New York: Crossroad, 1989); Delwin Brown, Ralph James Jr., and Gene Reeves, eds., *Process Philosophy and Christian Thought* (Indianapolis: Bobbs-Merrill, 1971). *Trinity in Process: A Relational Theology of God*, ed. Joseph A. Bracken and Marjorie Hewitt Suchocki (New York: Continuum, 1997) is a serious effort to elaborate trinitarian themes in terms of process metaphysical categories.

[27] See especially Jürgen Moltmann, *The Trinity and the Kingdom: The Doctrine of God*, trans. Margaret Kohl (San Francisco: Harper and Row, 1981); Wolfhart Pannenberg, *Systematic Theology*, vol. 1, trans. Geoffrey Bromiley (Grand Rapids, Mich.: Eerdmans, 1991); Robert W. Jenson, *Systematic Theology*, vol. 1, *The Triune God* (New York: Oxford University Press, 1997); Eberhard Jüngel, *The Doctrine of the Trinity: God's Being Is in Becoming* (Grand Rapids, Mich.: Eerdmans, 1976) and *God as the Mystery of the World*, trans. Darrell L. Guder (Grand Rapids, Mich.: Eerdmans, 1983).

classical theism and process theism and intends to allow the primacy of God's economical self-revelations in Israel and in Jesus Christ to become the critical focus for understanding who God is. The church continues to struggle to find an adequate trinitarian formulation, but it has been terribly burdened with the elemental conceptuality that God is essentially simple, immutable, and impassible, and therefore unrelated to the world and unaffected by the world. In rethinking the Trinity, these elemental concepts must be *dismantled and deconstructed* so as to have a sense for the complex, living, self-determining movement of God who has a history with the world and is affected by the world. With regard to process theism, in my judgment it cannot affirm a radical incarnation in Jesus, cannot affirm much of a trinitarian doctrine, cannot develop an adequate account of the freedom of God, and has to say God requires some world in order for God to be God.

Puzzles in the Contemporary Discussions of Trinity

We now turn to some of the most remarkable issues of our time among theologians who are dedicated trinitarians. With a measure of oversimplification, we have on one side the two most important proponents in this past century for the rejuvenated centering of Christian theology on the doctrine of the Trinity, namely, Karl Barth and Karl Rahner. On the other side we have a congeries of theologians who argue in various ways for a 'social Trinity.' And both sides think they are interpreting accurately the 'real sense' of classical orthodoxy. All of these theologians agree that the economic Trinity is the prime starting point for trinitarian constructions.

Let me first state in my terms what I regard as some of the focal issues of this contemporary discussion. Is the triune God to be thought of as *one subject* in a threefold way of being and relatedness? Or, is the triune God to be thought of as *three subjects* who are united in some special way? I use the terms 'subject' and 'subjects' instead of the traditional terms of *hypostasis, prosopon, persona,* and *person* in order to prescind from any question begging interpretation of these terms. But what is at issue is how the *real distinctions* between Father, Son, and Spirit are to be identified and explained, and how the *unity or oneness* of Father, Son, and Spirit is to be explained and defended. All the theologians agree with the Eastern definition of 'one being [*ousia*] of God in three hypostases [*hypostaseis*]' and the Western definition of 'one substance [*substantia*] in three persons [*personae*].' Yet the problems arise in interpreting what these formulae mean. Put simply, a key issue is whether the term *person* means 'a distinct center of consciousness, intentionality, and activity,' and whether there are three such persons or only one in the Trinity. Finally, this is tied to the issue of whether the unity of the Trinity is the unity of a single subject or the unity of a common essence or even the unity of a community of persons.

The following quotations from Barth and Rahner show strikingly how the issues are posed:

> By Father, Son and Spirit we do not mean what is commonly suggested to us by the word "persons." This designation was accepted—not without opposition—on linguistic presuppositions which no longer obtain today. It was never intended to imply—at any rate in the main stream of theological tradition—that there are in God three different personalities, three self-existent individuals with their own special self-consciousness, cognition, volition, activity, effects, revelation and name. The one name of the one God is the threefold name of Father, Son and Holy Spirit. The one "personality" of God, the one active and speaking divine Ego is Father, Son and Holy Spirit. Otherwise we should obviously have to speak of three gods. . . . Christian faith and Christian confession has one Subject, not three.[28]

> [There] is the danger of a popular, unverbalized, but at bottom quite massive tritheism. Whenever efforts are made to think of the Trinity, this danger looms much larger than that of Sabellian modalism. There can be no doubt about it: speaking of three persons in God entails almost inevitably the danger . . . of believing that there exist in God three distinct consciousnesses, spiritual vitalities, centers of activity, and so on.[29]

---

[28] Barth, *Church Dogmatics*, IV/1, 204–205; see also I/1, 351, 355–58; II/1, 284ff. It is for this reason that Barth prefers 'modes of being' (*Seinsweisen*) to the traditional 'persons.'

[29] Karl Rahner, *The Trinity*, trans. Joseph Donceel (New York: Seabury, 1974), 42–43. See also Rahner's entry on "Trinity" in *Encyclopedia of Theology: The Concise Sacramentum Mundi*, ed. Karl Rahner (New York: Seabury, 1975), 1755–1764. It is odd that the doctrine of the Trinity plays no explicit role in his major systematic statement: *Foundations of Christian Faith: An Introduction to the Idea of Christianity*, trans. William V. Dych (New York: Seabury, 1978).

[W]hen *today we* speak of person in the plural, we think almost necessarily, because of the modern meaning of the word,
of several spiritual centers of activity, of several subjectivities
and liberties. But there are not three of these in God. . . . But
there are not three consciousnesses; rather, the one consciousness subsists in a three fold way. There is only one real consciousness in God, which is shared by Father, Son, and Spirit,
by each in his own proper way.[30]

Note the following agreements between Barth and Rahner: (a) The
meaning of *persona* or *hypostasis* in the tradition is different from the
meaning of *person* today, and hence it can be misleading to speak now of
three persons in the Trinity; (b) God is a single Subject or I; (c) there are
not three centers of consciousness or three I's in God; and (d) three conscious subjects in God would be tantamount to tritheism.

The extraordinary development today is the rise of social trinitarians
who dispute all four points of the Barth-Rahner consensus, though their
perspectives and reasoning are not all the same. Their key point is that
the contemporary understanding of person is precisely what is needed in
trinitarian reflection because it emphasizes both person as an intentional
center of activity and awareness and the sense that persons are constituted by their relationships. Jürgen Moltmann has launched a vehement,
if not always convincing and clarifying, attack on Barth and Rahner, ac-
cusing both of Sabellian modalism and arguing for a plurality of persons
in the Godhead.[31] David Brown advocates a social Trinity in which the
persons are distinct centers of consciousness, intentionality, and will.[32]
Colin Gunton argues that a proper understanding of the Cappadocian
theory of the distinctions and relations of the persons is the true foundation for a theory of person that fits both an adequate trinitarian doctrine
and contemporary anthropological needs.[33] Catherine Mowry LaCugna

[30] Rahner, *Trinity*, 106–107.

[31] Moltmann, *Trinity and the Kingdom*, 139–148.

[32] David Brown, *The Divine Trinity* (LaSalle, Ill.: Open Court, 1985). See
also "Trinitarian Personhood and Individuality" in *Trinity, Incarnation, and
Atonement*, ed. Ronald J. Feenstra and Cornelius Plantinga Jr. (Notre Dame,
Ind.: University of Notre Dame Press, 1989), 48–78.

[33] Colin E. Gunton, *The Promise of Trinitarian Theology* (Edinburgh: T &T
Clark, 1991). See also Christoph Schwöbel and Colin E. Gunton, ed., *Persons,
Divine and Human* (Edinburgh: T & T Clark, 1991). Gunton acknowledges par-
ticular indebtedness to the Orthodox theologian John D. Zizioulas's *Being as*

proposes a rebuilt doctrine of Trinity in which 'relational personhood' is the key both to the persons of the Trinity and to the normative meaning of human persons for today. Cornelius Plantinga, Jr., probably presents the clearest account of the essentials of social trinitarianism as biblically and traditionally grounded and as able to address carefully, if not convincingly, the charges of tritheism.[34] Robert W. Jenson and Wolfhart Pannenberg[35] are cousins to these theologians, sharing similar criticisms of Barth and Rahner, but also having other axes to grind. But in all of these thinkers the decisive reversal from Barth-Rahner is that a modern understanding of *person* is not contradictory to the traditional *persona* and is in fact what is needed to construe God's triune life adequately for our time.

For the social trinitarians the charges against Barth and Rahner are two-fold: (1) that they are modalists insofar as they do not adequately recognize *real distinctions* within God; and (2) that they have God as one person, while there are actually three such persons in God that are relational to one another. This charge only makes sense if the only acceptable way to mark the distinctions within God is by affirming that there are three persons as centers of intentional action and awareness. But for Barth and Rahner the charge of modalist is absurd, since for them modalism is the view that the eternal God remains distant from and uninvolved in the work of the Son and the Spirit. The social trinitarians believe that Augustine's emphasis on the oneness of the substantial subject undermined the real threeness within God and that this tradition of trinitarian construal has led to the loss of the real triuneness of God.

How can we get a handle on these issues? The social trinitarians start with the economic distinctions within the Trinity, especially the biblical sense of the obedience of Jesus to the Father, in which there is a recognition of a difference between the Father and Jesus. The grammar of contemporary personhood as involving intentionality of action and awareness and relationality to others seems well suited for grasping the difference between the Father and Jesus: they are different and they are interrelated to one another. This does seem to be a net gain.

But the social trinitarians are vulnerable on the issue of the oneness or unity of God and whether they have adequately accounted for the

---

Communion: Studies in Personhood and the Church (London: Darton, Longman and Todd, 1985).

[34] See footnote 19.

[35] *Systematic Theology,* vol. 1, 319–327, 384–391.

strong intuitive sense among Christians that God is One, or monotheism. Their reply is that God is one in the sense that the persons share a common essence, now understanding that essence to be structure or nature and not another agent subject, and that the persons are interrelated in their very constitution as the persons they are. But if each person is divine because of the common essence or nature each possesses, then it looks strikingly as though we have a divine essence with three instances, which seems about as clear a conception of tritheism as one can imagine.[36] Can the perichoretic interaction of the three persons as a community of persons rescue this tritheism? It might, but the social trinitarians still want to maintain a vestige of the traditional view that the persons always act as one in their action *ad extra*—action beyond the triune Life in relation to the world, which suggests a unity that their prime concepts do not support. And when we inquire how a community of persons is divine, the reply has to identify some trait of the relations within the community that comprise the divineness of the community. Hence, it seems inexorably to follow that that trait or quality is what is really divine and the social trinitarian begins retreating again to the unity of essence.

We should be grateful for the vigor of these discussions aimed at retrieving and elaborating a viable doctrine of Trinity for Christian faith. But it is well to recall—at just this point of seeming impasses in the construals of God's reality—the fundamental theological rule that God is *incomprehensible mystery*. As such, God cannot be captured in concepts that have the character of being class concepts with vigorous entailments and precise references. This becomes apparent when, for example, the concept of person is pushed too far and too much is expected of its grammar in application to God. It is, after all, an analogical concept when applied to God, and that at least means that its grammar has some limitations in syntax and semantics that simply cannot be overcome. The *pragmatics* of Christian faith can live with those limitations without supposing that we really cannot know or construe God at all.

---

[36] Brian Leftow has pushed an excruciating critique of social trinitarians in his essay, "Anti Social Trinitarianism," in *The Trinity: An Interdisciplinary Symposium on the Trinity*, ed. Stephen T. Davis, Daniel Kendall, and Gerald O'Collins (Oxford: Oxford University Press, 1999), 203–249. Leftow concludes that social trinitarians cannot account adequately for the oneness of God. He contrasts the social trinitarians to what he calls the "Latin Trinity," which makes the unity of God as a subject central. Leftow does not explore, however, whether the Latin Trinity adequately accounts for the economic distinctions among the persons.

I propose that we understand our construals of the Trinity as models with limiting grammars.[37] One model, for example the social model, may be more adept at grasping the differences among the persons of the Trinity, whereas the model of Barth and Rahner may be more adept at grasping the unity of the Trinity and the sovereign singularity of God. With our limited analogical language, then, we might move *back and forth* between the models without too much confusion but perhaps with greater theological responsibility.

I propose further that nothing should be said which subverts the following *rules of any Trinitarian grammar*:
1. that it is one and the same God who is self-revealing in the identifying references of the Father, of the Son, and of the Holy Spirit;
2. that the grammar should accommodate the differences or otherness evident in the NT narrative among the Father, the Son, and the Holy Spirit.

I will also propose that much of the traditional grammar presupposed an understanding of God's essence and actuality that is inadequate and needs revising. Such a revision will empower us to honor the real otherness within the divine life and to construe God's interactive economic life with the world. Yet in all of this grammar, we must remain mindful of our conceptual limitations.

---

[37] I mean nothing highly technical in using the word 'model' here. A model is simply that grammatical cluster of both syntax and semantics that gathers around a primary analogy or even a set of interrelated analogies. The surfeit of discussions about metaphor, models, symbols, etc. has become so unwieldy that I prefer simply to work with the grammatical understanding in which a word does not have to have singular and comprehensive definition in order to have a working syntax and semantics. Much of our ordinary language functions with adequacy and without serious confusion with words that are "open textured" and variously used. The concept of open texture is dependent on F. Waismann, *How I See Philosophy*, ed. R. Harré (New York: St Martin's, 1968), especially 91–121. Waismann understood himself to be 'explaining' the later philosophy of Wittgenstein. See especially Waismann's *The Principles of Linguistic Philosophy*, ed. R. Harré (New York: St. Martin's, 1965).

The Grammar of God's Self-Identifications:
The Economic Trinity

I will start with the confessional affirmation that the God of Israel has definitively self-communicated Godself in Jesus Christ through the Holy Spirit. I am relying here on the authority of the biblical narrative testimony to God's interactive life with the world. The biblical narrative will supply the foundational identifying references as to who God is in the form of this locution: *'God is the One who . . .'* The narrative will then supply the particulars of the identifying description which serves as the semantical guide to reference.

The three foundational identifying references give epistemic priority to the *economic Trinity*. The locution 'economic Trinity' was developed in the post-apostolic tradition as a way of talking about God's active plan and management [*oikonomia*] of the world and its history. God manages creation and history in a way analogous to how a competent house owner manages a household. It comes to have reference especially to God's historical self-revelations in which God discloses God's plan for the world—a plan which has been a mystery from the beginning of the world.[38] In giving primacy to the economic Trinity, we are emphasizing the ways in which God has made Godself known in the world of human history. Thus, the concept of the economic Trinity is distinct from the concept of the immanent Trinity, which affirms that God is triune within Godself and not simply in relation to the world.

I am claiming, then, that we learn who God is by looking at what God does. God is who God is in God's acts of self-disclosure in creaturely history. Hence, these self-communicating acts of God we can call *God's being-in-acts*. If God's actuality is in these acts in history, then we have no reason for positing a *more real God* hidden behind these living acts. It would not be appropriate here to speak of *self-revelation* if there were a more basic semantic principle which authorized identifying a more real God than the God revealed in these acts. This is the basic reason for not adopting a systematic metaphysics in advance to rule how the self-revelations of God are to be understood. That is why I emphasized the priority of proceeding by *analogia fidei*.

Everywhere in the NT the reality of the God of Israel—who is also identified as the Father of Jesus Christ—is presupposed. Yet it also speaks of Jesus as Lord, Son of God, Messiah, Savior, Word, Wisdom,

---

[38] See Eph 1.9–10; 3.2, 9; Col 1.25.

and these have decided overtones of divinity. It further speaks of the Holy Spirit in numerous ways as the divine movement which gives life, new life, and redemption. In saying these things the texts seem to assume some *distinctions* among the Father, Jesus Christ, and Holy Spirit. Let us look now at these quasi-trinitarian passages:

> Matthew 28.19: baptizing them in the name of the Father and of the Son and of the Holy Spirit.
>
> John 14.26: But the Advocate, the Holy Spirit, whom the Father will send in my name, will teach you everything, and remind you of all that I have said to you. [see also 14.16–17; 15.26]
>
> 2 Corinthians 13.13: the grace of the Lord Jesus Christ, the love of God, and the communion of the Holy Spirit be with all of you.
>
> 2 Corinthians 1.21–22: But it is God who establishes us with you in Christ . . . ; he has . . . given us his Spirit in our hearts as a guarantee.
>
> Romans 8.11: If the Spirit of him who raised Jesus from the dead dwells in you, he who raised Christ Jesus from the dead will give life to your mortal bodies also through his Spirit which dwells in you.
>
> Jude 20–21: But you, beloved . . . pray in the Holy Spirit; keep yourselves in the love of God; wait for the mercy of our Lord Jesus Christ.
>
> Ephesians 2.18: For through him [Christ] both of us have access in one Spirit to the Father.
>
> Ephesians 5.18–20: But be filled with the Spirit . . . giving thanks in the name of our Lord Jesus Christ to God the Father.
>
> 1 Peter 1.2: who have been chosen and destined by God the Father and sanctified by the Spirit to be obedient to Jesus Christ. . . .

Other passages as well suggest trinitarian trajectories.[39] This rich and fluid language suggests that not all the issues of how we must talk of God are settled in the NT itself.

As we now look at what I am calling the three foundational identifying references to God, we must remember that they are being con-

---

[39] See also Mk 1.9–11; Rom 1.1–4; 5.1–5; Gal 4.4–6; 1 Cor 6.11; 1 Cor 12.4–6; Eph 4.4–6; Acts 2.32–33; Rev 1.4–8.

fessed and described from the perspective of Jesus Christ as the definitive self-revelation of God. It is not as though the church first must become convinced that the God of Israel is real and *then* move to the reality
of Jesus Christ. Rather, it is the reality of Jesus Christ that moves the
church to accept the truthfulness of Israel's witness to God.

First Foundational Identifying Reference

God is the One who elected, liberated, and covenanted with Israel
and thereby is the One who is the sovereign Creator of all things.

The God of Israel is everywhere presupposed in the NT. Hence, it is
presupposed that the God of Israel is known and has a history of self-
disclosures in Israel. Here we are distilling what Christian faith understands to be essential to the self-identification of God as the God of Israel.

The giving of the distinctive name of Yahweh is God's self-
identification to the people of Israel: "I am who I am" or "I will be who I
will be [Ex 3.13–15]."[40] Yahweh is the One who freely moves, acts, becomes, and is self-determining. As freely self-determining, Yahweh
freely elects or chooses Israel as covenant partner, freely liberates Israel
from oppression in Egypt, chooses to have a covenantal history with Israel, teaches Israel in covenantal Torah what constitutes obedience to
Yahweh, and shows justice and mercy to Israel. In electing and liberating
Israel, Yahweh confirms that he[41] is the One—previously named '*El*
Shaddai'—who called and made promises to Abraham and Sarah, Isaac
and Rebekah, and Jacob and Rachel. [Ex 6.3]

In electing, liberating, and covenanting with Israel, Yahweh is
thereby the sovereign Creator of all things. When we insert the word

---

[40] The original Hebrew word was four consonants—YHWH—and has become known as the 'Tetragrammaton.' In its original setting YHWH was pro-
nounced like 'Yahweh,' but around the beginning of the third century B.C.E. the
practice emerges among Jews of not pronouncing the divine name and hence
substituted 'Adonai,' which means 'Lord,' for YHWH. I will observe the practice of returning to the plausibly original pronounceability of the divine name of
the God of Israel as Yahweh. See *The Oxford Dictionary of the Christian*
Church, 3d ed., ed. R. L. Cross and E. A. Livingston (Oxford: Oxford University Press, 1997), 1593; hereinafter referred to as *ODCC*.

[41] Without retreating from my suggestion to not use 'he' for God, I am using male pronouns when I am talking about the peculiar witness of the OT
wherein this was the way Israel talked.

'thereby,' we confirm that the One who elects, liberates, and covenants can be none other than the One who creates all things creaturely. This shows the priority in Israel's life of the *soteriological* identification of Yahweh to the *creational* identification. Or, to put it another way, the soteriological identification includes and grounds the creational identification. It does not appear to be the case that Israel first believed that Yahweh was Creator and then asked 'will Yahweh save us and covenant with us?' Rather it is precisely in electing, liberating, and covenanting with Israel that Yahweh confirms himself as the liberator who is also Creator. In this respect, then, Israel has to be told who is the Creator of the world and Creator in what sense.

In focusing on the identification of Yahweh, I do not mean to omit the importance of the prophets for understanding who the God of Israel is. Yet, as most scholars now agree, it is the covenantal identification of Yahweh that is the linchpin of the prophetic leverage against Israel in its apparent disobedience to the covenant and therefore its disobedience to Yahweh himself. Yahweh simply is the God of the prophets and therefore is One who expects justice and mercy from Israel.

As Creator, Yahweh has no rivals or superiors but is the ruler of the whole creation. There is thus a sharp distinction between Yahweh the Creator and everything else, for they are all creatures created by him. In this respect, Israel was clear that Yahweh was sovereign over the whole world as his creation. This God is not only the 'One who . . . ,' but is the only God there is. God is One Sovereign Subject. It is only because Yahweh is the only God that all the other gods of the world are shown to be no-gods and prohibitions against idolatry become imperative for Israel. Note the *shema* of Israel: "Hear, O Israel, Yahweh is our God, Yahweh alone [Deut 6.4]."[42] The grammar of Yahweh provides the rule of *Sovereign Singularity of God*.[43] Christian trinitarian theology always intended to honor this rule and refused to think that trinitarian concepts challenged the rule of Sovereign Singularity. But it is also true that trinitarian thought *amplifies* how the rule is to be applied.

---

[42] See also Deut 4.35; Isa 44.6, 8; 45.5–6. See Mk 12.29 wherein Jesus recites Israel's shema.

[43] This can also be referred to as the rule of monotheism, if we are not too complicated in translating 'monotheism' and allow it to stand in plain contrast to 'polytheism': one God in distinction from many gods. However, monotheism does not as such posit the radical distinction between God and everything else that is created by God.

In this soteriological and creational identification, Yahweh is characterized as Almighty, Holy, Righteous, Steadfast love, Merciful, and Gracious in his life with Israel and the whole creation. As I indicated in the discussion of revelation in the OT, Yahweh is throughout understood in personal analogies: Yahweh takes initiative to reveal himself, to speak to Israel and its prophets, and he demands personal obedience to himself from Israel. This initiating, personal, revealing activity of God is important for the NT understanding of God.[44]

All of these identifying marks of Yahweh are put in a new light when Jesus the Israelite refers to Yahweh as 'his Father' and 'our Father' and is obedient to the Father in proclaiming the Father's kingdom and is raised from the dead by the Father, the God of Israel.

Second Foundational Identifying Reference

God is the One who is singularly incarnate in and thereby definitively self-revealed in the life, death, and resurrection of Jesus of Nazareth.

The self-identification here is that the God of Israel—whom Jesus called Father—has sent his only Son for the salvation of Israel and the world. This identification is rooted in the NT church's salvific encounter with the risen Jesus of Nazareth. In calling Jesus Lord [*Kyrios*], Savior, Son of God, Messiah, Word made flesh, Wisdom of God, Emmanuel, the apostolic church confirmed the trajectory that the life, death, and resurrection of Jesus of Nazareth is none other than the very life of the God of Israel. Here we use the language of Incarnation and self-revelation to emphasize the decisive dimensions of God's self-identification in Jesus the Jew.

In addition to the 'trinitarian' passages mentioned above, the following passages were especially important to the early church:

> Matthew 11.27: All things have been handed over to me by
> my Father; and no one knows the Son except the Father,
> and no one knows the Father except the Son and anyone
> to whom the Son chooses to reveal him. [see Lk 10.22]
> Philippians 2.5–11: Let the same mind be in you that was in
> Christ Jesus who, though he was in the form [*morphe*] of

---

[44] Brevard S. Childs's *Biblical Theology of the Old and New Testaments* (Minneapolis: Fortress, 1992), especially 351–402, has been especially helpful in stating this identifying reference to God.

God, did not regard equality with God as something to be exploited, but emptied himself, taking the form [*morphe*] of a slave, being born in human likeness. And being found in human form [*schema*], he humbled himself and became obedient to the point of death—even death on a cross. Therefore God also highly exalted him and gave him the name that is above every name, so that at the name of Jesus every knee should bend, in heaven and on earth and under the earth, and every tongue should confess that Jesus Christ is Lord [*Kyrios*], to the glory of God the Father.

2 Corinthians 5.18–19: All this is from God, who reconciled us to himself through Christ . . . that is, in Christ God was reconciling the world to himself. . . .

John 1.1, 14: In the beginning was the Word, and the Word was with God, and the Word was God. . . . And the Word became flesh and lived among us. . . .

John 20.28: Thomas answered him, 'My Lord and my God'!

Colossians 1.19–20: For in him all the fullness of God was pleased to dwell, and through him God was pleased to reconcile to himself all things. . . .

Hebrews 1.2–3: [God] has spoken to us by a Son, who he appointed heir of all things, through whom he also created the worlds. He is the reflection of God's glory and the exact imprint of God's very being [*hypostaseos*], and he sustains all things by his powerful word. [45]

Central to the NT church was the confession that God in Jesus Christ brings salvation. In Jesus Christ's life, death, and resurrection, God speaks and enacts God's gracious, forgiving, and loving reconciliation of sinful humanity to Godself. In this Jesus of Nazareth, God is incarnate, takes up the human cause, confronts the principalities and powers of evil, suffers death at their hands, and rises from the dead as the eschatological hope for all humanity. In what I will later call the work of Jesus Christ, Jesus is the Prophet who proclaims and enacts the kingdom of God, the Priest who remains obedient to the Father even unto death on the cross at the hands of sinful powers, and the Victor who is raised from the dead and manifests himself to some others as the One who is vindicated by the Father and victorious over the powers of evil. In this work, then, Jesus' destiny reveals the destiny of forgiven sinners now reconciled by God and given new life.

---

[45] In addition to these passages, see also: Gal 4.4–5; Rom 8.3–4; 1 Cor 8.6.

If this Jesus is God incarnate, does this challenge the sovereign singularity rule: that God is utterly distinct from all creatures, even though God works through creatures? In seeing deity in Jesus Christ, the early church begins to *stretch and transform* what further can be said about the God of Israel. These matters are not directly settled in the NT, but the direction of their resolution is given there. The doctrines of the Incarnation and the Trinity are thus inseparable as the church begins to explain to itself and the world how God has graciously brought salvation to all in the human Jesus of Nazareth.

The question of *who God is* cannot finally be separated from the question of *who Jesus is*. Is the uniqueness of Jesus' life, death, and resurrection merely the particular historical uniqueness of a compelling prophet of the God of Israel—one among many of Israel's prophets? Or is the uniqueness of Jesus' life, death, and resurrection the uniqueness of a *new and definitive salvific* act of the God of Israel for the salvation of the world? If this salvific uniqueness of Jesus is a *self-identification of God*, then we cannot adequately identify the God of Israel apart from this self-identification. Hence, however much God has identified Godself to and in Israel, this new identification in the Jewish Jesus of Nazareth is essential for understanding who God is. I agree with N. T. Wright that the issue of 'who God is'—which is also a christological issue—is the primary issue that finally leads to the separation of church from synagogue.[46] But it was strong trinitarian doctrine that kept this issue from resulting in the misguided solution of Marcion, who denied that the God in Jesus Christ is the God of Israel.

Further, what is so radical and compelling for the apostolic and post-apostolic church is that this identification of God in Jesus seems to posit an *otherness*, a *differentiation,* and a *becomingness* in God's life that requires clarification. Hence, it becomes apparent that God's acts in Jesus Christ are essential to the identity of the God Christians worship and in whose name they baptize and partake of Holy Communion.

---

[46] N. T. Wright, *Christian Origins and the Question of God*, vol. 1, *The New Testament and the People of God* (Minneapolis: Fortress, 1992), especially 444–476. See also vol. 2, *Jesus and the Victory of God* (Minneapolis: Fortress, 1997), 624–631, for a discussion of how Jesus' own life and work began the process of stretching and transforming Jewish monotheism.

The Third Foundational Identifying Reference

God is the One who empowers the church into being and moves within creaturely life to draw all creatures into a redemptive future.

This is the Holy Spirit who is none other than the Spirit of Yahweh and the Spirit of the incarnate Son of God. In all likelihood the Spirit language of the OT and the NT could have been handled without trinitarian implications if the church had not confessed the deity of Jesus Christ. It is this confession which transforms the understanding of the Spirit of God as not only the breath of life but as the giver of new life in the calling of persons to say 'yes' to God's reconciling action in Jesus Christ.

In the NT we see how the Spirit is crucial to Jesus' conception, baptism, and prophetic mission, and we see how Jesus redefines the Spirit as his Spirit. [Jn 20.22] Spirit language becomes trinitarian in the NT: the Spirit of the Father and the Spirit of the Son.[47] There does not seem to be any doubt in the NT that the Spirit of the Father and the Spirit of the Son is the Spirit of God and therefore divine as well. Hence we have not only the otherness and differentiation in God's Life of God's identity with the life, death, and resurrection of Jesus, but the otherness and differentiation of God's movement to empower persons to participate in and appropriate Jesus' salvific work.

Seeking the Intelligibility of the Economy of God

These three self-identifications of God thus provide a narrative connection in which the selfsame God has been engaged in *communicative transactions* with the people of Israel and with the world. These three self-identifications of God affirm that God is the One who created all things, elected Israel in special covenant, became human in Jesus of Nazareth for the salvation of the world, and moved in the Spirit to give life, renew life and redeem the world. These self-identifications of God I am calling *God's triune self-identifying being-in-acts: God is who God is as God acts to disclose Godself.* This is the *triune matrix* of the Christian doctrine of God. Intrinsic to this matrix is that God is the Father as One bound to the Son through the Spirit. The obvious relationality within God

---

[47] See the several combinations of 'Spirit of . . .' in Mt 10.20; Jn 15.26; Gal 4.6; Acts 16.7; Rom 8.9; Phil 1.19; 1 Pet 1.11.

and between God and the world is a salutary outcome of starting confessionally with these economic transactions of God.

This triune matrix, however, confronts the church with critical questions for its grammar. The church never forsook in its own mind that God is sovereignly one God. But given these triune self-identifications of God, how are we to understand the *oneness or unity* of God? If we are to avoid the heresies of modalism and tritheism, then there appear to be three options in conceiving the unity of God: (1) the unity of a common essence; (2) the unity of a community of persons; and (3) the unity of a complex, living, tri-moded person-subject. I will support option 3: that God has the unity of a person-subject, and therefore God's essence is itself triune.

How, then, are we to understand the *distinctions and otherness* within God, the plurality in God? The NT never seems confused about the Father, the Son, and the Holy Spirit being in some sense *different*. How do we affirm this difference or differentiation without subverting the oneness or unity? Further, how must deity be understood such that God can become incarnate in a particular human being? Some concepts of God would make this understanding impossible. Grammatically, Arius's god could not become incarnate; it is doubtful that either Schleiermacher's or Tillich's god could. Or, to put it sharply, *what is the grammar of intelligibility that makes it possible to say God dies a human death on the cross of salvation without thereby ceasing to be God?*

In order to answer these questions I will engage in a form of reasoning that is sometimes called *transcendental reasoning*. Such reasoning starts with some given actuality and then asks: what must be the conditions of possibility for this actuality to be the case?[48] Hence, the reasoning will go something like this: given the actuality of God's self-communicating self-identifications in Israel and Jesus Christ and through the Spirit, what must be the case about God such that these self-identifications become fully intelligible to us? A grammar of God that

---

[48] Harkening back to Kant, transcendental reasoning is simply that project of starting with a given statement of actuality and then seeking to explore how such an actuality is possible. It asks, if this is the case, then what must also be the case in order for this to be possible? This does not mean, however, to look around to find an existing ontology that will endorse the actuality and its possibility. I think this latter exercise is the sort of reasoning which Rahner calls transcendental, with deep dependence on Heidegger, and which appears suspect to me. To be sure, the search for the intelligible shape of possibility does involve some imaginative construals.

repeatedly renders these self-identifications unintelligible would be an inadequate grammar.

It should be clear here why this theological grammar I am constructing should be called *confessional theology*—I know of no noncircular way of demonstrating that God did in fact reveal Godself in Israel and Jesus Christ. But confessional theology can begin reflecting on the given actuality of God's self-identifications and then elucidate the grammar of discourse that takes this seriously as having to do with the salvation of the world.

A final word before we engage in the further construction of a grammar of the triune God. Our grammatical constructions—which in this chapter are primarily syntactic and semantic—intend to be no more than the empowering rules for telling coherently, consistently, truthfully, and faithfully the multidimensional *narrative* of God's creative, reconciling, and redemptive self-communicating love in the history of Israel; in the life, death, and resurrection of Jesus of Nazareth; and in the church for the world. In one sense, the narrative precedes the grammar. But in another sense, the grammar is already rooted in the narrative itself. When I say the narrative is about the economy of God's life with Israel, God's life in Jesus the Jew from Nazareth, and God's life through the redeeming Spirit, I am already discerning the grammar in the story. I am trying to articulate *the narrative grammar of God's interactive life with and within the world.*

The Grammar of God's Unity, Multiplicity, Relationality, and Complexity

Even as this grammar strives to speak coherently of God's economic self-identifications, we must remember the basic rule that God is mystery and is incomprehensible in strict categories of description. We must not forget the analogical character of our basic concepts and their inherent limitations. But we should not suppose that we have nothing really to go on and that we are just confronted with an Unknown X, defying all our human language. No, God has identified Godself to us in and through deputized human language. As I now try to construe a grammar of the triune God, I advert to the two rules mentioned above: (1) that it is one and the same God who is self-revealing in Israel and in the human Jew Jesus of Nazareth and in the calling of the church; (2) that the narrative differences and relationalities of the Father, the Son, and the Holy Spirit in the witness of the NT be preserved from any unity that would obliterate them. I acknowledge that the social analogy seems to preserve the differences and relationalities, while the analogy of God as a single subject seems to preserve the unity and oneness of God more adequately. Hence, some balancing of these models of unity and multiplicity will be required as we confront the limitations of our language and conceptions.

The Unity of God as the Unity of a Person-Subject

Here I am using the *analogia fidei* of the biblical talk of God as analogous to talk of a *person as an intentional agent*, who knows, intends, wills, decides, and feels and is thereby a center of consciousness and agency. Admitting all the limitations of our human language to conceive God, we know that conceiving the unity of God will have limitations as we seek those analogies in our human talk that seem to best fit talking about God's unity or oneness. I am claiming that analogy to the human person is the best analogy to use for describing God's oneness. *The unity or oneness of God is the unity of a person-subject.*

In choosing this analogy, I am denying the appropriateness of other ways of conceiving God's unity. First, it is denied that God's unity is the unity of a *common essence* with three instantiations. This would be vulnerable to tritheism, insofar as it would seem to say there are three entities or subjects that have one common essence and each is an instance of that essence. It seems to me that at the heart of the tritheism threat is the notion of there being three gods, and that is the logic of this conception of God's unity. Hence, if essence is understood as a structured nature that makes something the sort of thing it is, and if God is one insofar as the Father, Son, and Holy Spirit—as person-subjects—bear that nature in common, then it is unavoidable that there are three subjects who are God and who are one in having the common essence. That is the inescapable logic of three gods, even as it is the formal syntax of having many gods.

Second, it is denied that God's unity is the unity of a *community of persons*: unity as a quality of the relationships among the persons. While this analogy has the virtue of making some prima facie sense out of the differences among the Father, the Son, and the Spirit in the biblical testimony, it still has difficulty conceiving wherein each person of the Trinity has divinity. What constitutes the persons divine? If we say the divinity is in the quality of their relationships, then we seem inevitably to come back to affirming that the quality has three instances. Suppose we then identify the quality itself as the quality of loving mutuality. Then, in effect, we have said that divinity itself is comprised of loving mutuality and wherever this relational quality happens, there we have God. Interestingly enough, the reply eviscerates the divineness of the persons as persons, unless we then say that any persons who instantiate loving mutuality are thereby divine. But this conclusion seems to subvert the biblical and traditional grammar of the sovereign singularity of God. While it is good grammar to say that the Father, Son, and Spirit enjoy relationships of loving mutuality, it is devastating to locate the divinity of the Father and the Son and the Spirit in that loving mutuality as such, for that mutuality is quite prior to and detachable from the narrative interactions of the God of Israel, Jesus Christ, and the Spirit. While I will use the concept of divine community in further talk of the interrelationship of the Father, Son, and Spirit, I do not think the concept *by itself* is sufficient for grasping the biblical sense of there being one God and not three gods and not even one type of relationship that is divine.

So I am claiming that the analogy to the unity of the human person is the most fitting—albeit limited—way of conceiving God's unity. So, God is in this sense *one person*, not three persons in that same sense of person. Basically I am claiming that God is an *'I'* who meets us as a *'Thou.'*[49] We will now inspect the limits of the one-person analogy.

God Is One Person in Three Modes of Being-in-Act

Here I continue to follow Barth: 'modes of being' is a translation of *seinwesen* and is close to Rahner's *subsistences*. But the word 'mode' is not illuminating in and of itself; it is a technical term, like *hypostasis*, that is being put to particular stipulated uses. I stipulate here that a *mode is a way of being and action, and in this usage a mode is a mode of a subject.* I claim that the 'persons' of the Trinity can best be understood as modes of the divine being and action. We can say either 'three modes of being-in-act' or 'three being-in-acts' of the one Subject. Or, God is a tri-moded Person-Subject.

The essential point is that *God has three decisive ways of being God*, wherein God's being is in God's modes of agency. 'Mode' has the virtue of avoiding 'person' with its sense today of three *individual* person-

---

[49] To this extent I am in agreement with Barth and Rahner over against the social trinitarians.

subjects. But I am not proposing the elimination of the practice of referring to the Father, Son, and Spirit as *persons*. Rather, I do not want us to
be misled by that language. We will continue to speak of the three modes
as *persons* but we want to avoid the translation of this into three individuals. It is my conviction that if the Fathers of the church had a sense
for our modern meaning of 'person,' they too would not have talked of
'three persons.' Incidentally, this linguistic situation illustrates how
words themselves have histories of usage and how that usage can change
over time.

   Each mode of God is equally a mode of God. Among the Father,
Son, and Spirit there is no ranking of superiority or priority. While there
has been a historical tendency to regard the Father as the source
of—'begatting' and 'spirating'—the Son and the Spirit, I find this language regrettable and unhelpful, for it leads into an implicit subordinationism. We can acknowledge an economy of 'sending' and 'obeying'
that is biblically appropriate, but we should be wary of converting this
into a causal ontology of the persons' interrelationships. Hence, I regard
the tendency to speak of the Father as the real God and to be puzzled
about the status of the other two as one of the significant heretical inclinations in our time. The Son and the Spirit are as decisively and really
God as the Father and are not derivative from the Father. The Father, the
Son, and the Holy Spirit, then, are equally modes of God's being-in-acts.
This further means that I am suspicious of inclinations to identify the
Father as the originating subject who is really the sovereign one.

   I question the tendency to say that God is primarily subject in the
Father, with the Son as the object of the Father and the Spirit as the relation between subject and object. Hence, I have some hesitation in following Barth here who speaks of Revealer, Revelation, Revealedness.[50]
There are at least two problems with this way of putting it: (1) it tends to
make the Father the real subject and agent; and (2) it tends to reduce the
Spirit to being only a relationship between Father and Son. On the contrary, the Father, Son, and Spirit are equally agencies of God.

---

   [50] Throughout Barth's *Church Dogmatics* he uses the model of the subject
who reveals, the revealing itself, and the impartation of the revelation in and to a
recipient. See especially *Church Dogmatics,* I/1/, Chapter Two, Part One: The
Triune God, 295–489.

God Is a Complex Person-Subject

We can now begin to qualify the respects in which God is a triune Person. I affirm that God is an *'I'* and a *'Thou'* in all three modes of be-ing-in-act: *three ways of being I and three ways of being Thou*. When I say this, I am acknowledging an element of truth in the social analogy of Trinity! God actually lives *in* and not behind these modes of being-in-act. God does not meet us except in these modes of being-in-act. These modes of being-in-act are God's living actuality—God is actual in these modes of being-in-act. Hence, let us be clear: the modes of being of God are not mere appearances of God behind which the real God hiddenly lurks. It is this emphasis—*that the modes are real distinctions in God and that God is real only in the modes*—that differentiates our grammar from that of modalism.

In this light, therefore, it is appropriate to say *that God is a self-differentiating person-subject*. As self-differentiating, God lovingly dif-ferentiates God's life. When we grasp this self-differentiation in God, we can reckon that God is a *complex person-subject*. But here I admit the analogy to the human person begins to break down, since we do not know in our own person a self-differentiating similar to the richness of God's self-differentiating life. Oddly enough, the closest analogy would be the ancient one regarding the meaning of *persona* as the actor's role: God is the one actor who lives actually in three ways of acting and being. The limit of the analogy, of course, is that in the ordinary meaning of 'actor,' as one person on the stage, he or she has a real life off the stage as well. I am affirming that God does not have a 'real life' off or behind the stage but only in the *personae* of the Father, the Son, and the Spirit. As self-differentiating, God can be incarnate in Jesus without ceasing to be the Father-Creator.

There is a serious negation we must confront, however, as we move to say God is self-differentiating and complex. I am *denying that God is a simple, undifferentiated monad*. All the traditions seem to agree that God is simple, and the primary point of this is to deny that God is com-posed of quantitative parts. If God were composed of such parts, then two consequences would follow: (1) God would be a quantity located somewhere; and (2) we must inquire how the parts stay together and form a whole. Hence, it is argued that God is simple. I do not wish to challenge that point. But the doctrine of simplicity was pushed further to deny any real distinctions within God, and it plays into the concepts of immutability and impassibility—for the simple God cannot change, since that would require a distinction in God between potentiality and actuality.[51] To that extent it is also doubtful whether the traditional doctrine of the simplicity of God could allow even the real distinctions within God of the modes or persons of God. It was only in Hegel that this hegemony of impassible simplicity was broken, and God was conceived as *self-moving, self-differentiating and thereby complex*.[52] Given its prohibition that God could change in any respect at all, the church could not previously accommodate the notion that God is self-moving.

In the interest of conversing with the traditions that assert the divine simplicity, *a new reformulation of simplicity might say that it is the constant self-identicalness of God throughout all God's self-differentiating life with the world*. But here we would have to say this simplicity of God permits internal differentiations, otherness, and becomingness in God. Hence, there is a special sort of simplicity that allows for a special sort of complexity.

The Modes of God Are Distinct, Interrelated, and Interanimated

The Father, Son, and Holy Spirit, as modes in communion within God's life, are distinct, interrelated, and interanimated. The modes of God are *distinct* insofar as no mode is reducible to another mode or to something else. Distinct does not mean 'separated,' but it does mean 'differentiated.' Each mode in its distinctness from the other modes has

---

[51] Aquinas articulated the concept of simplicity with clarity in *Summa Theologiae*, Ia. 3; see St. Thomas Aquinas, *Summa Theologiae*, vol. 2, *Existence and Nature of God*, trans. Timothy McDermott (New York: McGraw-Hill, 1964), 18–47. The concept that God might be self-moving and complex and therefore have a nonquantitative distinction between essence and existence and between potentiality and actuality and therefore with the power to become is never seriously explored in Aquinas. Below I will propose a distinction between God's essence and actuality that will help us grasp the dynamic actuality of God's triune Life within Godself and with the world. The dismantling of the concept of God's simplicity includes the dismantling of a whole grammar of God's being and life.

[52] To be sure, Hegel conceived this self-differentiation within God in a linear, historical fashion, whereas I think the self-differentiation is eternal, and as such it is the immanent basis for God's genuine interactive life with the world in its temporality.

its own focus of being-in-act. As I will explain when we talk of their interanimation, the modes participate in one another's actions but do not do
one another's work. For example, understood economically, in the mode
of the Father, God primarily creates and governs the world; in the mode
of the Son, God primarily communicates and speaks in and to the world
and is incarnate in Jesus; and in the mode of the Spirit, God creates life,
moves prophets and others to participate in God's life and especially
moves within persons to bring the church into being. We can summarily
say that the Father is the Creator/Covenant Maker, the Son is the Encountering Reconciler, and the Spirit is the Life-Giving and Life-
Renewing Redeemer.[53]

As distinct from one another, the Father is not the Son or the Spirit,
nor is the Son the Spirit. When we put matters this way, we acknowledge
how profoundly there is *otherness* in God. It is this real otherness in God
that becomes decisively manifest in the otherness of Jesus the human
being from the otherness of the Father/Creator. The Father is not incarnate in Jesus; God the eternal Son is incarnate in Jesus. The differentiation between the Father and the Son is an eternal differentiation.

Yet even as distinct, each mode is *interrelated* to the other modes.
Each mode is what it is only in *relationship* to the other modes: no Father
without the Son and Spirit; no Son without the Father and Spirit; no
Spirit without the Father and Son. And each relationship is not the same.
The Father does send, abandon, and raise the Son, though the Spirit does
not. The Son does do the will of the Father and feels abandoned by the
Father and is resurrected by the Father as the Son's own work as well,
though the Spirit is not abandoned and resurrected. The Spirit does move
within creatures to bring life and new life as given by the Father and by
the Son, and the Spirit is the Spirit of the Father and the Son. Hence,
there are these interrelationships: Father to Son, Father to Spirit, Son to
Father, Son to Spirit, Spirit to Father, Spirit to Son. And these relationships cannot be collapsed into one another.

It is true that the relationship among the modes is that of mutual love

---

[53] The tradition has generally affirmed that all of God's action toward the
world, as action *ad extra*, is done in unity by all three persons. This does not
seem sufficiently nuanced and seems to lead to the conclusion that the Incarnation—as the premier action toward the world—was done by all three persons.
Here it seems to me that *perichoresis* can help us say both that no action *ad extra* is done by one person in isolation from the other persons and each person
can be the primary focus of an action.

in freedom, but this grammar can only be maintained if the modes are themselves agents in love. It is the strength of the social analogy that this relationality among the Father, Son, and Spirit is more vividly indicated. But the Spirit does not fit the notion of person quite so easily, as Pannenberg alone admits.[54] I think the concept of mode does, however, maintain the Spirit's identity. I should point out that I am rejecting the belief that the Spirit is the *relationship of love* between the Father and the Son; this would be a binity of two terms in a relationship. This affirmation about the Spirit is common in the tradition, but it has the effect of making the real agents of the divine life the Father and the Son, with the Spirit being simply their interrelationship to one another. Hence, we can understand the Spirit as also being in mutual love with the Father and the Son without simply being the name of the relationship between the Father and Son.

These relationships among the modes constitute the real interrelated life of God as a *complex Subject*. It is obscure to me how we could maintain the sorts of distinctions and interrelations among the modes of God and still employ the traditional concept of God's simplicity. Now, in affirming that these interrelations among the modes are constitutive of the divine life, we can analogically speak of *communion* within the complex reality which God is. This grammar of communion within God among the modes is evident in the traditional concept of *perichoresis*, which I am translating as the *interanimation* of the modes.[55] The *perichoresis* of the triune divine life is the lively—*dancing*—way in which the Father, the Son, and the Spirit have their life together. Not only are they in particular relationships with one another, they also interpenetrate one another as modes of the One Living Subject. The Father does not create/govern the world and call Israel without the interpenetration of the Son and the Spirit. Yet the Son as such does not create the world. Neither the Father as such nor the Spirit as such is incarnate in Jesus; only the Son is—though the Son is not incarnate without the actions of the Father and the Spirit. It is only the Spirit that moves within creaturely life to renew it and to redeem it, but this is not done without the interpenetration of the Father and the Son, for the Spirit is the Spirit of the Father and the Spirit of the Son. But their interanimation does not

---

[54] See Pannenberg, *Systematic Theology*, vol. 1, 383–384. I think Pannenberg becomes very confusing when he wants to identify the Spirit with the essence of God and conceive that essence as a 'force field.'

[55] In the Latin West, the Greek *perichoresis* is translated as *circumcisssion*.

abolish their distinctness. Their interanimation is the communal permeation of love among the Father, the Son, and the Spirit. *It is in love that the triune Subject lives and interacts both within Godself and with the world.*

Hence, in affirming that the triune modes of God are distinct, interrelated, and interanimated, I also affirm that there is real otherness, communion, and complexity within God's Life.

Some Important Negations and Qualifiers

It is important now to summarize what is being denied when I say God is a triune Subject. First, I am denying that God is an isolated, unrelated, simple monad, who is impassible, unmoving, and lifeless. Even within God's own life there is movement, relatedness, and dynamic self-differentiations. Second, I am denying that God is a more primordial One whose modes are *accidents* or *passing appearances*, but are not internal to God. This would be modalism. Be careful: though I am using the term 'modes,' what I affirm is decidedly different from what has traditionally been called 'modalism.' Do not be misled by the surface grammar of similarity of terms; the signs, as concepts, are quite different.

It is also being denied that the concept of *three* modes of being is derived from anywhere else than from the Scriptural language of Father, Son, and Holy Spirit. There is nothing magical or ontologically necessary about the number 'three' except this givenness of the name of God in the narrative of God's economic Life with the world. Hence, while there is indeed multiplicity in God, it is not sheer unlimited multiplicity but is the particular multiplicity of the interacting Life of the Father, the Son, and the Holy Spirit together.

In affirming that God has God's Life in the being-in-acts of the modes of God as these are seen in the economic self-identifications of God, we are speaking of a God who is active in relationships with the world. Whatever we might also say about God's transcendence of the world, *this Christian grammar of the Trinity will not allow us to place God in a remote, unrelated, and detached aloofness from the world.* The triune God has an interactive Life with, for, and within the world. It will require, however, the further development of the grammar of the distinction between God's essence and God's actuality in order to speak aptly of how God can and does have such an interactive and interrelated Life within Godself and with the world and without collapsing God's reality into the world.

I must now render a qualifier on what I have said about the grammar of God's unity and multiplicity. I have conceived the unity of God in terms of the analogy with what today we would call the human person as an intentional agent who is conscious, willing, knowing, affective, and active. I affirmed that such a unity is the unity of a complex person subject who is different from the human person. But I denied that God's unity should be conceived in terms of the perichoretic community recommended by the social trinitarians. *It should now be apparent that we cannot exclusively choose one analogy and completely dismiss the other. The unity of the person-subject grasps the unity of God better, but the social analogy grasps the multiplicity within God better.* Having chosen the person-model of the oneness of the Trinity, I also tilted a bit toward the concerns of the social-model. Here it seems to me we must confront and admit the limitations of our language in trying to conceive God's triune Life. God's Life is not a geometric puzzle that we will someday solve and then move on to another puzzle. God's Life is a mystery that we can describe and approach analogically, but we can never reduce God to our manageable grammar. After all, it is part of our grammar that God is mystery and incomprehensible. The pragmatics of the Christian life in worship, prayer, and in faith, hope, and love can certainly thrive in the face of that mystery but only if we attend carefully to the self-communications of that mystery that names Godself. Every time the church and theologians retreat behind the mystery to simple apophaticism, they verge on denying that God has been self-revealing and self-identifying.

The Grammar of God as the Triune One Who Loves in Freedom

In all that God does in interaction with the world, in self-communicating Godself, in self-identifying as the One who will be who he will be, in willing to become incarnate for the sake of the salvation of humanity, God communicates Godself as the One who loves in freedom, as the living Person-Subject who is free, self-determining love. *At the heart of the definitive self-revelation of God in Jesus Christ is the conviction that God loves and that God loves freely.*

In tracking now the grammar of God as the triune One 'who loves in freedom,' a locution that Barth has aptly used, I claim that *freedom and*

love are the two fundamental attributes of God which shape our under-
standing of all the other attributes or characters or traits of God.[56] In
God's triune self-identifications we have emerging a consistent characterization of God as one who is free and as one who is loving. God will
be who God will be and God wills to be the loving Creator, Reconciler,
and Redeemer of the world. In the mystery of God's triune Life, God is
freely loving and lovingly free.

The Basic Grammar of God's Grace

The grammar of God's free love and loving freedom becomes decisively manifest in the NT concept of *God's grace*. In clarifying what is
meant by God's grace, we will have to reckon with the deep grammar of
God's freedom and God's love. Certainly at the root of the concept of
grace is the concept of the love of God. God's grace is God's loving gift.
It is by God's grace that God has acted in Jesus Christ for the salvation
of creatures.

God's grace is always God's free gift.[57] God gives the gift of salvation without compulsion, necessity, or as a warranted reward for demon-
strated merit. But essential to this giving, then, is that it is *free, voluntary
giving*. Hence, it is not sufficient merely to understand the gift in terms
of its obviously *beneficial effects*; it must also be seen as *beneficial effects freely bestowed in love*. And it is not sufficient just to emphasize
beneficial effects that are *undeserved*. It is an extended use of 'grace' to
cover any beneficial effect that comes undeserved and therefore is not
one's due.[58] But this extended sense is not the primary sense for the gift
of salvation which God freely gives. To say it succinctly, *grace is beneficial effects undeserved and freely given*. The characterization of God's
love in the gift of salvation would be changed dramatically if we did not
clearly identify *God's freedom in the giving*. And the grace talk of the

---

[56] This section is dependent on Barth's brilliant articulation of God's freedom and love in *Church Dogmatics*, II/1, 257–321. But I do not pretend that
mine is simply an exegesis of Barth, as I deploy some concepts that are not explicitly identified by Barth.

[57] See Acts 15.11; Rom 3.21–26; 5.15–21; 6.15; 11.6; 2 Cor 8.1, 9; Eph
2.4–5; 3.7.

[58] In his otherwise illuminating book, *The Gifting God: A Trinitarian Ethics
of Excess* (New York: Oxford University Press, 1996), Stephen H. Webb focuses too broadly on this extended sense of grace.

NT would be rendered unintelligible to its authors if the love of God could be characterized as in some sense *necessary or compelled* for God to be God or something given as a reward for meritorious actions. As our presiding model of the Gospel states it: "the God of Israel . . . has in freedom and love become incarnate in the life, death, and resurrection of Jesus of Nazareth . . . to enact and reveal God's gracious reconciliation of humanity to Godself."

I emphasize this NT sense of God's grace because it pulls together into concentrated focus all the biblical narrative characterizations of God as freely giving, merciful, loving, and forgiving. This concentrated focus on grace, therefore, provides insight into the understanding of God's love and God's freedom. Were either one of these attributes neglected, the whole economic communicative transactions of God would be ill-conceived and produce an inadequate grammar.

Therefore, in our discourse about God we cannot prioritize or separate God's love and God's freedom. Keeping these two essential attributes of God together is decisive for the explication of the biblical witness to God as a personal agent who is freely and lovingly gracious to the creature. It has, however, been a profound temptation to the church to separate and explicate God's freedom and God's love independent of one another. When this separation occurs in the church's discourse about God, we have, on the one hand, a freedom that makes it appear that God is free not to love, as though freedom is more basic than love in God. This is the tendency of emphasizing that God is primarily *potentia absoluta*—absolute and unconditioned power. Or on the other hand, we have a love that makes it appear compelled or necessitated by God's essence or nature, as though God's loving is not a personal, free decision, relationship, and gift of God. In the church's discourse, therefore, we must grammatically keep God's freedom and God's love dialectically distinct and interrelated in such wise that they are never interpreted in independence of one another or that one is made more basic than the other.

The Grammar of God's Freedom

In the first instance, *God's freedom is God's unencumbered power to will and enact God's own life and actions.* God can do whatever God decides to do. Such willing and enacting are uncompelled and unnecessitated. God is not in the grips of a higher power or metaphysical principle that necessitates or limits God's actions. What God does is what God freely wills to do.[59] Hence, God freely and lovingly decides to create a cosmos, to elect and covenant with Israel, and to become incarnate in Jesus of Nazareth. In this sense, God's freedom is God's willing unencumbered by any external necessities or higher principles.

God's freedom is also God's free self-determination. The biblical testimony never contradicts the original meaning of Yahweh: that *God will be who God will be,* which is the essence of self-determination. As self-determining, God freely deploys and determines God's own actuality and life. In a way that the tradition could not affirm with its semantic rules about God's immutability, impassibility, and simplicity, we can now say that *in God's freedom God can self-determine Godself to-be-conditioned-by-another.* God is thus free to decide to-be-conditioned-by-another. The sense of 'conditioned-by-another' is that God can decide to be internally related to another, to be affected in God's actuality by another, and to be acted upon by another. But we must not grammatically violate this *basic rule: God is never affected by another actuality except as God freely decides or self-determines Godself to be so affected.* That God is free to be acted upon is nowhere more obvious than in the Son's being crucified by the powers of sin.

God's freedom is God's self-movement. God is not unmoved or immobile or unaffected, but profoundly self-moving. Implicit in this grammar of freedom as self-determination is the grammar of God's *becoming.* God is not sealed up in Godself as an unchanging monad. This grammar is explicit if we are realistic about God's having an interactive triune Life with the world, even to the point of becoming incarnate in a human life. The tradition found itself cut off from any concept of the self-moving freedom of God because of its commitment to the concepts of immutability, impassibility, and simplicity.

This grammar of God's freedom has important negations. God is not conditioned by another except as God's self-determination to-be-conditioned-by-another. There is no metaphysical principle that requires God to be determined by or conditioned by another reality. Hence, I do not say that being affected by another or being passible to another is *necessary* for God.

Also, God is not indeterminate and inchoate; this is why I am worried by the traditional practice of saying God is simply infinite—as

---

[59] Eberhard Jüngel says Luther believed 'free will' (*liberum arbitrium*) could only be properly predicated of God: Jüngel, *God as the Mystery of the World*, 36.

though that means that God is indeterminate, is no-thing of any sort. A god who is simply infinite is not a god who can become incarnate in a finite human being. But if *infinite* means no more than God's unencumbered and unlimited free self-determination, then that sort of infinity is acceptable. Also, this concept of God's freedom challenges the notion that all aspects of God's actuality are determined by an essence that necessitates all of God's actual determinations.

Does the grammar of God's freedom mean that God is free not to love? If we said that, we would be interpreting God's freedom as more basic than God's love. That would seem to imply that somehow in God's freedom God *contingently* decides to be loving and therefore could have decided not to love. To prevent that implication I now say that *God's free self-determination is the self-determination of love.* Hence, God does not *decide* to becoming loving. However—since the loving is God's own free act and is not imposed on God—*God does decide how and what to love.* The objects God loves do not necessitate God's love. However, that God is loving qualifies all the abstract possibilities of God's freedom; nothing is possible to God that contradicts God's loving. This is why we must never be lured into reflecting on abstract possibilities of God as though God is *potentia absoluta*—sheer unrestricted power.[60]

Finally, *God's freedom is also God's transcendent sovereignty over the world.* As the self-determining triune Subject, God can bring a nondivine world into being and interact self-determinately with that world. This does imply that God does not need the world in order to be God. To clarify this further requires developing the distinction below between God's essence and God's actuality.

The Grammar of God's Love

God's love is God's giving of Godself to another, to the beloved object. This is God's self-communication to another. God's giving of Godself is at the heart of God's self-revelations, which is why such revelation is not merely a datum of information; the revelation is God's giving of Godself. I have interpreted all of God's self-revelations as God's loving action of creating fellowship with the creature. In the NT God's love is called *agape.*[61] God loves insofar as God lives in and with another. It is

---

[60] Barth rightly objects that *potentia absoluta* is demonic in its implications. See *Church Dogmatics*, II/1, 524.

[61] See Jn 3.16; 16.27; Rom 5.5, 8; 8.35, 39; 2 Cor 13.11, 13; Gal 2.20; Eph 1.5; 2.4; 5.2; 2 Tim 2.16; 1 Jn 3.16; 4.7–16; Rev 1.5.

this love that is decisively evident in the relationships of the Father and the Son and the Spirit in God's economic Life.

God's love is God's capacity to will the good of another and God's actually willing that good. In loving the other, God desires and seeks the good of the other. The Father wills the good of the Son in raising the Son from the dead, and in so willing the Son's good, the Father also wills the good of the creature. The Spirit is God's loving empowerment of the creature. God's love is fundamental to our understanding of God's purposes in creating a world to love and redeem.

God's love is God's openness to the being of another, to letting the other be, and to being affected by the other. God is not jealous of another having life and actuality. God is not threatened by the actuality of another. God's love is God's capacity to be affected by another, to be conditioned by another. In love God becomes vulnerable to the world's life and actualities. This is God's *empathetic compassion* for another. The sharpest focus of God's love in the economy of God's life with the world is God's loving vulnerability and suffering for the world in the cross of Jesus Christ. This relationality of love involves being affected by the other as well as God's willing the good of the other.

In love God desires a reciprocal loving relationship with the other. But God's love does not depend on reciprocity. God does not merely love those who love God. In this sense, God's loving another arises out of Godself and is God's free self-determination. God's desire for reciprocity and mutuality is not a desire that *befalls* God but is the self-determined desire of God's love. God's desire issues from Godself; God does not have desire imposed on God by *falling in love*. It is herein that we must remember that God's love is God's *free love*. However, even as we affirm that God's desire for mutuality arises wholly from God's own self-determination, I must admit that *being-loved makes a difference to God and affects God.* This is God's loving self-determination to be affected by another.

There are two types of 'others' that God loves. First, there is the other that is internal to the triune Life of God—the communion of love the Father, Son, and Holy Spirit have among themselves. Second, and subsequently, there is the other who is a creature—God creates creatures in love and works in love to redeem them. If we did not give ontic priority to the sufficiency of the internal love within God's Life among the Father, Son, and Spirit, we would have to say that God *has to have* a creature in order to fulfill God's loving nature. But if we said that, we would blunt God's freedom in the loving. God's internal loving among the modes is sufficient in itself, but in loving freedom God also decides to create a world to love. But it is the internal love of God within the otherness of the divine Life that is the ground for God's capacity to will the otherness of the world and to love the world.[62]

In keeping love dialectically related but distinct from God's freedom, I say God's loving is always God's self-determined act of loving, of self-giving, of being vulnerable to another, of willing and desiring the good of another.

The Grammar of God's Aseity

God's aseity is God's power to be the triune One who loves in freedom. The aseity of God, in the tradition, was God's power of independent self-sufficiency, of not needing any other being. When this concept was combined with God's immutability and impassibility, we had a god who, in god's aseity, was utterly unaffected by the world. By holding freedom and love together in God, we can *reconceive God's aseity as God's power to live in loving self-determination.* This loving self-determination God has from Godself and as such does not require God to create a world and become incarnate in that world. How to make this clear requires the grammar developed below between God's essence and God's actuality. Without this distinction, the grammar of God's aseity will seem to hedge God into an unrelated and unaffected life apart from the world.

The Grammar of God's Essence and God's Actuality

In order to talk more consistently about God's free, self-determined life of love in Jesus Christ, it is my intention to reconstruct the traditional grammar of essence and existence in God. Without this distinction, the grammar of God's love and freedom becomes terribly confused. The reconstruction I propose is not developed in traditional or contemporary discussions of God's triune Life, though it is adumbrated in the Cappadocians and in Barth and is suggested in nontrinitarian ways in the proc-

---

[62] Pannenberg insightfully ties the possibility of a creaturely other distinct from God to the otherness within God of the Father and the Son. See Pannenberg, *Systematic Theology*, vol. 2, 20–35.

ess theology of Charles Hartshorne.[63] Remember, we are still asking transcendental questions: what grammatical distinctions are necessary to render intelligible that God is the self-identified triune Subject who loves in freedom?

What Do We Mean by 'Essence'?

What sort of talk is this talk about *essence*? It goes back at least to Plato and Aristotle, but it is deeply rooted in ordinary discourse about many things. Typically the *essence* of something is an answer to the question *'what sort* of thing is this?' Or, *'what* is it that makes this thing to be the *sort* of the thing it is?' So, we might ask 'what sort of things are Fred, George, and Priscilla?' The answer might be, 'they are humans.' *Being human* is the sort of thing they are; it is the *essence* or *nature* they have in common.

But Fred, George and Priscilla are *more than* just this human essence. They are also concrete, particular, individual, actual humans that have lives that change and become in time and are different from other humans, however much they may also have in common. Accordingly, we need to distinguish between the essence they have in common and the particular individuals who have that essence. Hence, we can say that particular human beings are *instances* of the common essence.

We must recognize that this *human essence* which humans have in common does not itself change, but particular human beings do change. The human essence is just what it is, and as such it is unchanging; it does

---

[63] The Cappadocians, as we have seen, at least recognized that the essence [*ousia*] of God is not another acting subject beyond the three persons. Barth's language about essence and actuality is notoriously unstable, but I do believe he saw that the Godhead as the essence of God does not do anything; only God the triune Subject acts. See *Church Dogmatics*, IV/2, 65. In utterly nontrinitarian ways, Hartshorne is quite clear about the distinctions between God's essence, existence, and actuality. For our purposes here, I am not concerned about his distinction between existence and actuality. While these distinctions are evident in much of Hartshorne's writings, they do not receive systematic clarity until he strives to state the ontological argument with logical rigor. See *The Logic of Perfection and Other Essays in Neoclassical Metaphysics* (LaSalle, Ill.: Open Court, 1962), 61ff and *Anselm's Discovery* (LaSalle, Ill.: Open Court, 1965), x. The genius of Hartshorne is in seeing that God's actuality is the inclusive concept even of God's essence.

not change from person to person. It might help here if we understand that we can also use other terms for essence: 'nature,' 'idea,' 'form,' 'structure.' *The essence of something is its unchanging structure of traits and powers.*[64]

Following this line of thought further, we can see what it would mean to say the essence of something is a logical subject but not an ontological subject. As logical subject, we can predicate of the human essence those traits that are necessary to something being a human. And the human essence with its traits can be predicated of particular humans such as Fred. But note: Fred as a particular individual cannot be predicated of anything—Fred is an ontological subject. Fred can act and do things and change, but the human essence is unchanging and does not act and do things.

Here now is the problem stemming from Plato: he thought the *essence* of something was what was *most real* about that something. And since the essence is itself unchanging, it was thought that it is more real to be *unchanging* than to be a thing that is subject to change. This principle—*that the unchangeable is more real than the changeable*—gets adopted in post-apostolic Christian theology and has played havoc with much of our God-talk.

The developed Christian tradition came to think that God's essence and God's existence—or actuality—are *identical*, and so we have the following:
   a. God's essence as such is unchanging;
   b. God's essence and existence are identical;
   c. So God's existence [or actuality] is unchanging;
   d. Hence, God is unchanging, simple, impassible, etc. in essence and existence.

This grammatical development in the church's discourse makes it difficult, if not impossible, to talk consistently about God acting in creation history, becoming incarnate, being affected by the world—matters that seem important to the biblical witness.

---

[64] The issue here is not whether there is an essence of human being upon which everyone can agree, but simply how the concept of essence works when it works. That the essence of humans, or of anything, has in the past been misidentified does not undercut the value of the concept of essence. I will, however, attempt to identify the essential structure of humanity in chapter six.

The Priority of God's Actuality

My fundamental revisionary proposal is that we must distinguish between God's essence and God's actuality. In making that distinction, we are free to insist that *God's actuality is the inclusive and basic reality of God.* I have referred to this *actuality as God's modes of being-in-act.* Hence, grammatically I want to affirm that *God is actual as the infinitely and eternally living triune Subject who freely and self-determinately loves in three modes of being-in-act.* This actuality of God has priority over God's essence in the sense that *the essence only has reality as the essence of God's actuality.*

Yet within God's actuality we have a need to talk of God's essence. Think of *God's essence as those unchanging traits of God that are present in every actuality of God's life.* These are the traits or characters which are present in God's actual life and without which God would not be God. In this sense, the essence of God is itself *immutable and unchanging.* In the same way the essence of humanity is immutable. So, here with regard to God's essence we do have an aspect of God's actuality that is unchanging. We can now say that *it is God's essence necessarily to be actual as the infinitely and eternally living triune Subject who freely loves in three modes of being-in-act as Father, Son, and Holy Spirit.* This is God's immutable essence—sometimes referred to as the 'Godhead' or '*Gottheit.*' Think of this essence or nature of God as God's *necessary structure.*

Yet, *while God's essence is itself immutable and does not change, God's actuality can change, become, can live.* Hence, we should not say that immutability is itself an essential trait of God's actuality. If immutability were an essential trait of God, then we could not say God changes in any respect. This can become quite confusing unless we note the distinction between saying: (a) 'God's essence is itself immutable' and (b) 'Immutability is an essential attribute of God.' I deny statement b. Recall again the discussion of humanity: the human essence is unchanging, but it is not one of the traits that comprise that essence that humans are unchanging. So too, God's essence is unchanging and immutable, but it is not one of the traits that comprise God's essence that God's actuality is immutable.

It should now be clear that *God's essence is not itself an ontological subject: God's essence does not do anything. Only God as actual Subject acts.* God's actuality is the ontological triune Subject who lives and acts.

The Cappadocians were right that God's essence is not an ontological subject over and beyond the three persons, but they were unable to affirm that God is One as a Living Subject. Hence, God's essence is a logical subject but not an ontological subject; the essence of God is predicated of the living tri-moded actuality of God.[65]

We know this essence of God only by inference from the actuality of God's life in the world—by virtue of God's self-revealing being-in-acts in the world. This is important: we do not first think abstractly about some idea of deity and then propose what is the essence of deity. We speak of the triune God's essence only on the basis of reflecting on who God is as the One who is Father, Son, and Holy Spirit in three modes of being-in-act with the world. Even as we speak of God's essence, we are only intending to refer to those traits of God that seem essential to God being the God we understand from God's self-revelation. We speak of those traits, of course, in analogical language, but we should not suppose either that the essence of God is utterly unknown or that we know it in precise categories of thought.

God's Actuality as Dynamic Becoming and Agency

Since this grammar does allow us to understand God's essence as an unchanging structure of attributes, we can speak more aptly of God's actuality. *In actuality God can change, become, be responsive to, be affected by, suffer with, and be in real relation with that which is other than God.* Precisely these powers seem required by the biblical testimony to God's living self-communications and self-identifying interactions with the world as the One who loves in freedom. But in affirming God's capacity for change, becoming, and suffering, we must not violate the rule that God's actuality in relation to others is always *God's self-determined decision-to-be-in-relation, to affect and to-be-affected-by-another, to condition and to-be-conditioned-by-another.* Hence, by giving priority to God's self-determining love, when we affirm God's being affected by the world in God's actual life with the world, we do not have to say that mutability is itself a necessary and essential attribute of God. Rather, we say that God in essence has the power to change and be affected by another, but that it is not necessary to God that God changes. It

---

[65] It should be clear how radically different this concept of the distinction between God's essence and God's actuality is from Pannenberg's. He still wants God's essence to be an agent in some sense, hence the identification of the essence of God with the Spirit. See *Systematic Theology*, vol. 1, 347–358.

is necessary to God for God to be self-determining love, but it is not necessary to God for God to be unchanging or changing in actuality. Whatever change God's living actuality does involve is always God's free and loving decision to change and be affected.

Hence, the God we know in God's historical actuality—God in God's economy of life with the world—is the *God who is freely and self-determinately lovingly actual as*:

a. the Creator of this world, this cosmos;
b. affected by and in real relation with this world;
c. incarnate in the life, death, and resurrection of Jesus of Nazareth and affected in God's actuality by this incarnation—the lineaments of the doctrine of atonement;
d. the Spirit who freely and lovingly moves the world toward a future yet-to-be-actual redemption;
e. the Tri-Moded Subject who self-determinately in love wills to have a history with the creation.

This is the actual God we know in the foundational identifying references.

The Essence and Actuality of God's Freedom and Love

Without the distinction between God's essence and God's actuality we could not talk aptly and fruitfully of the triune actual Life of God. My distinction challenges those theologians—certainly some process and feminist theologians—who have wanted to say, largely on the basis of saying love is God's nature, that: (a) it is God's essence to have an object of love and therefore, (b) it is God's essence to create a world to love and therefore, (c) it is necessary to God's actuality that God create a world. But to say God necessarily creates a world to love is to make the world co-eternal with God and necessary for God to be God. As I have argued, *this is a false separation of love and freedom.* Further, I have difficulty understanding what it would mean to talk of *grace* on these terms: we would have the beneficial effects without the free gift, the free and voluntary giving. What is of essence necessary is not something that is freely self-determined in love.

Hence, to preserve God's freedom in love, I propose that God's essence does not require or necessitate that God be creator in order to be God. God is in God's essence the God who loves within God's triune Life, and hence God does not need a nondivine object in order to be loving. By essence God is Father, Son, and Holy Spirit lovingly together. By essence, God *could* be God without any world. By essence, God does not need the world in order to be actual. God could be actual, and in a peculiar sense, God *was actually* God even *before* the creation of the world. We will call this being-actual-before-creation the *Primordial Actuality of God*, and will further specify that it is the *Primordial Trinity*.[66]

We also hereby avoid the mistakes of the tradition. The tradition wanted to say: (a) that God's essence does not require or necessitate God to create; and (b) that God freely creates a world; but (c) because God's essence and actuality are identical, and God is in essence self-sufficient and immutable; then (d) God is not affected by or actually related to the world that God creates. We must avoid accepting the principle that anything predicated of God's actuality is an essential predicate of God, and that the only way God can have an attribute or character is by necessity of essence, and therefore that God cannot have any attributes contingently.

Rather I affirm that God has some attributes or traits essentially, i.e., necessarily, as those attributes of God without which *God could not have any actuality*. Essential attributes are those without which God cannot be God. But we also affirm that God has some attributes by virtue of God's self-determined contingency. These are primarily those attributes that presuppose the world. But it does not follow from this distinction that self-determined attributes are less real or actual for God. In the section below, we will explore the essential and the contingent attributes of God.

Hence, with these concepts in mind, we can more clearly affirm:

a. that God's essence does not require God to create;
b. that God does in actuality freely create a world;
c. that God is lovingly and self-determinately affected in God's actuality by this creating and by the world so created;
d. even though God's essence is unchanged and not affected by this creating;
e. God's essence is just what it is and is immutably present in the actuality of God's life with the world.

Therefore, the distinction between God's essence and God's actuality allows us to affirm:

a. God's triune essence as Father, Son, and Holy Spirit;

---

[66] The locution 'Primordial Trinity' I obtain from Moltmann, though I do not claim that I am developing the same concept as he. See Jürgen Moltmann, *The Spirit of Life: A Universal Affirmation*, trans. Margaret Kohl (Minneapolis: Fortress, 1992), 292, 299.

b. living, free, self-determining love as the essence of God;

c. that God loves within God's life in the modes of God's being;

d. that God's actuality is always more inclusive than God's essence;

e. that God's essence [Godhead, *Gottheit*] does not do anything and only has reality as included in the actuality of God's life;

f. that in essence God could have been God without creating a world;

g. that God's actual life now is free, self-determining love with and for the world;

h. that God freely and lovingly creates a world, covenants with the world and Israel, is incarnate in the Palestinian Jew Jesus of Nazareth for the salvation of all creatures, and moves vitally among creatures to bring them to a redemptive future with Godself.

This distinction also enables us to speak of an appropriate *sequentiality to God's triune Actuality*. As the Primordial Trinity, *God was actual*—in a peculiar sense—even *before* the creation of the world. God does not first become actual in creating a world. But God did actually create a world with the positing of creaturely space and time full of creatures, and God does actually continue to create and govern the world. God did actually elect, liberate, and covenant with Israel and does have an ongoing, promissory covenantal life with Israel. God the eternal Son actually became incarnate in Jesus of Nazareth at a particular point in creaturely time. God was not incarnate before this time. God actually calls creatures toward a not-yet-actual future redemption and consummation. Hence, God in self-determining love does have a sequential actual life with and for the world. We cannot escape, as much of the classical tradition tried to escape, the peculiar sense in which there is a *before*, a *with*, and an *after* in God's actuality. This is a key to what we might mean by God's *eternal Life*.

In sum, *God the Actual Primordial Trinity self-determinately becomes the Actual Economic Trinity. Thus God self-determinately becomes—acts and is acted upon—in having a sequential, interactive Actual triune Life with the world.*

Recapitulating

Since this has been a conceptually strenuous section, let me recapitulate some points. I am arguing that without the distinction between God's essence and God's actuality, we could not talk intelligibly of God's actual free and loving triune life with the world. Without this distinction, one is tempted to make every attribute or character and every action of God's actuality to be an essential trait, and thereby necessary for God to be God. With that misleading grammatical rule, when we affirm that God is incarnate in Jesus Christ, it looks like being so incarnate has to be a metaphysical necessity for God—which of course negates it being a free and gracious action of God.

Further, this distinction between God's essence and actuality alleviates some of the misgivings about using the model of God as a single Subject; it makes it clearer than Augustine does, for example, that this single Subject is tri-moded with real distinctions and dynamic actions among the modes themselves in relation to the world. An Augustinian divine single subject who is immutable and impassible does in conceptual fact obliterate the distinct persons of the Trinity.

Also, when we want to affirm strongly that God is affected in God's deepest actuality by becoming incarnate in Jesus Christ, and therefore that it is impossible to say that God is in all respects immutable and impassible, it looks like we must say that mutability itself is a metaphysical necessity for God. Hence, by virtue of the distinction between God's essence and God's actuality and with the priority given to the actuality, we can say that God in actuality has a free, self-determining life of love with the world—without having to say that this life is itself a metaphysical necessity for God to be God. Neither classical theism nor process theism is able to keep this grammar straight and intelligible for a God who is triune in essence and actuality and who becomes incarnate in Jesus Christ for the salvation of the world.

The Grammar of the Immanent Trinity

The distinction between God's essence and God's actuality enables us to speak more aptly of the immanent Trinity. The concept of the immanent Trinity has had a tortuous history, full of confusion and needless debate. The locution 'immanent Trinity' has variously been used to refer to: (a) God *in se*, or God-in-Godself or God as internally related among Father, Son, and Holy Spirit; (b) God *in se* as distinct from God-in-relation-to-the-world; (c) God's essence; and (d) the deepest reality of God.

The first point to emphasize is that everything we say about the immanent Trinity is derived from what we say about the economic Trinity. The grammar of the immanent Trinity is derived from the economy of God's self-identifying interactions with the world. The actuality of God's triune Life with the world is the epistemic priority. We do not first know God in Godself and then deduce what God does in the world.

The next point is that the *concept of the immanent Trinity affirms that God is not just triune in salvation history but is actually triune in Godself [God in se]*. I stressed this by saying that God is actually who God is *in the being-in-acts* of God's history of self-revelations. There is not a more primordial and more real God *hidden behind* the economic Trinity who may only be a simple monad without internal distinctions. By saying that God is immanently in Godself triune, the concept of the immanent Trinity helped ward off modalism, which argued that the manifestations of the Father, Son, and Holy Spirit did not affect God's own internal reality. So, God is triune in Godself and not merely triune in relation to the world.

The concept of the immanent Trinity has also been used to affirm and preserve the freedom of God in relation to the world. God *in se*—God in God's immanent and eternal self-relations—is self-sufficient in love among the Father, Son, and Spirit, and therefore God does not need the world in order to be the loving God. That God does create a world of nondivine creatures and has an economic life with the world is God's own free decision; the world is not necessary to God. Thus far the distinctions developed in the previous discussions about God's freedom and love and about God's essence and actuality were in support of the interests of this understanding of the immanent Trinity. Without this concept of the immanent Trinity, the economic Trinity is vulnerable to the interpretation that it is a single, necessary unfolding of the divine reality, such that God becomes God only in and with the world. Hegel succumbed to this temptation.

But the peril to the doctrine of God comes when this concept of the immanent Trinity is combined with the concept of God's impassibility and immutability. These concepts require, then, that the immanent Trinity remain immutably and impassibly self-sufficient and unaffected by the economic Trinity's life with the world and that this immanent Trinity is the *innermost real being of God*. This peril—which subverts any proper understanding of the Triune Actuality of God's Life with the world—can be avoided by maintaining the distinction developed above between God's essence, which is unchangeable and necessary structure, and God's actuality, which lives, acts, and can become.

The concept of the immanent Trinity has also been used to affirm God being triune and actual even *before* the creation of the world. Even granting the paradoxical character of this *before*, we do need to affirm that God is actually God before self-determining Godself to be Creator of the world. Using a term of Moltmann's, I have called this triune actuality of God before the creation of the world the Primordial Trinity—God is primordially actual as triune even before the creation of the world. This concept of the Primordial Trinity denies that God first became actually God only with God's economic life with the world. We can now say: *the triune Primordial Subject becomes the triune Economic Subject creating and interacting with the world.* Hence, in God's Primordial Triune Actuality God has the power or potential to become the Economic Triune Actuality. We will further extend this analysis of God's actuality by referring to the eschatological actuality of God as the *Triune Consummating Actuality.* Hence, the sequentiality of God's triune Life is from the Primordial Life to the Economic Life to the Consummating Life.

Remembering that in the grammatical usage developed earlier, the term 'essence' does not mean 'that which is most real,' but simply means 'necessary structure without which something could not be what it is,' we can affirm that God is in essence triune. It is necessary to God's being God that God is Father, Son, and Holy Spirit. This denies that God is first a simple one or monad who *becomes* triune by becoming incarnate. Rather, God is already triune in essence as Father, Son, and Holy Spirit.[67] Yet if we did not now have the distinction between essence and actuality in God, it would look like we had to say it was a necessary character of God's actuality that God became incarnate in Jesus. So, without saying the Incarnation is an essential necessity of God, we can say the Son *actually becomes* historically incarnate as Jesus of Nazareth. This affirmation of God's essence as triune also denies that God has an essence that has three instantiations. God's essence has one instantiation as the tri-moded Subject.

Given the priority of God's actuality, we should never say the triune essence of God is some life of God *apart* from the world. *And we must never identify God* in se *with God's essence.* God in Godself or God *in se*

---

[67] In using the names Father, Son, and Holy Spirit, I am simply affirming that the givenness of these names in the economy of God's life with the world is the only ground for identifying God's internal life. The distinctions and the interanimation among the modes of God's actuality as manifest in the triune self-identifications of God are thereby maintained as internal to God.

is simply the internal relatedness within God of God's actual triune Life, both primordially and economically. Yet interior to God's life with the world, there are real relations among the Father, the Son, and the Spirit, and these relations are affected by the actuality of God's living with and for the world. So, God's actuality always has an internal relatedness among the Father, Son, and Holy Spirit, but also, as we know it in the economy of God's acts, a real relatedness to the world. Hence, we should never say the essential Trinity is the immanent Trinity.

In self-determined actuality, God is the Creator, Reconciler, and Redeemer of the world—and being all this affects God's living actuality. And yet, in order to affirm the freedom and love of God's actuality, we can say that God is in essence a tri-moded Subject as Father, Son, and Holy Spirit, and would be this if God had never determined Godself to become the Creator of a world. In this connection it should be grammatically intelligible why we cannot simply identify in scope of meaning of the set of names 'Father, Son, and Holy Spirit' with the set of names 'Creator, Reconciler, and Redeemer': *in essence God is not Creator, Reconciler, and Redeemer, but God is in essence the three modes of Father, Son, and Holy Spirit. And in God's Primordial Triune Actuality God is not Creator, Reconciler, and Redeemer, though God has the power to become those.*

In sum, immanent Trinity talk becomes less confusing by saying:

a.   God in essence is triune.
b.   God *in se* is triune.
c.   God's living Actuality includes God's essence and God *in se*.
d.   God in Primordial Actuality is triune.
e.   God in Economic Actuality with the world is triune.

The Grammar of God's Essential Attributes

The traditions have not been consistent either as to the content of God's attributes or their derivation and order. For our purposes, an attribute of God is a *characterizing trait* of God. It characterizes the actuality of God in some way. The proposal here is that God is being characterized on the basis of God's self-communications in the history of Israel, in Jesus Christ, and in the calling of the church. In the previous discussion I have proposed a distinction between those attributes which comprise the essence of God and those attributes that are comprised by God's own self-determined relations with the world. I have also argued that freedom and love have a constitutive centrality in God's triune self-identifications. Therefore, these two attributes will be controlling for how we describe the other attributes of God.

It is obvious from the church's actual discourse to and about God that there are innumerable ways in which we can describe God in human language. In the midst of these rich images, metaphors, and parables of God, why do we bother to sort out those concepts called the 'attributes of God'? The reason is precisely that in the midst of such rich possibilities, the church needs some grammatical guidance as to how to determine appropriate and inappropriate—faithful and truthful—language about God. In addition, then, to the self-identifications of God that we have discussed, we need to focus on those crucial traits of God that govern the many other images we might apply to God. Once we understand the grammar of God's attributes, we will be in a better position to interpret and apply a plethora of metaphors, images, and parables to God's actuality. Obviously, our earlier discussion of *analogia fidei* of the biblical witness will itself guide our understanding of the attributes of God, and the attributes will help guide the interpretation and use of the many analogies of God in that Scriptural witness.

What then is an essential attribute? *An essential attribute is a characterizing trait of God that is necessary to God and without which God could not actually be God.* In other words, God's actuality—as we know it in God's triune economic Life—would be inconceivable without the essential attributes. While all the essential attributes are manifest in all of God's actuality, I have further stipulated that the essential attributes simply of themselves do not necessitate that God create a world and have an interactive life with the world. But given that—in actuality—God does freely create a world, the essential traits are present in all of God's actual Life with the world.

The essential attributes comprise the essence of God. To that extent they are the immutable structure of God's actuality. But remember, the essence of God is not another subject: the essence of God is predicated of God the living triune Subject. I am claiming that *it is essential that God is a Subject who has the attributes of being triune, free, loving, almighty, living, eternal, and wise.* These attributes are the necessary structure of God being God as we know God in the economic Trinity. God is these attributes unchangeably, immutably. Accordingly, I say God does not *decide* to have these attributes. But *how* God deploys these attributes in relation to the world is a free and loving self-determination of God who is the almighty, living, eternal, wise, and triune Subject.

Hence, I am making a distinction between those attributes of God that are essential to God being God and those attributes of God that are freely and lovingly self-determined by God in relation to the world, which God has freely and contingently created. So we have essential attributes and self-determined attributes in relation to the world.[68]

With the traditions I want to affirm that there is no distinction between God as the triune Subject and the essential attributes. In being the triune Subject, God is simply the one who is these attributes. God does not *have* the attributes in the sense that maybe some other actuality might have the attributes as well. God is not in a class of objects that have the attributes. Hence, there is no distinction between God the Subject and the attributes. God is the actual Subject who uniquely possesses these attributes.

We must remember that *God is a Person-Subject* on analogy with human personhood. God is that person-subject who is a tri-moded center of activity and life. As such a subject, God is an indissoluble *I* who can be apprehended and known as a *thou*. But as this indissoluble *I*, God has three ways of being *I*. I am, accordingly, denying that God is better characterized as 'being-itself' or '*esse ipsum*,' as though these impersonal names or traits are somehow more basic to the actuality of God than being the almighty self-determining loving triune Subject.

As I have already argued, I am decentering and dissolving the function of the traditional *negative attributes* of God: immutability, impassiblity, and simplicity. The further traditional negative attributes of infinity and eternality are being significantly redrawn. God is infinite only in the sense that God is unencumbered by any limitation in God's actual life that is other than God's own self-determined limitation and conditionedness. Without the centrality of God's freedom to self-limit and condition Godself, the attribute of infinity would seem to make it obscure how God could be affected by the world and become incarnate in the world. The attribute of eternality will not be conceived below as primarily a negation of temporality.

The *Essential Attributes of God* are:

a.   God is Triune.

b.   God is Free.

---

[68] Since the traditions have not wanted to distinguish between God's essence and God's actuality, there is likewise no prior concept in the traditions between essential attributes and self-determined attributes.

   c. God is Love.
   d. God is Almighty.
   e. God is Living.
   f. God is Eternal.
   g. God is Wise.
   h. God is Necessarily Actual.

Since we have already investigated the attributes of God's freedom and God's love, I will not further discuss them in specifics below. But it should be remembered that the dialectic between God's freedom and love is basic to all the other attributes.

God Is Triune

In distinction from the traditions, I contend that tri-unity is an essential attribute of God insofar as God is the triune subject in all of God's life. In naming tri-unity as an essential attribute, I thereby block any grammar which would suppose we can first name the traditional attributes of divinity and then turn to talking about the Trinity of God. That approach runs the peril of developing a concept of God's essence, which—when it finally turns to talking about God's tri-unity—cannot avoid the slide into saying that there are three subjects who have the essential attributes. This is the peril of tritheism. But we block this tritheistic inclination when we make tri-unity an essential attribute of God, and therefore there is the one Subject who is triune in essence.

It is of the essence of God to be Father, Son, and Holy Spirit in eternal distinction, interrelatedness, and interanimation. And all the essential attributes are attributes of God the triune Subject. Hence, triune internal relatedness is essential to God, without which God is not God. In affirming essential triuneness in God, we block any grammar that says God *becomes* triune in becoming creator and becoming incarnate. Further, we block any grammar that says God's tri-unity—as seen in God's economic life with the world—requires God to be Creator and Redeemer in order to be God.

God Is Almighty

The subject matter of this attribute is *God's power*. But I am veering away from using the traditional term 'omnipotence.' It is my contention that this term has created needless confusions in the church's life and language about God's power. The traditional concepts invite inappropriate abstractions.[69] Hence, I reject the following possible meanings of omnipotence. First, I reject the claim that God has all the power there is. If all power is God's, then this seems to deny any power to creatures and moves inexorably in the direction of pantheism or monism. If God is simply all the power there is, then there is no reality beyond or different from God. Second, I reject the claim that God is absolute power as such and without restriction. In tradition this was called God's *potentia absoluta*. This would make God's power utterly arbitrary and unrestricted, which Barth claims is more nearly power as demonic.[70] Christians do not worship power as such and without further characterization. I have argued earlier that *God's power is always the power of God's love, and hence there is no unrestricted power of God that is prior to God's love.*

It is sufficient for our grammar of God's power to say first that *as Almighty, God has the power to be actual as the triune Person-Subject who loves in freedom.* In this sense, God has the power to be God and therefore the power to execute God's own self-determining and loving Life that we know in God's self-revelations to Israel and in Jesus Christ. Whatever is affirmed of God's triune Life with the world affirms God's power to be and enact that Life. *God's power, therefore, is manifested in all God's other attributes as the power of God to be God.* All the attributes of God are powers of God.

Second, *as Almighty, God is the sovereign power in relation to the world: power to create nondivine actualities, power to order the nondivine world, power to reconcile and redeem the world.* There is no other power as strong and effective as God, and there is no power superior to God. While there are other powers in the world, all these other powers have their power only under divine creation and permission. None of their powers derives from a source that is other than God, and they all exist under the permission of God.

Third, *as Almighty, God has power sufficient to accomplish all God's purposes in creating, governing, reconciling, and redeeming the world.* Without abandoning God's own sovereignty in relation to the world, God has the power, for example, as we discern in God's economic life:

a.   to self-determinately limit God's power;

---

[69] For an exacting and dismantling analysis of omnipotence in Aquinas, see Anthony Kenny, *The God of the Philosophers* (Oxford: Clarendon Press, 1979), 91–117.
[70] Barth, *Church Dogmatics*, II/1, 524.

b. to become vulnerable to nondivine powers and actualities;

c. to become incarnate in a human life and suffer a human death;

d. to raise dead human beings to redemptive life;

e. to persuade and empower humans to respond in faith.

Fourth, it should now be clear that *as Almighty, God has the power to decide among possibilities and to enact possibilities*. There is no possibility that God decides to enact and yet lacks the power to enact. Decision and enactment—as the constitutive concepts in talking about God's will—go hand in hand. What God wills, God decides and enacts.[71]

We should not look for only one paradigm of God's power, such as saying all God's power is *persuasive power*—which is the claim of some process theologians. This omits, however, God's power to create—to posit nondivine creatures in being—and God's power to become incarnate and die a human death and to raise a dead person from the grave. Hence, while God is marvelously persuasive in many of God's actions, it is abstract and inappropriate to the economic Trinity to say all God's power is persuasive.

We can avoid saying—as some traditions say—that God's power is complete and eternally actual: God as *Pure Actuality*. Rather, I say God has potency, potentiality, power yet unused. This sense of God's potency is crucial to our understanding of God's eternality as involving sequentiality with the world of creaturely time. And, in denying that God is utterly simple, we have also become conceptually empowered to affirm a distinction between God's potentiality and God's actuality. But we can say *God is the prius of all actuality*, without saying that God is Pure Actuality without any potentiality.[72] As prius of all actuality, God is the sovereign source of all other creaturely actualities.

---

[71] In the doctrine of creation in chapter five, I will explore a further differentiated way of talking about various aspects of God's will.

[72] See the insightful essay by Austin Farrer, "The Prior Actuality of God," in Austin Farrer, *Reflective Faith: Essays in Philosophical Theology*, ed. Charles C. Conti (Grand Rapids, Mich.: Eerdmans, 1972), 178–191. It seems to me Farrer did not yet have his grip on this essential point in the earlier Deems Lectures of 1964: Austin Farrer, *Faith and Speculation: An Essay in Philosophical Theology* (New York: New York University Press, 1967), especially 131–170. I think it is clear that throughout Farrer's brilliant early work, *Finite and Infinite: A Philosophical Essay* (Westminster, U.K.: Dacre, 1943), he asserts the belief that God is Pure Act.

God Is Living

In affirming God is Living, we pick up the biblical affirmation that God lives and is the source of all other life. *The primary feature of life is its power to be active, to move, to have energy.* As living, God is self-moving, self-actualizing, self-determining in love. This attribute thus denies that God is fundamentally immobile, unmoving, immutable, impassible, and frozen in eternal stasis—which are the features of lifelessness and death. It is peculiarly the work of the Holy Spirit to be the constituting source of life in those creatures that have *psyche* and *pneuma*, soul and spirit.

Because God is living we can openly admit that God has the power to become, to self-move, to be affected by other actualities in time. Only a living God could genuinely suffer, as we must affirm about God if there is any sense to the belief that the incarnate Son suffered human death on the cross. But even further, in suffering up to and in death, the life of the Son overcomes death as the last word about human beings. Here we are reaching toward the affirmation that God's Life is eternal Life.

As with all the other interanimations of all the essential attributes, the attribute of living is simply God's way of being triune, free, loving, almighty, eternal, and wise.

God Is Eternal

As eternal, God is everlasting, imperishable, and without beginning and end. God's actuality does not begin sometime, does not conclude sometime, does not absolutely perish and die even in its appropriate sequentiality. Eternity is simply God's living actuality, whether without the world or with the world.

I do not begin this discussion of eternality by way of the negation of time in which God is sheer *timelessness*. This has been a misleading concept of the traditions. To be sure, time itself is a condition of the creature in which there is before and after and perishing. As eternal, God is in *contrast* to creaturely time, without simply being the antithesis or negation of creaturely time. If God were sheer timelessness, then God would not be free to have time for the creature, to be affected by the creature's time or by its perishing and finitude.

Because the incarnation of the eternal Son is precisely God's Life

under the conditions of time without being defeated and completely determined by creaturely time, we must conceive God's eternality as open
to being in and including creaturely time. And because God is actual
even *before* the creation of the world and *will be actual* everlastingly,
God's eternality has a *sequentiality* of *before, with, and after* that is
uniquely God's Life. God is eternal as the One who is actual before
creaturely time, is interactive with the creature in time, and will be actual
in the Consummation of all time and creatures. Here we are revising the
tradition's grammar about God's eternity as the sheer negation of any sequentiality in God's life. But in God's own sequential life, *there is no
absolute perishing in the movement from 'before' to 'with' to 'after.'* In
this sense, then, God has a constancy of living endurance and persistence
in the sequentialities of God's life.

However, even though I am granting sequentiality in God's life, I am
wary of saying that God's eternality is merely God's infinite and everlasting extension in time. This is the position of process theology. Insofar
as I regard time itself to be peculiarly created by God and therefore
creaturely, I see no need to conceive God as being wholly and completely subject to time in all of God's living actuality. Further, creaturely
time, I claim, is finite and therefore has a beginning and end, whereas
God is without beginning and end. The biblical concept most appropriate
here is 'everlasting,' if we can shear from it the notion that God is merely
the infinite extension of time. In our sense of eternity, God is everlasting
in that God is without beginning and end in time.[73]

I also eschew the grammar of eternality in which God is pure duration and simultaneity, which is typically associated with Boethius and
seemingly embraced by Barth. This is the notion that God simultaneously is present to past, present, and future. Not only does this require the
future to 'already' exist in some sense for God, but its root problem is
that it depends on the concept of God as pure actuality in which there is
no potency for becoming in God.[74]

When I say that God does not perish absolutely, I am not denying
that the eternal Son dies a human death on the cross. For crea-

---

[73] See the interesting article by Nicholas Wolterstorff, "God Everlasting," in
God and the Good, ed. Clifton Orebeke and Lewis Smedes (Grand Rapids,
Mich.: Eerdmans, 1975), 181–203.

[74] See Boethius, *The Consolation of Philosophy*, V, 6: "Eternity is total, simultaneous, and perfect possession of unlimited life." [*Aeternitas est interminabilis vitae tota simul et perfecta possessio.*] See Boethius, *The Consolation of
Philosophy*, trans. W. V. Cooper (New York: Random House, 1943), 115ff.

tures—simply considered in terms of their own finite powers—death is perishing as ceasing to be in any sense. In dying a human death, the eternal Son does experience and endure this creaturely perishing and ceasing to be, but this is not the absolute perishing of ceasing to be divine. It is precisely the Son's eternal life that does not absolutely perish and cease to be God, though now he suffers the perishing conditions of human death. A concept of God's eternality that cannot handle the dimensions of Jesus' death and resurrection—which the concept of eternity as sheer negation of time cannot—is not a satisfactory grammar of eternality.

God Is Wise

The usual formulation here is to refer to the attribute of omniscience, God's power of knowledge, of knowing everything. However, this formulation invites some abstract questions that can obscure the more important point that God's knowing is always God's loving knowledge. Hence, I will use the concept of God's wisdom [*Sophia*] to discuss God's knowledge.

First, *God's wisdom is God's own internal knowings, relatings, and communications as Father, Son, and Holy Spirit.* God is wise within God's own complex and interanimated Life. Fundamentally I am saying that God first knows and apprehends Godself in that Father, Son, and Spirit are three ways of being an apprehending subject who relates to that which is other. This internal self-knowledge of God is also manifest in the transactions between Father and Son in which the Father knows the Son and suffers in the knowing and the Son knows the Father in his otherness and distance, and these knowings are both God knowing God.

Second, *God is wise as the fount of all truth, of cosmic order and purpose, of loving knowledge.* As wise there is no truth that is not rooted in God's living actuality, and therefore all truth is coherent with God's Life. This is truth both as that which is the case and that which is authentic and normative. It is the wisdom of God that is the ground of both senses of truth.

Third, *as wise, God provides order and purpose in the bringing to be of the creaturely world.* God provides—envisages, foresees—the creation and its needs. It is out of God's wisdom that God creates a world and engages in an interactive history with the creation.

Fourth, *the wisdom of God is manifest in the cross of Jesus Christ, and stands in contrast to the truth-claiming—the authenticating purposes and ordering—of the human social worlds.* [1 Cor 1.18–31] Herein we understand that God's cosmic wisdom is at heart the wisdom of God's reconciling and redemptive love in the weakness and vulnerability of the cross of Jesus. Here we can also place Jesus as the enacted Word of God, manifesting wisdom and truth. Or more sharply, *Jesus is the incarnate Wisdom of God.*

Fifth, *as wise, God knows all there is to know.* Nothing—no creature and no falsehood—can hide from God's knowing. Nothing escapes God's knowing. God's knowing is thus the standard of all truth and knowledge. If there is any primary meaning to the locution 'objective truth,' it is God's knowledge. Oddly enough—though contrary to the human sense that to be objective is to be neutral and uninvolved—God's knowing is the knowing of passionate love. Hence, God's truth never intends neutrality or apathy but life and authenticity. It is this truth that sets persons free. It is in this respect that God lovingly communicates with and speaks to the human creature, disclosing the truth and authenticity of creaturely life.

There is a lingering grammatical quandary: should we say God knows the future even before the future has happened? To say God does eternally know all of the creaturely future suggests that in some profound ontological sense the future has *already happened before God.* But this seems to conflict with our saying God gives the creature relative independence and permits the creature to have an interactive life with other creatures and with God. I propose saying that God's eternal wisdom does not require that God knows everything in the future. But I am not thereby denying that God's wisdom—as the beneficent fount of order and purpose—might place limits on historical outcomes and that therefore God does know in advance these limits. Further, that God's almighty power is the power to accomplish God's purposes does not require that God knows every event before it happens. But *God's wisdom is so penetrating that God does know—and suffers often in the knowing—the potentiated trajectories of human lives and societies.*

God Is Necessarily Actual

That God is necessarily actual is an odd attribute of God that has come to the fore in recent discussions of the ontological argument. Without endorsing the ontological argument as a sound noncircular argument, I can affirm that for Christian grammar it is an attribute of God that God is necessarily actual. Given who we otherwise think God is, it is inconceivable to us that God could not be actual. This means that it is inconceivable that God could cease being God. Whatever someone might conceive to be God and then wonder whether that God exists is not yet the conception of God we have been developing in this Christian grammar. This is the point of saying God is necessarily actual.

But the attribute is 'necessarily actual.' This does not make every *how* of God's actuality necessary. God does *not* freely and lovingly choose *whether* to be actual, and God cannot choose to be nonactual. But, in ways consistent with God's own essence, God can choose *how to be actual*, how to be self-determining love. Similarly we can say that God does not choose to be triune, free, loving, almighty, living, eternal, and wise. God is all these attributes necessarily. These attributes are the essential structure of God; they are God's essence. But God does self-determinately decide how to be actual with this structure of attributes and powers. God's actuality is always fully under the sovereign control of God. And in this sense, all of God's essential attributes are actual only in God's living self-determining actuality.

In line with points previously made, while it is impossible for God to cease being God, it is not impossible for God to die a human death. Hence, the essential actuality of God can encompass human death and perishing within its own eternal life.

The Grammar of God's Self-Determined Relational Attributes

In addition to God's essential attributes, which characterize all of God's actuality, some attributes of God's actuality *presuppose nondivine actualities, or creatures,* and therefore characterize God's self-determined relationality with those actualities. As self-determinations of God's loving life, these attributes are not less real than the essential attributes. Take God's mercy: being merciful is certainly an attribute of God's relational interaction with the world, but we would not know what it means to say God is merciful in essence. God is loving in essence and this essential love of God is the root of God's mercy in relation to the world of sinners. But God's mercy is a self-determination of God's life with the world. *These are the attributes—in addition to the essential attributes—which in particular characterize God's actuality as Creator, Reconciler, and Redeemer of the world of creatures.*

God Is Perfect

God is perfect in all of God's relationships with the world: perfect as the One who is undivided and integral in all relationships; perfect as the One who is never deficient or lacking in God's relationships; perfect as the One who is the measure of all other life and its fulfillment. Hence, God is perfect in love and freedom, perfect in becoming incarnate and suffering on the cross and in rising from human death.

I am contending perfection is an attribute of God's relationships with the world in order to negate those traditions which affirmed God's perfection as God's self-sufficiency as the supremely simple, immutable, and impassible One. Hence, the model of perfection in the traditions became that which is unrelated, untouched by others and self-sufficient unto itself, which is directly antithetical to God's love and the love Christians are to practice in their relationships. In opposition to this tradition, I emphasize God's perfection precisely in God's self-determined Life in and with and on behalf of the world and therefore in integral actions and relationships with the world. In those relationships God lacks nothing and does not suffer deficiencies.

Thomas Aquinas's discussion of the attribute of perfection did not have to eventuate as it did in affirming God's lack of real relationship with the world. It is altogether consistent with the grammar I am developing to say with Aquinas that what is perfect lacks nothing with respect to actuality. But this means for Aquinas that the perfect therefore has no potentiality yet to be actualized, for to have such potentiality is to be in a state of lack and need. Hence, God being fully actual—Pure Actuality—needs nothing.[75] While I agree that God in essence and even in primordial actuality needs nothing beyond God in order to be God, I have argued that God does in actuality create a world and enter into interactive relationships with the world. This living actuality of God has potentiality but lacks nothing necessary to the enactment of God's own self-determining life with the world. Thus, having developed the distinction between God's essence and God's actuality, I am not obliged to think of God's perfection as implying God's self-sufficiency—unaffected by and independent from the world.

When we are counseled to be perfect as our heavenly Father is per-

---

[75] See the discussion of the attribute of perfection in St. Thomas Aquinas, *Summa Theologiae* [Ia. 4], vol. 2, *Existence and Nature of God (Ia. 2–11)*, trans. Timothy McDermott (New York: McGraw-Hill, 1964), 48–59.

fect [Mt 5.48], we are not being counseled to be supremely self-sufficient and unaffected by others. Rather, we are being counseled to lovingly give of ourselves to others in the way in which God has lovingly given of Godself to the world.

God Is Omnipresent

According to the biblical testimony, God has supreme and unique powers of being present to creatures. But saying God is present *everywhere*, which is the first meaning of 'omnipresence,' does not help us much. We need a grammar of the *various ways in which God is present in the world of creatures*. We must resist the grammar that talks in undifferentiated ways about the omnipresence of God. God has different ways of being present in, to, and with the creature.

First, everything to be affirmed about God's presence in the world is affected by the *definitive presence of God in Jesus of Nazareth*. This radical presence is the presence of identity: God the eternal Son *is* Jesus. It is this presence that we call *Incarnation*, and therefore, in its radical uniqueness, it is not as such a general concept of God's presences in the world. Therefore, it is conceptually confusing to speak of God's presences in the world as *incarnations of God*; God is incarnate only in Jesus. But God's incarnate presence in Jesus does centrally affirm that God can be and is present in the world in multiple ways.

Second, *God is always free in God's multiple presences to creatures in the world*. Hence, God's presence is never a property of the creature, and therefore under the possession and control of the creature. In being present to the creature, God remains distinct from and sovereign over the creature.

Third, *all creaturely times and spaces, and therefore all creaturely actualities, are open to the presence of God*. The world is not sealed up in itself and closed to God. There is no time or place absolutely closed off to God. Hence, no creature, as creature, is ever beyond the reach and power of God's presence. [Ps 139.7–12]

Fourth, *God has multiple ways of being present to the creature*; I will call these *modes of presence*, which follow the modes of actuality of the triune God. First, God is present to the creature in the *mode of the creative ground of the creature's being and life*—the mode of the Father/Creator. No creature is without this creative presence of God. Second, God is present to the creature in the *mode of encounter with the creature*—the mode of the eternal Son or Word of God. In this mode God meets the creature, communicates to the creature, confronts the creature as an *I* being received as a *thou*. Last, God is present to the creature in the *mode of empowerment within the creature's life*—the mode of the Spirit of God. The Spirit's presence does not displace the creature; creatures are *permeable* to the Spirit's presence. In short, God is present to the creature in all God's relationships with the creature. In all the modes of God's presence, God is giving of God's own life and power.

Fifth, *there are also different and multiple configurations of God's presence*; I will call these *modalities of presence*. These are configurations in which God is diversely present to the creature; we do not need to have only one paradigm of presence. Such modalities of presence are God's presence at Sinai, in the giving and sustaining of Torah, in worship, in the Lord's Supper, in preaching, in prayer; in other words, the many configurations of God being *under, to, with, and within* the creature's life. Think also of God's presence in suffering companionship.

God may be present in one mode without being present in another. For example, God is always present in the mode of the creative ground of the creature's life, but God is not always present as the One who encounters the creature. And God may be present in one modality of presence and not in another. Here we have the possibility of the creature experiencing the *absence of God*. In the many contours of the creature's life, God may not be experienced as a present and nurturing *I*, though in fact God is always present as creative ground. But God is in fact never absent as the Triune Ultimate Companion of all creatures.

God Is Holy and Righteous

As Holy, God's life is infinitely differentiated from all creaturely life, and yet as Holy, God is the ground of all life. God's presence to the creature, as the infinitely differentiated presence of One who is freely present, is always *holy presence—awesome presence not under the control of creature.* As the Holy One, God's Life solicits the creature's gratitude, respect, awe, and acknowledgment of the infinite differentiation between God and the creature.

As Holy, God is supremely *Good and Righteous*. As Good and Righteous, God is the sovereign founder and determiner of right relations and right order between God and creatures and among creatures. This righteousness determines what is God's due from the creature and what is the creature's due from God and others. God's justice obtains when God's righteous order is effective. But God is righteous in relationships with the creature for the creature's own good and flourishing. In this sense, God's righteousness is teleologically ordered to the flourishing of the creature before God. So, we can never articulate God's righteousness independent of affirming that it is the Holy Righteousness of the God of Israel who becomes incarnate on behalf of the sinful creature and confers and summons the creature to a new righteousness of flourishing in grace. Without a firm grasp on God's righteousness, we could never fathom the meaning of Jesus' atoning life.

God Is Patient, Merciful, and Gracious

As *patient*, God freely and lovingly gives the creature actuality and space and time in which to live and enjoy God's righteous order of fruitful living and well-being. God *consents* to the actuality of the creature and gives the creature a relative power and independence.[76] God creates and permits creatures to live in the interacting world of other creatures. In patience God permits the doing of evil, the human rebellion against God's righteous and good order, as one of the possibilities of the creature's power. But God's patience is not unlimited: God does not ultimately leave the creature to its own devices and choices.

As *merciful*, God freely and lovingly comes to the rescue of the creature in distress and espouses the cause of the creature. It is this mercy which limits God's patience.[77]

As *gracious*, God freely and lovingly atones for the creature's sin, forgives the sin, seeks fellowship with the creature, and summons the creature to embrace freely new possibilities of living in love. This grace is not the creature's due; it is free gift. Remember: it was reflection on God's grace as free gift that precipitated the depth grammar of keeping God's freedom and love interrelated.

God's patience, mercy, and grace are God's free self-determinations

---

[76] The young Jonathan Edwards grasped well God's consenting to the being of the creature. See his early essay on Mind in *Puritan Sage: Collected Writings of Jonathan Edwards*, ed. Vergilius Ferm (New York: Library Publishers, 1953), especially 14–16, 30–33.

[77] Mercy and patience are seen powerfully together in Karl Barth, *Church Dogmatics*, II/1, 411. Much of my thinking on God's patience, mercy, and grace has been deepened by Barth.

in love to be affected by the life and actuality of the creature. We can summarize these attributes of the concrete openness of God to the creature as the *empathy of God*: God chooses to have life with the creature, to be moved and affected by the creature's life, and to suffer with the creature's misery and to suffer from the creature's rebellion and sin. And God is perfectly empathic, supremely and completely feeling and knowing the creature's situation. The remarkable point about God's empathy is that it is also God's almighty power and wisdom that do not merely suffer but also act mercifully and graciously to rescue and redeem the creature.

God Is Constant

The paradigm of God's constancy is not some abstract immutability and impassibility. Rather, God is One who is self-revealing and self-communicating to the creatures so that the creature can know and trust God as Creator, Reconciler and Redeemer of the creature. God is constant as the One who can be trusted and relied upon in the life of the creature. God's Life is not fickle and arbitrary and capricious: God is not an elusive and ineffable and unknown infinite power that arbitrarily disposes of creatures. God makes promises and self-communicates with creatures, and these can be trusted by the creature.

All the attributes of God are testimony to the constancy of the ways in which God is God in God's triune Life with the world. Hence, we are talking about constancy of character of a living person-subject. In these senses God is unchangeably the One who loves in freedom and is perfectly powerful in coming to the rescue of the creature. We affirm the constancy of God when we confess that—in spite of the obscurities and ambiguities of our lives—we can trust God's self-revelations as the *One who has been, is, and will be the Ultimate Companion of all creatures.*

The Grammar of God's Transcendence and Immanence

The uses of the terms 'transcendence' and 'immanence' are often quite confusing and have tortured histories. Mostly these terms are attempting to talk about how God is *both distinct and differentiated from the world* and *present in the world.* I have affirmed God's transcendence in our talk about God's distinctness, differentiation, self-determining freedom, and aseity. I have insisted that God is not the world but is the Creator, Reconciler, and Redeemer of the world. But I have avoided and critiqued the grammar of a transcendence that renders God immutable and impassible and unaffected by the world. Instead I have stressed God's infinitely self-determining ways in love of being God as essential to God's distinctness and transcendence of the world. And I have insisted that the transcendent God is the one who has a triune Life of interactions with the world.

With regard to the ambiguities of the word 'immanence,' I have avoided speaking of immanence in one way only or under one paradigm. God is *in* the world in multiple ways, as was affirmed in our grammar of omnipresence. But I have affirmed an immanence of God in the world that refuses to collapse God into the world or to render God indistinct from the world. God is not the world, and any concept of immanence that affirms that God is the world is contrary to the deep grammar of the Christian doctrine of God. God is not identical with the world, and God and the world do not simply share the same way of being actual. There is no univocal category of actuality of which both God and world partake. Hence, God and world are not to be added together to make up a greater whole.[78]

In the light of this doctrine of the triune God, I propose *these basic rules for talking about God's transcendence and immanence*:

a. God's immanence in the world is not simple *identity*; God is not the world.
b. God's transcendence of the world is not simple *separation from*.
c. It is always the transcendence of the God who is multiply immanent in the world.
d. It is always the immanence of the God who is freely immanent in the world and never the property of the world.
e. It is always the free and loving self-determined transcendence and presence of the triune God we know in God's self-identifications in and with and to the world.

In concluding this long chapter, it is well to remember that everything we say in the whole of Christian theology is saying something or implying something about God—about who God is and how God is to be characterized. Hence, the fullness of our account of God's triune Life is

---

[78] I fear Charles Hartshorne never grasped this grammar of Christian faith inasmuch as he continually thinks of God and world as univocal concepts and as related as whole to part. See especially Charles Hartshorne, *Divine Relativity: A Social Conception of God* (New Haven, Conn.: Yale University Press, 1948), 1–59.

not exhausted in this chapter. We will be exploring further in subsequent chapters how God is Creator of the world, the Reconciler of the world, and the Redeemer of the world, though we have adumbrated all these points already in our discussion.

Further, in this discussion I have concentrated primarily on some *syntactic and semantic* considerations peculiar to and definitive of the church's discourse about God and witness to God. It will require other sections to sketch more fully the *pragmatics* of the life of Christian faith, love, and hope in which it finally makes sense to talk of the triune God. I recognize that some of the reflections in this chapter have *seemed* unduly abstract and unavailable—perhaps even irrelevant—to practical faith. But the pragmatics of Christian grammar do not exist simply unto themselves; Christian pragmatics are formed by the syntactic and semantic concepts of identifying and talking about God. When the syntax is in profound disarray, such that anything goes in Christian grammar, then the pragmatics themselves are in disarray and confused.

I hope it is clear that we have been in quest of that deep grammar which helps us rule and generate further ways of talking about God. If this project has been successful, then we should see that the grammar being developed intends to be *generative* of further ways of using images, analogies, metaphors, parables, and stories to talk about and witness to God. Hence, this grammar of the triune God is not exhaustive of our linguistic witness to God: it is properly generative of the fullness of our witness.

Chapter Five

God the Creator:
Creation, Providence, and Evil

Orientation to the Doctrine

Belief in God the Creator of all things is foundational to Christian belief and is essentially trinitarian in content. But the approach to or interest in God the Creator in both the OT and the NT is primarily a function of soteriology. It is not: we believe in God the Creator but will God *save* us? Rather: we believe in the God who saves us, and this God is the Creator of all things. This is the priority in the OT to Yahweh being the One who liberates, and therefore is the One who creates the whole world. Hence, Creator and creation talk is not basically driven by curiosity about origins, and even the genuine interest in origins is an attempt to understand the present situation and the hope of salvation.

For Christian theology the God of Israel, the Creator of all things, is none other than the One who is definitively revealed in Jesus Christ and becomes thus incarnate in the world and is known through the Spirit. Therefore, the Christian belief in God the Creator does not sit on its own bottom unaffected by the self-revelation of God in Jesus Christ through the Spirit. The grammar of God the Creator is essentially the grammar of the self-revealing God who is triune in essence and actuality. Hence, I speak of God the Creator from the perspective of God's self-identifying communications and not on the basis of some presumed natural theology or metaphysical inferences from our experience of the world and its finitude. I remain in the sphere of the confessional grammar that speaks of the self-revealing triune God.[1]

Accordingly, we should distinguish between 'natural theology' and a 'theology of nature.' A *natural theology* is a theology that claims to identify God and establish God's existence on the basis of what we know about the world independently of God's self-revelation. It need not deny God's self-revelation, but it argues independent of that revelation. A *theology of nature* is simply theological reflection on the nature and value of the whole creation in relation to God and in relation to human stewardship. But the perspective from which such theologizing is executed can be either natural theology or revealed theology. Since I have already given reasons for being suspicious of a foundational natural theology, I will be exploring a theology of nature from the perspective of God's self-revelation. It should therefore become apparent that a theology of nature can be developed quite appropriately from a confessional theological basis that does not abandon the context of God's self-revealing triune work.

A Conviction of Faith

The belief in God the Creator is a theological, faith conviction. As a fundamental theological belief, the belief in the triune God who creates all things visible and invisible is a faith conviction: a construal of the world from the perspective of faith in the God we know in Jesus Christ. As a faith conviction the belief is self-involving, existential, and passionate in character, involving a whole way of life. It involves the everyday practice of regarding one's life as a gift of the loving Creator, and the practice of regarding the whole world as created and sustained by the free love of God. Hence, this grammar denies that one might—in the Christian sense—believe that there is a creator simply as a detached, non-self-involving belief. Put another way, one has not yet believed the Christian convictions about the Creator if one is not morally and spiritually shaped concretely by that belief. This shows again the intrinsically soteriological pragmatics of the conviction.

---

[1] The trinitarian context and content of the doctrine of creation are well-maintained in Colin E. Gunton, *The Triune Creator: A Historical and Systematic Study* (Grand Rapids, Mich.: Eerdmans, 1998). Gunton has also edited a useful discussion of current and classical issues in the doctrine of creation in *The Doctrine of Creation: Essays in Dogmatics, History, and Philosophy* (Edinburgh: T. & T. Clark, 1997).

As a faith conviction, this belief is one that the believer has *to learn* from the witnesses of the discourses and practices of the church. *These discourses are essential to the experience of the world as a world created by the triune God.* This is a construal of the world that is quite at odds with many other construals that have been prevalent in the history of humanity. Accordingly, our grammar *denies* that belief in the triune Creator is: (a) a belief that can simply be *read off* the perceived order of the world from a detached theoretical standpoint; or (b) a belief that basically arises from an aesthetic experience of the apparent harmony or beauty of the world—or of some aspect of the world; or (c) a belief that is rooted in some empirical sense of the purpose of all things in nature, and therefore is particularly supported by the so-called arguments from design. However, I do not deny that these beliefs and experiences might be important along the way of some person's route of faith or that they might finally be included as beliefs founded on the Christian understanding of God's self-revealed purposes in creating the world. But I am concerned that they not be understood as the *grounds* for the Christian belief in God as Creator of the world, and therefore of the meaning of the concept of Creator.

The doctrine of the Creator and creation is a *faith conviction about the reality of God.* Semantically, it is making a truth-claim about the reality of God as the One who is Ultimately Real and who has made God-self known in a history of self-revelations. The doctrine is also a *faith conviction about the reality and destiny of the world—of the whole cosmos.* Further, *it is a faith conviction about the meaning of being a creature.*[2] The Christian belief in the creation of the world by the triune God is, therefore, a *defiant and subversive belief* in the face of the many other tempting beliefs and practices about self and world. We should therefore be wary of assuming that the word 'Creator' always has the same grammar in its many uses in the discourses of the world.

---

[2] Donald D. Evans, *The Logic of Self-Involvement: A Philosophical Study of Everyday Language with Special Reference to the Christian Use of Language about God as Creator* (London: SCM, 1963) is a splendid examination of the self-involving character of Christian belief in God as Creator. But he virtually eliminates the truth-claiming character of that same self-involving language. My whole theory of the grammar of Christian discourse is designed to dismantle the common contrast by some theologians between Christian discourse as the passional language of faith and as the language of judgments and truth-claims.

Theology and Contemporary Science

In the discussion of norms and sources of theology, I identified contemporary learning as one of the possible sources of theological understanding and formulation. Clearly, such contemporary learning includes
the many diverse fields of inquiry, description, and explanation that we
call 'sciences.' Hence, it is appropriate that some of our theological understanding will use some of the descriptions, truth-claims, and explanations of these sciences. However, I also said that there is no *in-principle*
way in which the sciences *must be used* by Christian theology. Included
in this refusal to grant an in-principle procedure for the bearing of the
sciences on theology is the refusal to grant the sciences the privileged
status of being the *primary reality claims* in relation to which theology
must find some accommodating place for itself. That is, science is not
granted that status of determining what is *truly real,* leaving theology to
find its place in the midst of these truly real perspectives, models, and
claims. This refusal is not *hostile* in character. It simply says that theology does not wait around until the sciences have done their work to determine what reality claims it might feasibly still be entitled to make. It is
true, however, that since the rise of modern science in the seventeenth
century, interpreters of science and theology have often found themselves in apparent conflict over reality claims.[3] In this postmodern world,
science has come to be seen as a fallible, corrigible, and profoundly human endeavor—influenced and shaped by human interests and social
practices—that is continually in some flux in the search to describe and
explain the realities of the world.[4]

---

[3] See John Dillenberger, *Protestant Thought and Natural Science: A Historical Interpretation* (New York: Abingdon, 1960).

[4] The philosophy of science has been much preoccupied with understanding
the human context in which scientific investigation and reasoning work. See the
important work of Thomas S. Kuhn, *The Structure of Scientific Revolutions,* 2d
ed. (Chicago: University of Chicago Press, 1970). Paul K. Feyerabend, *Against
Method* (London: Verso, 1978) is a stringent critique of the presumed neutrality
of scientific methodology. Stephen Toulmin's *The Philosophy of Science* (London: Hutchinson University Library, 1953) and *Human Understanding* (Oxford:
Clarendon Press, 1972) are helpful. William C. Placher has an accessible discussion of science in *Unapologetic Theology: A Christian Voice in a Pluralistic
Conversation* (Louisville, Ky.: Westminster/John Knox, 1989), especially
24–54.

With the rise of quantum physics and chaos theories, one of the most dramatic changes in the perspectives of science is the repudiation of the Newtonian world in which the events of the temporal world are tightly determined by their preceding causes. I call this the 'billiard ball theory of cause and effect.' In its place is a view of the cosmos as an evolving and emerging order of actualities and events that are not simply and completely determined by antecedent causes. Instead the world is open to novelty, and the causal nexus is not an order of absolute determinism.

It is also the case that recent developments in astrophysics have posited a so-called big bang theory, whereby there is a primordial originative event many billions of years ago in which something first explodes into being and from which the whole cosmos to date has evolved and emerged. This originative event is said to be the 'beginning of space and time.'[5] This is an interesting scientific development, and while most of the theorists do not regard it as having anything to do with a god, it does suggest some fascinating considerations about the presumed paradoxicality of there being a *beginning to time*. But I would caution Christians about rushing to conclude that this new theory is evidence for the truth of the Christian doctrine of creation.

In general, the most controversial areas between the apparent claims of science and the claims and interests of Christian theology are: (a) the status and import of the theory of biological evolution and whether it conflicts with the Christian understanding of God's creative work and the origin of humanity;[6] (b) whether it makes sense to say 'God acts within the world'; and (c) whether purpose can be discerned in the evolving and emerging order of the world. I will discuss these questions in our ongoing exploration.

To the extent science proffers theories about how the universe has emerged, it is preoccupied with physical explanations and not purposive explanations of the world. It is too easy and is misleading to say that science is about the *how* of the world process and theology is about the *why*. Theology is interested in how the world process unfolds before God and

---

[5] See Stephen Hawking, *A Brief History of Time: From the Big Bang to the Black Hole* (New York: Bantam Books, 1988).

[6] See Svend Anderson and Arthur R. Peacocke, eds., *Evolution and Creation* (Aarhus, Denmark: Aarhus University Press, 1987); Langdon Gilkey, *Creationism on Trial: Evolution and God at Little Rock* (Minneapolis: Winston, 1985); and Ernan McMullin, ed., *Evolution and Creation* (Notre Dame, Ind.: University of Notre Dame Press, 1985).

in interaction with God. But there is no real investment of Christian belief in any literal rendering of the account in Genesis 1 as a description of the processive order by which God created in the beginning. The doctrine of God the Creator does, however, occasion questions about how God is involved in the processes of the world—how God acts in the world.

Christian theology has no interest either in demonizing or deifying contemporary science. In fact there are reasons to believe that an interesting rapprochement is possible in our time.[7] But I propose that we decide point by point just how science and theology interrelate, without deciding in advance how they *must* interrelate. It seems quite beyond serious controversy for Christian theology that: (a) the universe is billions of years old; (b) some sort of evolutionary development has taken place in the emergence of the universe from its earliest moments; (c) the universe has a size and extent so vast that it is hardly even imaginable; (d) the earth is possibly not the only place in the universe inhabited by what we call sentient and rational beings; and (e) the emergence of the earth as just the sort of place that has diverse forms of life is itself an improbable probability in scientific terms.[8]

'Creationism'

Among the more dreadful grammatical developments in our time is the rise of so-called creationism, which describes itself—and is accepted as such by the secular world—as 'the Christian doctrine of creation.' The confusions produced in the media and even in the church are so delete-

---

[7] For interesting discussions of the relation between theology and science, one of the most accessible and brief introductory discussions is John Polkinghorne, *Serious Talk: Science and Religion in Dialogue* (Valley Forge, Pa.: Trinity, 1995). See also Ted Peters, ed., *Cosmos as Creation: Theology and Science in Consonance* (Nashville, Tenn.: Abingdon, 1989); Arthur R. Peacocke, *Theology for a Scientific Age* (Oxford: Blackwell, 1990); Ian G. Barbour, *Religion in an Age of Science* (San Francisco: Harper and Row, 1990); and Vincent Brümmer, ed., *Interpreting the Universe as Creation: A Dialogue of Science and Religion* (Kampen, Netherlands: Kok Pharos Publishing House, 1991). John Polkinghorne's *The Faith of a Physicist* (Princeton, N.J.: Princeton University Press, 1994) is a virtual systematic theology conceived in direct and continual conversation with scientific reasoning and scientific theories.

[8] This last thesis is plausibly developed in John D. Barrow and Frank J. Tipler, *The Anthropic Cosmological Principle* (New York: Oxford University Press, 1986).

rious to serious Christian grammar that I must say something about it here.

Creationism intends to be an epistemic challenge to contemporary science on such issues as the age of the universe and the evolutionary emergence of human life from lower forms of life. In this sense, creationism pretends to patterns of scientific reasoning in order to stand as an alternative scientific theory to evolution. It intends to wed Christian faith to being anti-evolutionary and to oppose the teaching of evolution in public schools.

While there are plausible scientific reasons for questioning some evolutionary theories and to even challenge the range of its explanations, it is not appropriate that Christian faith should see itself as pretending to set up an alternative 'science' against evolution. To be sure, the theory or theories of evolution are to be continually tested and perhaps revised by critical thinking. And to be sure, evolution does not explain everything interesting and true about human beings. But the intellectual credibility of creationism as a science is suspect, and it is furthermore a misrepresentation of the Christian doctrine of creation. Lastly, some of our prime beliefs developed in this doctrine do not pretend to be 'scientific, empirical generalizations.'[9]

Further Orienting Notes

Among the topics to be discussed in this chapter is the cluster of issues around the understanding of *evil* in the world. It is decisive to understand that this is a Christian topic with a Christian grammar, and therefore will have to include the whole of how God deals with evil in the world. We are always talking about the triune God who creates, reconciles, and will redeem the world. *In christology and eschatology we come most fully to grips with the problems of evil in the world and how God deals with such evil.* We cannot grasp how we are to understand a world so full of evil powers without seeing that the Creator and the Reconciler and the Redeemer are one God in three modes of being-in-act. The so-called problem of evil will always be grammatically misconstrued if it is seen primarily as a problem for a non-triune creator god.

---

[9] For a discerning history and analysis of 'scientific creationism' see Ronald L. Numbers, *The Creationists: The Evolution of Scientific Creationism* (Berkeley: University of California Press, 1993).

Given the current interests in ecology and in scientific cosmologies, issues of creation are much discussed in contemporary theoretical writings. Yet sustained theological treatments of the doctrine of creation are still needed. The compelling discussions pivot around the widespread appeal of process theism, with its emphasis on an emergent world process and its denial of the classical doctrine of *creatio ex nihilo*. The resulting position posits an infinite everlastingness to time and the ontological need of God for some world. Obviously, if God needs the world in order to be God, then the world must have the same temporal and ontological extension as God. I will be developing a doctrine of creation that joins issue with the process account, while acknowledging the need for a revised grammar of God's interactive history with the world.

Langdon Gilkey's early work, written with strong affinities to Tillich and Reinhold Niebuhr, is still interesting on the existential dimensions of the doctrine: *Maker of Heaven and Earth*.[10] Karl Barth's doctrine of creation in *Church Dogmatics*, III/1, III/2, III/3 merits careful attention and has influenced some aspects of the grammar I will develop. Jürgen Moltmann's *God in Creation*[11] has stimulated renewed interest in the doctrine. Kathryn Tanner, bringing unique analytic skills to the discussion, has challenged such theologies as process theology, with their synergistic understanding of God and the world, in *God and Creation in Christian Theology*.[12] I will have occasion to discuss her and others' work on how to understand God's action in relation to creaturely actions. Wolfhart Pannenberg's treatment of creation and providence in *Systematic Theology*, volume 2, is sweeping and historically insightful.[13]

---

[10] Langdon Gilkey, *Maker of Heaven and Earth: A Study of the Christian Doctrine of Creation* (Garden City, N.Y.: Doubleday, 1959).

[11] Jürgen Moltmann, *God in Creation: A New Theology of Creation and the Spirit of God*, trans. Margaret Kohl (San Francisco: Harper and Row, 1985).

[12] Kathryn Tanner, *God and Creation in Christian Theology: Tyranny or Empowerment?* (Oxford: Blackwell, 1988).

[13] Wolfhart Pannenberg, *Systematic Theology*, vol. 2, trans. Geoffrey W. Bromiley (Grand Rapids, Mich.: Eerdmans, 1991), 1–174.

Biblical Notes

Old Testament

Belief in God the Creator is rich and is spread throughout the OT. It is centrally articulated in the creation texts of Genesis 1–3. Genesis 1–2.3, the Priestly account, affirms that "in the beginning God created [*bara*] the heavens and the earth" [1.1].[14] The Hebrew verb *bara* only has God as its subject in the OT, affirming the unique activity of God in creating the world. God summons the world into existence over six 'days.' God's *ruach*—Spirit—is involved in the activity of creation. [1.2] It is clear that God does not create the world under any complusion or necessity, but does so in utter freedom and with almighty power. In contrast to other world origination accounts, God's creating does not involve any conflict or war and is not the outcome of conflict among other gods.[15] God speaks, and it is so.[16] God needs no cooperation from other powers in order to create the world.

What God creates is "good," indeed "very good" [Gen 1.4, 31]. Genesis 2.4–3.24, the Jahwist account, focuses less on the days of creation than on the coming to be of human being [Adam] in the Garden of Eden. But belief in God as Creator of the world is also expressed vividly in other passages of Scripture.[17]

It is essential throughout the OT witness that there is a fundamental distinction between Yahweh and all creatures. Yahweh creates the crea-

---

[14] This is the traditional reading of this verse, but in the NRSV it is considered an alternative reading to "In the beginning when God created the heavens and the earth." This "when" obviously changes the meaning considerably, implying that God's creative act is not the absolute beginning of all things but only the relative beginning, with the chaos or formless earth being the stuff that needs to be subdued by the creative action of God. For an engaging discussion of these issues see Bernhard W. Anderson, ed., *Creation in the Old Testament* (Philadelphia: Fortress, 1984), especially the essays by Anderson, who supports a chaos theory of creation, and by von Rad and Eichrodt, who support an absolute beginning to creation.

[15] See Isa 2.1–4.

[16] See Ps 33.6.

[17] See Pss 8; 19; 86; 100; 136; and in the 'Royal Psalms' 89; 74; 47; 91; 93–99; and in Am 4.13; 5.8–9; 9.5–6; Jer 4.23; Deutero Isaiah 40.28; 44.24; 45.18; 45.7; 45.9–13; 46.10; 51.9ff.

tures, and they are one and all dependent on Yahweh for their being and life. The basic character of all idolatry is that it takes that which is only creaturely and worships it as though it were God.

The OT remains bound together around the conviction that Yahweh is not only the Creator of all things but is also that One who acts in and upon the creatures of the world. Yahweh communicates to the creatures, to Israel, and is present to and in Israel. The world created by God is therefore never thought of as self-contained and functioning independently on its own. The order of the creation reflects God's wisdom in creating.[18]

New Testament

Throughout the NT, God the Creator is everywhere assumed, though the interest in Jesus Christ begins to interpret further who the Creator is. It is the God of Israel who is the Creator of all things and is called 'Father' by Jesus and repeatedly referred to as 'Father' throughout the NT. It is this God of Israel as the Father of Jesus Christ who is the one who creates in *the beginning*.[19]

The God of Israel as the Creator is that power that brings things to be and upon whom all things depend for being and life.

> Romans 4.17: [God] calls into existence the things that do not exist.
> Romans 11.36: For from Him and through Him and to Him are all things.
> Acts 14.15: to the living God, who made the heaven and the earth and the sea and all that is in them.
> Hebrews 2.10: that God for whom and through whom all things exist.
> Revelation 4.11: You are worthy, our Lord and God, . . . for you created all things, and by your will they existed and were created.

As Creator of the world, God shows continuous concern for the world.[20] And "[God] gives to all mortals life and breath and all things [Acts 17.25]."

---

[18] See Ps 104.24; Isa 45.18.
[19] See Mk 10.6; Heb 1.10; Jn 1.1–4, 14; Rev 21.6; 22.13.
[20] See Mt 6.25ff; 10.29ff; Lk 12.6.

The most decisive new development in the NT in the understanding of the God of Israel as the Creator is that Jesus Christ, the very Word of God, the Son of God, is involved in the work of creating the world.

> John 1.3: All things came into being through him, and without him not one thing came into being.
>
> 1 Corinthians 8.6: yet for us there is one God, the Father, from whom are all things and for whom we exist, and one Lord, Jesus Christ, through whom are all things and through whom we exist.
>
> Colossians 1.16–17: for in him all things in heaven and on earth were created, things visible and invisible . . . all things have been created through him and for him. He himself is before all things and in him all things hold together.
>
> Hebrews 1.2: but in these last days he has spoken to us by a Son . . . through whom he also created the worlds.
>
> Revelation 22.13: I [Jesus] am the Alpha and the Omega, the first and the last, the beginning and the end.

These passages also were important to the church in construing Jesus as divine.

The whole of the witness of the New Testament pivots around the conviction that the God of Israel—the one who created heaven and earth and who elected and liberated Israel—has brought salvation to the world in the life, death, and resurrection of Jesus of Nazareth. The witnesses are thus emboldened to claim that what has been done in Jesus Christ and what will finally be done in ultimate consummation is what God the Creator intended from the beginning in creating the world. Hence, there emerges in the NT—deeply rooted in the Hebrew Scriptures—the conviction that *God had purposes and a plan in creating the world* and that God's life with the world has been fundamentally the execution of that plan.[21] Hence, it would be inconceivable to the NT grammar that the creation of the world might be a cosmic accident.

---

[21] See Eph 1.3–14; 3.8–12; Col 2.25–27. This is the central theme of G. B. Caird, *New Testament Theology*, compiled and edited by L. D. Hurst (Oxford: Clarendon Press, 1994), especially 27–73.

Basic Elements of the Grammar of God the Creator

The Triune Creator

For Christian grammar, God the Creator is inextricably trinitarian: God is the One who is known in self-identifying disclosures in Israel; in the life, death, and resurrection of the Israelite, Jesus of Nazareth; and in the calling of the early church as the Father, the Son, and the Holy Spirit. In the chapters on revelation and the doctrine of God, I have referred to these self-communications of God as the *economic Trinity*: the history of God's self-revealing acts in the world. It is in this history of self-communicating actions that God identifies Godself as the one who created heaven and earth and elected, liberated, and covenanted with Israel, as the one who becomes human in Jesus for the reconciliation of the world, and as the one who empowers creaturely life to a redemptive future. I have thus identified this God as triune in essence and actuality: the Father, Son, and Holy Spirit; the Creator, the Reconciler, and the Redeemer. This is the one eternally actual Person who lives in three modes of being-in-act.

Because this triune Subject is known definitively in Jesus Christ as the one who graciously and mercifully in love comes to the rescue of the creature and seeks the creature's fellowship and redemptive fulfillment, I have identified God as the one who loves in freedom and thereby the one who lives eternally in loving self-determination. If what we know of God in Jesus Christ is not God's free and loving self-determination, then we would stand in conflict with the fundamental convictions of the Old and New Testaments. All that we know of the triune God is known on the basis of God's economic self-communications.

God Creates in Loving Freedom

God the Creator is the one who creates the world in loving freedom. That God creates the world *in freedom* means that God does not create the world from any imposed internal or external necessity. If God created by internal necessity—which is the claim of those theologians who assert that God's love necessitates that God create an object to love—then we would have to conclude that the world is necessary to God for God to be God. If creating the world was fundamentally a necessity of God's presumed nature, this would make it difficult to talk about God's life with the world as 'gracious.' If God created by virtue of some external and necessary metaphysical principle, we would have to conclude that there is some structure or power that is superior to God, which would undercut the very grammar of God's almighty power as well as the sovereign singularity of God.

That God creates the world *in love* means that the activity of creating arises freely out of the sheer loving generosity of the triune actuality of God. This also implies that God values the creature, is not jealous of the creature's actuality, and seeks the creature's good. God lovingly consents to the actuality of the creature.

To clarify this grammar of God's loving freedom, I introduced earlier the concept of the distinction between God's essence and God's actuality. God's actuality is the inclusive reality of God. God's essence is simply that structure of powers and characters without which God could not be God and which are essential to all of God's actual life. It is as eternal actuality that God acts and lives, and it is this actuality of God that includes God's essence. We must not say that the essence is the more real God. Hence, *God is not Creator in essence, only in God's self-determined actuality.* God could be God without creating the world. But in living actuality God is not God without the world.

I also introduced the concept of the *Primordial Trinity*—God was actual as triune even 'before' the creation of the world. This helps keep grammatically clear that the triune God who creates the world does so in loving freedom and not under any sort of necessity. That God creates the world in loving freedom means that the actuality of the creature so created is a *loving gift of God.*

We can now go on to say that *God's activity of creation is a free and loving self-determination of God to-be-Creator.* Out of God's primordial triune actuality, God determines Godself to be Creator of a world of nondivine creatures. In unconditional freedom, God self-determines Godself to create a world of creatures that are other than God. In the language of election, we can say God *elects* Godself to be the creator of a nondivine world of creatures. In this sense as well, we can say that God chooses to be God in relation to a world of creatures, and therefore not God alone in God's primordial internal triune life.

In self-determining Godself to become the Creator of a world of nondivine creatures, *God also thereby self-determines Godself to be limited and conditioned in God's actual life by the world.* We can call this God's freely chosen *self-limitation.* In creating, God determines Godself to have an interactive life with the world, and therewith to-be-affected by the world, to-be-conditioned by the world, to have a 'real relation' to the world. This is God's self-determination to-be-conditioned-by-another. From God's incarnate activity in Jesus Christ we know that God does not stand in any self-sufficient apathy and impassibility, removed from and unaffected by the world's suffering and miseries and joys. But God still retains freedom in *how* God interacts and is affected by the particular unfolding of creaturely history. The central point here is: in creating a world of nondivine creatures, God determines Godself to be with and for the world, and therefore to not exist in isolation or aloofness from the world.

The economic Trinity itself is precisely the revelation that God self-determinately wills to not actually be God without the world. These doctrinal considerations show again why it is good theological grammar to say that in actuality God *becomes*: God *becomes* the Creator; God *becomes* in having an interactive history with the world; God *becomes* incarnate in Jesus at a particular point in creaturely space and time.

God's Purposes in Creating a World

In self-determination the triune God has purposes in becoming the Creator of a world of nondivine creatures. Epistemically these purposes are not so strongly evident in the OT, though there it is evident that God finds the created world good and pleasing in being created. We can interpret this to mean that God *values* the world of creatures. Also in the OT, with the creation of human being, it is evident that God desires fellowship with the human creature. It is the fellowship of obedient response of the creature to God in which the creature celebrates being a creature, enjoys God, and does not seek to be or replace or repudiate God's sovereignty over the creature. This fellowship can be called a *covenant* between God and human being, and this covenant is renewed again and again in the history of creation and especially in the history of Israel within the history of creation.

In the NT Jesus Christ is understood as the one who was with the Father in the beginning and through whom all things came to be created.[22] And Jesus Christ is that human being who is obedient to the Father and who thereby fulfills the covenant as that fellowship between God and the creature which was God's purpose in creating. We can interpret this to mean that in God's primordially triune self-determination,

---

[22] See Jn 1.3; 1 Cor 8.6; Col 1.16–17; Heb 1.2.

the Father elected the Son to be the fulfiller of the creature's covenantal life with God and elected the Spirit to be that empowering presence that brings creatures to participate in the Son's gracious and merciful fulfillment of the covenant.[23] These internal elections of the triune God can be understood as God's self-determinations in love to create a world to love.

Hence, I propose *that God's purposes in creating a world of nondivine creatures are*:

a. that the creature might enjoy life and actuality;
b. that God might communicate Godself to the creature and have fellowship with the creature;
c. that God might become a creature in order to bring the creature to fulfillment of life and actuality;
d. that God might be enriched in God's own living actuality by the life and actuality of the creatures;
e. that God might be glorified in and by the creature: the final teleology of God's creative action and life with the world is that God will be glorified by the creature precisely in and through God's sharing God's glory with the creature.

These purposes of God in creating the world we can also name *God's desires*. In loving freedom God desires the actuality of the creature and desires the creature's fellowship and so desires the creature's enrichment of God's own glory and life. These desires and purposes do not arise in God's primordial life from any internal necessity or need, but are simply and profoundly the freely self-determined desires of God arising out of the eternal love among the Father, the Son, and the Spirit.[24] In such purposing and desiring, God makes Godself vulnerable to the situation and vulnerabilities of the creature.

It should be noted that I have not included the reconciliation of the world in these purposes of God. Reconciliation, of course, presupposes sin and the need for reconciliation. In discerning the purposes of God in creating, we are dependent on the discernment that is forthcoming in understanding the reconciling act of God in Jesus Christ. But sin itself is

---

[23] See Eph 1.3–12; 3.8–12; Col 1.15–17.

[24] I say this in disagreement with an otherwise outstanding book: Paul S. Fiddes, *The Creative Suffering of God* (Oxford: Clarendon Press, 1988), especially 71–76. I think my distinction between God's essence and God's actuality and my dialectical interpretation of God's freedom and God's love prevents the fall toward a process understanding of God and the world that seems evident in Fiddes's thoughtful account.

not something that God wills to exist in the creation, and therefore it is not a necessity of there being a human world. God does *permit* sin to exist, which I will explain more fully below. But because reconciliation is the work of God's love and freedom, we can reckon that even in the absence of sin, God would become human for the purpose of enhancing the flourishing and fulfillment of the creature and for the purpose of fulfilling God's desire for the good of the creature and for fellowship with the creature. As Austin Farrer aptly puts it: "The humanization, the incarnation of God, would still have a place, if the heart had never hardened, if sin had not become habit, nor selfishness second nature."[25]

To recapitulate, Christian discourse is entitled to say these things about God's purposes only on the basis of what God has revealed of Godself in God's triune self-communications in the world of creatures. These things are not said on the basis of some metaphysical necessities or perceived designs we otherwise know. God self-determinately elects Godself to be the creative Father who brings a world to be, to be the Son who fulfills God's desire for fruitful fellowship with the creature, and to be the Spirit that empowers the creature to embrace that fellowship, and in these triune ways of being God, God will finally embrace all creatures as their Ultimate Redemptive Companion.

Creatio Ex Nihilo

Creation by God is *creatio ex nihilo*: creation out of nothing. It is a disputed exegetical judgment whether the account in the first chapter of Genesis is to be interpreted as creation out of nothing. Given the irrevocable rule in Israel that Yahweh is utterly different from the creature and is the one who creates the creature, I do not see how Israel could be interpreted as understanding God's creative action as primarily the action of contending with some primordial void or chaos that preexists God's creative action. The phrase 'creation out of nothing' can be found in 2 Maccabees 7.28, which shows that the belief is rooted in OT grammar; and it is adumbrated in Romans 4.17 and Hebrews 11.3. In the post-apostolic times, near the end of the second century, Justin, Athenagoras, and Tatian mention something similar, and Theophilus of Antioch and

---

[25] Austin Farrer, *Saving Belief* (London: Hodder & Stoughton, 1964), 112.

Irenaeus develop it as an explicit implication of revelation and in repudiation of Platonism, Gnosticism, and Marcionism.[26]

There is a Greek distinction between two different meanings of 'nothing.' First, there is nothing as *ouk on*—absolute nonbeing in distinction from all being. Second, there is nothing as *me on*—relative nonbeing, as that which something is not: e.g., that tree is *not* full grown. This is comparative nonbeing. Meonic nothing was thought to be part of the finitude of temporal beings that can change and become. In the hands of tradition, the meaning of 'nothing' as used in the formula was that of absolute nonbeing—*ouk on*; out of absolute nothingness, God creates the world. Were the nothing in the locution understood as *me on*—relative nonbeing—then it would be a creating out of something.

The grammar of the doctrine of *creatio ex nihilo* has *two negative* functions. First, *it denies that God creates the world out of Godself.* This would divinize the world and eradicate any distinction between the Creator and the creation. The creation is not a diminution or emanation of divinity. Second, *it denies that God creates the world out of some pre-existing or everlasting stuff or matter or chaos.* This would reduce God to being primarily a *shaper* or *molder*—like an artist—of some pre-existing matter or reality. As used by Plato, this would be the image of the *demiurge* who shapes the prime matter into things but who does not create the prime matter as such.[27] This would have the grammatical effect of positing something else as uncreated and as ultimate as God, which would be an ultimate ontological dualism. Such would deny the sovereign singularity of God.

The doctrine also has *four positive* functions. First, it clearly states *that anything that has nondivine actuality or reality is brought to be by God's creative action.* There is no *something else* that can explain the sheer contingent actuality of the whole creation. So if some nondivine actuality exists, it exists solely by virtue of God's creative action.

Second, it asserts *that the creation has a beginning.* This affirms that the creation is finite in having a beginning and an end, and therefore is not infinite or everlasting or eternal in itself. This reinforces the notion that God does not need the world in order to be God. Aquinas believed that philosophically considered, without reference to revelation, creation

---

[26] See Irenaeus, *Adv. Haer.*, II,1,1; 10,4, and the full discussion by Gerhard May, *Creatio Ex Nihilo: The Doctrine of 'Creation Out of Nothing' in Early Christian Thought*, trans. A. S. Worrall (Edinburgh: T. & T. Clark, 1994).

[27] See Plato, *Timaeus*, 27c–30c.

from nothing only shows that the world is absolutely dependent on God's originating act of creating but does not require that there must be a beginning of time. Revelation, however, does posit a beginning to time and the world.[28] That the world has a beginning is a disputed point in contemporary theology, with most process theologians affirming that the world is necessary to God and that therefore both God and the world are infinite in time. The doctrine of creation out of nothing, however, couples with Augustine's notion that in creating the world, God creates space and time as the conditions of the world. Hence, God does not create *in time*, but creates time itself as the beginning of time. So, the sense of God *before* the creation of the world and time is itself a difficult notion, which I have affirmed above in the doctrine of the Primordial Trinity.[29]

Third, it underlines the inescapable grammatically limiting fact *that God's creative action is singularly unique and without analogy in the creaturely world.* All the analogies we might imagine are analogies of *making something*—even something new—out of some pre-existing materials or actualities. Think of all the various images of the artist cre-

---

[28] See Thomas Aquinas, *Summa Theologiae*, Ia, 46. Since Aquinas also believes that the world is freely created by God and not out of necessity, he plunges into difficult waters in trying to put all this together with the simplicity, immutability, and identity of essence and existence in God. See F. C. Copleston, *Aquinas* (Baltimore: Penguin, 1955), 136–141.

[29] See Augustine, *City of God*, XI, 6, and *Confessions*, XI, 13. See also William A. Christian, "The Creation of the World," in *A Companion to the Study of St. Augustine*, ed. Roy W. Battenhouse (New York: Oxford University Press, 1955), 315–342. If the locution *before time* is difficult, so too is the notion of infinite time when combined with any sense of a present moment. Hartshorne clearly wants: (a) an infinite extension of temporality; (b) a thick present moment; and (c) to have God always existing and dependent on some world. For him there is an infinite extension of worlds to which God stands dependently related. But how can you have a past that is infinite, if that implies that the present moment and all future moments are *infinite plus one, plus one, ad infinitum*? I suggest that this notion of infinite is as paradoxical and difficult as my notion of God being actual *before* time and time itself being created with a beginning and a finite extension. Obviously, the *before* here does not mean *some moments before*. It simply means *prior to temporality*. The function of the locution 'time is finite' is simply to deny that time is infinite. Likewise, God preexists time and the coming to be of the world. See Charles Hartshorne, *Man's Vision of God: The Logic of Theism* (Chicago: Willett, Clark, 1941), especially 230–250.

ating something; think of the conceiving and giving birth to new creatures. All are suggestive images or metaphors of bringing something new to be but not quite applicable to God's creative action. These images may be useful, however, when we talk below of God's providential governing of the creation. The strongest image of God creating is expressed in Genesis 1: God speaks or summons [amer] the world into existence. God speaks and it is so. God does not use something intermediary to create the world. At the grammatical and imaginative limit we say God's creative action is simply the action of positing something in actuality, in being.

Fourth, it positively underscores *that the God who creates all creatures is the One who is Almighty in power, the sovereign and supreme Power.* We should not, however, construe this power as that sort of omnipotence that is all the power there is. In granting actuality to the creation, God also thereby gives the creation its own creaturely powers. But no creature shares God's almighty power to create out of nothing.[30]

Creation as Triune *ad extra* Work

The work of creation is an *ad extra* work of the triune God. In calling God's creative activity an *ad extra* work, I am simply affirming with the traditions that God does the work freely and lovingly, and that it is not a work that is essential to God being God. But it is work that is central to the living economic actuality of God. Internal to the triune Life of God, the relations among the modes of God's actuality involve otherness and interanimation [*perichoresis*] and in their work beyond God's life, there is a tri-unity of action: *opera trinitas ad extra sunt indivisa.* I further affirmed, that in their tri-unity of action, there is also a sense in which each mode of being has a distinctive focus of action or focus of being-in-act, though never in the absence of the other two modes. Hence, without supposing that the Father acts alone, we can, with Scripture and tradition, say that *the creative action of God is primarily the action of the Father.* The Father is the creative ground for the actuality of the creation.

---

[30] A helpful further examination of *creatio ex nihilo* can be found in David Kelsey, "The Doctrine of Creation from Nothing," in McMullin, ed., *Evolution and Creation*, 176–195. See also Jaroslav Pelikan, "Creation and Causality in the History of Christian Thought," in Sol Tax and Charles Callender, eds., *Evolution after Darwin*, vol. 3, *Issues in Evolution* (Chicago: University of Chicago Press, 1960), 29–41.

Yet the Father does not create without the Son's action as well. The Father creates through the Son in the sense that the Son is the evident order and purpose of the Father, called the Word or *Logos* of God and the Wisdom or *Sophia* of God. But this Word and Wisdom of God, in Christian grammar, cannot be separated from the performative Word God speaks in the life, death, and resurrection of Jesus of Nazareth, and which is the peculiar Wisdom and Word of God. This reconciling and salvific suffering in Jesus is a wisdom that the world otherwise does not know and would never on its own impute to the created order and purpose of the cosmos. But it is Jesus Christ as this *Logos* and *Sophia* through whom the Father brings all things to be.

The Father does not create without the Spirit that empowers life in the creature and summons the creature to covenantal life of obedience. It is this same Spirit that empowers new life, that redeems the creature and calls the creature to live in the light of the forgiving covenant revealed in Jesus Christ. It is this Spirit that is the promise of an ultimate redemption and fulfillment of the creature.

I also affirm that the otherness of the Father, Son, and Spirit within God's primordial triune actuality is the prefigurement of that otherness which is posited in the creating of the creaturely world.[31] *Otherness* is not foreign to God. This is another reason why some interpretations of the simplicity of God which did not allow for real otherness to exist in God also made it difficult to conceive God having an actual life with the otherness of the world. Yet we cannot say that the actions of creation and providence are the actions only of the Father, or say that the actions of reconciliation are the actions only of the Son, or say that the actions of redemption are the actions only of the Spirit. Hence, we say that in *ad extra* actions of the triune Subject, there is no quantifying division among the Father, the Son, and the Spirit. But there are *ad extra* differentiations of actions [*perichoresis*] among the Father, the Son, and the Spirit.

God Creates Creatures

God creates nondivine actualities—called creatures—that are utterly other than God. The basic ontological distinction in Christian theology is that between the Creator and the creature: this is radical and incommen-

---

[31] See this concept developed in Pannenberg, *Systematic Theology*, vol. 2, 20–35.

surate. The otherness between God and the creature is an otherness that precludes assuming God and the creature under some more general category of actuality—a univocal concept of actuality that applies to both God and creature. God's ways of being actual are unique to God and only analogically available to us in understanding the actuality of the creature. Here we simply have to admit that our grammar comes to its limits. The concept of actuality is analogical, and we cannot eliminate the sense in which God is not actual in quite the same way we say creatures are actual. Given this basic distinction, we must also say that God and the creation cannot be included in some more general and *inclusive whole*. God and the creation are incommensurable actualities and grammatically cannot be treated as comparable entities that can be added together to make some larger whole. And God is not the whole of which the world, in its plurality of creatures, is the parts. If so-called *panentheism* means that the world *in its actuality* is *in God* as the whole of all actuality, then our grammar precludes that concept.[32]

Yet even though there is this basic otherness between the Creator and the creature, God the Creator is not imprisoned in this otherness. It is not such an otherness as to prevent the Creator from becoming a creature, from dwelling with the creature under the conditions of the creature. Hence, this otherness is not best described as the otherness of the finite and infinite, for such would suggest that the infinite ceased being infinite and simply became finite. Rather, I say God in becoming incarnate overcomes the distinction between Creator and creature by becoming a creature without ceasing to be God the Creator who is incommensurate and radically other. This language, however, would fall into profound disarray and unintelligibility without a trinitarian conceptuality. Further, the overcoming of the distinction in the particularity of Jesus Christ does not collapse the radical distinction between God and all other creatures.

The otherness of the creature's actuality affirms its distinctness and relative independence of God. The creature is unconditionally dependent on the Creator for its actuality, for its standing out from nothingness, for its having actuality. Without the creative action of God the creature would 'fall into nothingness.' The creature, therefore, is never simply an

---

[32] Charles Hartshorne has never understood this grammar of the Christian doctrine of creation. See his discussion of panentheism in *The Divine Relativity: A Social Conception of God* (New Haven, Conn.: Yale University Press, 1948), 88–92. In arenas outside process theology, the word 'panentheism' is very popular and prone to getting up and walking around on us.

autonomous, self-creating actuality. But the creature is a real actuality empowered with genuine action and movement in distinction from God. As relatively independent, the creature has the gift of actuality as distinct and differentiated from God. To be sure, the creature does not have actuality without ultimate dependence on God's creative activity. But it is God's creative activity that confers relative independence—not absolute autonomy—on the creature. In its relative independence, the creature has finite powers of activity.

In their otherness from God, creatures are *individually centers of activity*.[33] As a center of activity, a creature has its own internal focus, physical form, movement, and unity that comprise its characteristic activity or types of activity. These creatures are thus actualities that are their own particular embodied being-in-acts. These creatures vary in complexity and activity from the simple creatures—the subatomic to the single cell—to the more complex creatures such as humans. The simpler creatures can be part of a larger, more complex creature. These larger and more complex creatures we can call 'organisms.' For example, human cells, as centers of activity with their characteristic being-in-acts, affect and are affected by the larger human organism in which they reside, and they 'do their own characteristic thing' within that organism.

As a finite center of activity, each creature has a beginning in time and ending in time in which it ceases to exist. Creatures have finite spans of life and actuality. It is the creature's created *essence* or *nature* that overall defines and delimits the sort of activity or activities the creature might possibly have. The essence sets limits to what the creature might be and become simply as the creature it is. Thus the oak seed has an essence that delimits and defines the range of possibilities that the seed might have and become; the seed cannot become a toad. Thus creatures are endowed by God with an essence and an embodied particularity which comprise their own delimited powers of activity and reactivity.

The radical otherness of the creature from the Creator implies the following negations. First, the actualities of God and the creature are not to be understood *monistically*. Monism says that all actuality is one and the same and that whatever plurality there is, is but a plurality of the one

---

[33] In this concept of actuality as a center of activity, I am not making *event* the fundamental concept, as is the case in process theology. I stand much closer to Aquinas and his modified Aristotelianism. I think my usage is quite similar to that of Austin Farrer in *Finite and Infinite: A Philosophical Essay* (Westminster, U.K.: Dacre, 1943).

basic actuality. Sallie McFague affirms such a monism.[34] Pantheism in its various forms is simply such a monism. All forms of monism and pantheism have the grammatical effect of making either the creaturely world a predicate of God the subject or reducing 'God' to no more than a name for the world. Yet, second, the actualities of God and the creature are not to be understood *dualistically*, as though there are two different but equally ultimate actualities. It is best, then, simply to say that the creature has an appropriate creaturely independence of God, is respected and valued by God in this relative independence and otherness, and we should grammatically refuse to further reduce that otherness to some systematic and necessary metaphysical categories.

The *otherness of the creation* is the condition for God having *relationships* with the creation and with the various creatures of the creation. In relation to the otherness of the creation, God interacts with the creation. Without such otherness there could be no relationality between God and the creation.

Creation as an Interdependent and Ordered Cosmos

In creating creatures, God creates a cosmos of creatures in massive interconnection and interdependence among themselves. By 'cosmos' I mean also 'creation' or 'world'; these terms may be used here interchangeably. In creating a cosmos, God creates *space and time* as the necessary conditions for creaturely actuality. Space and time thus determine every creature to be finite: to be limited by a particular bodily location in space and in a particular period of time. In their own particular space and time, creatures are *processes of becoming.* They become, act, interact, affect and are affected by the larger historical and cosmic environment in which they reside and have actuality. Hence, becoming is a necessary feature of being a creature. Creatures are agents using their potentialities in the actualization of possibilities.

As a cosmos of creatures, the creation has structures of relationality that order the creatures among themselves: orders of causality, dependence, interdependence, complexity of activity, and emergence of novelties. Here we can think of the regularities we sometimes call 'laws of nature.' There is thus a *necessary relationality* that affects the actuality of all creatures. Negatively put, no creature exists just by itself and unaf-

---

[34] *Models of God,* 71ff.

fected by the cosmic environment of other creatures. Here we can stipulate a distinction between a *relation* and a *relationship*. A relation exists when an actuality is affected in its actuality by another actuality. In this sense, the actuality is affected internally. A relationship, however, is a relation in which an actuality is intentional toward another actuality. The claim here is that all actualities are in relations, but only actualities such as humans are in relationships.[35]

We can also identify in the creation various *force fields of power*, adopting a concept from natural science. A force field of power is a set of relations and structures that exercise power over the various actualities that reside within the field, and the set or field cannot be reduced to the power of any particular actuality or group of actualities within the field. The field of power transcends but includes the particular actualities over which the power is exercised, but is not itself another actuality.[36] In addition to the use of force fields in physics, force fields are easily evident in human social worlds. For example, think of the force fields of economic powers and relations. This concept of force fields helps us interpret the 'principalities and powers' and 'elemental spirits' referred to in the NT.[37] But remember, as used here, force fields are creaturely realities.

The order of the world can be thought of—in line with most contemporary science—as an *emerging world in process of becoming*. It is a process of becoming in which there are novelties, and while there are genuine causal regularities, the present and future are not simply and completely determined by the past. The future is the field of possibilities yet to be realized and open to emerging actualizations. Further, there is no compelling theological reason why some of this emergence of the world through time cannot be thought of along the lines of evolutionary theory. That God might use evolutionary structures in governing the world is not an offense to Christian sensibilities. But Christian confessional theology differs from some evolutionary theories in that we assert

---

[35] These concepts, will be explored further in the next chapter on the doctrine of humanity.

[36] Pannenberg uses the concept of force field as a way of talking about the Spirit of God; see *Systematic Theology*, vol. 1, trans. Geoffrey Bromiley (Grand Rapids, Mich.: Eerdmans, 1991), 382ff. I am not using the term here as a way of talking about God.

[37] See Gal 4.3, 9; Rom 8.38; Eph 3.10; 6.12; Col 1.16; 2.8,15,20; 1 Pet 3.22. This concept of force fields will be useful in identifying the systemic character of human sin.

that God rules teleologically or with purpose over the evolving. The evolving of the world is not merely a blind emergence. Yet this teleology of purpose we do not pretend to read off from the created order considered simply in and by itself. It is not an empirical generalization; it is a teleology we understand from the perspective of the Christian doctrine of creation.

The created cosmos is ordered by spiritual structures and actualities that are more than the order of physical causality and activity. The compelling biblical concept of this spiritual order is '*covenant,*' and it applies primarily to the human creature who is created in the image of God. Later I will develop the notion that human beings are constituted by the Spirit of God and are originally endowed by the grace of God for relationship with God. In and by the Spirit, God summons the human spirit to exist in covenant with God and with other humans. God has a history of summoning the human to a covenant of right relations among humans, among humans in relation to other creatures, and in relation to God. These right relations are what we can identify as the structures of justice and love God summons humans to obey. The summons in Israel and in humanity as created is a summons to the promise of well-being and fulfillment for the human who lives in obedience to God.[38] The refusal to heed the summons and the violation of the right relations lead to a deep rupture in the spiritual order of the world. God thus is engaged in time in an interactive struggle with humanity to rescue persons from this rupture and disorientation. We will explore this spiritual disruption in our discussion of evil below and in our chapter on human being as created and as sinful.

This finite world of an immense plurality of creatures is a cosmos of creatures with competing goods and losses. Not every possibility is equally possible at the same time; the actualization of one possibility eliminates other possibilities for that moment. Real creatures—as dynamic centers of activity—impinge upon and collide with other creatures in the world. Thus creatures as such, in their relational interactions with other creatures, have real *vulnerabilities* to harm, distortion, pain, and death from the activities of other creatures. Consider, for example, the use of other creatures for food, the swirling forces of weather that afflict other creatures, the infectious diseases in which the infecting creature is simply doing what it characteristically does. Even God could not create a

---

[38] See Isa 56.4–5; Heb 8.10–12.

human being who is absolutely preserved from pain and harm. Whatever else such a being might be, it would not be a *human being*.[39] Hence, in this world of an immense plurality of creatures in interdependence and interaction, *some dimensions of suffering are built-in to being-a-creature*. Later in this chapter we will explore what this means for understanding evil.

The Creation Is Good

The creation as created by God is basically 'good.'[40] In saying that the creation is good, Scripture and tradition are affirming the following: (a) the creation and all the creatures are of *value to God*; (b) God says a fundamental *'yes'* to the creation; and (c) the creation of creatures is a *positive purpose* of God in creating. That the creation is of value to God is affirmed in our confession that God creates in loving freedom. It also means that the creature, in relation to God, will affect God and be positively embraced by God. That the creation is valuable to God and worthy of God's 'yes' is the context for God's 'no' to sin and God's reconciling 'yes' in Jesus Christ. Or, to put it another way, in Jesus Christ we come to see and understand just how valuable the creation is to God and how remarkably gracious is God's self-determined 'yes' to the world. This affirmation includes the bodily reality of the creatures: bodies as such are good and valuable to God. The traditions had a tendency to forget or neglect this important assertion.

To avoid confusion, we must understand that 'good' does not mean that the creation is *morally good* or that the creation is *perfect*. Hence, that human being is good and thus of value to God does not mean that human being is *as such* morally good. To be morally good requires actions of obedience to God. Though human being is valuable to God even in its moral disobedience, it is not morally good as such. Also, there is no need to impute to the creation a perfection, which would seem to imply that all actual states of affairs are as such perfect. We would hardly know what we mean if we said that.

The affirmation that the creation is good entails some important denials. First, it denies that the world is itself the creation of an evil principle or god [Marcion] or that the world as physical material is in itself evil [Gnosticism]. Second, it denies that being finite is itself a sign of being

---

[39] Notice how clearly these remarks are grammatical remarks.
[40] See Gen 1 and 1 Tim 4.4.

evil or corrupt. That the world of creatures is valuable to God is included in the concept that God is affected by the creature, suffers the creature's pain and suffering, and rejoices in the creature's spiritual obedience and flourishing.

This doctrinal belief in the goodness of the creation is important as we face the current ecological crisis in which humans have abused the systemic interrelations with the nonhuman world of creatures and have thereby endangered the future of the earth. This crisis represents a refusal to see the whole creation as valuable to God and is a reduction of the nonhuman world's value to being an instrumental value for human use, consignment, and disposal. However, contrary to some ecological theologians, there is nothing in Scripture to support the notion that all the creatures are of 'equal value' to God. *'Universality of value' to God does not imply 'equality of value.'*[41] Does God value the weed with the same value as the little child?[42] We do have reason to believe that God places a superior value on human beings, even to the point of becoming a human being for the sake of the salvation of a fallen humanity. Without reduction to being an instrumental value for some other creature, however, each creature as such has its own dignity and value before God. That the world is of value to God does mean that God ultimately seeks the redemption of *all creatures*.[43]

The Grammar of the Providence of God

The grammar of creation thus means that we can speak of a *beginning, a middle, and an end for creation*. Out of loving freedom and with the purpose of sharing life with that which is other than God, God brings the creation into actuality and reigns over the whole of its existence in space and time. It is a grammar of an ultimate beginning: the world with its space and time comes to be out of nothing but the divine will. The world, therefore, is not infinite and everlasting in time. It is a grammar of a long and meaningful middle: God continues to sustain and govern the world

---

[41] Kathryn Tanner seems to affirm an equality of value of all creatures. See "Creation, Environmental Crisis, and Ecological Justice," in *Reconstructing Christian Theology*, ed. Rebecca S. Chopp and Mark Lewis Taylor (Minneapolis: Fortress, 1994), especially 117–118.

[42] See Mt 6.26ff; 10.31; 12.24; Lk 12.4–7, 24.

[43] See Ps 36.6; Rom 8.19–21.

as it emerges in creaturely time. Here I affirm that God has an interactive history with the world. It is a grammar of an ultimate end: the world has destiny or end, both as *telos* or goal and as *finis* or conclusion. Under God's ordained purposes, the world is moving toward its destined goal. These grammatical matters are affirmed in saying that the triune God—as the Creator, the Reconciler, and the Redeemer of the world—is the Alpha and the Omega of all things in heaven and on earth.[44] This is the grammatical context for considering the providence of God.

To understand the providence of God, we must draw out the implication of God being the Creator of the world: *the creation is open to the action of God within the world.* The world is not created so that it is closed up and sealed up in itself and impervious to any action of God within its creaturely relations and becomings. God creates a world that is open to God's ongoing interaction with the world and therewith God's action within the world. Thus the doctrine of creation by the triune God denies the fundamental tenet of *deism*, namely, that God creates the world in the beginning—like creating a machine that can run on its own—and the world unfolds without any further interference or interaction by God. Hence, deism asserts that God does not, need not, and cannot act within the world. Deism, in cryptic forms, has been widespread in much contemporary theology, and it does believe that the cosmos is sealed up and self-contained in itself.

God the Preserver of the World

God the Creator is also God the Preserver of the World. Even though God's creating out of nothing means that there is a beginning to the world, it does not mean that God created *only* at the beginning and the world then runs along quite well on its own. Rather, in the requisite sense that the creative activity of God is that which gives actuality to creatures out of absolute nonbeing, absolute nothingness [*ouk on*], it also follows that the creation requires God's continuing creative activity to sustain it in actuality and to keep it from lapsing back into nothingness. The creature does not have the creative power of itself to keep itself in actuality and thereby to sustain a whole world of which the creature is a part. I will call this continual creative activity of God *creatio continua*.[45] This continuing creativity of God we can also call God's preservation of the

---

[44] See Rev 1.8; 4.8; 21.6; 22.13.

[45] See Moltmann, *God in Creation*, 209ff.

world. *God's preservation of the world is God's continuing preserving of the world in its relative and endowed independence in created space and time.* In preserving the creature, God grants it extension in space and time. Thus God's preserving is always the preserving of a whole cosmos of creatures.

God the Governor of the World

As the Governor of the world, God reigns over the life of the world in its creational space and time. This includes God's reigning over the process of temporal becoming whereby creatures emerge in creational history. As Governor, God sustains the created structures of order and interacts with the world's becoming, thus shaping by such interaction the emergence of the world in time. In this sense of interactive shaping of the creation, we can cautiously speak of God as *Shaper of the world.*

Under this rubric of governance, I am acknowledging a *difference* between God creating *in the beginning* and God creating in the *ongoing bringing things to be out of that which has preceded them.* God creates a child, for example, out of the stuff of parental sexual activities, genes, and processes of growth and birth. And yet, even as God creates through these antecedent actualities, there is a sense of God sustaining and preserving the whole process of insemination, gestation, prenatal growth, and birth that is this very preserving of things in existence. This is God creating out of that which God has already created, and therefore is not a creating out of that which is uncreated and as ultimate as God, which was what we denied in our previous grammar of *creatio ex nihilo.* Hence, we can say that in interactively governing the world, God not only preserves a whole cosmos in being but creates out of that cosmos succeeding cosmoses of creatures.

The Governor is, of course, the triune Governor, and hence, God has several ways of interacting with the world. I have already spoken of the multiple ways in which God is present in the world and the permeability of creatures to the presence of God. While God does not displace the creature or destroy the creature's relative independence, God does not simply leave the creature to no more than the interdependence of creatures to each other. There is no place in all creation where a creature can hide from God or escape God's wise presence. In the mode of being-in-act of the Father, God is the creative ground of the creature's actuality. In the mode of being-in-act of the Son, God is the encountering presence that meets and guides the creature, that communicates with the creature, and confronts the creature from time to time. In the mode of being-in-act of the Spirit, God empowers the creature's life as a process of becoming and pulls the creature into the future. In all these ways, God as the triune Governor sustains and leads the creature into the future and wills the good of the creature.

The grammar of governance is the grammar of *God's interaction with the world*. Having already affirmed that God is affected by the happenings in and to all the actualities of the world, we have good reason to move further and affirm some ways in which God responds to the emerging life of the world. These affirmations were not possible to the tradition that maintained God's immutability and impassibility, but they do become conceivable insofar as we affirm God's self-determination to be affected by the world and therefore to be open to the world. It is also a world that is not sealed up away and independent of God.

Keith Ward has been discerning in identifying these ways in which God interacts with the world process:[46]

   a. particular imaginative shapings of the contingent emergence of the world with ordered and persuasive possibilities;
   b. personal acts relating to persons: self-communications, inspiration, withdrawal, movements of the Spirit;
   c. direct acts affecting emerging probabilities of the creation, such as 'miracles.'

As the Governor of the world, God governs with the Wisdom and Word we know in Jesus Christ. Thus we are never to think of God's governance simply as that which is evident in the physical regularities of nature.

The Providence of God

The providence of God is God's preservation and governance of the world. In speaking of God's preservation and governance of the world, we are speaking of the traditional topic of the providence of God. But we must remember that the grammar of God the Provider is essentially informed by what we know of God and God's purposes in Jesus Christ. Such purposes are not discernible simply by looking at how the world

---

[46] Keith Ward, *Divine Action* (London: Collins, 1990), 111ff. Aside from some conceptual traps he falls into at the beginning of the book, Ward shows wide-ranging sound judgments in accounting for the interactive life of God with the world.

unfolds, at how the events of the world happen. We can determine little about the provident purposes of God in creating and governing the world simply by observing the course of events in the world. We do not know a God whose will and purpose are simply as such the unfolding of all events, for such a god would be 'fate.' Thus we never talk about any other activities of God than the actions of the triune God who is the Creator, the Reconciler, and the Redeemer of the whole world. Hence, for Christian grammar the providence of God is simply the sovereign and orderly ways in which God pursues God's own purposes in relation to the world. It is God's management [*oikonomia*] of creation history: God interacts with the world, leading the world toward the fulfillment of God's primordial purposes in creating the world. Hence, under the providence of God we include what we have previously said about God's preservation of the world, God's continuing creativity, and God's governance of the world. In all these ways God brings forth successive worlds and provides for their orderly sustenance and preservation.

This doctrine of God's providence is, therefore, a Christian convictional construal of the world, confessed and learned on the basis of God's self-communicating with the world in Israel, in Jesus Christ, and in the Spirit. Thus, our experience of God's providence—as the providence of the God we know in Jesus Christ—is always dependent on the construal powers of the language of faith. We learn through the witnessing power of the discourses of faith to experience the world as God's world, and thus we learn to practice being grateful to God for life and to trust God in the unfolding of our lives.

Another Question

Should we think of the world as God's body? Sallie McFague makes a persistent argument for this understanding.[47] McFague thus argues for a monistic understanding of God and the world, and she assumes that this understanding will have the beneficial effect of making humans more appreciative of the physical world in which they live and which they are destroying. McFague also argues that the image of *giving birth* is a suitable metaphor for God's creative activity in the world. Most process

---

[47] See Sallie McFague, *Models of God: Theology for an Ecological, Nuclear Age* (Philadelphia: Fortress, 1987) and *The Body of God: An Ecological Theology* (Minneapolis: Fortress, 1993).

theologians also argue—though a bit differently—that the world is God's body. These arguments trade heavily on the alleged similarity between the soul-in-the-body and God-in-the-world. God is the soul of the bodily world.[48] It is a metaphysical principle for process theologians that all actual events, including God, must have a mental pole and a physical pole.

I object to this grammatical understanding of God and creation for the following reasons. First, it diminishes the incomparable distinction between God and the creation. Second, McFague tends to suppose that only things 'divine' are of real value, which contradicts the fundamental Christian conviction that creatures are as such of value to God. Christians do not need to divinize the world in order to be reminded that we are responsible for the care of the earthly world and that other creatures are as such of value to God. Third, giving birth is a vivid and useful metaphorical image if used with grammatical care. But birthing is the act, as we know it, of giving birth to that which is *of the same kind as the birthing mother*. But God and creation are not of the same kind of actuality. Birthing might be a powerful image for talking about what God is doing in the death and resurrection of Jesus Christ. These objections are not based on some presumed metaphysical principle that *God cannot be a body*. Christian theology is insistent that God does become a particular human body in Jesus Christ. Hence, while there is utter otherness between God and creation, neither creatureliness as such nor creaturely bodiliness is alien and impossible to the actuality of God.

Further Issues in the Grammar of God's Action in Relation to the World

The Problematic Grammar of Traditional Theism

In order to clarify a few issues about God's action in the world, I begin this section with an examination of the grammar of traditional theism. By *traditional theism* I am referring here primarily to the views of

---

[48] See Schubert M. Ogden, *The Reality of God and Other Essays* (New York: Harper and Row, 1966), especially 58ff and 175ff.

Thomas Aquinas,[49] some Thomists, and sometimes Calvin. In contemporary theological discussion, traditional theism's account of God's action in the world has been defended by Austin Farrer,[50] Kathryn Tanner,[51] David Burrell,[52] and to some extent, William C. Placher.[53] In addition, numerous volumes have addressed the issues of how God might be understood to act in relation to the world.[54]

Etienne Gilson states the conundrum of Aquinas aptly:

> The problem in the final analysis comes to this. We must hold firmly to two apparently contradictory truths. God does whatever creatures do; and yet creatures themselves do whatever they do. It is a question of understanding how one and the same effect can proceed simultaneously from two different causes: God and the natural agent which produces it.[55]

---

[49] Aquinas's focused discussion of God's causality and the causality of creatures is in *Summa Theologiae*, Ia, 103–106 and *Summa Contra Gentiles*, III, 64–68, 70, 72, 77, 89, 90, 99–102.

[50] See especially Farrer, *Finite and Infinite* and *Faith and Speculation*. See also Brian Hebblethwaite and Edward Henderson, eds., *Divine Action: Studies Inspired by the Philosophical Theology of Austin Farrer* (Edinburgh: T. & T. Clark, 1990).

[51] Tanner, *God and Creation*.

[52] David B. Burrell, *Aquinas: God and Action* (Notre Dame, Ind.: University of Notre Dame Press, 1979).

[53] William C. Placher, *The Domestication of Transcendence: How Modern Thinking about God Went Wrong* (Louisville, Ky.: Westminster John Knox, 1996). It seems to me that Placher slips so uncritically into the incomprehensibility of God with its attendant emphasis on immutability that he can hardly retrieve matters when he attempts to develop a christology in the later parts of the book.

[54] See Owen C. Thomas, ed., *God's Activity in the World* (Chico, Calif.: Scholars Press, 1983); Thomas V. Morris, ed., *Divine and Human Action: Essays in the Metaphysics of Theism* (Ithaca, N.Y.: Cornell University Press, 1988); Thomas F. Tracy, *God, Action, and Embodiment* (Grand Rapids, Mich.: Eerdmans, 1984); Thomas F. Tracy, ed., *The God Who Acts: Philosophical and Theological Explorations* (University Park: Pennsylvania State University Press, 1994).

[55] Etienne Gilson, *The Christian Philosophy of St. Thomas Aquinas*, trans. L. K. Shook (New York: Random House, 1956), 182.

Traditional theism asserts a central and fundamental *distinction be-tween God's causality and creaturely causality*. The term 'causality' is here being used analogically in these two locutions. We cannot semanti-cally spell out exhaustively in what sense God is 'cause'; we cannot 'conceive' God's causality in the same terms in which we conceive creaturely causality. God's causality is God's creating all that is, just as it is, in the whole created order. This can be called the *vertical dimension* of God's causality. Aquinas also refers to this as the order of *'primary causality.'* Creaturely causality pertains to the ways creatures exercise power or causal efficacy among themselves within the created world. We can call this the *horizontal dimension* of causality. Aquinas also refers to this as the order of *'secondary causality.'* These two dimensions are on-tologically incommensurate and incomparable and therefore are not to be conceived of as in *antithesis* or in a zero-sum relation. That is, in regard to the created world, between these two dimensions of causality there is no competition or conflict in which what one does *diminishes* what the other does or can do. Tanner draws a distinction between "contrastive and non-contrastive" understandings of the two ontologically distinct spheres of causality. She recommends that God's causality is non-contrastive to creaturely causality, which means that their different cau-salities are not in mutual competition, such that what one causes as an ef-fect the other cannot cause as well.[56] I prefer the term 'antithesis' to her term 'contrastive.'

With these distinctions in mind, let us look at an analysis of a crea-turely causal action:

a. Creaturely agent C can be said to causally act so that effect E is produced, or C-causes-E.

b. God, as causal agent G in the vertical order, can be said to cause C-causing-E, or G-causes-(C-causing-E).

c. Because these are two different orders of causality, there is no competition or antithesis between God's causality and the crea-ture's causality, or G-causing-(C-causing-E) does not exclude or compete with C-causing-E. In their own proper spheres, each cause has its own proper causality.

d. Hence, it is inappropriate to say: if God causes effect E, then it could not be caused by creaturely agent C.

e. But it does seem necessary to say that for every creaturely agent and for every creaturely caused effect, it is the case that God

---

[56] Tanner, *God and Creation*, 136–148.

caused every creaturely agent to be and to be the causal agent it is and to produce the effect it produces.

This grammar of traditional theism intends to say firmly:

a. that God causes to be every creature and every creaturely event; and whatever God causes to be God also wills to be;

b. that, in the horizontal sphere of secondary causes, creaturely agents are properly causal agents of effects;

c. that God is not a secondary cause among the secondary causes of the creaturely horizontal order of causal efficacy, and God's causal efficacy does not compete with the creature's causal efficacy and freedom on the horizontal level;

d. that there are two different and incomparable orders of causal agency and efficacy: God's primary or vertical causal agency that causes to be anything that is and the creature's secondary or horizontal agency that causes effects among creatures;

e. that 'God causing effect E' does not exclude 'C causing effect E': these are logically compatible statements, or these statements are not antithetical;

f. that if a critic says these two statements are antithetical or logically incompatible, then he is with a sleight of hand using the term 'cause' univocally and not analogically;

g. that we thus have what some call a *theory of double agency*: for any event it is logically compatible to say that God is fully active in causing the event *and* that some creature is fully active and is causing the event;

h. hence, God's creative causal action does not displace the creature's causal action; rather it is God's action that creates, grounds, and empowers the causal action of the creature.

What do the critics identify as some of the implications of this grammar? First, some critics contend that it cannot render the concept of cause relative to God sufficiently intelligible to make any sense; the concept is not really analogical but simply empty when referred to God. This can also be phrased as the issue of the term 'cause' being used equivocally with two utterly different meanings, though the term is obscure in its application to God. Second, to the extent the concept of cause, even as analogical, is intelligible, it seems to assert that God is the only real causal agent and only that which God wills to happen happens. Third, if for every event that happens we can say 'God willed the event to happen,' then it would seem that nothing happens that is *contrary* to the will of God. This seems to say that the evil events of the world are willed to happen by God, which does challenge the belief that God does not cause or will evil. Fourth, it has the unhappy consequence of saying that we can read God's will off what happens in the world, since everything that happens is caused by God and therefore must be willed by God. But this seems contrary to the belief that we know God's will for the world primarily in Jesus Christ. Further, this seems to make the understanding of God as Creator and Governor the simple equivalent of the Greek grammar of *moira* or fate. Fifth, the grammar is rhetorically devastating for Christian discourse and practice because it seems to authorize the following: 'It was the will of God that the van ran over and killed baby Fred.' Sixth, it is not sufficiently trinitarian in considering the full range of God's actions in relation to the world and therefore not able to talk of God's *interaction* with the world. It is no intellectual accident that traditional theism is wedded to the concept of the simplicity and pure actuality of God as one unaffected by the world. Precisely because the causal activity between God and the world is asymmetrical from God to the world, there is no way God can be thought of as being acted upon by the creatures of the world.

What does my sense of trinitarian Christian grammar regard as basically right about this grammar of traditional theism? First, it does take seriously the doctrine of creation and continuing creation as the singular and incommensurate activity of God. Second, with regard to God's creative action, it refuses to place God and creatures in one single order of causal agency. God's creative action is of a different order of action than the action of creaturely causal agents. Third, it refuses to say that any creature is self-creating in any respect, from which it would follow—if the creature were partly *self-creating*—that some aspect of the creature's actuality is beyond the power of God's creative action. If some creature were, in this sense, self-creating, then we could not say God creates all that is actual. We would be putting God into the position of being no more than a molder and shaper of the world but not its Creator. Fourth, therefore, it does not want to place God and the creature in competing actions, such that whatever either one does as agent takes away from what the other as agent does or can do. To reduce God and the creature to a zero-sum situation would force us into a grammar of *synergism*: for any event, God is causal agent of some aspect of the event and the creature is the causal agent of some other aspect and both are necessary to the production of the event. Such synergism is the solution of process theology, but it renders *creatio ex nihilo* unintelligible, and it reduces the concept of causal agency to a univocal concept, applying it with the same meaning to both God and creature. Thus the strength of traditional theism is in seeing that God solely accounts for there being anything at all and for all that exists. This is the ontological dependence of all things on God, without which no thing would be. And it wants to understand God as working though creaturely actions rather than working in such a way as to exclude creaturely actions. Double agency helps in some regards, but it renders unintelligible that God might have an *interactive* history with the world. Hence, we need to sort through some different concepts in order to relieve ourselves of the theological cramps produced by traditional theism.

Critiquing Traditional Theism

Critiquing traditional theism requires that we focus on its tendency to join the doctrine of creation from nothing with a misleading understanding of God's triune actuality and omnipotence and thus has difficulty conceiving how creatures have power that is distinct from God's power. Also it tends to treat these themes of creation and power independent of the themes of the triune actuality of God. Hence, it tends to make unintelligible that God might self-determinately decide to be affected by the created world and thus to have an interactive history and life with the world. Aquinas's God, for example, is unaffected by the world in any respect. Finally, it tends to obscure how we are to understand evil and sin as realities that are contrary to but permitted by the will of God. Much of what I developed in the grammar of God's triune life in the doctrine of God can be seen as a critique of much of traditional theism.

We must take seriously that Jesus Christ is the definitive self-revelation of God and that we are to *think from this revelation.* Then we must take Incarnation seriously and see Jesus Christ's incarnate life, death, and resurrection as the forgiving reconciliation of the sinner. According to this christological insight, we must think of the world as open to God, of God as interactive with and affected by the world—indeed as suffering the cross on behalf of the world—and of sin as that which is contrary to God's purposes in creating a world.

We further need to say that in creating and preserving the world, God creates, endows, consents to, and permits the creature to have its characteristic essence and particularity of powers of activities and thus powers of actuality. This is the creature's relative independence of God and is a precondition of the creature being one who might respond to God in fellowship. God wills this creaturely independence and wills to preserve the creature in the created matrix of its cosmos. This willing of God I call the *permitting will of God*: God permits the creature to have life in distinction from God, over against God, and with the possibility of not cooperating with or rebelling against God's purposes for the creature.

Reconstructing the Grammar of God's Will

We now need to reconstruct the grammar of God's will. Christian discourse has often been misled by the assumption that whatever *God wills to be* in some sense *God causes to be*. While we can accept that whatever God causes to be in some sense God wills to be, we need to distinguish between several dimensions of God's will. The concept of will here is analogous to human intentional willing. But we must allow that God's intentionality might have complexity of scope and focus. Without that allowance, the concept of God's will might be construed in undifferentiated and confusing ways.

First, there is God's *primordial will* as those large purposes intended in the creating and governing of the world. This includes such willing as God's self-determination to become Creator and to be limited and affected by the creation. This concept of God's self-determination to limit Godself in relation to the world is a concept that always eludes traditional theism. The primordial will of God also includes those purposes of God that I have identified earlier. Among these are that God wills the existence of a world of creatures that are genuinely other than God and can be in fellowship with God. The concept of God as pure actuality cannot handle either of these purposes in God's primordial will.

Second, there is God's will as *creational positing and preserving* of the world in the beginning and across creational space and time. God wills to be all that is. But this positing and preserving cannot be adequately articulated without understanding that God's positing will is also God's *permitting will* that the creature be endowed with relative independence of actuality and to have actuality in the midst of the creaturely causal nexus. We cannot draw a sharp distinction between God's positing will and God's permitting will in that to posit the creature is also to endow the creature with appropriate creaturely powers of action and interaction. To create and preserve the creature means in Christian discourse that the creature is permitted to have actuality in relative independence of God. When we say *creatio ex nihilo* we grasp the absolute dependence of the creature on the creative activity of God, without which the creature would not be at all. But when we see this creation from nothing as sustaining and preserving a whole cosmos in actuality in otherness from God, we grasp this best when we emphasize that God *permits* the creature to be actual with powers of action and reaction, even though God does not permit the creature utter independence of God.

Fourth, we must also allow for God's *covenantal will* as that intentional order of moral and spiritual commands, virtues, and values of right relations among humans, between humans and the other creatures, and between humans and God. But, of course, the covenantal will of God would make no sense if the creature had not the power of obeying or disobeying that will.

Fifth, there is God's will as the *particular direct will* to affect the creature's actuality as, for example, (a) the will to be present to the creature in the Spirit through the various modalities of presence; (b) the will to be incarnate in Jesus; (c) the will to govern the emergence of the world in various ways; (d) the will to liberate and redeem the creature from desperate situations; and (e) the will to respond to a prayer. It is this will and action of God that is repudiated by the various forms of deism.

Of these senses of the divine will, it is intelligible to say it is possible for the creature to act contrary to God's will in the senses of God's primordial will, God's covenantal will, and some types of God's direct particular will. But it would not be clear what we could mean in saying the creature acts contrary to the creational positing and preserving and permitting will of God, for without that will, there is no creature to act. Thus, from the considerations of these meanings of the *will of God*, we do not have to say that God wills and therefore causes every event to happen just as it does happen.

With these distinctions in mind, we can *reconstruct the grammar of the creation of individual creatures.* We tend to think that God's primary creative action is the creation of discrete individual creatures. But this is misleading, for God creates individual creatures only by also creating the larger cosmos in which the creature is actual. And this larger cosmos is, as I have affirmed, massively interconnected and interdependent, structured with laws and relational principles, without which no creature could be. So, for God to create a human being involves creating a whole world in which the human being can be systemically supported and given definiteness. In creating, then, God creates the systems and structures of relations that locate and support the particular creatures, and God cannot be continually suspending these structural, systemic relations and regularities. Therefore, God's creative action must be seen as bringing to be a whole cosmos of such systemic structures and sustaining that cosmos in actuality. This is helpful to remember because it requires us to see how *creatio ex nihilo* is unintelligible without seeing it as implying *creatio continua,* or what I have called the preserving work of God. And even though ontological dependence of the world on God is maintained at every moment of time and not just at the beginning, God's preserving activity is precisely the permitting activity of God.

Hence, God creates Adam and Eve within a structured world, in which there is night and day and a world of other creatures and structures that can sustain them. Adam and Eve, within that world, are also endowed with appropriate creaturely powers of action and self-determination. In creating Adam and Eve, God gives them, for example, the powers of rebelling against God's covenantal will and commands. It would seem odd, however, to say God 'caused' them to rebel against God. So, our account of the creation of individual creatures must take account of God's creating them within a structured, relational world and God's creating and endowing them with the appropriate powers of action which comprise their essence or nature. God has purposes in creating this cosmos and permits the creature to have powers of actions in rebelling against these purposes and their covenantal expression. *Thus the locution 'the will of God' covers a family of meanings that must be discriminately used and not reduced to just one meaning and use.*

God's Interaction with the World

Thus, I hope it is clearer *that God not only creates and preserves the world, but governs the world and has a life of interaction with the world and thus acts upon and within the world.* Christian grammar should refuse any attempt to reduce God's action in relation to the world to only one type of action. God has many types of actions with, within, and upon the world. Therefore, all forms of deism must be repudiated as unacceptable to Christian theology. Further, the understanding of God's primordial will as God's primordial self-determination in love to be affected by the world shows that God's interactive life with the world is not only God acting in relation to the world but also the world's acting upon God. Granted, such terms as 'vulnerability,' 'suffering,' and 'rejoicing' as applied to God are analogical and therefore resist attempts to depict exactly how God is affected. Suffice to say that Jesus is the incarnate life of God and he suffered brutally on the cross, and that is itself sufficient for asserting that God suffers not only in the cross but suffers as well in relation to the sufferings of the world.

Interpreting the character of God's interactive life with the world, we can say that *God acts freely and contingently within the cosmos and is therefore self-determinately limited and conditioned by: (a)* God's own antecedent decisions; (b) the general lawlike structures of order God wills for the governance of the world; (c) the indeterminacies God has built into that structure and system of relations with its possibilities of emerging novelities; and (d) the free decisions of humans. Among God's antecedent decisions are such matters as promises to Israel and promises in Jesus Christ. Certainly it makes sense to say that in freedom and love God binds Godself to the world. Hence, two extremes are ruled out: (1) that God can do absolutely anything at any time; and (2) that God cannot act contingently within the cosmos.[57]

While I have affirmed that God can act directly on the world to effect particular outcomes, I am wary about saying that God *intervenes in the world.* The language of 'intervene' and 'intervention' is wedded to assumptions of the Enlightenment and deism. Among these assumptions are that there are strict and inviolable laws of the world by which the world operates and endures more or less on its own powers. This is the distinctively *modern* assumption that the world is a sealed up causal nexus and the assumption that epistemically excludes any agency that is not of the world or locatable in the world. On the basis of these assumptions, talk of divine intervention is mythical talk of what is naturally impossible, so the deist says.

But the Christian angle of construal is different: (a) the world is created, preserved, and governed by God; (b) God has an interactive history with the world; (c) the world is an open and emerging process of becoming, not a deterministic causal nexus; (d) God is thus constantly acting within the world in a variety of possible ways and modalities; and (e) it is not inconceivable in such a world that God might directly act to affect the emerging world in such wise as to produce an effect that is unexpected and unpredictable. Thus we have the possibility of '*miracles.*' Hence, if we carelessly talk of 'divine intervention,' we might be importing the assumptions of the Enlightenment and deism.[58]

---

[57] Ward handles these points helpfully; see *Divine Action*, 111–112.

[58] See the interesting discussion of the meaning of 'laws of nature' and 'miracles' by William P. Alston in Tracy, ed., *The God Who Acts*, 41–62. See also the discussion of C. Stephen Evans, *The Historical Christ and the Jesus of*

We can now reconstruct how we understand the *grammar of God's purposes and the events of the world.* I have already identified God's primordial purposes in creating a world. In addition to these overarching purposes of God, Scripture and tradition testify to God's having short-term and more limited purposes relative to the unfolding events of the world. But even God's limited purposes must be consistent with God's primordial purposes. For example, God's purpose in establishing a Christian community in Ephesus was specific and limited in character but consistent with God's primordial purposes. And it is theologically appropriate to affirm that the Spirit was at work in the founding of the church in Ephesus.

We must pose the question of *whether we should suppose that for every event in the world, there is a specific divine purpose just for the occurrence of that event.* If there is, then it would suggest that there is a divine answer to every 'why question' we might ask: 'why did this event happen?' Did God will it to happen? But here in the word 'will' we have a lurking dilemma. In what sense did God or did God not will the event? That God has general and encompassing purposes for the world does not of itself imply that God must have a specific willed purpose for every event that happens in the world. However, for any particular event, it is possible that God does have a direct purpose for the occurring of that event. But we do not have to say that every particular event *must* have a direct divine purpose in its happening. In God's preservation and governance of the world, God's permitting will plays an indispensable role. Hence, *God may permit much to happen without explicitly and directly willing it to happen.* Thus, there may be no particular divine purpose in its happening, except the divine purpose of permitting it to happen in the creature's life. Yet we can say that in God's permitting will, there is the general purpose of God to honor and preserve the relative independence of the creatures' actions and interactions.

Having made these points, we can say that for humans, in relation to the events in the world and especially to the events that happen to them in particular, it makes sense to ask: '*how does God want me to respond to these events?*' God is always in the Spirit summoning humans to spiritual actions in the world and therefore also to spiritual responses to the events of the world. Accordingly, it is fair to say that the Spirit has purposes in mind in so summoning and moving us. We need not suppose there is a direct divine purpose in answer to every human *why question*—'why did God take little Johnnie from me?' There is here, however, a genuine *spiritual question*—'how does God want me to respond to this terrible early death of my little son Johnnie?' Often in situations of profound grief at the loss of a loved one, the depth grammar of the above utterance is: 'how will I ever cope with this loss and grief; perhaps God will help?' Or, 'I cannot cope with this loss from my own resources unless I, my loss, and the death of Johnnie are encompassed by the reality and love of God.' It is not the triune God's pattern to send bad things to persons *in order to* make them better: 'God caused the deaths of the ninety-nine persons on the airliner, including my daughter, for the purpose of making me give up drink and become a Christian.' This would suggest that God has no regard for the dead persons except as their deaths might be the occasion for another's good.

I affirm, however, that God's governance, in ways often hidden from us, is continually working *to bring good out of evil*. Even though we are not encouraged to expect God to 'intervene' continually in the creational order, it is true that within God's almighty power God *could have* affected the outcome of an event differently. That is, it is always possible that God—in God's interactive governance—might have directly affected the outcome of some event or series of events differently. Christian grammar—because it affirms the sovereign loving freedom of God—precludes saying of any event that it was *impossible for God to have directly affected it differently.* Yet, to the pathos of the question, then, of 'why did God *not* affect the outcome of this terrible event differently?' there is no direct Christian answer. We trust in God's purposes and wisdom, knowing God as we do in Jesus Christ through the Spirit, and we hope in God's eschatologically salvific will. But there is a decisive limit to what we can understand about the wisdom of God's governance of the world in relation to the occurrences of particular events.

Let me now summarize these points. *First*, God does have primordial purposes in creating the world. *Second*, this does not imply that God has a specific willed purpose for every event that occurs, and therefore we do not say God directly causes and wills every event to happen just as it happens. *Third*, many events in the world are contrary to God's primordial and covenantal will—though they are permitted by God. *Fourth*, it is possible that for any particular event God could have been the direct cause of the event, and therefore God could have had a particular purpose for that event. *Fifth*, it is always the case that God is working to bring good out of evil, and therefore God does summon human beings to respond in faith, love, and hope to the ordinary and the evil events of the world. *Sixth*, while I do not believe that God's will is revealed in the happening of every event—that would reduce God to being mere fate—I do believe that God *could have affected the outcome of an event differently*. But this is an abstract qualifier about God's sovereign freedom, love, and power. We are not invited to second-guess God's permitting will and ask why God did not affect some events differently. And I have admitted that God would contravene God's own purposes if God continually contravened the orderly processes of the world. *Seventh*, we cannot presume to understand God's wisdom in the occurrence of every event, though we can believe and hope that God's primordial purposes will be ultimately realized.

With these considerations under our belt, we can turn to issues of evil and theodicy.

The Grammar of Evil and Theodicy

Let us first consider an orienting distinction about the so-called *problem of evil*. There are two quite different senses of the term *problem*: (a) evil as a problem of understanding and explanation; and (b) evil as an existential-personal, practical problem of coping with its concrete reality, as experienced in personal suffering, pain, injury, harm, and injustice, for example. It is the existential sense that has priority in human life and in the Christian life. But how can we cope effectively with this experienced evil without also raising the question of how we are to understand the nature, status, and causes of the evil? To be sure, people obviously do cope with the evil they experience without any clear explanation of its causes and nature. Yet, in questing for some understanding of evil, regrettably some philosophical formulations of the problem of evil seem detached and isolated from the existential problem of evil, and thus those analyses often skew the practical grammar of the problem in its existential dimensions.[59]

The existential problem of evil becomes more sharply focused when it involves belief in the reality of one and only one God. How does God relate to the evil? Hence, the existential problem of evil is differently ex-

---

[59] I take this as the main point of Kenneth Surin's sobering book, *Theology and the Problem of Evil* (Oxford: Blackwell, 1986).

perienced when it involves belief in the reality of God. It is when evil is understood in relation to God that we have the conceptual problem of evil emerge as a *theodicy question*: how can we justify belief in God in the face of the evil in the world and/or how are we to understand the reality of evil in light of believing in God? But surely the theodicy question is deeply affected by the grammar of the term 'God' which is being used. The problem of evil changes with different conceptions of the god. For Christian grammar, we cannot easily pry apart the existential sense of the problem from the conceptual problems of understanding: what does it mean to call something evil? and how do we understand the status of evil in relation to the triune God? Yet the grammar of the issues is never the detached and neutral grammar of theory isolated from passion and practice.

In the grammar of Christian discourse being developed herein, I contend *that evil and theodicy cannot be adequately dealt with—either existentially or conceptually—apart from understanding God as the triune Creator, Reconciler, and Redeemer of the world.* Evil—its nature, status, and causes—cannot be handled abstractly on philosophical grounds independent of the full doctrine of the triune life of God: the Father who creates and governs all creatures, the Son who incarnately lives among and reconciles creatures, and the Spirit who moves redemptively among creatures to bring them to salvific fulfillment.

Biblical Notes

The Bible spends little time trying to analyze evil. It deals mostly with evil as that harm to creatures—mainly human—as a phenomenon that happens under the sovereignty of God the Creator. It consistently attributes most evils to effects of the human violation of God's covenant. In this respect, such violation of the covenant is itself that which is contrary to the will of God. And this violation has consequences for human relations and for the human relations to God.[60] Much of the Scriptural testimony is about the drama of how God contends against evil as this human violation of God's covenantal will given in creation and given to Israel.

There is extensive concern, especially in the OT, with the question of how to interpret the events of both good and evil that historically seem to

---

[60] See 2 Sam 12.9–10; Judg 2.11–15; 13.1.

befall humans individually and collectively. Are these goods and evils evidence of the recipient's morally good or evil will and behavior? Are they evidence of divine reward and punishment? The Book of Job is essentially about these issues, and tries to hold together several theological points:

a. that God is the sovereign Governor of the whole world and nothing happens without the consent of the divine will;

b. that the goods and evils that befall persons are not simple and straightforward evidence of either divine favor or divine punishment—the rain falls on the just and the unjust;

c. that, hence, humans should stop trying to figure out God's governing wisdom by trying to infer it from the way things happen in the world;

d. that the good and evil that humans do to each other do not escape the divine reckoning, but such reckoning is not simply administered in how good and evil events happen to the human agents of good and evil;

e. that God's relation to the creation—to the good and evil that befall humans and to the good and evil that they do—is an inscrutable mystery beyond human understanding and explanation.[61]

In the NT the primary focus is on that evil called *sin* and its consequences, which pivots around the drama of God's incarnational defeat of sin as the presumed determiner of human meaning and destiny and the gracious work of the Spirit to redeem the world. Neither testament shows any extended concern for the harm done to nonhuman creatures, except maybe domestic animals. Paul does assert:

> [T]he creation was subjected to futility, not of its own will but by the will of the one who subjected it, in hope that the creation itself will be set free from its bondage to decay and will obtain the freedom of the glory of the children of God. We know that the whole creation has been groaning in labor pains until now . . . for the redemption of our bodies.[62]

This clearly places the whole creation, with its groaning under perishing and decay, in the ultimate context of God's redemptive purposes.

---

[61] These remarks are embarrassingly slight in comparison to the complex narrative of the Book of Job. See the excellent discussion in J. Gerald Janzen, *Job*, Interpretation Bible Commentary (Atlanta: John Knox, 1987).

[62] Rom 8.20–23.

Sorting the Grammar of Evil

In *ordinary discourse* even today we find the following important contrastive terms: 'good and bad,' 'good and evil,' 'right and wrong.' Sometimes these contrastive terms are mutually exclusive, and sometimes they are graded, tending to possibilities of more or less. One of the most common uses of 'good and bad' and 'good and evil' is to performatively express *approval* or *disapproval* of some state of affairs: 'that shirt looks good on you' expresses approval. Deep within much of our discourses are criteria or rules for how we determine approval and disapproval with regard to differing states of affairs, though much of the time the *good and bad* are used by reference to the *preferences* of the speaker. With 'right and wrong' we are mostly dealing with moral appraisals, though we do say such things as 'you did not put the saddle on right,' meaning something nonmoral by that judgment. *Good and evil* seem to be more serious than *good and bad* and often close to *right and wrong*, but not simply reducible to either pair of contrasts. But however we might further provide criteria for applying *good and evil*, we are aware that the two terms will be defined by their contrastive meanings: we cannot talk of *good* without talking of *evil*.

As contrastive terms, *good and evil* can be semantically applied to either *states of affairs* or *agents or causes of state of affairs*. The logically prior consideration is how *good and evil* apply to states of affairs, for it is in terms of those states of affairs, appraised as either good or evil, that we might talk about the good or evil agents or causes that brought about a particular state of affairs.

In theological traditions there are *three definitions of evil* that are prominent:[63]

a. evil as the privation of good;
b. evil as harm to some creature's good;
c. evil as that which is contrary to the will of God.

Evil as the privation of good is most commonly associated with Augustine. It avoids saying that evil is primarily a metaphysical *agent* that is as ultimate as God, as for example in Manicheanism. This view retains the sense that what God has created is good or of value to God, and hence what God creates is not evil as such. Evil, then, is that state of

---

[63] A reasonably helpful survey of concepts of evil in Christian traditions can be found in John Hick, *Evil and the Love of God* (London: Macmillan, 1966).

affairs or condition in which there is a privation—a diminution, a default, a deprivation, a corruption—of some good. When applied to creatures—mainly human creatures—we are referring to some respect in which the creature's good or well-being has been deprived or diminished. Hence, the concrete meaning of evil is dependent on the concrete meaning of good with regard to the creature. We can then ask about the causes of this privation of good.

Evil as harm to some creature's good is a close variation on evil as privation of good, but invites more promptly the inquiry into the causes of the harm. It requires that the creature's good be understood normatively and teleologically and not simply by reference to experiences of pain and suffering. Normatively, a creature's good is that state of affairs we can call 'well-being' or 'flourishing.' For Christians this always at least includes responsive and obedient fellowship and communion with God and fellowship with other humans. Whatever prevents, frustrates, or causes injury to the creature's well-being is thereby *harm to the creature's good*.

Evil as that which is contrary to the will of God is a strong biblical theme and is certainly at least a dimension of evil, especially with regard to humans violating the covenantal will of God. But it does not seem to help much in clarifying the respects in which evil might afflict the nonhuman creatures and the ways in which natural forces might cause evil. For example, are hurricanes that destroy creaturely life contrary to the will of God?

My constructive proposal is that we fundamentally think of evil as harm to some creature's good. This definition of evil can accommodate the concerns of the other two definitions. We now need to sort the grammar of the agents and causes of evil.

Sorting the Grammar of the Agents and Causes of Evil

Among the *agents and causes of evil*, we can identify the following:
a. nonhuman creaturely agents and causes;
b. human agents;
c. transpersonal powers or causes.

Considering *nonhuman creatures as agents and causes of evil*, we can come to grips with how such creatures do inflict harm to the good of other creatures. In all their great variety and differences, creaturely centers of activity, either in their simple forms or their complex forms, afflict each other and humans in ways that harm the good of the other creature. We do not impute any intentionality or purpose or moral responsibility to these creaturely agents of harm. Because we do not so impute intentionality to the creature, we do not view their afflicting action as culpable, and therefore they are not agents of evil in such wise that we can call them agents with an evil will. They are merely doing their created creaturely sort of thing that has the consequence of bringing harm to other creatures.

Human creatures as agents and causes of evil is the most prominent meaning of evil in the biblical testimony and in the traditions. For our diagnostic purposes we can distinguish between human action that causes evil inadvertently or accidentally and human action that intentionally causes evil. This intentional action violates the structure of right relationships established by God's covenantal will. We are mainly concerned with those intentional actions that violate God's covenantal will and thereby afflict other humans with harm to their good.

Transpersonal powers as causes of evil refers here to those *force fields of power* in the human social relations and relationships that exercise causal efficacy that produces harm to creatures. They are also called 'principalities and powers' in the NT.[64] These are still creaturely powers but they are not reducible to the power of human agents individually: hence they are *transpersonal*. Think, for example, of those force fields of power that cause great harm to human beings: the powers of nationalism, ethnicity, class, gender, and the powers of economic systems, traditions of rivalry and enmity. Of course, none of these powers could exist without human consent and complicity.[65]

It is appropriate to ask where the *devil* fits in these categories, since the traditions have repeatedly referred to the devil as the opponent of God and doer and provocateur of much evil. Nowhere, however, in the traditions is it suggested that the devil is as ultimate as God, and it is

---

[64] See Eph 1.21; 2.2; 6.12; Col 2.10–15; Rom 8.38.

[65] See substantive examinations of this concept in Hendrikus Berkhof, *Christ and the Powers*, trans. John H. Yoder (Scottsdale, Pa.: Herald, 1962). See also Walter Wink, *Naming the Powers: The Language of Power in the New Testament* (Philadelphia: Fortress, 1984); *Unmasking the Powers: The Invisible Forces That Determine Human Destiny* (Philadelphia: Fortress, 1986); *Engaging the Powers: Discernment and Resistance in a World of Domination* (Philadelphia: Fortress, 1992). Wink's new book, *The Powers That Be: Theology for a New Millennium* (New York: Doubleday, 1998), is a recapitulation and extension of the earlier three books.

typically affirmed that the devil is a creature, sometimes thought of as a fallen angel. While there is good reason to impute agency to the devil, there seems less reason to make the devil into a singular agent existing somewhere. Rather, I propose that we think of the devil as comprised by the principalities and powers—those force fields of powers—that have been corrupted by humans and which corrupt humans in vicious cycles and trajectories of destructive power. These demonic powers do indeed bring about much suffering and evil among humans and nonhuman creatures.

On Distinguishing Natural Evil and Moral Evil

This is, with some variations, a traditional distinction and has to do with discriminating between types of causal agency of evil. *Natural evil* is defined negatively *as that evil that is brought about by nonmoral causal agency.* Natural evil is the many forms of evil that occur in the natural functioning and malfunctioning of creatures in their interactions and collisions as historical processes of becoming. Consider, for example, the afflictions of weather, natural disasters, natural diseases, malfunctioning bodies, and creatures consuming and preying on creatures.

In contrast, *moral evil is that evil done by humans—or by humans in complicity with transpersonal powers—that violates the covenantal will of God.* It is a precondition of such actions that they are that sort of intentional actions that can be called *human finite freedom.* But they need not be actions that have as such the *intention* to violate God's covenantal will and they may or may not have the intention of harming some creature or creatures. But human moral evil also includes the unintended consequences of actions that are harmful to some creature and for which we assign moral responsibility. For example, Fred, driving his car while intoxicated, did not have the intention of colliding with Mary's car and causing her death. Nevertheless, Fred is morally responsible for this consequence. Moral evil is that human action which either intends harm to some creature's good or results in such harm. Hence, the test is not simply whether the harmful action was intentional toward doing the harm but was the intentional action one that also resulted in harm. Humans are the sort of creatures that are summoned by God to be responsible for their actions and the consequences of their actions. But even here, without becoming unduly complicated, moral evil is that evil done, whether by intentional or by omission of action, to which we can assign moral responsibility.

When I include transpersonal powers as agents of moral evil, I am pointing to the human complicity with these powers in which harm results to creatures. They may not be intended as such, but nevertheless the force fields of powers do inflict harm. The subtle grammar here is that the harm done by the powers may not be attributable to one person or set of persons, but nevertheless the powers could not exist without the complicity of many persons.

The full nature of this evil is further evident insofar as such harmful actions also violate the relationship to God that God summons humans to have. It should now be clear that the more serious uses of the contrasts between *good and evil* bear on the evil that humans afflict on each other and on themselves in violation of God's covenantal will. This meaning of evil we also call *sin*, and it encompasses much of what is meant in the assertion that evil is that which is *contrary to the will of God*, meaning thereby the covenantal will of God.

Formulating Theodicy Issues

The classical formulation of theodicy starts with the following assumed beliefs:[66]

a. that God is the Creator of the world;
b. that God is omnipotent;
c. that God is perfectly good and loving;
d. that evil exists.

The following questions are then posed:

e. If God is omnipotent, then God has the power to prevent evil, and if God is good, then God must want to prevent evil; so then why does God permit evil?
f. Wouldn't a good and loving God want to prevent evil happening to creatures?

From these questions it draws the following conclusions:

g. Either God is not omnipotent with the power to prevent evil or God is not good and loving;
h. Logically, God cannot be both omnipotent and good in the face of the existence of evil;

---

[66] For helpful formulations of some traditional theodicy issues, see Stephen T. Davis, *Encountering Evil: Live Options in Theodicy* (Atlanta: John Knox, 1981) and Robert Merrihew Adams and Marilyn McCord Adams, eds., *The Reality of Evil* (Oxford: Oxford University Press, 1990).

i.   Therefore, God is either not omnipotent or not good.

The standard classical response to the theodicy questions attempts the so-called free will defense, attributing the primary evil in the world to the freely willed actions of humans. It argues that evil exists because God created human freedom. It can sometimes further argue that the freedom of humans to do evil contributes to a greater good than if there were no humans with finite freedom. Since God is surely not culpable in creating human freedom, God can conceivably be both omnipotent and good. It further argues, however, that the reality of God is such an inscrutable mystery that we humans cannot know how to explain the existence of evil in a world created by an omnipotent and good God.[67] This response has to admit that the natural evil in the world is a consequence of God's creating this sort of world, and therefore God is in some sense responsible for this evil. My previous discussion of God's permitting will was designed to deal with this question as well as the question of human finite freedom.

Process theology concedes the legitimacy of the critique of the classical theodicy formulation and offers a reconstructive response. First, it accepts that God is not creator in the traditional sense as the one who creates the world from nothing. Rather, creativity is something shared by God and all creatures, for every actuality is at least partially *self-creating*. It further concedes that God is not omnipotent; rather God's power is metaphysically limited by the self-creating power of actualities other than God. It contends that God's goodness is preserved because God is doing *the best God can do* in the face of the creative independence of the other actualities; God seeks and struggles to persuade the agents of the world for their and others' good. Finally, it affirms that the existence of evil as such is simply a precondition for there being any world at all, which does not mean that any evil in the world must be complacently accepted and tolerated.[68]

But note the following diagnostic points about the classical theodicy and its reconstructive responses. The arguments are carried out without reference to the triune Life of God, but simply consider God in terms of being creator of the world—and a nontriune creator at that! Further, the

---

[67] For an accessible discussion of the free will defense, see Alvin Plantinga, *God, Freedom, and Evil* (New York: Harper and Row, 1974).

[68] For thorough critiques of traditional theism and for careful defense of the process perspective, see David Ray Griffin, *God, Power, and Evil: A Process Theodicy* (Philadelphia: Westminster, 1976) and *Evil Revisited* (Albany, N.Y.: SUNY Press, 1991).

incarnation of God in Jesus Christ and the promise of an eschatological redemption are not brought to bear on any of the issues. Most defenses of classical theodicy remain staunchly in the framework of classical theism, and the process theological alternative gives up any strong sense of God as Creator of the world. For process theology the 'principle of creativity' is the ultimate given and applies to both God and all other actualities.

A Trinitarian Theodicy and Its Limits

In distinction from most formulated theodicies, I do not start with God the Creator as an independent theme. Rather I start with the triune God we know definitively in Jesus Christ. Given the epistemic priority of the economic Trinity, we have argued that God has in love and freedom self-determinately created a world with gracious purposes in mind and has been contending with the world's creaturely independence and frequent resistance to God's governance. God also created human creatures in God's own image, who, under the conditions of finite freedom, inevitably rebel against God's covenantal summons. Hence, in response to human evil, God elected Israel as covenant partner and light to the nations, has become incarnate in the Jew Jesus of Nazareth for the salvation of humankind and the whole world, and moves in the Holy Spirit to redeem creatures ultimately. Assuming this kerygmatic grammar of the Gospel of Jesus Christ, and assuming what has been developed above about God's creative and governing activity, I propose the following theodical responses.

In creating a whole cosmos—at whatever stage of its unfolding creation history—God is creating the structures and orders and sorts of creatures that will necessarily involve some colliding and harm to some creature's good. I will admit that in God's creating this world, natural evil is to some extent inescapable, without saying that God directly causes any particular harm to be. Hence, *God is responsible for the conditions under which natural evil of some sorts unavoidably takes place.* Does this impugn God's loving regard for and valuing of the various types of creatures? It might, though these are limiting grammatical matters that escape our easy formulation. I do not want to argue that natural evil contributes to some greater good and is therefore justified. And I do not want to argue that this world is the best of all possible worlds. These sorts of arguments are much too abstract, and I must admit that we, like Job, do not know how to stand in judgment on God's creative activity with arguments that will vindicate God. That is, I do not know how to appeal to a set of concepts that will of themselves justify God creating *this world*, with its obvious array of evils, as distinct from some other world that might have fewer evils. But there remains *the grammar of God's eschatological work*: God in transcendent vertical and horizontal ways redeems and will redeem the creature from absolute perishing and thus will fulfill the creature. If there were not some such ultimate eschatological redemption, then it would be utterly obscure how we could say God loves all the creatures of the world.[69]

In creating human beings, God endows them with finite freedom: the freedom of intentional actions, including rebelling against God's summons to covenantal life with God.[70] Inexplicably—that is, without any ontological necessity or explanation—humans do rebel and commit sin. In committing sin and being sinned against, humans become encumbered by the consequences of sin: disintegration of the self, alienation from other persons, and alienation from God. Hence, humans bring harm to their own good and to the good of other creatures. It is a built-in consequence of sinning that human becoming is mired in this alienation and its spiraling trajectories and thereby becomes subject to enmity, violence, and a despairing death. Does God cause humans to sin? No. Does God cause the consequences of sin? In a sense, yes, because the consequences of sin are those structures of destruction that intrinsically and inherently follow from sinning. Sin is fundamentally the choosing of life without God, which is choosing death.

In Jesus Christ, God comes to the rescue of the human creature, engaging the sinners and the principalities and powers of evil, disarming them of their power to determine human destiny before God, and forgiving the sinners their sin; this is God breaking the destructive powers of sin.[71] In the Spirit of Jesus Christ, God moves humans to respond to the invitation to a new life no longer under the domination of sin and moves humans in hope to look to an ultimate redemption. Hence, *trinitarianly understood, evil is permitted by God, engaged by God, and finally defeated by God. This is the only theodicy that makes sense of the full range of God's triune life with and for the world.*

---

[69] For further exploration of this theme of God's eschatological redemption, see chapter thirteen on eschatology.

[70] See the discussion in the next chapter on humanity as created and as sinful.

[71] See 1 Jn 3.8; Heb 2.14–15; 10.12–23.

Creaturely Pain and Suffering

I have acknowledged that the world God created is a world with competing goods and real losses among the creatures of the world: creatures collide with other creatures and harm one another's good. And I affirmed that some pain and suffering are inescapable in this world. For humans we can distinguish in most instances between pain and suffering that are basically physical and pain and suffering that are basically psychical and spiritual. But, of course, all pain involves the mind. And there are complex interactions between the physical and the mind that are beyond any easy tracking and discernment. Yet pain and suffering are experiences of embodied persons.

We should not suppose that every pain and suffering as such of any creature is itself an evil, for the capacity of sentient creatures to experience pain and suffering is in itself a positive capacity. The capacity for pain is not a sign of divine punishment, but is intrinsic to our creaturely finitude. The experience of pain can alert the creature to threatening possibilities of danger and harm and thereby stimulate reactions of avoidance or coping. My middle daughter had a rare spinal cord stroke several years ago that left her immediately paralyzed from the chest down. Through courage, persistence, and the empowerment of the Spirit, my daughter regained the capacity to move her legs and walk. But she still has no feeling in her body from the chest down. Hence, her body cannot alert her to the functioning of her internal organs, and she is often surprised by an upset stomach. Except for possible fever, she would not know if her appendix ruptured. She cannot feel the bruising or straining of her leg muscles, and therefore does not know when they need special rest and care. She would only know she has suffered a cut if she sees it; she could not feel it. My daughter would love to have the capacity in her lower body to experience pain and its incumbent suffering.

The experiences of pain and suffering are always also the particular experience of a particular person in some concrete set of circumstances, which has its own causes. Hence, the causes of pain and suffering vary immensely, and we respond to the pain in terms of what we might perceive to be its causes, though often the causes are hidden from the sufferer. At its excruciating extremities, pain and suffering are destructive and debilitating of the person and cut to the core of the person's life, thus diminishing her coping powers. These are experiences of great harm to one's well-being. Current studies in severe human traumas lay starkly before us just how destructive the experience can be to the individual. There are many experiences of pain and suffering as experiences of evil that are occasioned by natural causes and many occasioned by human intentional affliction. Note: *to afflict* is to cause pain and suffering. Indeed we can say that experiences of pain and suffering are often the crucial signals or symptoms of our encounter with the agents and causes of evil, both natural and sinful.[72]

Because pain and suffering are so distressing, for most humans the basic dynamic of their life is the avoidance of pain and the pursuit of pleasure, as the opposite of pain. However, this dynamic is to be differentiated from Christian life and its experiences of pain and suffering. There is nothing in Christian grammar that says Christians will be preserved from experiencing pain and suffering in this life. There is no theological reason to believe that Christians will be protected from the contingent harms occasioned by their encounters with other creatures and the vulnerabilities of their embodied personhood. This given creaturely vulnerability to harm and its consequent suffering is not a condition from which the believer can expect exemption and protection.[73] This given situation, however, is not a reason for the Christian to accept complacently any particular harm and suffering that other creatures might inflict. Yet, to the extent Christians are followers of Jesus Christ in the world, they will probably suffer for their witness as they encounter the powers of the world. But the extraordinary point of Christian belief and practice is that the believer trusts that no harm inflicted by any creature can separate her from the love of God. This is not to say that the believer will be protected from harm or to deny that some great harm might befall the believer with such severity as to diminish or even extinguish her capacity to experience the love of God.

---

[72] This is not to say that all situations of evil are accompanied by pain and suffering in any obvious sense. But there are those often silent sufferings, without physical pain, that afflict the persons who are in one way or another in despair. See Søren Kierkegaard, *The Sickness unto Death*, ed. and trans. Howard V. Hong and Edna H. Hong, *Kierkegaard's Writings,* vol. 19 (Princeton, N.J.: Princeton University Press, 1980).

[73] Precisely because Jesus himself suffered and died on the cross, that strand of Hebraic theologizing that proposes that God will protect from harm those whom God favors, as expressed in Psalm 91, is brought under serious questioning. Of course, it had already come under scrutiny in Deutero–Isaiah. This insight on Psalm 91 I owe to J. Gerald Janzen.

Essential to Christian grammar on suffering is that all the sufferings of the world of creatures are known and experienced by God and that thereby God suffers with the creature. This is the clear import of God's becoming human and suffering affliction from other humans and suffering finally an ignominious death on the cross. It is in the cross of Jesus Christ that God encounters most profoundly the inimical powers of sin that afflict humans constantly, and Jesus disarms these agents of suffering of the power to be the final determination of the meaning and scope of human life. No suffering of any creature, of whatever sort, happens without God's empathetic and suffering response. I have consistently denied that God should be understood as impassible and apathetic, incapable of being moved by another and incapable of suffering with and for another. I have affirmed that God suffers as the creature suffers. This emphasis on the suffering of God in the midst of the evils humans experience was consistently missing from the theodicy defenses given by classical theism.

In emphasizing the suffering of God, I do not mean to suggest that all sufferings of whatever sort and under any circumstances are thereby justified. We protest insistently against the unjust human inflictions of evil that cause great suffering in the lives of humans. God is at war against these inflictions, and God suffers in the midst of them. But because we know of God's love for us and because we trust the Spirit of God, we are given power to cope with the sufferings we meet. Sometimes this power to cope is no more than the power to hope beyond the suffering. And Christian faith affirms that even when we are so diminished by the afflictions of evil that we cannot cope or resist—similar to Jesus' affliction on the cross—God will eschatologically redeem the world from the power of evil to determine our whole destiny.

There is yet a lingering question. In some of the traditions of the church, there is a strand of teaching, rooted in the OT, that asserted that all the sufferings of humans are the consequences of sin and signs of God's punishment of the sinner; as though without sinning, there would be no suffering. This is closely associated with the belief that the goods and evils that befall a human in the course of her life are respectively signs of divine reward for obedience and divine punishment for sin. The Book of Job, as I have mentioned, seriously challenges this view. This view is hard to sustain in the face historically of the profound suffering of many of the faithful for their witness to God. While human sinning does itself have an inherent structure of disintegration and destruction of human well-being, we would be unwise to try to correlate this structure straightforwardly to the goods and evils that befall persons in history. Empirically and by some standards, it may appear that some evil agents flourish and are not afflicted as are some of the faithful. But such is a profound deception and illusion: the corruption of their evil hearts is a repudiation of any genuine flourishing before God. At points such as these we come to understand how radically different the grammar of Christian faith is from the grammars of many of the views of life that reign in the worlds of human affairs.[74]

Creation Pragmatics

While the full range of practices that express the Christian belief in God as Creator and Provider will unfold throughout this grammatical exercise, I can note some that have particular urgency in our time. But over all of the Christian life there are those wise practices of celebrating our life as a creature who exists by the love of God. That we exist at all is a gift of God. Hence, Christian grammar denies that our life is nothing but a burden to be rejected and a bitterness to be hated, though we are reminded not to be glib in the face of those tragic diminutions of life that afflict many individuals. Precisely because the believer knows herself as a creature of God, she knows herself and her afflicted neighbor as existing before a loving Creator who is her Redeemer. Christian discourse and practice do not know a Creator who may or may not be our Redeemer. Any pragmatics of life that denies this goodness of creatureliness is a pragmatics alien to Christian faith.

We must especially affirm this in those situations in which our life may be full of misery and physical handicaps. Even in these challenging circumstances, our life as creature is to be affirmed and celebrated. Hence, creation belief entails the practices of protecting life from harm, seeking ways to build up life and encouraging its flourishing before God. Here flourishing does not mean realizing some abstract human potential, but it does mean knowing God and having fellowship with God. This knowledge and its pragmatics of life are not limited to those whose lives

---

[74] Insightful discussions of evil and human suffering can be found in Douglas John Hall, *God and Human Suffering: An Exercise in the Theology of the Cross* (Minneapolis: Augsburg, 1986); Arthur C. McGill, *Suffering: A Test of Theological Method* (Philadelphia: Westminster, 1982); and Fiddes, *The Creative Suffering of God*.

are 'healthy' and 'successful' according to the world's grammar of well-being and success and good.

It is urgently the case today that Christians confront honestly the whole range of issues involved in our undeniable ecological crisis. Our human practices of the past have presumed that the whole of the created order was fundamentally at the disposal of human decisions and values. Not only was this negligent of the ways in which our past practices threatened long-term human well-being, it is also alien to the Christian belief that we humans are created from dust and deeply interconnected with a creational order of other creatures. We must rediscover practices that acknowledge this interconnection of creatures, including both living and nonliving creatures. God has given us a complex and interrelated world in which to live and has called us to be *stewards of this world.* Stewards are not owners, but they are the responsible managers of the owners' purposes and desires. In this sense, God is the owner of the world, and humans are merely—but importantly—the well-furnished yet limited agents of God's ownership. We are not led to believe that God's sole purpose in creating a world is that humans might thrive and be redeemed, though that is among God's primordial purposes in creating. I have affirmed this sense of stewardship in the statement of the Gospel: *humans are summoned in the Spirit to "caring for the whole creation."*

I propose also the practice of affirming the value of other creatures as God's creation and not giving in to valuing such nonhuman creatures only as means to our human ends and happiness. This is the practice of appreciating the *otherness of the creature as God's creature.* Here we encounter the difficult questions that have become urgent in our time, namely, the questions of the so-called rights of animals. Stephen Webb and others have written soberly on how we are to engage in practices that do not use animals merely for our human purposes and ends. Animals have a divine right, they claim, to their lives, protected from the harm of human use as food and as subjects of experimentation. The claim is that the animal creature has a good that is not morally at the disposing of the human and that should be honored by humans.[75]

While the full range of these issues demand our further consideration and attention, I can here note that even the continued use of animals as food must be a practice that expresses gratitude for the animal as a crea-

---

[75] See Stephen H. Webb, *On God and Dogs: A Christian Theology of Compassion for Animals* (Oxford: Oxford University Press, 1998).

ture of God. This sense of gratitude precludes wantonness, cruel indifference, and waste in our consumption of animals and in our ways of taking their lives. Gratitude also precludes indifference to the animal's value as such as a creature of God. Even when the Bible suggests that some animals are given to humans as sources of food, it does not mean they are simply at the disposal of humans under any and all conditions of slaughter, indifference, and extravagance. While I am not prepared to recommend the practice of eating only plant life—called 'vegetarianism'—I do appreciate the solemnity of the vegetarian's regard for the life of the animal creature. But in all of our human actions toward animals we must avoid the assumption that they exist merely for our pleasure and good. This, of course, is not to deny that animal companionship is a rare and privileged gift to us humans.

We should forgo the temptation of some animal rights advocates who assert that the animal has the *same value* before God as any human creature. While I disbelieve this assertion and worry about its implications for the regard for humans, I do believe that animals have a value before God that is not merely instrumental to human good.

These new practices of Christian stewardship must include such matters as preserving and using wisely the earth's resources, protecting the larger ecosystem from human abuse and destruction, and limiting our human appetite for more and more of the world's limited resources. We must resist the belief that because we have the technological knowledge necessary to subdue some aspect of nature that we are thereby morally free to apply our knowledge and technology. Further, we must create practices of living on behalf of—and for the benefit of—future generations who may be consigned to experiencing the brunt of centuries of human neglect of its nonhuman environment.

Chapter Six

Human Being as Created and Sinful

The doctrine of humanity—like the doctrine of God—is a continuous subject of the whole of systematic theology. A complete treatment of the nature and destiny of human being thus includes the following topics: humanity as created; humanity as sinful and fallen; humanity as reconciled and called into community; humanity as eschatologically destined and redeemed. Humanity in its fullness of being is seen through a prism in which its various dimensions and shades of light are refracted. In this chapter we are basically asking about humanity as *created* and *sinful*.

The basic questions of human identity and destiny are intensely existential and universal. Who am I? Who are others? What must I do? Where am I going? How can I be fulfilled (saved)? Is there release from this bondage of finitude, vulnerability, and sin? Humans concretely are puzzling to themselves.

These questions asked by human beings have many answers historically and contemporarily. *Who the human truly is* is as elusive and disputable as *who God is*. Think of the big alternatives in our contemporary world—that humans are primarily biological, primarily physical, primarily psychological, primarily spiritual, primarily social, primarily economic, primarily political. We cannot develop a Christian grammar without being aware that there are powerful principalities and powers that want to tell humans who they are, to be the dispensers of human self-understanding, and thereby to be the controllers of human identity and destiny. Hence, we must not suppose there is some *general rational agreement* about human being on the basis of which Christians can build their theological understanding of humanity.

We will need, however, to reckon with the vast amount of learning about the human which is available in the contemporary world. But this learning, to the extent that it is scientific, will not be able to address some of the most fundamental questions about human being. Yet what we do otherwise know about human beings from sources of contemporary learning can influence how we understand theologically the human situation. For example, we seem to know more about the physical and social systemic character of human existence than our forebears.

In developing a Christian grammar of human being, we must remember Calvin's rule: *true knowledge of humanity cannot be separated from true knowledge of God.* To know self and others truly is to know God truly, and to know God truly is to know self and others truly.[1] What then is our starting point in systematic theology? I will start with Scripture and tradition as normed by the Gospel of Jesus Christ. I will look there to provide the basic contours and diagnostic points for understanding humanity, even as this is supplemented by other learning. But basically we must remember that Jesus Christ is not only the normative revelation of God but is also the *normative revelation of true humanity.* One of the salutary contributions of Karl Barth is his building a doctrine of humanity around Jesus Christ, instead of proceeding with the traditions by adopting first some philosophical anthropology to frame and ground the basic grammar of human being. However, in ways Barth would neither admit nor counsel, I will draw on much contemporary learning to discern a shape of human being that is also deeply biblical and that is illuminated and normed by Jesus Christ.[2]

But which Jesus is the normative revelation? The Jesus of historical research? That is, the Jesus that might be projected by the canons of historical research as applied to the past—what these canons permit one to say about Jesus. This is problematic because historical research, by virtue of its canons of description, can never say anything about Jesus' relationship with God or about Jesus being the perfect model for humanity. Historians who speak this way qua historians have confused their categories and have surreptitiously slipped in theological descriptions or moral appraisals.

---

[1] John Calvin, *Institutes of the Christian Religion*, I, 1.

[2] See Barth, *Church Dogmatics*, III/2, for the full development of his doctrine of humanity as created being.

But historical canons are not the only way we have of making reality assertions about the past or about past figures. I will be talking about the *actual Jesus* on the basis of the biblical testimony in and through narratives, character descriptions, pictures, and images, which are used to say *who Jesus was and is.* From these we can knit together something about the actuality of Jesus' humanity, even as we also use judgments from historical research.[3]

In the whole of this systematic theological grammar, humanity will be described in the following *diagnostic categories* as normed by assertions about Jesus' humanity:

a. Human Being as Created Being
b. Human Being as Sinful Being
c. Human Being as Reconciled Being in Jesus Christ
d. Human Being as Redeemed Being in the Holy Spirit

All of these doctrinal foci comprise the Christian doctrine of humanity, or what is sometimes called 'Christian Anthropology.'

In the doctrinal topics of this chapter I will discuss:

a. Human Being as Created Being
    1. as creaturely being: creature among creatures
    2. as personal being: person among persons
    3. as spiritual being: spirit among spirits
b. Human Being as True Being in Jesus Christ
c. Human Being as Sinful Being

In later chapters I will complete the doctrine of humanity by addressing the grammar of Human Being as Reconciled and Redeemed.

Under the topic of Human Being as Created Being in this chapter, then, I will be aiming to discern and describe the grammar of the multidimensional structures, powers, and possibilities of human being as created by God. *Our basic question is*: what are the essential and constituent structures and powers of human being—as created by God and without which we would not have the actuality of human being—which Scripture, tradition, and contemporary learning suggest?

---

[3] For a more extensive discussion of these recalcitrant issues, see the section on faith and history in chapter seven on the Person of Jesus Christ.

Human Being as Creaturely Being:
Creature among Creatures

Human being, as creaturely being, is created by God the Creator. As
with other creatures, human being is posited in being by God.[4] Humans
could not be or exist except for the creative action of God. Hence, human
creatures are ontologically dependent on God for their existence. In saying this, it is also denied that human creaturely being is ontologically
autonomous or simply self-created. Further, as developed in the doctrine
of creation, creaturely being is a *gift* of God, created by the free love of
God.

In this section I will explore the ways in which human being shares
in the general conditions of being-a-creature in continuity with other
creatures of God. In emphasizing here the continuities with other creatures, I am not denying there are also discontinuities in which human
being is distinguished from other creatures. These distinguishing traits
will be explored in the discussions below of human being as personal and
as spirit.

*As creaturely being, human being is distinct from and other than
God.* As creature, human being is utterly different than the being of the
Creator, conforming to the basic ontological distinction—for Christian
grammar—between the Creator and the creature. As other than God, human being has real being and agency distinct from God, though not independent of God. Hence, as thoroughly creaturely, human being is not
quasi-divine, not part-divine, not an emanation of God, not descended
from God, not a diminution of God.

As creaturely being, human being is finite being. Space and time are
forms of finitude and of the fields of the possible and actual. Human being is always a *particular* limited human being, conditioned and delimited in the field of the possible and the actual. Human being does not
have unlimited possibility. As with all other creatures, humans are temporal actualities that have a beginning in time and an end in time. Humans are born and die as given conditions of life and are, therefore,
mortal. But as a gift of God, humans have their lives as a temporal sequence in which to live, to act, to become, to develop, to flourish as possibilities of their lives. As this temporal sequence of living, humans have
a past, a present, and a future as the dynamic conditions of their living.

---

[4] See Gen 1.27; 2.7; Isa 45.12; 64.8. See as well the discussion of God the
Creator in chapter five.

This temporal finitude is not a prison or punishment, nor is it—in the light of Jesus' resurrection—the full scope of human being and destiny.

As creaturely being, human being is a physically embodied being. Human being has *spatial location* as a material body [*soma*] related to other bodies. As physical body, humans are strikingly similar to and in continuity with other creatures that have physical bodies. The human body as such may differ in complexity from other creaturely bodies, but the similarities and continuities are essential to a Christian grammar of human being. As physical body human being is in part comprised of in-herited, genetically particular traits and tendencies. As a material body, human being is both dependent upon other creatures for food and sus-tentation and vulnerable to the invasion of other creatures in the form of disease and injury. As a body, human being in time is subject to the growth and decline of the body over time, and thus subject to inevitable diminution, deterioration, and decay.

A human being's body is also essential to her being known and identified and located by other creatures and humans. It is certainly ap-parent in the Bible and in everyday experience that the human face is central to being known by others. Our face and bodily shape are a given presence that is easily discernible and important to human transactions. Bodily features, bodily capacities, and bodily descriptions are inescap-able in human interaction with other creatures and among themselves.

As with many other creatures, but not all, embodied human beings are *sexually differentiated into male and female.*[5] We should distinguish at this point *sexual differentiation*—which is inescapable and bod-ily—from *gender roles*—which are by and large socially constructed. The church has often not been able to maintain this distinction between bodily sexual differentiations and gender-constructed roles for man and woman. It is the feminist movement that has dramatically identified and insisted on this distinction. We must acknowledge, however, that most of the biblical witnesses tend to a patriarchal construction of both sexuality and gender. We will revisit some of these issues when we explore the grammar of male and female being created in the image of God in the next section on personal being.

As embodied being, human being's particular body is a *given raw*

---

[5] I do admit that such sexual differentiation in its bodily characteristics is sometimes confused and ambiguous for some humans. But the extraordinarily miniscule ratio of such phenomena only goes to prove the virtual universality of differentiation into male and female.

material of her or his life. Every human has to contend with her or his bodily actuality. And of course, our bodies are subject to great change over time.

As creaturely being, human being is living being. In the OT and NT to live is to have vitality, movement, and activity. This basic organic and biological life is not peculiar to humans. In the OT life is *nephesh* and *hayyim*; in the NT, *zoon*.[6] In continuity with other living creatures, human being has life as a gift of the Spirit of God. The Spirit of God [*ruach*] 'breathes' [*neshamah*] life into human beings [Gen 2.7]. Job 33.4: "The spirit [*ruach*] of God has made me, and the breath [*neshamah*] of the Almighty gives me life."[7] As such living creatures, humans require air, food, water, and shelter to sustain their lives. As living creature, human being faces death as the cessation of life.

The biblical witness does not seem concerned to call nonliving beings, such as salt, rocks, etc., 'creatures.' Tradition, in developing a fuller doctrine of God and creation, came regularly to include nonliving beings in the category of creature. Contemporary biology and physics are not clear about exactly where to place the demarcation between the living and the nonliving beings. Whitehead and Hartshorne have tried to bridge any distinction between the living and nonliving by including all realities (i.e., 'actual entities') as events of mental and physical prehensive feelings. I will follow the tradition and speak of the category of creatures as including more than what we might ordinarily call 'living,' reserving also to say that the distinctive *life* of humans reaches into a realm of actuality that is not reducible to the lower forms of creaturely actuality.

As creaturely being, human beings are centers of activity. As with all other creatures, a human being is—in his given individuality—a center of activity. Human being's center of activity is complex and yet is in large ways defined by the human form and essence that delimit the sort and range of possibilities his activities might enact. As a center of activity, human being is a process of becoming in time, of enactments in time and over time. To fully describe the sort of center of activity that is distinctive of human being we will need to consider below the categories of personal being and spiritual being.

As creaturely being, human being is interdependent with other creatures, with the rest of the creation. Human being sinks deep into and emerges out of the created matrix of creaturely interdependence. Hence,

---

[6] See Gen 1.20, 21, 24, 30; 2.19–20; 9.10, 12, 15–16.
[7] See also Job 27.3.

humans do not and cannot exist without other creatures. Remember, human being is formed out of 'dust'—out of atoms, elements, chemicals, etc.[8] This creaturely interdependence is thoroughly biblical, and it is quite compatible with an evolutionary theory of human emergence. But whatever the process of human emergence in creation history, Christian grammar must affirm that humans emerge from the dust by the active Spirit of the Creator and in the light of the eternal Son.[9]

This physical interdependence with other creatures can be seen in *microscopic interdependence*—this physical body in the immediate environment of these other physical bodies, and *macroscopic interdependence*—this physical body in this larger earthly environment, and *cosmic interdependence*—this larger cosmos of astronomical physical entities and structures. In all aspects of creaturely interdependence, human being is dependent upon structures of relations among creatures, such as physical laws and regularities of nature. This image of human interdependence with a whole creation is aptly captured by Moltmann's concept of human being as *imago mundi*—in the image of the world.[10]

As creaturely being, human being is good and valuable to God. Along with all other creatures, simply as God's creatures, human creatures in their singularity and interconnection are good and valuable to God. This is not to say that all creatures have either 'the same' or 'equal' value to God. But it is especially important to Christian grammar that nondivine creatures have their own properly creaturely value to God and therefore are not worthless or evil simply because they are creaturely and not divine. Human being has a value which cannot be eradicated by any other creaturely being and which should be respected by other humans.

When we say with Scripture and tradition that human being is good, we are not saying humans are as such morally good or perfect. We are simply affirming that humans are valuable to God and important to God's purposes in creating a world. The further goodness of human being—as intrinsic to God's purposes—is explored in asserting that human being is made in the image of God, an assertion that Christian grammar does not make about other creaturely beings.

---

[8] See Gen 2.7; 3.19; Ps 103.14; 1 Cor 15.47–49.
[9] See Jn 1.3–4; 1 Cor 8.6; Col 1.15ff; Heb 1.2–3.
[10] See Jürgen Moltmann, *God in Creation: A New Theology of Creation and the Spirit of God*, trans. Margaret Kohl (San Francisco: Harper and Row, 1985), 186.

Human Being as Personal Being:
Person among Persons

In this section we begin to wrestle with the ways and dimensions in which human being is different than other creaturely being and is that special creature called into being by the Spirit of God, formed in God's image, and intended for living fellowship with God and for being God's co-partner in having the dominion of stewardship over other creatures. We will not be able to answer fully what is meant by being created in *the image of God* without also considering in the next section what it means for human being to be *spiritual being*. The discussion of this section is intended to identify those preconditions in human actuality that open into the actuality of humans as spiritual beings. Here we begin to understand why human personal being and agency are used in Scripture as an analogy of faith to the personal being of God. Also in personal being we begin to see some of the dimensions of Jesus Christ as both the personal being of God and the personal being of humanity.

It is to be hoped that much of what is developed in this section will be accessible and credible to persons outside of Christian faith. Contemporary learning will play an important role in the various diagnostic categories I develop for identifying those structural powers and relations that are essential to human being as personal being.

It should be noted here at the beginning of this discussion *that both male and female are created personal beings in the image of God.* [Gen 1.27; 5.1–2] However much tradition may have tended to understand this differentiation in patriarchal terms that subordinated women to men, already present in Genesis 2.5–3.19, it is my affirmed task in constructing this contemporary witness to the triune God to recover the biblical fact that both male and female are in the image of God. Hence, I join with many feminist theologians in refusing characterizations of women that subordinate them to men and thereby diminish their being created in the image of God. I will strive to avoid and critique any interpretation of the concept of image of God that is sexist or androcentric.[11]

---

[11] See the serious, however flawed, work of Rosemary Radford Ruether that traces understandings of the meaning of 'image of God' and its predominant interpretation as defined by the male, *Women and Redemption: A Theological History* (Minneapolis: Fortress, 1998), especially 1–178.

Personal Being Is Embodied Soul/*Psyche*

Both terms, 'psyche' in the NT and the traditions and 'soul' in contemporary usage, have a family of uses. This family of uses pivots around the ways in which the soul is peculiarly *the living intentional consciousness* of a human body. There is no tendency in Scripture to treat soul as something that is independent and separable from the body. Such independence and separability were definitely asserted in much Greek and Hellenistic philosophy and religion, especially in Plato and the Platonists. Yet the Scripture also resists the tendency to describe the human person *only* in terms of bodily traits. It recognizes the same need, as in the Greeks, for speaking of human being as also *more than mere body*, hence the need for the terms *'psyche'* [soul] and *'pneuma'* [spirit].

While there may be a *distinction* between body and soul, there is no soul without body, and personal being is always *embodied soul.* The relations between body and soul are multiple and complex, and we should not grammatically look for any precise lines of demarcation or simple interconnection. In the NT, belief in the resurrection of the body held in check any talk of an immortal soul that is separable from the body and immortal by its very nature. But the traditions early on reverted back to the Greek immortal soul as a created given in the Christian understanding of humanity. I regard this reversion as an infelicitous development.[12]

The grammatical focus of saying 'human being is embodied soul' is to affirm the distinctive human ways of living as a conscious, intentional, linguistic, epistemic, emotive, agential subject—the subject that is a living 'I,' but all this as embodied actuality. Hence, as an embodied soul, a human person is a particular living subject.[13]

---

[12] While there may be some misgivings about the various analyses in his book, I think Oscar Cullmann's *Immortality and Resurrection*, ed. with introduction by Krister Stendahl (New York: Macmillan, 1965), has shown decisively that immortality of the soul is not a theme of the NT. For an account of how the doctrine of the immortal soul became adopted in Christian tradition, see Jaroslav Pelikan, *The Christian Tradition: A History of the Development of Doctrine*, vol. 1, *The Emergence of the Catholic Tradition (100–600)* (Chicago: University of Chicago Press, 1971), 45–52.

[13] Christian grammar of the human person as subject neither has to flee from Ryle's critique of the soul as the "ghost in the machine" nor be unmindful of the concrete ways in which being a subject of thoughts, judgments, actions, feelings, and much more are legitimately intrinsic to talk of human beings as en-

Personal Being Is Relational and Social

To explicate this point properly, I will begin by stipulating a *distinction between my uses of the terms 'relation' and 'relationship.'* My definition of *'relation'* is: an entity is in relation to another entity if it is conditioned in its actuality by that other entity. In this sense, then, to be related to another means that one's actuality is in part conditioned or influenced by that other. My definition of *'relationship'* is: an entity is in relationship with another entity if its relation to that entity is intentionally acknowledged, engaged, and shaped. Hence, a relationship is a special type of relation that requires intentional responsiveness to the other entity.

In affirming the interdependence of creatures within the creation, I acknowledged the multiple ways in which *all creatures have and are conditioned by relations.* But it seems in Scripture and traditions that among creatures, *only humans have relationships as intentional relations.* Hence, humans have relationships to other creatures, other humans, and to God, and this is distinctively human. This sense that only humans have relationships might seem dubious to those who want to posit intentionality throughout the creaturely world. The full sense of intentional and intentionality that is crucial to my restriction of relationships to human beings will be further clarified below in the complete discussion of personal being and spiritual being. But any imputation of intentionality to other creatures must be by analogical extension and diminution of how we speak of humans as intentional in various ways.

A person may be in *relation* to another person and to God without thereby having a *relationship* with either. For example, I may be in relation to the farmer and the system of persons and processes that brought bread to my table, but I may have no relationships with any of these other creatures. Hence, personal being is in relation to—conditioned by—all sorts of other creatures and God, but has many fewer relation-

---

during subjects. See Gilbert Ryle, *The Concept of Mind* (London: Hutchinson, 1949). Ryle's tendency to translate all 'mental' language into dispositional and behavioristic language is often quite helpful, but as a full account of how we speak of the human subject, it is just as often misleading. While the literature on these issues has grown exponentially, I have found these early responses helpful: Peter Geach, *Mental Acts: Their Content and Their Objects* (New York: Humanities, 1957); G. E. M. Anscombe, *Intention* (Oxford: Blackwell, 1958); Stuart Hampshire, *Thought and Action* (London: Chatto and Windus, 1960); and Anthony Kenny, *Action, Emotion, and Will* (New York: Humanities, 1963).

ships with creatures and God. It is important to remember here our earlier discussions that God has relationships and that all God's relations to
creaturely actualities are self-determined relationships.

This distinction should help us grapple with personal being as *social
being*, or the structure in which personal being is always *co-humanity or
co-personal*. The most primitive and elemental signal of this given sociality of personal being is that affirmed in the biblical narrative about
male and female being created in the image of God. While I affirm that
there is a sense in which male and female—in their individuality and
otherness—are each in the image of God, to leave this as the only meaning of the text would be misleading. It is their basic *togetherness* that
also comprises their being in the image of God. This togetherness includes their *radical otherness and differentiation* and their *mutual orientation one to the other*. We do not have to reduce their togetherness to
sexual complementariness to affirm that male cannot be male without the
female and female cannot be female without the male. This primitive
otherness and togetherness is basic to all other differences and togetherness that will also comprise humans as social beings. The male who
wants to be human without—or in disregard of—the female or the female who wants to be human without—or in disregard of—the male is
desperately defying a basic structure of human existence. In saying this
we do not have to say also that every male and every female should be in
some mutual marital union. Male and female are human persons without
marriage, however desirable marriage might also be for other reasons.[14]

Further, persons are inextricably related to and formed by relations
and relationships within some human society/culture. Previously, I called
this use of 'society/culture' one meaning of the word 'world' in the
church's discourse. For our purposes here, we use the terms 'society' and
'culture' interchangeably, while for other purposes one might choose to
make a distinction. A *society/culture* is an interconnected system or matrix of relations and relationships ordered through specific arrangements

---

[14] As important as Barth has been to the recovery of the basic male and female differentiation and togetherness as the basic form of "fellow humanity," I
must disagree with him that this fellowship of male and female "is fully and
properly achieved only where there is the special connexion of one man loving
this woman and one woman loving this man in free choice and with a view to a
full life-partnership." Certainly agapic love, as the paradigm of Christian love,
can be achieved in male-female relationships that are not "full life-partnerships."
See Barth, *Church Dogmatics*, III/2, 288.

of language, custom, values, structures, institutions, and traditions. There are large spheres of systemic interconnections that shape a particular society/culture, including economic production of and distribution of goods, government and systems of laws, communications, arts and entertainment, educational institutions and practices, systems of approval and disapproval and of coercion and persuasion, etc. This social world is, in significant measure, contingently *constructed* by human beings and handed on in *traditions of discourses and practices* and in material artifacts.

This sociality of persons being the case, therefore, no human being is an isolated, monadic, unrelated individual who is autonomously self-made. This social world can be seen either as microscopic or macroscopic in space and time—from my family in Okemah to my family in the global world. Every personal being thus has some microscopic and macroscopic social worlds as the given *social raw material* of her life. Our lives are always bound up with some other lives and other social institutions and processes. The social world conditions how persons are linguistic, epistemic, emotive, and agential, and these dimensions of personal life condition the social world. Yet *how* a person is *in* a social world is also a matter of her individual responsiveness and actions and not merely a matter of her being completely determined by that social world. Being formed and shaped by social worlds does not mean being completely determined in all respects by that world. There is always some measure of dynamic interaction with that world that is peculiar to the individual person.

Personal Being Is Linguistic and Communicative

It is striking that at the beginning of the canonical narrative of Scripture it is boldly asserted that not only does God speak the cosmos into being, but God speaks to the first human beings, and more striking yet, they hear and understand. [Gen 1–3] The high value of language is also expressed in the divine Word being an essential way God communicates Godself to humans, and it is in the communicative action of the life, death, and resurrection of Jesus Christ that the Word that gives light, order, and hope to the world was made flesh. [Jn 1.1–14] Having language and communicating are, therefore, essential to personal being, without which we would not have human persons.

Just as Adam came into a relationship to the other living creatures by virtue of his naming them [Gen 2.18–20], so too language is the basic medium for human knowing, understanding, and having a cosmos and a so-cial world. Through language humans have possibilities of being open to God and to other humans, to acknowledge them, to hear them, to see and identify them, to address them and be addressed by them, and to conduct life in relationships with them. And it is by virtue of language that hu-mans can have relationships to other creatures. Additionally through lan-guage, personal being is empowered to rise above and contend with the given systems of natural creaturely interrelations and processes.

Personal being requires language as a medium of its becoming, of its having a world, and its having any relationships, knowledge, emo-tions, intentional actions, and practices. Put another way, language is the fundamental medium in terms of which all other media of human rela-tionships are distinctively *human* media. Or again, language is the indis-pensable precondition for any social world.

Language, theologically understood, is a gift of God intended for good and truthful communication and understanding between God and humans and among humans. It is intended by God to *build up* human life and community. To be sure, the good gift of language is misused repeat-edly by humans as an instrument of lies and falsehood, of closure and mystification, of alienation and suspicion, of hatred and enmity. The Tower of Babel [Gen 11.1–9] symbolizes the peril of language that does not communicate truth, goodwill, love, trust, and hope—utter confusion and estrangement come among persons and societies. Acts 2.7–11 can be understood as the Pentecostal recovery of language for communicating truth, understanding, love, and hope among diverse people.

As indicated in the first chapter, language is more than just a syntac-tic system of signs. It is a system of signs comprised of syntactic, se-mantic, and pragmatic dimensions. These dimensions of language are the living grammar of language.

Personal Being Is Epistemic

Under this term *epistemic*, from the Greek word *episteme*—to know—I group the various ways in which humans are *knowers*—have beliefs and convictions, make judgments about what is the case. It is taken for granted throughout the biblical text that human beings can know God, know their world, and know others, even know themselves. When Adam is addressed by God, Adam recognizes God, and knows that it is God speaking. There is a great variety of epistemic terms: perceiving, seeing, seeing as, apprehending, believing, judging, discerning, recognizing, understanding, comprehending, construing, experiencing, etc. Even the emotive potencies of human being have epistemic powers of construal and discernment. All these epistemic terms are in some sense concerned with 'the truth'—about what is actually the case about some subject matter or object or reality.

The basic conviction here is that human beings are endowed by God with the power to know the world. This orientation to knowing the world in which we live is a fundamental human propensity. Christian grammar must celebrate the power to know and encourage the desire to know whatever there is to be known. Curiosity, searching, inquiring, questioning, probing, and judging are cognitive actions essential to human personal being.

But all epistemic actions and events are relative to the objects being known. We should not try to reduce all knowing to knowing appropriate to one type of object or to one type of action, position, and procedure. To know God is not the same as knowing geometry or the distance to the moon. The various ways of knowing each have their own actions and procedures for getting into a position to know the appropriate object. We can remember here that the semantic identification of objects cannot be separated from syntax and pragmatics. Every kind of knowing is impossible without the appropriate discourses and practices. *What* we know and *how* we know cannot be separated from or sustained apart from the contextually appropriate discourses and practices. We cannot expect to know astrophysics without putting ourselves in the position of disciplined study of the subject matter. Even though Christians always confess that God is finally known by someone only to the extent God chooses to reveal Godself, it is also a well-known and central *belief and practice* of the church that we cannot expect to know and understand God without positioning ourselves in the church's discourses and practices that aim at knowing God. Further, knowing God involves such pragmatics as, for example, doing the will of God and living in the Spirit.

All knowing claims—as truth-claims—invite checking and confirmation by others. Knowing that is in principle private and incommunicable or unrepresentable is everywhere suspect. Even the knowledge of God is intended for communication to others, though the communication itself depends on the action of the Spirit. The point here is the locution 'in principle incommunicable,' which means that the knowing cannot be communicated under any circumstances or in any way. To be sure, persons may know something in a fully credible way without being *able* to explain or justify their knowing. But this is not an *in principle* condition of their knowing; they could learn how to explain and justify their knowing, which means they could learn the discourses and practices of such explaining and justifying.

Should we say then that all persons do know God in the sense of possessing some genuine claim about God that is true? Even Scripture does not say this. All persons in God's creative work were *intended* to know God. Below I will construe this intention of God in creating humans as the endowment of the original grace of the Spirit. But this created and conferred capacity to know God—in the full richness of that knowing—has been obscured, forgotten, and repressed by humans in the midst of their sin. Hence, from the perspective of Christian grammar, we can say that all humans are created to know and rejoice in God—created with the *capacity* to know God. Yet even this capacity needs the activation of God's actual presence and address to become real knowing. We do not say this from the perspective of a presumably neutral epistemic theory, such as some philosophies often propose.

Christianly understood, all knowing should finally aim at freeing humans from ignorance, falsehood, and sin. Unhappily, much human knowing is used on behalf of oppressive and alienating powers of domination, subjugation, possession, and retaliation.[15]

Personal Being Is Emotive

The Bible throughout attributes a multiplicity of emotions and feelings to persons in the various transactions of life with God and other persons. Emotions are recognized as strong energizers and motivators of actions. Many of the characterizations of human responses to God are in terms of the power of the emotions they feel: e.g., awe, fear, anger, shame, joy, hate, envy, compassion. Emotions are also intertwined with knowings and actions in the biblical narrative.

Under this heading of 'emotive' I am gathering a family of terms in an attempt to map some of the capacities for and interconnections among the ways in which persons have emotions, feelings, and affections. I am not striving for an all-inclusive definition of 'emotion' or 'feeling' or 'affection,' for there are ranges of meanings in the ways in which the Bible,

---

[15] For further discussion of some of these issues see chapter two on "Revelation and the Knowledge of God."

the traditions, and we today talk of the emotive life of persons. Note, for example, how the term 'feeling' has wide flexibility and can be combined with a variety of different types of objects, as shown in the uses of the expression 'feeling of . . . ,' wherein many types of emotive states or objects can be inserted. Consider *feelings of* anger. And consider *feelings of* insignificance. This feeling is not just a matter of having the belief that one is insignificant, in some relevant sense, but that one *feels* this throughout one's consciousness and it *disposes* one to have other feelings and to perform or refrain from particular actions.

I aim here to sort through the decisive features of a grammar of human emotions as essential to understanding humans as personal being. *Most emotions are aroused, sustained, and expressed by two different but interrelated dimensions of human intentionality: (a) Concerns, cares, interests, and passions; and (b) desires, erosic attractions.*

Concerns, Cares, Interests, and Passions

Let us first consider concerns, cares, and interests—being used here interchangeably. I propose that the grammar of these emotive potencies includes the following minimal conditions:

a. the *construal* of something as the object of the concern—the construal of that about which one is concerned;

b. an *emotion-disposition* relative to the object—the disposition to have certain feelings in response to construals of the object of concern;

c. an *action-disposition* relative to the object—the disposition to act in certain ways in response to construals of the object.

We would not say someone has a concern about feeding the poor if there was no disposition to feel empathy relative to the poor, and if there was no disposition to actions of feeding the poor or seeing to the feeding of the poor. Seeing the rich ignore the poor might occasion anger. The concern for one's own security involves feelings of fear, uncertainty, and anxiety in situations construed as threatening to oneself. Hence, many times if we want to understand someone's *feeling-state*, we can inquire about her concerns.

Not all concerns, cares, or interests of a person are of the same strength for that person, so we can roughly grade the strength of a concern by:

a. the felt intensity of relevant emotions;

b. its power of duration;

c. its power to express itself in actions;

d. its power to override other concerns.

Persons typically have a host of concerns of more and less transience and strength. But those concerns of a person that concretely have the greatest strength during some span of a person's life I shall call 'passions.' *Passions are those focal and primary concerns that are most efficacious in the concrete shaping of a person's emotions and actions.* Think, for example, of a dominating passion for racial justice or for sexual gratification or for being admired and respected. It is also grammatically correct to describe a particular passion as intense and overriding other interests, but short-lived. Nevertheless, the long-term passions of a person are integral to shaping the life and career of that person.[16]

Thus far I have said nothing about appraising concerns and passions relative to their moral and spiritual impact on a person's life and world. The biblical witness is interested in those concerns and passions that are destructive of life and those that are upbuilding of life and well-being. Christian grammar talks about these matters in terms of spiritual sickness and health, of life and death, of sin and redemption.

Desire and Erosic Attraction

We turn now to the other great engine of emotions and actions: *desire and erosic attraction.* In the grammar of desire, a *desire* has the following minimal conditions:

a. a *construal* of some object as valuable to the desirer, or 'good-for-me'; the object may not in fact be good for the desirer, but

---

[16] Admittedly the term 'passion' has other uses that are different from this one, but I am following a usage of Kierkegaard's that is spread throughout his writings. Contemporarily, the important but neglected writings of Robert C. Roberts have been especially helpful to me. See his *Spirituality and Human Emotion* (Grand Rapids, Mich.: Eerdmans, 1982); *The Strengths of a Christian* (Philadelphia: Westminster, 1984); *Taking the Word to Heart: Self and Other in an Age of Therapies* (Grand Rapids, Mich.: Eerdmans, 1993). See also the fascinating essays in Robert C. Roberts and Mark R. Talbot, eds., *Limning the Psyche: Explorations in Christian Psychology* (Grand Rapids, Mich.: Eerdmans, 1997). I think this concept of passion can be grammatically helpful and discerning to Christian speech and action. This use might also help us recover a more vivid sense of what we mean when we talk of Jesus' passion toward the cross.

she at least posits its goodness-for-me in the very act of desire;

b. feelings of *being attracted* by the object, of wanting to obtain or possess the object;

c. *strong* desires also have the further condition of involving an action-disposition to obtain or attain or possess the object;

d. the attaining of the object of desire involves feelings of satisfaction, even though the satisfaction may be intense but transient.

The Greeks were fascinated with the curious and mysterious *power of attraction* that is evident in desires of various sorts and for various sorts of objects. The *objects of desire* are indeterminately multifarious: other persons, other creatures, relationships, virtue, the good, future possibilities, etc. This multifaceted and omnipresent power of attraction in human beings they referred to as *eros*, and the grammar of *eros* is related to the grammar of *appetite* and *want*. To have a desire is to experience a *need for* the object desired, which means to have an appetite for the object. Eros is this power of attraction that expresses itself in desire for union with the object of desire, wherein *union* is some form of possession. An unfilled desire is therefore experienced as a lack or dissatisfaction or frustration. While eros always included sexual attraction—which was often identified as a paradigm of eros—it was not typically *reduced* to sexual attraction. With Freud and others the concept of eros was reduced to sexual attraction [termed *libido*], with the result that the adjectival use of eros became 'erotic' and was basically sexual in nature. In order to resist this reduction of eros and desire to dimensions and manifestations of sexual attraction, I recommend a new word/sign, *erosic*, to refer adjectivally to the general power of attraction in human life. Hence, I will say that our *desires are concrete manifestations of the general power of erosic attraction in human life.*

We are now in a position to recognize how pervasive desire is in human life and how our concrete desires can be graded according to their strength in shaping a human life. I say 'concrete desires' here because there may well be a difference between a person's professed or self-identified desires and the concrete desires working in her actual life. The deep and dominating desires of a person's life dispose her to feelings and actions commensurate with those desires. Of these desires it is appropriate to say the person is also 'possessed' by the desire and its object. These erosic desires—in their infinite variety and power—are very much what the world calls 'loves'—those erosic attractions that pull humans forward and *energize* their feelings, construals, decisions, choices, and actions. How persons come to have their particular desires or erosic loves is the complex tale of human life: from those desires that seem 'to befall' a person—for example, erotic or sexual love—to those desires that require long-term discipline and cultivation—for example, the desire to become an expert violinist.

These erosic loves involve powerful construals and dispose persons to emotions and actions commensurate with the loves. Hence, we can call these primary or focal desires of a person the erosic loves of her life. Later I will be concerned to differentiate the grammar of erosic love carefully from the grammar of *agapic love.*

Passions and dominant desires are, of course, interrelated in multiple ways. Sometimes a strong desire can empower a passion, and sometimes a passion can elicit strong desire. For example, his passion—dominating concern—for being admired for his intelligence elicited his desires to please his scholarly peers and these desires expressed themselves in specific actions. And we may have passions that are not functions of erosic attraction but which involve desires commensurate to the feelings and actions elicited by the passion. For example, the passion for feeding the poor may elicit desires for objects that involve getting the poor fed. Further, desire and passion are almost indistinguishable in 'her desire to be a great violinist was the passion of her life.'

The Human Heart

The complex intertwining of passions and dominant desires in a person's life forms what I call the person's *heart* [*kardia*]. This is a good biblical term, used in both testaments, and very useful even today in ordinary speech. *A person's heart is those core passions and desires—with their accompaniment of construals, convictions, and dispositions to emotions/feelings and actions—that form the dynamic center of a person's life and character.* We can now see Scripture's concern for the concrete dynamic shape of a person's heart, inasmuch as there can be 'hard hearts,' 'evil hearts,' 'good hearts,' 'new hearts,' etc. There are 189 uses of *kardia* in the NT, all occurring in the family of uses referring to the core passions and desires of the person and the attendant emotions and actions, both good and evil, happy and unhappy. This language of the heart obviously involves moral and spiritual considerations. This concern for morally and spiritually appraising a person's heart points to the discussion below of spiritual being.[17]

We may further say that *a person's heart shows forth what the person regards as of self-involving value to the person: passions and desires are value relations.* Hence, hearts have treasures—those objects of compelling value, as urgently good-for-me, that shape and express passions and erosic loves.[18] We can thus say that the human heart is possessed by the values toward which her central passions and desires move.

These *emotive potencies and structures* of human personal being I have identified are, as such, *givens* in human life. The grammar here is not, as such, peculiarly Christian. As such, it is neither morally good nor bad that humans have passions and desires. The spiritual question is: what are the objects of passions and desires that bring human flourishing and well-being and what bring human disintegration and alienation? We still have the complex question of how a person comes to have the passions and desires she does have.

Personal Being Is Agential

I use this term 'agential' as an umbrella term to refer to that dimension of human personal being in which persons *will* something, make *decisions, choose* something, and *enact* choices—*human persons as agents.* The biblical narrative repeatedly assumes and asserts that human beings—in acts of willing—make decisions and choices. The grammar of *willing, deciding,* and *choosing* is related to the grammar of *intentional action.* I will strive here to map some of the grammar of intentional action as a way of understanding human agency. Remembering that intentionality is a more general power of human action and interaction that is present even in emotions and various acts of human construal, I am restricting the analysis here to those actions for which the following questions can grammatically apply when addressed to the agent of the action: '*What* did you do?' and '*Why* did you do it?' Likewise, persons other than the agent can answer these questions in *ascribing* an action to the agent. It is critically presupposed in such ascriptions and descriptions of actions that they take place in a social context of agreement and practice in identifying actions.

---

[17] See the penetrating essays concerning the human heart written under the impetus of the concerns of Kierkegaard and Wittgenstein: Richard H. Bell, ed., *The Grammar of the Heart: New Essays in Moral Philosophy and Theology* (San Francisco: Harper and Row, 1988).

[18] See Mt 6.21; Lk 6.45; 12.34.

The following are proposed as some of the minimal conditions of the grammar of the *concept of intentional action*. First, the agent *construes* the action as a real possibility-for-him. I am not positing, in every case, a prior act of construal *before* an action is done. In fact, we can say that in the enacting itself the construal shows itself. But it is the lack of such construals that is at the root of possible actions not enacted. That is, many possible actions do not arise for an agent precisely because he does not construe it as possible-for-himself. Hence, while intentional action often happens without a prior act of construal, it is also the case that many such possible actions never arise for an agent because he cannot or does not construe them as possible-for-himself.

Second, the action is such that we can say the *agent willed or decided or chose the action*. In this sense, the action is decided from among other possible actions. Hence, the concept of intentional action excludes the action being involuntary—as in a quick movement in response to a sudden loud noise—but does not exclude the action from being coerced by some other agent. The armed bandit may coerce me to lie down, but the act of lying down is my intentional action. The minimal condition is that there is a choice from among alternative possibilities. Notice about the action of coughing that it can be either an intentional action or an involuntary action.

Third, the action involves a *purpose, goal, or aim*. This is the clearest respect in which the action is intentional—it intends some goal. It is here that the question of 'why did you do it?' is appropriate and facilitates understanding *what* the action was. Most actions are such that they could be described by others in several different ways. We see a man in a boat casting a lure into the water; we can describe the action as 'he is casting a lure.' We can also legitimately, if we are familiar with lakes, boats, and the art of fishing, say 'he is fishing,' which is another possible ascription of action to him. But if we ask him *why* he is doing what he is doing, he can tell us his intention or purpose in the doing, which is probably that he is fishing. Answering the why question can, however, become more complicated. There can be a whole subset of actions performed in the course of enacting a larger, supervening action. For example, in order to fish, I had to gather my tackle, choose a rod and lure, go out in the boat, and choose a place to start casting my lure—all done in the course of enacting the action of fishing. At any point along the way, I could have been asked what I am doing and why, and different accounts could have been adduced, such as 'I am gathering my fishing tackle.'

Fourth, the agent and others can regard the *agent as accountable for the action*. As accountable, the agent can and can be expected by others to give an account or explanation of the action. *Accountable* does not have to mean 'morally accountable'; it simply means the agent is expected to *own* the action as his action and to be able to answer the questions of *what* and *why*. Hence, we can use such locutions as 'my action' or 'Fred's action' as grammatically sound understandings of the concept of intentional action. I say that the agent is *expected* to own the action and explain the action, but obviously in fact sometimes the agent is not able to explain his action to others. This brings us to reasons and motives in the explanation of actions.

Fifth, the description of the action and its explanation can involve both *reasons* and *motives*. The distinction between reasons and motives is easily obscured for us because both can be given in response to the question '*why* did you do that?' A *reason* for an action is usually contained in the description of the action as its goal or is implied in its description. So, the goal of fishing is to catch fish. The goal of walking to Ft. Gibson is to get to Ft. Gibson. A *motive explanation* for an action usually is given when the goal of the action is not contained in or implied in the description of the action. A motive explanation usually has the form of 'for the sake of,' wherein the motive explains why the action was done. So, 'for the sake of getting the poor and hungry fed, Fred gave his inheritance to the church.' Or, 'his motive in taking Priscilla fishing was to show off his skill in catching fish.' Motive explanations draw upon understanding the concerns, cares, interests, passions, and desires of the agent. Motive explanations become very important in making moral appraisals of actions.[19]

Often humans do intentional actions but are obscure in their own understanding of the action. Notice what we get into when we try to unravel the following biblically induced question: 'David, why did you send Uriah to the front?' Even David tried to obscure from himself what desires motivated him and what purposes he had in sending Uriah to his certain death. But David could recognize himself finally in the narrated

---

[19] The grammar of reasons for actions and motives for actions is extremely more complicated than I have suggested here. For a discerning and helpful discussion of intentional actions and of reasons and motives, see Eric D'Arcy, *Human Acts: An Essay in Their Moral Evaluation* (Oxford: Clarendon Press, 1963).

description of his actions by Nathan.[20] These situations of being confused or deceived about oneself and one's actions and motives point us to the profound depths of how arduous it is to gain *self-understanding*.

Finite Freedom

Intentional actions always occur in circumstances that are finite and delimited. *Some of the following conditions delimit every intentional action*:

a. the agent's previous history of knowings, feelings, and decisions, including the agent's capacity to construe possible actions;

b. the agent's bodily conditions;

c. the microscopic social setting in which the action occurs;

d. the macroscopic social setting in which the action occurs.

Hence, every intentional action presupposes a specific world in which it occurs and which conditions its occurrence. Human agents do not create of themselves the total environment in which they act. Therefore, every agent's willings, decidings, and choosings are profoundly conditioned by the particular environment or context in which they occur. Tillich's locution *"finite freedom"* refers to this universal fact that all human intentional actions occur in a matrix of given conditions.[21] Hence, there are no human unconditioned decisions and actions. This diagnostic fact should make us suspicious of some extravagant claims concerning human 'autonomy.' Yet there may still be choices in our actions without there being utter autonomy of action.

Relative to intentional action, we now inquire about the grammar of *freedom*, which is to inquire about the various uses of the term 'freedom' and their differences. The basic sense of freedom for us in this analysis is that expressed in the givenness of intentional actions—persons make decisions, make choices from among alternative possibilities. However delimited the possibilities, there are at least some alternative possibilities. This general capacity to choose and decide is traditionally referred to as

---

[20] See 2 Sam 11–12.14. This point about human opaqueness about their own motives for actions raises important questions about the grammar of *unconscious* intentions and desires. But we will remain hopelessly confused about the grammar of such matters if we are muddled about the grammar of conscious intentions.

[21] See Paul Tillich, *Systematic Theology*, vol. 2 (Chicago: University of Chicago Press, 1957), especially 31–33.

Chapter Six

liberum arbitrium. The contrary of this sense of freedom would be to say the action was *totally determined* or *totally necessary*—there being no other *real possibilities.* Where there are no real choices, there is no human freedom relative to that situation.

Because our actions are always conditioned—and these conditions are infinitely variable—and because the goals of actions are infinitely variable, we have reason to qualify further what we mean by 'freedom' as it pertains to agents and actions. If we understand a *person's will as the power to choose,* then a person's will can be *encumbered* by her situation as it pertains to: (a) her capacity to construe possibilities as real 'possibilities-for-me'; and (b) the strength of her willpower to choose and enact a possibility.

With regard to the first type of encumbrance, human beings concretely are repeatedly encumbered by an incapacity to construe possibilities as being real possibilities for themselves. The will is encumbered because the present situation is so inadequately understood and the imagination cannot project possibilities beyond that situation. Relative to the power to choose a possibility and the power to enact the choice, notice how intertwined are construals, desires, passions and the power to enact a choice. In some weak sense, a person may desire or want to enact a possibility but does not have the willpower to choose and enact that possibility. This shows us that desires and concerns do have their differing strengths, which become evident in their power not only to *dispose* a person to some possibility but also to move her to the enactment of that possibility. It is herein that we should understand how easily we humans have *divided wills*—that we are torn between conflicting desires and passions and disperse thereby our power to choose and enact some possibilities.[22] It should also be clearer to us how the grammar of *weakness of will* might play itself out. The *power of our wills and the power of desires and concerns are profoundly intertwined.*

Hence, the *conditions* pertaining to a person's will can be both *internal* and *external* to the person. The internal conditions I am calling *emcumbrances.* Internal to a person are those epistemic and emotive dimensions that might severely encumber her construals and powers of enactment. For example, drug addiction encumbers the will of the agent and inhibits the power to choose not to take drugs. Conditions which are *external* to the person are those conditions that are beyond her control and simple manipulation. For example, being in prison severely condi-

---

[22] See Rom 7.14–20.

tions the will of the prisoner relative to many possibilities. Because any person is always interacting with some creaturely and social world, it can sometimes be a murky question just where the differentiation between internal encumbrances and external conditions limits the agent's possibilities. Also, an agent may retain the power of choice and enactment relative to some very limited possibilities, but have lost the power relative to other possibilities. So, the addict can choose between apples and oranges for dessert but is not able to choose to stop the drug consumption.

It is in reference to these *conditions and encumbrances of the will* that I now introduce the expression *freedom from*—'liberation from' also captures this sense nicely. Here we are talking about that freedom from those conditions that in various ways restrict a person's:

a. capacity to construe possibilities as real possibilities for her;
b. power to choose and enact her choice;
c. actual range of possibilities that her situation permits.

Think about the myriad ways in which relationships to other persons and God are affected by the encumbrances on our choices and actions. Consider here how intelligible it is to talk of freedom from despair, freedom from a parent's malice, freedom from male oppression, freedom from hunger and poverty, freedom from fear, freedom from prison, freedom from the illusion of helplessness, freedom from self-deception, etc. To be *free from* such conditions and encumbrances of the will as these is also to become capacitated to will what was previously impossible in some way. Hence, freedom of choice is not only always delimited and conditioned, it is also encumbered in the ways we are here mentioning. *Human finite freedom is never fully free from all conditions and encumbrances.*

We can note here that *Christian faith is interested in freeing persons from the power of sin to encumber their choices, their actions, their lives.* The movement of being freed from an encumbrance can now be interpreted as a *freedom for* new possibilities and actions with the power to decide for and enact those possibilities. It should be abundantly clear that all human intentional action is interconnected in complex and differentiated ways with the person's knowings, construals, and feelings and passions and desires.

Personal Being Is Vulnerable Being

'Vulnerable' refers here to the personal being's capacity for *being-acted-upon*. There are at least six general forms of human vulnerability:

a. being-acted-upon by *other creatures*; remember the interdependence of creaturely bodies as centers of activity that sustain each other but often collide and impinge on one another;

b. being-acted-upon by *other persons*; persons always live in a world of significant others that condition and shape them;

c. being-acted-upon by *transpersonal powers*, by principalities and powers that are not reducible to the power and activity of a singular creaturely agent; these are inescapable large spheres of social worlds with their systemic interconnections and powers, which I have referred to as *force fields of power*;

d. being-acted-upon by *one's own past* of knowings, feelings, and actions;

e. being-acted-upon by construed future possibilities;

f. being-acted-upon by *God*.

Personal being cannot escape the *givenness of these structures of vulnerability*. But the extent and character of particular vulnerabilities may vary greatly from person to person and from time to time for the same person. Yet vulnerable personal being is also responsive and interactive with the larger cosmos and social worlds in which she lives. To this extent, personal being is in some measure always self-determining. In response to her many vulnerabilities a person is confronted with the question of *how* she will *cope*—in denial, in escape, in belligerent self-protection, in fear, in despair, in courage, trust, and hope?

Personal Being Is Dialogical

The capacities for being linguistic, epistemic, emotive, and agential are conditioned and shaped by the dynamic interaction of persons with their social worlds. This interaction I call *dialogical*. These social worlds condition and shape how persons have language and can communicate; become knowers in various positions of knowing; become persons of concerns, passions, and desires and their attendant emotional potencies; and become persons who construe possibilities for themselves and make choices. These social worlds—constructed by humans as they are—*dialogically inculcate what persons in their social locations should value and desire and how persons should identify themselves and their possibilities in life.*

In this dialogical social world we see especially the importance of *significant other persons and significant communities* in the formation of personal being. These significant others and their relations and relationships shape persons by virtue of the *fact of being recognized and identified* and the *sort* of recognition and identity conferred. Being an Israelite was an identity that was conveyed by the family, the communal leaders, and the discourses and practices of the community of Israel. Here is the power of the social world to give identity and value to persons.[23]

Within the social world are also those transpersonal powers that convey identity and value. It is appropriate to follow and expand NT usage here by designating these transpersonal powers of the social worlds as principalities and powers or force fields of power. As such they are creaturely, not quasi-divine. And as such, they are neither good nor evil, though they may become either in any particular situation.

In terms of this dialogical interaction of self and world, consider René Girard's theory of *mimetic desire*. He contends that human desire [erosic attraction] is shaped by our social world which inculcates in a variety of ways *what* and *how* we should desire. But the basic inculcation comes in the power of *mimesis*: by imitating the significant others in our lives we learn what to desire. Yet this mimetic desiring—or learned erosic attraction—lays the foundation for *rivalry* and *envy* among those with similar desires for the same objects. This rivalry and envy create covetousness, which is the source of much violence and destruction among humans.[24] Clearly such mimetic desiring need not be destructive; it could also be *constructive* of human well-being. But structurally, this dialogical character of human personal being's identity—including mimesis—shows the *peril* of social worlds that are conflictual and destructive and the *promise* of social worlds that are empowering, liberating,

---

[23] While the concept of dialogical other is rooted in Hegel, see Charles Taylor, *The Ethics of Authenticity* (Cambridge: Harvard University Press, 1991), especially 32ff, for an insightful discussion of the dialogical character of the human need for recognition, identity, and value.

[24] See René Girard, *A Theater of Envy* (New York: Oxford University Press, 1991) and *Things Hidden Since the Foundation of the World*, trans. Stephen Bann and Michael Metteer (Stanford: Stanford University Press, 1987). For an interesting discussion of the theories of Girard with respect to mimesis and violence and Christian faith, see Gil Bailie, *Violence Unveiled: Humanity at the Crossroads* (New York: Crossroad, 1995).

and peaceful.

Personal Being Is Self-Determining

Given the fact of our creaturely and social worlds in the formation of personal being, we might be tempted to conclude that personal being is no more than what the creaturely and social worlds dictate. This would make the creaturely and social worlds completely or virtually determinative of human actuality and identity. Yet we must remember that personal being is an *irreducible subject* who is not only *related* to social worlds and the larger creation but is potentiated to have *relationships*—intentional relations. As intentional relations, the human person is interacting through intentionalities of awareness—intentions of action, intentions of emotion, intentions of construals—to the social and creaturely worlds. Remember, there is a distinction between being *conditioned* by other entities and being *completely determined* by others. I am claiming that the human person is not dissolved in relations and relationships and therefore is not a mere function of these.[25] There is some measure of *self-determination* in all relationships, if not in all relations. Persons are not only formed by their creaturely and social worlds but they dynamically interact with those worlds, expressing their finite and conditioned power of self-determination. The concrete dimensions of this self-determination may vary in degree, integrity, and richness among persons and among the moments of a person's life. As we have seen in the earlier discussion of agency, the self-determining possibilities in a particular situation may be severely delimited and diminished without thereby completely eliminating all possibilities. The prisoner may not be able to escape the prison, but he is confronted with *how* he will respond to the multitude of other possibilities of living in the prison. The poor certainly have their actual choices severely delimited by their poverty, but there remain other possibilities of self-determination in relation to that poverty itself.

Hence, in personal being there is *irreducible otherness in the subject,* and there is likewise *an irreducible otherness in the others* with which

---

[25] Sometimes the so-called social self can be so emphasized that the self becomes no more than a function of the social relations. Julian Hartt reminds us of the "terminal individual" that cannot be reduced to being simply a function of his relations. See Hartt's "The Situation of the Believer," in *Faith and Ethics: The Theology of H. Richard Niebuhr*, ed. Paul Ramsey (New York: Harper & Brothers, 1957), 225–244.

the subject has relations and relationships. In the social worlds, the human person is an irreducible *I* in relationships to other persons who are irreducible *I's*. Herein we see that personal being is always a *singular subject* interacting with others in her creaturely and social worlds.

Even as I have now affirmed a measure of self-determination in human persons, we must emphatically refuse to characterize this self-determination as 'autonomy'—if we mean by 'autonomy' that a person's will is ever unconditioned by her physical and social worlds. Self-determination is and remains dialectically conditioned by our creaturely and social worlds.

Personal Being Is Historical Becoming

All creatures—as centers of activity—become in time and are thereby processes of actualizing possibilities and being conditioned by past actualizations. Actual creatures are not static, unchanging entities. Persons, like other creatures, become in time as processes of actualizing possibilities and being conditioned by past actualizations. But persons-becoming-in-time is also differentiated from other creaturely becomings. Persons can have a *relationship to their own becoming* and to many of the possibilities they are actualizing. Their becoming can be a matter of intentionality: of decisions, desires, passions, and construals. Persons can ponder their possibilities, muse over alternatives, and enact choices among the possibilities. This peculiar becoming-in-time of personal being I will call *historical becoming*. Personal becoming can thus involve *projects* of intentionality which are trajectories of becoming with purposive direction and defining character over a period of time.

We are here encountering the peculiar ways in which persons are temporal, in which there is a *past*, a *present,* and a *future*. It is in relationship to all three of these dimensions of temporality that human persons are confronted with the use of the powers of personal being we have been exploring. In relation to the past, persons are capacitated with *memory*—the intentional power to grasp one's past, to feel it, to know it, to learn from it, to respond to it. And with other creatures, human persons are loaded with bodily relations to their own past of interaction with other creatures; these can often become objects of intentional apprehension. In relation to the future, persons are capacitated to envisage possibilities and are thereby confronted with the task of how they will decide in the present among the many possibilities. The encounter with future possibilities also capacitates the person with attitudes toward the future. Herein, *anticipation*—the power to envisage possibilities and to assume attitudes toward them—is directed toward the future. Among the attitudes toward the future is that of *hope* as desire for prospective possibilities as real possibilities. But the capacity to envisage possibilities and to assume attitudes toward them is also the capacity for fear, for apathy, for despair concerning the future and the construal of its real possibilities. In both memory and anticipation, as intentionality toward the past and intentionality toward the future, the person is in self-determinative interaction with given creaturely/social worlds.

In the dimensions of memory and anticipation in historical becoming, persons are to an extent the *narrative or story they embrace, live, and enact, and thereby the narrative conveys and builds an identity and meaning for them.* The narrative of a person's life—whether thin and spare or thick and rich—is essential to human becoming, self-understanding, and historical identity: who am I? who are we? what is life about? what is my life about? where is life going? In the narrated grasp of one's life, we see again the importance of the dialogical character of persons. What communal narrative is internalized is formative of how the person understands and enacts her life. Hence, as historical becoming in time, personal being has the capacity to confront the question of *how one becomes in time:* how one self-determinately puts together in living desires, passions, decisions, and construals the raw material—*the given physical and social matrix*—of one's life. Personal being—as historical becoming in time—points toward humanity as *spiritual being.*

Human Being as Spiritual Being: Spirit among Spirits

In this section we will explore the grammar of human beings as spirits. The grammar of spirit has not been sufficiently exploited in much of the doctrines of humanity of the past, but it seems to me that it is the point at which the distinctively Christian concerns with human life and destiny can best be identified and articulated. Much of the preceding grammar of human being as creature and as personal being is shared with some of the grammars in the world. But in beginning now to introduce the distinct concept of spirit, I intend to show how Christian grammar has profound sense-making power about the universal situations in which humans find themselves. In the grammar of the spirit, the moral and theological dimensions of human existence will come to the fore. Herein I will deal with the respects in which human beings are especially to be understood as created in the *image of God*.

While it is not decisively clear that the NT has a consistent way of describing human beings as spirit, it is the case that spirit language is prominent in talking about the relationship with God. Being in the Spirit of the Lord is critical for understanding Christian life. But from this usage in the NT, we can in the full grammar of Christian understanding infer that the relation to God, in both its possibilities of positive relationship and disrelations, is grounded in the spiritual capacities of the person. Kierkegaard says simply that "a human being is spirit . . . [and] spirit is the self . . . [and] the self is a relation that relates itself to itself."[26] It is this potential for relating oneself to one's own becoming that is the dimension of spirit. It is herein that Christian grammar construes human beings as created by God for relationship to God; the grammar of spirit is about the possibilities of that relationship and its disrelations.

In the Bible human being is that special creature:
a. called into embodied being and life by the Spirit of God;
b. formed male and female in the image of God;
c. addressed and commanded by God;
d. made accountable to God for how one lives;
e. called into the future for covenantal fellowship with God and fellowship with other humans in communal life defined by right, peaceful, and fruitful relationships among humans;
f. called into stewardship of the creation.

All these powers of human being would be impossible without the powers and structures I have previously described as creaturely being and as personal being. Yet those descriptions of human being did not yet fully reach into the depths and heights of human being as a spirit constituted by the Spirit of God. We will now explore the grammar of human being as spiritual being.

Spiritual Being as Constituted by the Spirit of God

Human being as spiritual being is an embodied person constituted by

---

[26] Søren Kierkegaard, *The Sickness unto Death*, ed. and trans. Howard V. Hong and Edna H. Hong, *Kierkegaard's Writings*, vol. 19 (Princeton, N.J.: Princeton University Press, 1980), 13.

the Spirit of God. Human being is peculiarly spiritual being—that being in the image of God that is constituted by the Spirit of God for relationship to God. Being constituted by the Spirit of God means that humans are constituted for *openness to God and to God's summons into relationship.* I call this constituted openness to God *the endowment of the original grace of God.* As original grace, being so constituted for openness is thus the distinctive gift of God's creative act of bringing human beings to be.

This constitutive openness to God affects the totality of ways in which persons are embodied creatures in their physical and social worlds. This openness, while given by the Spirit, does not make the Spirit of God a property of the person—it is a gracious and inviting presence of the Spirit that summons the person to a responsive life with God. This constitutive openness to God is what makes human being more than embodied soul but embodied spirit. Hence, it is the Spirit of God that by its action constitutes created human being as *spirit.*

I do not pretend that this grammar of the spirit is grounded in empirical generalizations available to anyone who might look at humanity. Rather, these descriptions of persons as constituted by the Spirit of God are peculiarly Christian theological descriptions articulated on the basis of God's self-identifying communications in the history of Israel, in Jesus Christ, and in the movement of the Spirit. They are not developed on some other foundation of natural knowledge or transcendental metaphysics. We are empowered by the self-communicating love of the Holy Spirit to discern the fact of this constituting by the Holy Spirit. But the basic ground for these construals of the human spirit is that these powers are revealed in and realized by Jesus Christ. In the *actuality of his life,* we can discern the original endowment of the grace of God for openness to God.

However, having affirmed these epistemic points, it is an astonishing fact of human history that humans repeatedly *repress and reject* their being constituted by the Spirit for a spiritual life with God. They choose in their lives to be animated by other spirits than the Spirit of God. But however much they may so repress, deny, or repudiate this constituting by the Spirit, humans can never completely eradicate their being so constituted. However, a signal of this endowed openness that is never eradicated is that humans find themselves restless and subject to despair in the absence of an intentional relationship with God. Yet because of their repression and rebellion—which Christian grammar calls *original sin*—humans require the revivifying of God's historical self-revelations in order to become opened again to God's life and love.

Spiritual Being Is Summoned into Relationship with God

The biblical witness is clear that human being is created to have relationships with God. Adam and Eve are given commands by God and summoned to obedience to those commands. [Gen 2.15–17] In repeated covenants with humanity and Israel, *God summons humans into obedient relationships with Godself through covenants of mutuality and promissory expectations.* Hence, in being summoned to acknowledge God as God, to obey God's commands, to speak the truth to God, to worship God alone, to not make any other relationship the central focus of one's life, humans are distinctively spiritual beings. This summoned relationship with God is to be the center of a human being's life. God is to be the supreme desire and passion of the human heart—there shall be no other gods! [Ex 20.3–8] To be a created spirit is to be summoned not only to life but to life in relationship with God.

In being so summoned to spiritual existence, *human being is made accountable to God for the self-determined shape of her life.* All the capacities for personal being are hereby brought under the summons and judgment of God—there is no other way truly to be personal being except as persons summoned to be spirits in relationship to God. In creating persons as spiritual beings, God lays claim to the totality of the ways in which humans possess and enact their creaturely and personal powers.

As summoned by God into covenant, spiritual being is summoned into *right relationships* with other creatures and with other humans. Right relationship with God is inseparable from right relationships to others. Hence, spiritual being is summoned by God to *moral existence* and confronted with the questions of *good and evil*, of *right and wrong*, of *virtue and vice*. This summons of God poses these questions for the becoming of spiritual being. These are the spiritual possibilities and potentialities for human dispositions and actions, passions and desires, construals and judgments.

Human being is summoned to accountability for her *heart*, for that dynamic center of passions and desires in which the construals, feelings, and actions of her life have their *energizing source* and *defining character*. Here, on the basis of our previous discussion of the human heart, we can talk discerningly about the *spirit* that *animates* the human heart. Spiritually there are possibilities of evil and destructive spirits animating the human heart, as well as the possibility of being animated by the Spirit of God, by the Holy Spirit, by the Spirit of Christ.[27] In saying human being is constituted by the Spirit of God I am affirming that the human heart is intended to be open to and occupied by the divine Spirit. But beyond the initial endowment and summons of the Spirit, the Spirit of God cannot occupy the human heart without human consent.

The whole of God's summons to spiritual being to have relationship with God is contained in one fundamental and total commandment: "You shall love the Lord your God with all your heart [*kardia*], and with all your soul [*psyche*], and with all your mind [*dianoia*], and you shall love your neighbor as yourself."[28]

In sum, as spiritual being, humans are summoned to accountability for all the ways in which they live in the relations and relationships of their worlds. This is to have all of life as *life before God*, from whom no secrets can be hidden and by whom all hearts are known.[29] In being so summoned by God, the human spirit is summoned to confront the ineradicable question of *how* she will live her life with its inescapable issues of self-determined character and trajectories of decisions in becoming.

One *signal* of this being summoned by God is the myriad ways in which many humans acknowledge that their lives are hauntingly only shrouds of death—that though they live in the biological sense, they do not live in a way that fulfills life, that gives life meaning and depth, and that gives it virtuous character and achieves flourishing. Humans long for flourishing, peace, and meaning—which Christian grammar identifies as the *longing for God*. This elusive longing for God is a faint echo of humans being constituted human spirits by the original grace of God. Such also signals that humans only have their *true home* wherever they enjoy communion and fellowship with God, their Creator, Reconciler, and Redeemer.

Spiritual Being Is Summoned to Communal Being

Genesis 2.18 asserts that in the primeval creation the only thing that "is not good [is] that man should be alone." I have identified this basic structure of *being-with-another* in the basic creation of male and female;

---

[27] In the Gospel of Matthew, see the stunning array of appraisals of the human heart: 5.8; 5.28; 6.21; 11.29; 15.8, 19; 18.35; 22.37.

[28] Mt 22.37–39; Mk 12.31–32; Lk 10.27; and see Deut 6.4–5.

[29] See Ps 44.21; Rom 2.16.

in the midst of radical otherness there is to be radical togetherness. Hence, it is biblically inescapable that persons are summoned by God to live together and forbidden to live in isolation and loneliness. Persons become what God intended in creating them only by realizing relationships of communal well-being with others. In communal being persons live in harmonious respect, concern, and mutual support. Communal being *builds up* its members, *protects* them from the demonic relationships that destroy life, and *enjoys* others as fellow creatures and *friends*. Humans as spirits are summoned to understand that their well-being is intimately connected to and dependent on the well-being of others in community.

The primary form of this communal summons by God to the human spirit is the establishment by God of *covenant* with humanity and then in particular with Israel to be the people of God and thereby to be a light to the nations.[30] Humans are summoned to a covenant with God that includes covenant with other humans. God's covenant with humanity—which we see clearly in Jesus Christ—is an inclusive covenant from which no human spirit is excluded.

In communal being persons live in relationships that are analogous to the triune life of God—distinct persons in interrelated passions and actions of love. It is in just, right, loving, and peaceful communities that persons realize what it is to be and become in the image of God. Hence, spiritual being is responsible before God for the character of the social worlds humans construct. Being so summoned to communal being raises the questions of what practices, construals, passions, desires, and actions are productive of human flourishing together in community and what are destructive of such flourishing.

In sum, *humans—as spirits constituted by the Spirit of God—are summoned to embrace the kingdom of God as that inclusive and ultimate community of loving communion with God and among humans.* This kingdom is the intended community sought by God in the establishment by God of all God's covenants with humanity.

---

[30] For an examination of the concept of covenant in Israel, see Walther Eichrodt, *Theology of the Old Testament*, vol. 1, trans. J. A. Baker (Philadelphia: Westminster, 1961). In fresh ways within the Reformed tradition, Barth has developed the interlocking character of creation and covenant; see *Church Dogmatics*, III/1, [¶ 41: Creation and Covenant], 42–329.

Spiritual Being Is Summoned in Freedom to Be Free

Insofar as the human spirit is originally endowed by the Spirit for openness to God, which we have seen involves being summoned into relationship to God and into communal being with others, it should be clear that *this openness itself is the gift of freedom.* It is the endowment to be the sort of creature that can live in self-determined relationship with God and others. So the freedom given the human spirit is also the freedom to be free from all that might encumber the relationship with God and to the community of other human spirits. Here the endowment is *power*, but it is not unconditioned power. It is power that must be used properly, or to put it another way, it is conditional on its right actualization and exercise. It is not a sheer autonomy of action in whatever way the spirit might desire. When the human spirit actualizes a life that is not in self-determined obedient relationship with God, the power of this gracious endowment is imprisoned and depleted. Hence, the gift itself of self-determination, which I have called *finite freedom*, is squandered and plunged into disrelationships with God.

In the section below on human sin, we will explore the human debacle of living in opposition to the original summons of God. There is no ontological explanation of why this gift of freedom, of authentic self-determination, is diminished amid the shackles of encumbrances self-inflicted. Hence, human beings, in diminished finite freedom, encounter the challenges of becoming in time amid the shadows of unfreedom—of enslavements to that which cannot confer well-being and flourishing. It is in this context that we will ponder the grammar of the human spirit as life in destiny.

Spiritual Being Is Life in Destiny

The biblical witness is throughout clear *that human life is created to be under God's summons or call and God's promise.* The summons is to obedient relationship with God and communal being with others, and the promise is fruitful life before God. Human beings, in their historical becoming in time, are summoned into the future as the time of confronting good and evil, as the time of accountability to God, as the time of promise, as the time of destiny. Being under God's summons and God's promise is distinctive of being a human spirit and marks humans as creatures of destiny.

The grammar of *destiny* refers to the *end of human life,* wherein end is both *telos* or goal and *finis* or conclusion. Destiny also includes the *route* or *process* by way of which the end of life is realized. Hence, humans as created spirits are prompted to questions of destiny—questions about the end of human life and the route to that end. Being spirit poses questions about the goal of human life before God—the promise of flourishing as human being before God and the threat of the misery of disobedience to God. But questions of *telos* also point to questions about the route to the goal—which trajectories of historical becoming promise meaning and flourishing. That human spirit is embodied also poses questions about the conclusion of human life—questions about death and its meaning. We must grant that the grammar of these questions is intensely self-involving for the spirit who asks.

There are two distinct but interrelated realms of human life that fall under questions of destiny that confront the human spirit. First, there is destiny as the temporal, finite historical route of human becoming and perishing. I call this realm *historic destiny*. For humans, historic destiny always unfolds as a particular route of becoming in interaction with given creaturely and social worlds under the conditions of finite space and time. Spiritual being is potentiated to ask about the meaning and purpose of what is happening to her in her time of becoming along her particular route of interaction. Historic destiny always *concludes in death*. Second, there is destiny as the ultimate goal and conclusion of human life. I call this realm *ultimate destiny*. Because humans are created spirits, they must ask about the relation between historic destiny and ultimate destiny.

It seems that questions of life and destiny pivot around how one understands human freedom and life, how one understands death, how one understands other powers that might affect human destiny, and how one understands God. I will now develop *three models of life and destiny that pivot around issues of who or what powers are the real determiners of human destiny.*

The *first model* accepts that death is the finis of life; there is no life beyond death. Hence, historic destiny is as such ultimate destiny. When we inquire about what powers are the real determiners of destiny, there are two possible types of answers. One type simply affirms that human destiny is whatever happens to a person in her temporal life, and there may be considerable variation in how one identifies the primary powers that determine 'what happens.' The other type can affirm that the only historic destiny that really matters is *how* a person lives her life, which presupposes that there is some standard for judging the various hows of the human spirit. Here the emphasis is clearly on the spirit's powers of self-determination as the real determiner of human destiny. Persons themselves decide their own destiny. What role God might play in this destiny is not as clear, but it could not be such a role that might violate the freedom of human self-determination. Curiously, this version of the first model cannot avoid positing a dual destiny: some live lives of blessed self-determination and others do not live blessed lives.

The *second model* does not accept that death is the finis of life and therefore posits a life beyond death. Its distinctive feature, however, is that it understands historic life and destiny as the *testing ground* of an ultimate destiny beyond this life. What then are the powers that determine historic life's bearing on ultimate destiny? The emphasis invariably falls for this model on some factor in human self-determination that is judged worthy or blessed. What that factor is might be various, such as how one morally lived one's life by some standard of morality or whether one has accepted Jesus Christ as Lord and Savior or some other condition. But in all these criteria of what is worthy in human life, the assumption is that the decisive power that determines destiny historically and ultimately is human self-determination. Hence, all other powers in human history are rendered irrelevant—or no more than the occasion in which self-determination takes place—to the desired quality of human self-determination. Obviously, this view of destiny posits a *dual destiny*, both in historic time and ultimately, which itself pivots around some understanding of *just deserts*: ultimately humans get what they justly deserve. However God might be conceived in this model, it is clear that the real determiner of human destiny is the individual human spirit.

The *third model* also does not accept that death is the telos and finis of all life, but it does not conceive the relation between historic and ultimate destiny as exclusively a matter of human self-determination. Further, this model does not conceive of historic destiny as the testing ground for ultimate destiny. And it cannot conceive either historic destiny or ultimate destiny without intentional consideration of how God is active in both. In short, this model reckons that what has happened in Jesus Christ decisively reveals the original endowment of human spirits now lost in rebellion and disobedience. But insofar as the emphasis is on the grace of God in Jesus Christ, both this historic life and the life beyond fall under the power of that grace. Hence, while human self-determination under the empowerment of the Spirit of God does shape historic destiny, thereby making a difference in how one lives, it is not

the sole ground for how ultimate destiny is resolved. Here this model, which I take to be the decisive *Christian model, hopes in the triumph of God's grace as the Ultimate Companion of the human spirit.*
We can now see how these models might form the *horizon* for human self-understanding in which the powers of life and destiny can be cast in some narrative framework. In terms of the narrative, the human spirit derives a sense of orientation to life and destiny and therewith a sense of identity. Precisely because humans inevitably confront questions of life and destiny, the construction of such narratives is inevitable; and such construction is a signal of the repressed but constitutive grace of God. In the narrative itself, the human spirit finds herself included in a larger story of the whence and whither of human life—the meaning and purpose of human becoming.
The Bible provides such a narrative framework for Christians to understand their spiritual becoming and destiny. Our construction of the grammar of human being as creature, as person, and as spirit is dependent on the biblical narrative. *It is essential to the biblical narrative—understood through the Gospel of Jesus Christ—that humans do not live out their destiny independent of the life of the triune God.* God is continually and dynamically interacting with humanity in historic destiny. The issues of destiny become more urgent as humans enact and live under the destructive and thwarting power of sin. For Christians, the crucial act of God's dealing with human destiny is in Jesus Christ, and ultimate destiny is finally the triumph of the grace of God revealed in him. But concrete issues of historic destiny may be full of suffering, misery, betrayal, and violent death. The vulnerabilities of humans, as identified in our previous discussion, and the potentiations of spirit are what Pascal has called "the grandeur and misery" of human being.[31]

Spiritual Being Is *Homo Religiosus*

On the basis of what I have thus far developed about human being as spiritual being, we are in a position to grasp theologically why humans construct religious communities. But there are some tricky issues in elaborating humanity as *homo religiosus*. What do we mean here by *re-*

---

[31] See Blaise Pascal, *Pensées,* frs. 397–409 in *Pensées, The Provincial Letters,* trans. W. F. Trotter and Thomas M'Crie (New York: The Modern Library, 1941), 127–130.

ligiosus, religion, religiousness? The semantics of these terms are controversial and difficult. Persons can propose definitions of these terms from many different theoretical and practical perspectives. But here I am interested in a Christian theological understanding of the human spirit as potentiated to religiousness.

Because I first understand created human being as spiritual being in the light of Jesus Christ, from Scripture, traditions, and human history I can propose the following definition of religion and religiousness. Affirming that humans of most times and places have created religious communities of shared discourses and practices, I propose that a community is *religious* to the extent that its discourses and practices intend to answer such spiritual questions as: what are we humans to do in life? for what do we hope? what is our destiny? what or who is truly *ultimate* or *divine* or *sacred*? With Tillich and others, I propose that *religiousness* is a matter of *ultimate concern* and how that concern is concretely embodied in discourses and practices.[32] An ultimate concern can also be called an *ultimate passion*—that which most deeply, profoundly, and persistently forms a human heart and shapes the values of its life. An ultimate passion is a religious passion. Hence, being religious involves shared discourses and practices, a shared *self-understanding*, a shared way of *being-in-the-world* and of *having-a-world*. Individuals within this community way of being may vary greatly as to the depth or extent of their concrete participation.

I am wary of saying further with Tillich that every human has an ultimate concern. That seems difficult of confirmation. Empirically human life often seems divided and confused within itself, with no dominating passion of any cohesive strength. But I can say that the propensity for having an ultimate concern or ultimate passion is rooted in humanity's spiritual constitution by the Spirit of God. I have also claimed that humans inevitably repress and stifle their being constituted by the Spirit of God such that it does not come to expression in genuine communities of love, justice, and mutual flourishing. Nevertheless, the echo of being spirit expresses itself in human religion-making in response to the human anxiety and fear in our encounter with the *Unknown* at many points of our experiences at the *edges of life*. Humans—as spiritual beings—strive to convert this massive and potent and frightening *Unknown* into something known, manageable, and relatively safe. Finitude and death are

---

[32] See Paul Tillich, *Systematic Theology*, vol. 1, 10–15, 106–159; and the encompassing discussion in *Dynamics of Faith* (New York: Harper & Brothers, 1957).

haunting provocations to religion-making. The discourses and practices that arise in constructing a religion have their aim and life in domesticating this *Unknown* into a manageable and negotiable *Known*.

Theologically understood, such human religion-making is a *signal* and *symptom* of the fact that humans are created by God, constituted by the Spirit of God, and called in their spiritual being to find ultimate meaning, goodness, hope, and destiny in *relationship to the triune God*. Hence, human beings in their spiritual potentialities—and in their repression of God's Spirit—*search for God*. But human religion-making is repeatedly prone to *idolatry*. In the conversion of the unknown into the manageable known, humans construct ultimates and divinities that are less than the true triune God. Humans *misidentify* the true God and therefore find meaning and hope in a relationship to what is not-God, to what is idolatrous. Paul, in commenting on the human quest for a justified life through works of the law—or what the early Barth called *works of religiousness*[33]—is addressing this universal human propensity to find a justification of life other than that freely offered in God's original grace and historically offered in the incarnate life in Jesus Christ.

What I have developed here about human religiousness is asserted from a confessional standpoint of Christian theology. I do not pretend to stand in some neutral, transcendent position from which to declare what human religiousness is *truly about*. I realize that other perspectives might find my understanding arrogant and presumptuous—but this would itself be articulated from some standpoint that pretends itself to know who God truly is or what is truly ultimate or what is the true meaning of all religion. I wonder where these other semantic rules about divinity and religion come from. Yet I admit that there is no neutral forum in which Christian faith, as dependent on the self-revelation of God in Jesus Christ, can be adjudicated as true. But I must further admit that my own understanding of human religiousness requires us to recognize how Christian religiousness—as concretely practiced by Christians in the world—is also prone to this same idolatrous quest to control divinity and to use divinity as a justification of a life we want on our own terms. *Nota bene!* An inevitable ambiguity stalks spiritual being in its historical life. Hence, Christian theology and Christian life must continually trust in the grace of God as an inclusive and ultimate answer to our being spirits who

---

[33] See Karl Barth, *The Epistle to the Romans*, translated from the 6th German edition, Edwyn C. Hoskins (London: Oxford University Press, 1933), especially 117ff, 182ff, 229–270.

are constituted for life with God and who long for God. Further, Christian theology can never forget that it is, at every point along the way of its reflection and witness, confronted with the *ineradicable question* of its own faithfulness and truthfulness.

Spiritual Being Is Steward of the Creation

God gives human being *dominion* over other nonhuman creatures.[34] While the other creatures are related to human good, it is not said they are created for the sole purpose of providing for human good. The other creatures are as such *good and valuable to God*. The dominion conferred on humans does not mean that they can do with other creatures as they please or simply for their own selfish purposes. The great sin of much church tradition is that this dominion was interpreted as conferring on humans the *right of total disposal of other creatures and the whole world*—hence, the Christian participation in many practices wantonly destructive of creatures and the creaturely world. The discourses and practices of this tradition of interpretation must be dismantled.[35]

The human dominion over other creatures enjoins the human acceptance of responsibility for the care and integrity of the rest of the creation in co-partnership with God. Adam names the animals and tills the land of the earth under the summons of God. But the creation is God's, not the possession or creation of Adam and his progeny. As was affirmed in the chapter on creation, the steward is the manager of the owner's valued goods. The steward does not own the goods, and therefore any management of the goods must be at the owner's behest. In being given dominion by God, the steward understands the creation as God's gift and expressive of God's love. Humans are to respect the created orders of creaturely relations and processes to the extent they produce and fructify life.

---

[34] See in particular Gen 1.26, 28–31; Ps 8; this perspective is not challenged anywhere else in Scripture.

[35] H. Paul Santmire's *The Travail of Nature: The Ambiguous Ecological Promise of Christian Theology* (Minneapolis: Fortress, 1985) is a balanced study of the misuses and promises of Christian discourses and practices in relation to the nonhuman creation. I have also found the writings of Richard Austin sobering and helpful; see *Environmental Theology*, bk. 1, *Baptized into Wilderness;* bk. 2, *Beauty of the Lord*; bk. 3, *Hope for the Land* (Atlanta: John Knox, 1987, 1988, 1988); and bk. 4, *Reclaiming America* (Abingdon, Va.: Creekside Press, 1990).

I have ventured here to use a locution that might be dangerous if misunderstood—*co-partners*. We are not co-partners of God in creating the world, though we are given dominion and co-partnership in the *management* of the world. Of all creatures, the human spirit is the only one who is capacitated for responsibility and culpability, for initiative and planning, for imagination and envisagement, for knowing and implementing, for care and compassion, for self-denial and for self-discipline, for sustained labor in hope. These—and many more—are the capacities summoned by God in granting humans dominion and co-partnership. Hence, it is always wrong to regard the dominion of the steward as the steward's right of possession and disposal. *Dominion is a trust given by God that confers responsibility.*

It is one of the great illusions of human history that humans—in a variety of societies and a variety of times—have considered themselves, usually some elite, the *owners* of the earth. The earth, in this way of understanding, is their property to do with as they please. This understanding has been incorporated in social and governmental systems and is assumed to be a human 'right.' For Christian grammar, however, the steward may till the earth and build upon it, but he does not presume that the earth is his. The earth is God's creature and given into humanity's *care* as a matter of *trust* from God.[36]

Spiritual Being Is the Image of God as Enacted Actuality

Human being is *actual* in and through the various dimensions of its being-in-act. This enacted actuality includes the being-in-act of its *creatureliness*—its inescapable dependence upon and interaction with the Creator and other creatures. It includes the being-in-act of its *personal being*—the distinctive powers of its intentionalities of life, of its subjectivity and its relationalities. Finally, it includes the being-in-act of its *spiritual being*—the comprehensive actuality in which human being has its creaturely and personal being in relationship to God, as summoned by God, made accountable to God, and destined by God.

Human being is thus *enacted actuality*. It is in the enactments of the dimensions of its life that it has actuality and is the singular and distinc-

---

[36] Douglas John Hall's *The Steward: A Biblical Symbol Come of Age* (New York: Friendship Press, 1982) is a fine attempt to recover the concept of steward for the church's discourses and practices in the face of the enormous ecological challenges we now face.

tive actuality it is in a world of other creaturely actualities. Here we must also emphasize that human being—as enacted actuality in time—is, in its temporality, always *coming-to-be.* Just as God's actuality is enacted actuality and God's actuality is more inclusive than God's essence, so too human actuality is enacted actuality and is more inclusive than the human essence. *It is in its spiritual being-in-act—as including its creaturely and personal being—that humanity is potentiated as the image of God.* Herein we can now see what a complex and multidimensional actuality human being is as a *center of activity.*

The full meaning of being created in the image of God becomes clear. In its being constituted by the Spirit of God—as an embodied creature with personal powers—humanity is created in the image of God. Being so created in the image of God must be firmly seen as both a *gracious endowment* and a *teleological task.* God constitutes human spirits in God's image and summons them into a future destiny of life with God and with other humans and with the whole creation. Being so created, human spirits are launched on a great adventure in which they are called to become—to fully enact—their potentiated endowment. This is their destined task and goal. Human being is thus created with a *promised teleological good—to find fulfillment in loving God, loving the neighbor, and being the loving steward of creatures.*

The frenzied history of humanity testifies to the repression, the renunciation, and the forsaking of this endowment and task. Nevertheless, being in the image of God is not something human spirits can *eradicate or destroy* on their own, however much they might *corrupt* the image and their created nature.

Though human spiritual being repeatedly forsakes his endowment of original grace, God does not withdraw; instead, God goes in search of the beloved creature who was summoned to fellowship and blessing. God's search for humans comes to definitive expression in Jesus Christ—God's own becoming human in which both the endowment and the task are fully actualized in historical becoming and enactment. *Jesus Christ is therefore the one human who lives out the power of the endowment and fulfills the task of being and becoming the image of God.*

Jesus the True Human Being

Jesus—as the true human being—is most fully what God intended in creating human beings. Here 'true human being' means 'normative human

being.' Jesus as norm fulfills the Creator's *purpose and promise* in creating human beings. Hence, *his destiny*—as enacted in his life, death, and
resurrection—reveals human destiny before God. Christian faith looks to
him and the shape of his life—the patterns of living he enacted—for our
normative understanding of human being. The term 'true' is here being
used in the sense of 'authentic'—Jesus is the supremely authentic human
being.

In saying Jesus is the true human, we must beware of misleading no-
tions which might suggest that Jesus is 'perfect' in all respects or that he
made no mistakes. Jesus is the true human being with respect to the personal and spiritual contours of *how* he lived his life and died his death.
There is no need to impute a false 'perfection' to Jesus in every aspect of
his concrete life—must Jesus have been the perfect carpenter?—or an infallibility from any sort of mistake or misunderstanding or misjudgment.
We can assume that Jesus' knowledge of geography and biology, for example, was limited to what was available in his time and place. That
Christian discourse will also describe Jesus as of the very reality of God
does not mean that Jesus is not fully of the very reality of created humanity. In fact, as will be shown in the discussions of christology, Jesus
is most fully God precisely in his being fully human.

Our discussion in this section will outline how Jesus enacts the fullness of actuality that human being was created by God to enact. Jesus'
being-in-acts are the fulfillment of God's intentions for human actuality.

Jesus Lives for and Loves the Father

*Jesus receives and enacts his life, identity, and destiny through his
relationship with his Father—the God of Israel—and the motherly
Creator of all things.* Given creaturely life by the Spirit of the Father and
sent and summoned by the Father into the future, Jesus fully accepts his
embodied creatureliness without rebellion or despair. He does not regard
finitude as a status to be despised or as unredeemably evil. Neither does
he reject or seek to escape from his physical and social particularity as a
first-century Palestinian Jew. In this sense, Jesus works with the raw
bodily and social material of his situation. But he does not assume that
this finite particularity is the sole determiner of his identity and destiny.
It is, of course, the inescapable contextual arena in which his life and
destiny are enacted.

The supreme determiner of his identity and destiny is his heavenly

Father who creates all things. Jesus wills and realizes the possible in obedience to the Father's will and purpose. He says 'yes' to the Father's will for him and his future. His will and the Creator's are distinct but not disparate or divided or opposed. Jesus the Jew accepts God's summons and keeps and fulfills the spirit of the *covenant* with the God of Israel. Jesus lives and dies, going to the cross, in obedience to the will of the Father, which is the will to save the world from its self-enacted destiny of violence, rebellion, and death.[37]

As the one summoned and sent by the God of Israel, Jesus wills to be one whom the Father loves. In such willing he is open to and animated by the Father's loving Spirit. He does not reject or ignore or forget the Creator's love for him. Yet Jesus does not act as though he is the only person the Father loves or as though the Father's love for him either excludes the Father loving others or diminishes others. Hence, Jesus does not receive the Father's love at the expense of others but on behalf of others.

Not only does Jesus accept the Father's love, he *loves* the fatherly and motherly Creator and wills to live in loving mutuality with the God of Israel. Jesus loves the Father in being open to the Father's Spirit and doing the will of the Father. He shows his love for the Father in his willing obedience to the Father. It is in this being loved and loving that Jesus' passions and desires are formed by his relationship with the Father. Jesus' *heart* is formed by the Spirit of the Father.

Jesus' pattern of life and his identity—as the Father's chosen one—is vindicated in his resurrection by the Father. He is the one sent and loved by the Father for the sake of the world, and therefore he is a norm for the world as to what it means to be God's creaturely embodied spirit. *He is the true human who lives fully for God and, in so doing, loves God above all others.*

Jesus Lives for and Loves Others

Jesus enacts love for other human beings in their singularity and unity. He wills the good of the other, intending to open the other to his or her own proper good before God. Jesus wills to be affected by the other's situation, to have passions and desires that embrace the other's life and good. He does not love humanity in general—but always in singular par-

---

[37] See Phil 2.8; Mk 14.36; Jn 6.38; 15.10; Rom 15.10, 19; Heb 5.8 among many other passages.

ticularity—and he does not sacrifice persons for the sake of some higher cause. It is always love for this or that particular person in his or her particular situation. Yet Jesus' love is indiscriminate in that it is not parceled out according to worldly distinctions. But in response to worldly distinctions and their power over humans, Jesus intends especially the loving of those the world rejects or marginalizes. His love for others does not segregate or exclude, though he challenges all to be loving to God and neighbor.

We should especially note that Jesus' love for the women he meets is never a love that is structured and determined by patriarchy. It is not the love of a superior male for inferior females. In fact, Jesus' love for women subverts the givens of patriarchal society about submission and domination. He embraces women as included in the co-humanity he loves and as the ones the Father loves.

Jesus' love for the other does not depend on reciprocity or mutuality. He does not restrict his love to those who seem to love him, for whatever reason. The most radical difference in the other or rejection by the other is not an occasion for Jesus forsaking the other or willing his destruction. Consistent with this practice, Jesus refuses to enact enmity, hate, or violence toward others. Instead he summons others to enact a radical love of the *enemy*.[38] He refuses to repay evil for evil. [Mt 5.39] He does not enact rivalry with others for goods that can be possessed only by the exclusion of others. The primary and defining goods of his life, and the goods he summons others to desire, do not deprive any others of their proper goods before God. In loving all others—in their singularity and unity as God's beloved creatures—*Jesus is the true human who lives for others*.[39]

Jesus Is the Free Spirit

Jesus is the singularly free embodied spirit. While Jesus' exercises of willing, of choosing, of deciding are all under the conditions of finite freedom, his willing is without the encumbrances of sin and inner division. Jesus is free in that his passions and desires are not encumbered by his own sinning in disobedience to the Father. While Jesus lives in the midst of sinners and is immersed in the sinners' world, he does not sin against the Creator or against other persons. As fully human, Jesus expe-

---

[38] See Lk 6.27, 35; Mt 5.43–44.
[39] See Barth, *Church Dogmatics*, III/2, 203–222.

riences the power of worldly passions and desires that alienate persons from God and other persons but does not yield to their inviting temptation. He is not encumbered by his own infelicities of disloyalty, of ambition, of selfish designs, and of inordinate fear. Hence, he is—in finite freedom—free from many of the enslavements of sin that oppress persons.

He says 'no' to the principalities and powers that seek to bestow worldly, coercive, civil, and religious power, glory, and identity on him.[40] Jesus is free in that his freely enacted obedience to the Father is not encumbered by the principalities and powers of sin. Their resistance and deadly domination of him on the cross do not cancel his freely chosen path of obedience and love of the Father and love of his neighbors. These powers of state and religion have the power to kill him, but they do not have the power to divide and defeat his will and to force him to relinquish his purpose.

Jesus is free in integral self-determination in interaction with the Father, with other persons and with principalities and powers. He is free in the constancy with which he pursues his summons to love God and neighbor and to announce the coming kingdom of God. In this respect, Jesus is *free from the encumbrances* of sin on his life's goals and enactments. And thus Jesus is *free for* obedience to the Father, for love of the Father, and for love of other persons. Jesus is freely open to the other without being coerced. Even his response to coercive evil is not coerced—*how* he goes to the cross is a manifestation of his obedient passions and desires animated by the Spirit of the Father.

Jesus is free in his manifold vulnerabilities in that he does not choose to deny or escape them but embraces them in doing the will of the fatherly and motherly Creator, the God of Israel. Jesus is manifestly vulnerable to pain and suffering and to the injury inflicted by others. He is finally vulnerable on the cross to the force fields of human evil and sin, and yet he does not confront the cross seeking by sundry means to escape its destiny and meaning. In all these ways his free decisions and enactments are *conditioned* by his worldly situation—as is the case with finite freedom as such. But his life decisions and passions are not dictated to him by the world. He is free from their power to shape his desires and passions and free for constancy of obedience to his heavenly Father.

In all these ways of freedom, as freedom from and freedom for, Jesus is truly the *free human spirit* that gladly accepts the original endowment

---

[40] See Mt 4.1–11; Lk 4.1–13; 2 Cor 5.21; Heb 4.15.

of the Spirit of God to choose obedience to the Father, to be unencumbered in his own intentional willing of the Father's will, to be the one who freely loves the Father and loves the human others he encounters. As this free spirit, he does not allow the powers of the force fields in which he lives to decide his identity and the meaning of his destiny.

Jesus Enacts the Kingdom of God

Jesus announces, brings, and enacts the kingdom of God as that communal reality that fulfills human life. He summons all others to the call of that community which God intends for humans and which God is bringing to humans. It is the summons to enjoy others in mutual obedience, service, and love in which each's flourishing does not exclude the flourishing of others though it may be differentiated from others. It is a summons to peace with God and other humans. This kingdom is the communal being of love in which the various stations and locations of persons in the human social worlds do not dictate their eligibility for participation.

In his own love of the Father and his love of others, including the least and the sinful, Jesus himself enacts the presence of the kingdom in the midst of human life. Jesus has a passion for the kingdom of God, with the attendant dispositions to emotions and actions appropriate to the passion. Jesus' erosic attractions are desires formed by his passion for the kingdom. Even in his explicit desires for others and their good in the kingdom, Jesus is not in quest of his own needs independent of others. The dominant and enduring *motive* of his actions in enacting the kingdom is *for the sake of* the Father's will that his fellow humans might live in and for the kingdom of God. In this sense, he is motivated throughout by his love of the Father and his love for others.

Jesus the Enacted Image of God

Jesus is homo theologicus—*the true and full human image of God.*[41] Jesus is the true human from God and for God. Jesus in his life, death, and resurrection enacts the will of the Creator and thereby is what the Creator intended in creating human beings. In his personal and spiritual life he enacts the true human image of the triune God. Jesus lives freely

---

[41] See 2 Cor 4.4; Col 1.15; Heb 1.3.

and lovingly the particular embodied existence of a first-century Palestinian Jew, conditioned by a creaturely and social world not of his own
making but which does not determine the *how* of his life and destiny as
obedience to the God of Israel, the fatherly and motherly Creator.

His enactment of the will of the Father for human life is the an-
nouncement, summons, and presence of the kingdom of God as God's
intended community with humanity and among humans in which communal mutuality and peace are realized. As the human image of God, Jesus is also the true human being. He is the new and definitive Adam, in
whose image all humans were created.[42] In his particular Jewish humanity Jesus is the normative human: in him—according to his pattern of
life—are both male and female *created, reconciled, and redeemed.*

We are now able in retrospect to see that the previous discussions of
humanity as created, as personal, and as spirit were deeply affected by
this understanding of Jesus as the true human being and norm for human
life. The descriptions developed in the previous sections are about the
basic structures and potencies of human being as creature, personal, and
spiritual. These descriptions can now be understood as describing the *essence or nature* of created human being. This essence identifies those
characteristic structures and powers that are definitive of human being as
created by God. This essence also identifies the basic potentialities of
human being. But this description of human essence does not identify
every possible trait human beings might have in common. Yet as the essence of human being, I am claiming that all humans share in this essence.

It is the essence of human being, as creature, personal, and spiritual,
to be an enacted actuality, to be and become actual in the enactments of
her life. It is as spiritual being that the comprehensive actuality of human
being is enacted. It is as spiritual being that the decisive issue of life and
death is posed to human being: *how does one enact one's true humanity?*

Christian faith claims that Jesus—as the true human being—is the
unsurpassable, historical enactment, fulfillment, and realization of the
human essence in its destiny as created by God. Jesus is, in this sense, an
eschatological happening in and for human being. In him Christians see
their own human destiny and fulfillment. In him, by way of contrast,
Christians understand themselves as creatures who have sinned against
God and violated their own proper creaturely essence or nature. *Jesus,
then, is the New Adam who overcomes the corruption of the primordial*

---

[42] 1 Cor 15.14,45; Rom 5.12–21; Jn 1.3–4, 10.

Adam's sin and who reconstitutes human being's destiny before God.
[Rom 5]

It is of this particular Jewish person he was and enacted that we also say in our full christology that his life, death, and resurrection are the very life of God as well. In the chapters on the Person and Work of Jesus Christ, I will explore more explicitly how Jesus' identity and destiny are not simply the identity and destiny of the normative human but of the self-determined identity, enactment, and destiny of the triune God.

Preliminary Observations on Human Sin

The doctrine of human sin is one of the most difficult concepts of Christian faith to keep clear, supple, discriminate, and pertinent. In this task of systematic theology we inquire as to what we mean when we speak of sin and with what right do we speak. What is the Christian grammar of sin? The biblical witness is consistent in both testaments in naming sin [Gr: *hamartia*] as human missing the mark and choosing to live in rebellion against God and in conflict with other humans. But we must note here at the beginning of our discussion of sin that the word 'sin' has many cultural uses that are quite different from the distinctive Christian use. This creates enormous problems for Christian discourse and practice, and we must pause to identify in advance some of these surrogate uses that are sometimes identified—both within and beyond the church—as the Christian concept of sin.

Primarily the Christian concept of sin is easily confused with a variety of 'deficiencies,' 'shortcomings,' 'wrongs,' 'evils,' and 'inadequacies' that play indisputable roles in every human culture. These assignations are part of social systems in their attempt to control and order human behavior and attitudes. These are the judgments about what is valuable and valueless, right and wrong, acceptable and unacceptable in human behavior and in human persons. As social instruments, these judgments become a source of a *diffuse sense of guilt* as a general human phenomenon.

The Christian concept of sin has often been co-opted, corrupted, and distorted by church and culture throughout the church's history. The term 'sin' has been used as a 'tag,' a 'name,' for all sorts of things that are socially unacceptable. Not rarely the distorted concept is used by the powerful in society to control and diminish the power of others. This is espe-

cially evident in the male diminution of females as prime agents and em-
bodiments of sin and in the focus on bodies and sexuality as the prime
sources and bearers of sin. Also there have been widespread racial abuses
of the meaning of sin. The history of these abuses is not pleasant, and
their occurrences in the life of the church are reason enough for us to use
discerning care in our development of the doctrine of sin for the witness
of the church today.

In our time the concept of sin is especially confused, distortable, and
co-optable in some cultural movements and in their discourses and practices of self-understanding. The rise of psychotherapeutic theories and
practices focuses on the sources of guilt and shame as pervasive illnesses
in human life. Then a presumed concept of sin is identified as that which
produces this guilt and shame inappropriately and therefore must be dismantled in therapy in order for the client to overcome her shame and
guilt. As even some psychotherapists have come to realize, some of their
theories and practices have had trouble distinguishing between what I
call 'junk guilt' and 'moral guilt.' By 'junk guilt' I mean that guilt and
shame humans experience that have nothing to do with their moral character and behavior but are foisted on them by their dialogically significant others. Let therapy exorcise this junk guilt! But let it not deal frivo-
lously with the depths of human moral guilt.

There is also the widespread *bourgeois common sense* that people
are a relative mixture of good and bad, that nobody is perfectly good and
nobody is fully evil or bad. Most people, it claims, are 'good enough' if
we are not too 'idealistic' or expect too much. Reference to sin is considered 'bad taste' and is to be omitted from our understanding of the human condition. Is this the misplaced confidence and complacency of
moral mediocrity?

In and out of the church we are confronted with the 'enlightened'
notion that sin is moral wrongdoing, wrong acts, committed by the free
choice of humans, and *correctable* by future free choices of humans to
do what is morally right. The capacity to choose what is right and just is
unimpaired, and people can improve their moral performance if they
only will to try harder. Does this grasp the depths of human incapacity to
will the right consistently? Does this grasp the sense in which humans
need to have their hearts healed and transformed if they are to have the
passions and desires appropriate to willing the good of the other?

We also have the contemporary use in social analysis and in religious
practice of distinguishing sharply between the oppressed—or victim—and the oppressor. This can become a sharp distinction between the

good and the bad, the innocent and the unjust, the saint and the sinner. We end up with a world divided between *the sinners* and *the sinned-against innocents*. As a comprehensive tool for understanding sin, this analysis has difficulty seeing any sin in the oppressed, or if it does, then sees sin only as a function of being a victim. Take away the oppressor and all sin vanishes. Is this sufficiently discerning about the universality of human sin and its multiple forms?

For our purposes we need diagnostically to understand that *sin* and *salvation* are corollary concepts, and a mistake or misreading of one will lead to mistakes or misreadings in the other. Relative to salvation, *what are we saved from and to what are we saved*? If sin and its consequences are what we are saved from, then it is vitally important to grasp deeply just what this sin is and what its consequences are. But we cannot help but notice how various the answers are in the contemporary life and discourse of the church about sin and salvation. It is obviously one of the purposes of constructing this grammar of sin and salvation to aim at creating and recovering some agreement in the life of the church.

Knowledge of Sin in Jesus Christ

Let us begin by asking these critical questions: 'how does one come to the knowledge of sin *as sin*?' Or, 'how does one come to understand oneself as a sinner?' Or, 'how does one become conscious of sin?' Or, in systematic theology, 'how do we develop and rule the concept of sin?' These questions are not the same, but they are interrelated.

Let us consider some inadequate possible answers. First, it might be claimed that we come to know sin by observing empirically the great and widespread harm and injustice humans do to each other and to themselves. There is no doubt that the phenomena of such harm and injustice are illuminated by the concept of sin, but as an empirical generalization such observations do not reach deeply enough into human existence. Second, we might claim to know sin by knowing one's own moral deficiencies. To which the next questions leads: 'moral deficiencies by what standard?' Third, we might claim to know sin by knowing one's own guilt. This is similar to the second claim, but its focus is on the presence of guilt in our consciousness. But again this can obscure the difference between the many socially inculcated junk shames and guilt and moral guilt. But it is apparent that we need some standard of measurement and assessment for grasping what counts as sin.

Kierkegaard can help us here. While he was one of the masters of the modern world in tracking the shape of sin in our lives, he urged us to distinguish between the concept of sin as an empirical generalization and the concept of sin as a dogmatic concept rooted in revelation. What he meant was that the standard or criterion for what it means to be sinner is given in divine revelation. Without the criterion, our empirical probings and analyses might simply wander around in the vast sea of theories about the nature of humanity. Hence, the concept of sin is given to us in God's revelation. We may know our miseries and our unhappiness and our festering guilts, but *we need God to tell us we are sinners.* This is because sin is first and foremost sin against God, not against some social mores.[43]

We need to distinguish, therefore, between the following human phenomena of consciousness: (a) *the consciousness of moral guilt*—the awareness that one has violated a moral principle or rule that has some claim on the person; and (b) *the consciousness of sin*—the awareness of one's violation of God's covenantal rule *and* the awareness of God's reconciling and healing forgiveness in Jesus Christ. It is my contention that consciousness of sin—in the distinctively Christian sense—is a consciousness that includes both the awareness of violating God's covenantal will and rule and the awareness of God's forgiving grace in Jesus Christ. Though it is evident in the OT that sin is identified as 'missing the mark' in relation to the covenant of God, the grammar of sin in Christian faith includes the further respects in which the knowledge of sin is affected by Jesus Christ.

This knowledge of sin is itself given in God's revelation in Jesus Christ as the one in whom true human being is revealed and who stands in contrast to the sinner, and as the one who loves, atones for, and forgives the human sinner. For Christian faith, sin is definitively and decisively revealed in Jesus Christ as that which is *judged, repudiated, and forgiven* by God in Jesus' atoning and gracious life, death, and resurrection. In the encounter with Jesus Christ, sin comes to light as to its *gravity, extent, self-involvement, and its consequences, defeat, and destiny.* The Christian doctrine of sin, therefore, must elaborate how these dimensions of sin interrelate and issue in discerning discourses and apt practices of faith.

As rooted in revelation, *this knowledge of sin is faith's knowledge*

---

[43] See Kierkegaard, *The Sickness unto Death,* 96–104.

and therefore from the first is confessional, self-involving, and existential knowledge. While we may have understood moral guilt in ourselves and others, sin—as sin judged in its profound depths and forgiven in Jesus Christ—is not yet grasped until it is known that *my sin* is forgiven in Jesus Christ. Hence, *I am a sinner.* Or, as discourse in the church, that *our sins* are forgiven and *we are sinners.* Without this elemental self-involvement and confession, the concept of sin is subject to much misuse and abuse. The concept of sin might then refer *only* to the sins of others. In this way the word 'sin' is used to refer to the sins of 'them,' the evil 'others' who are now demonized. It goes without saying that this trap of misunderstanding is one into which Christians and the church have fallen repeatedly over the centuries.

Hence, *Jesus Christ is himself the criterion for discerning how deeply enmeshed in sin we are and the criterion for discerning the unfathomable graciousness of God's atoning and forgiving love of sinners.*[44]

Jesus Christ Brings Sin to Light

Jesus Christ brings to light[45] *that I have refused to be the creaturely, personal, and spiritual being I was created to be. In the passions, desires, and decisions of my life—in my heart—I have not wanted to be:*

    a.   dependent upon the living Creator of all things;

    b.   finite and vulnerable, subject to pain, suffering, and death;

    c.   a creature in interdependence with other creatures;

    d.   before God in covenant, to be God's co-partner;

    e.   personally accountable to God for how I live and become in

---

[44] There have been some discerning books on sin in recent decades that are worth perusal. But not one pursues consistently the theme of seeing sin primarily in terms of Jesus Christ. See William F. May, *A Catalogue of Sins* (New York: Holt, Rinehart and Winston, 1967); Cornelius Plantinga Jr., *Not the Way It's Supposed to Be: A Breviary of Sin* (Grand Rapids, Mich.: Eerdmans, 1995); Marjorie Hewitt Suchocki, *The Fall into Violence: Original Sin in Relational Theology* (New York: Continuum, 1995); Ted Peters, *Sin: Radical Evil in Soul and Society* (Grand Rapids, Mich.: Eerdmans, 1994).

[45] It is to Karl Barth that I am indebted for articulating so vividly that Jesus Christ is the one who brings sin to light, though Barth may not appreciate all the uses to which I have put that fundamental insight. See the orienting discussion which focuses the christological character of his account of sin in *Church Dogmatics*, IV/1, 358–413.

time, for my enacted actuality;

f. responsible for and open to the other—to my brother and sister,
    my neighbor, the stranger, and the enemy;

g. accountable and fully aware of the extensive and destructive
    harm I inflict on others and on myself.

In sum: how I have not wanted to be and become that spiritual being created in the image of God and constituted by God's Holy Spirit.

Jesus Christ brings to light how *uneager and fearful* I am of being
the one for whom he lived and died, of being forgiven, of being in need
of grace in order to be whole and healed and of seeing all human others
as forgiven as the ones for whom Jesus Christ also lived and died. It is
with fear and trembling that I fall into the hands of the living mercy of
God.

*Jesus Christ brings to light that I have violated and broken all the
right relationships, intended in God's creating, with God, with myself,
with the human others, and with the whole creation.* I want life on my
own terms or on terms that I can control. I want to choose my own value
sources—my own gods—that will give me the meaning, direction, and
hope I determine I need. I have yearned for autonomy—utter independence of others—and I have fallen into slavery to others, wanting them
to sanctify my decisions and my life. I have wanted only those covenants
that might serve my own interests and have feared being bound to others
in obligations and promises. Jesus Christ brings to light how deeply corrupt my heart is, how my passions and desires pivot around my own perceived advantage and security at the expense and disadvantage of others
and how I refuse to be responsible for my heart. He brings to light how
death strikes such fear in my life, how it haunts my relationships, how it
provokes selfishness and alienation and violence.

*Jesus Christ decisively brings to light the universality of God's grace
and forgiveness and therefore the universality of sin.* God's forgiving
grace in Jesus Christ is wholly God's gift and is offered unconditionally,
without dependence on personal merit or distinction or moral achievement. The forgiveness of sin is *for me* and is my forgiveness, but it is not
a forgiveness *only* for me. If Christ died for us "while we were yet sinners" [Rom 5.8], then are not all who sin universally included in the love
of God revealed in his death? Ponder Romans 3.23ff: "For there is no
distinction, since all have sinned and fall short of the glory of God; they
are now justified by his grace as a gift, through the redemption that is in
Christ Jesus, whom God put forward as a sacrifice of atonement by his
blood, effective through faith." That *all have sinned* is not an empirical

generalization from the 'experience of evil,' to which there might in principle be an exception. Hence, *the dogmatic grammar of sin and forgiveness is this*:

All humans are loved and forgiven in Jesus Christ.
Therefore, all humans are in need of God's love and forgiveness.
Therefore, all humans are sinners.

By way of contrast, the grammar is not: some are sinners and the world is divided between saints and sinners. And neither is it: only I (and those like me) are forgiven because I have repented and received Jesus Christ.

Jesus Christ brings to light the seriousness of God's judgment and wrath against human sin, against the human violation of the covenantal order of relationships. God says 'no' to human sin and identifies it as that which cannot secure flourishing and blessing and as that which cannot of itself bring peace and hope. The forgiveness of sin is not a mere heavenly decision of God unknown to humans. It is a forgiveness that costs God something. It is not that forgiveness of sin is contrary to God's nature and therefore difficult. It is that the revelation to humans of sin's defeat is costly to God. In Christ God takes upon Godself the burden of human sin and its consequences. Here the doctrine of the work of Jesus Christ as atonement and reconciliation will have to be fully identified and elaborated. Without this elaboration of atonement, the concept of forgiveness of sin can easily deteriorate into a bourgeois sentimentality in which humans pronounce themselves fundamentally 'O.K.' It can become a glib and empty 'God loves us all just as we are,' wherein there is no profound self-involving grasp either of oneself as a sinner or of the God who loves us in the cross and resurrection of Jesus Christ.

Jesus Christ brings to light the full depth and range of sin. His life, death, and resurrection vividly reveals how we are both *doers of sin* and *victims of sin*, of our own sin and the sins of others—reveals how deeply intertwining and consuming sin is in human social life. Sin alienates us from God, from self, from the human other, and from the creaturely world. Sin infects and corrupts *the totality of our spiritual being* and thereby the creaturely and personal depths of that being. Sin renders our linguistic, epistemic, emotive, and agential potencies captive to lies, misconstruals, hatred, enmity, rivalry, covetousness, and violence. Sin is present in social structures and institutions.[46] This is the *systemic* character of sin that infects human social worlds. The principalities and powers of the world become force fields and instruments of sin. Sin infects the discourses and practices of everyday life, becoming the instruments of falsehoods, lies, self-deception, oppression, and death. In all these ways sin is death-dealing and life-forfeiting.

Hence, being-in-sin is not a 'more or less,' not a 'here and there,' not 'sometimes.' This is not to say that all sinful acts of harm against others and oneself are leveled out as being simply of the same moral gravity. But it does warn us against trying to find exoneration for our sinning by comparative looking at the 'worse' sins of others. It is also the case that Jesus Christ brings to light that the sin done against us, the harm from others that seeks to disable us, *is not something we otherwise deserve.*

While Christians are called to practice forgiveness of others, sin is not something we can overcome by forgiving ourselves, not something the world can forgive and heal, not something another can identify and rectify. Sin is not the sort of disorder within human life that can be set right and healed simply by a person or persons deciding and doing the right thing. The human heart needs to be forgiven and reconstituted and freed from the encumbrances of past sins, and only God has the power and right to enact the forgiveness that can finally heal and give new life and hope. When we confess our sins in communal worship, we do not pronounce ourselves forgiven and healed but hear the declaration of God's forgiveness and healing.

Jesus Christ brings to light the many manifestations and symptoms of sin that are discernible even apart from Jesus Christ, but now become discernible as sin. These are the multiple, complex, and life-encompassing ways in which humans violate God's created and covenantal order. These are the things we 'know' from 'experience' as evil or unhappy or harmful or as undesirable or wicked, which we might now see as the manifestations of sin. It is not as though humans have not experienced betrayals, lies, violence, selfishness, and evil in their lives. They have. But Jesus Christ brings to light the respects in which all these are against God and yet the respects in which these are forgiven and defeated by God. Reinhold Niebuhr showed the great power of the Christian concept of sin to illuminate empirically many areas of human individual and social life. But Niebuhr sometimes confused this empirical

---

[46] The 'world as infected by sin' was one of the three meanings of the word 'world' in the earlier discussion of the dialectic between church and world in chapter one.

illumination by treating it as the *dogmatic foundation* of the concept of sin. Nevertheless, the full elaboration of the Christian doctrine of sin does have *compelling sense-making power* for how we construe and understand ourselves and our social worlds.

Jesus Christ brings to light the perils of a doctrine of sin cut loose from or detached from the forgiveness of sin. When such detachment happens, the discourse about sin becomes a general negativity toward human beings and human life. It becomes a severe and inescapable judgment that cannot confer life but brings only denunciation, debilitating shame, death, and annihilation. It becomes a repudiation of human life—a 'put-down'—to which humans will often respond by refusing to be put down and rejected and therefore become vulnerable to Promethean self-assertion at the expense of others: 'I am better than . . . ,' 'I am as good as . . . ,' 'We are better than. . . .' Does this not deepen sin and produce resentment? Is this an idolatrous self-esteem? But also when the discourse about sin is cut loose from the mercy and forgiveness of God, persons are vulnerable to accepting the repudiation and put-down as what one deserves anyhow. Plunged into a self-loathing already present, does not this declaration of sin simply plunge one further? Isn't this an idolatrous lack of the divinely given self-esteem that comes in knowing the love of God for oneself? Therefore, doesn't this misuse of the discourse of sin only increase the human unwillingness to hear the grace of Jesus Christ as life and hope? It is the temptation of much prophecy to judge too harshly and to assume too easily that anyone can overcome sin by her own purposeful efforts. Isn't this prophecy cut loose from the Gospel? Here we must affirm that the church is the prophet *only* of God's judging grace in Jesus Christ. Judgment of sin without grace only entrenches sin more deeply into the matrix of human life. Is not this what troubled Paul about how the law can drive sin into fortresses of hard hearts and mean spirits?[47]

Jesus Christ brings to light that sin is both a 'condition' of human life and an 'act' of the individual person. As condition, sin is already there universally in the matrix of human life, especially in the *habits and actions of the human heart.* Sin forms human beings, and from that formation arises the acts that confirm the sin and—in their repetitions—strengthen and harden the habits. It is the condition of having such an encumbered will that it chooses possibilities that only further

---

[47] See Romans *passim*, especially chapter seven.

empower and entrench the encumbrances, thus intractably imprisoning human life.

The Origin of Sin

In Christian grammar there does not seem to be any satisfactory answer to the questions of *'why do humans sin?'* and *'why do all humans sin?'* Jesus Christ brings out the fact and universality of sin. But why does sin happen? The church has refused to say there is a necessary ontological explanation positing a universal cause whereby all sin. Is sin a necessity of human nature as created by God? If so, then that would seem to indict God and leave humans helpless victims of their created nature. Is sin caused by some transcendent negative principle of evil that seduces all—by, say, the devil? There are demonic powers, of course, but they are functions of and manifestations of human sinfulness, not therefore the *ultimate* explanation of human sinning. Such demonic powers do, however, perpetuate sin through human social worlds. But it does not clarify matters to posit a demonic principle that universally *causes* humans to sin, and the church has refused to say the devil is as ultimate as God. The devil and the demonic powers are no more than creaturely.

With the traditions of the church, I claim that sin is not necessary to the essence or nature of created human being. Hegel tried to argue that sin was simply part of the necessary process of human maturation and individuation from divinity—to be other than God entails standing against God.[48] However, for us, since Jesus lived and fulfilled the human essence, it cannot be said that it is a necessity of the human essence that humans sin. So sin is not the same as being finite and creaturely in distinction from God. The human problem of sin is not that we are not God; it is that we somehow fall into the wrong and rebel against God.

---

[48] It is singularly mischievous when the 'fall' of Adam and Eve is interpreted as the natural maturation of human beings in coming to the knowledge of good and evil. After all—it is contended—is not such knowledge desirous, as opposed to that dreadful preceding state of innocence and ignorance? But this construction of the story utterly hides from us the presiding point that God had first *commanded* Adam not to eat of the tree of the knowledge of good and evil. In Adam and Eve's eating of the tree they are already violating God's command and arrogating to themselves the power to decide what is good and what is evil. The heart of their rebellion is refusing to hear God's command, which is the proper source for knowing and identifying what is good and evil.

What about Adam and 'Original Sin'?

Taking a lead from Paul in Romans 5 and First Corinthians 15, the tradition developed the notion that Adam and Eve's sin was the *original sin*, which then plunges all human offspring into sin as well. From this original sin, the rest of humanity *inherits* sin—are born into sin. After Adam, sin preexists the coming to be of Adam's progeny and thereby enslaves them as they come to be. They have no choice in the matter. Augustine struggled mightily with these issues and finally taught that Adam had the possibility and the power not to sin [*posse non peccare*], but Adam's progeny do not have the power not to sin [*non posse non peccare*]. This is why humans need a new power from God to overcome sin and to not sin. Hence, Adam's original sin infects and enslaves us all.[49]

But even here it is not clear *why Adam* and *Eve* sinned. There was no *had to* in their sinning. Finally, we are confronted with the conclusion that sin is somehow rooted in the freedom of self-determination that God created humans to have. *Sin simply happens in the finite freedom of human persons.* In creating human beings God constituted them with the possibility of not responding to the summons to obedient fellowship with God. God permits sin to happen. Hence, relative to God's creative intention, *sin is a surd, an inexplicable but permitted irrationality. It is what God did not will and what should never have been.*

The notion of original sin as something biologically inherited and transmitted through sexual conduct—of which women came to be seen as the primary *seducers* of an otherwise unsuspecting male—has done great harm to persons historically and has misled Christian discourse and practice concerning human sexuality and women. This tradition of original sin teaching and practice must be firmly repudiated and dismantled from authentic Christian discourse and practice.

But the image of sin as transmitted through sexual intercourse and human birthing was a clumsy way of trying to explain the universality of sin and the transmission of sin from generation to generation. We can retrieve some elements of the notion of *original sin* by noting that humans are born into and raised in the midst of sinful humans and sinful human social structures. Sin seems to preexist in our social worlds even before a particular individual comes to exist in those worlds. Hence, per-

---

[49] *The City of God*, bk. 22, chap. 30.

sons live in the midst of sin and ingest sinning into their hearts without
ever having some *first moment* in which they clearly and decisively first
choose to sin. Mimetic desire—which we discussed previously—has the
power to induce rivalry, envy, enmity, fear, and violence. In our dialogical situation with significant others—others both as individuals and as
force fields of social relations—the turn in upon oneself in selfishness is
cultivated and reinforced. Hence, we humans reproduce Adam's sin in
our own peculiar self-determined sinning. This is not a necessity of human existence, but it does seem an *inevitability*—to use the language of
Reinhold Niebuhr.[50]

Let us look again at the story of Adam. In Hebrew *adam* simply is
the general name for *man* or *human being*. Consider Genesis 1.27:

> So God created *adam* in his image,
> in the image of God he created him;
> male and female he created them.

Yet *adam* is also used as the proper name for a particular human being: the first human male created by God and the one who violates God's
command. There are no decisive theological reasons for regarding *Adam*
as the historically first male human who sinned and from whom our sinning is destined. But Adam is also *prototypical human being*—the story
of everyone. 'In Adam we sinned all' is our story of our willing to sin.
"Everybody's last name is Adam."[51]

Therefore, I do not want merely to trash the concept of original sin,
however much I do want to reinterpret it. Further, the concept of original
sin and its sexual transmission was used in traditions as a way of asserting the universality of sin. While we can see a usefulness in the doctrine
insofar as it points us to the social and historical transmission of sinning,
I have asserted here the universality of sin from a christological basis.
We do not need the older concept of original sin to accomplish this task.

I do also abjure from the position that says God cannot hold us responsible for our sin unless there is some identifiable point in a person's
life in which he self-consciously confronts the question of whether he
will be obedient to God or not, and then chooses 'freely' to be disobedi-
ent. This analysis is bloodlessly abstract and completely fails to grasp the

---

[50] See Reinhold Niebuhr, *The Nature and Destiny of Man*, vol. 1, *Human Nature* (New York: Scribners, 1955) 251–254, 262–263.

[51] Leander E. Keck, *The Church in Conflict* (Nashville, Tenn.: Abingdon, 1993), 61.

deep grip sin seems to have on us humans. We are responsible for our sinning because such sinning is our own choice and enactment, but Augustine has correctly seen that we cannot simply, by further choices and enactments, eradicate the sins we have already committed and prevent more sins.

We must acknowledge a temptation to which the church has succumbed repeatedly in the past. I have argued that human being's created nature is not the cause of sin. But, given the universality of sin and its inescapable clutches and enslavement, it is sometimes said that it is 'human nature to sin.' While I think the point here was to interpret the universality of sin, the use of the term 'nature' is deeply misleading and confusing. I propose that we reserve the locution 'human nature' to designate only humanity's created essence—which as such is not sinful. Humans are not *enslaved* by their created nature. But when we take cognizance of the habitual and intractable character of human sin, we can see the meaning of talking about our 'sinful nature' or 'second nature.' These locutions do thus acknowledge the givenness of the *condition of sin.*

Human Anxiety and Sin

While it is not an explanation in the sense of telling us exhaustively why sin happens, the account of Søren Kierkegaard is illuminating and about as much as can be said. Greatly simplified, *sin is rooted in the self's anxiety occasioned by its awareness of temporal possibility.* The confrontation with the uncertainty of the future—with future possibilities, with alternatives, with the unknown—fills the self with *anxiety* as to *which* possibility or alternative to choose and actualize and fills with *dread* as to the possible consequences of the choice. This anxiety occasions the self's quest to be secure and free of anxiety, to have a future that is safe, secure, and nonthreatening. The quest for security precipitates *closure* to God, to one's theologically related self, and to other humans. But why should or must it precipitate such dread and closure? There is no answer. *And in Jesus such encounter with possibility does not precipitate anxiety, dread, and closure.* That we can recognize ourselves in Kierkegaard's analysis confirms the power of our temporal anxiety. But that we do not in our anxiety flee to the everlasting mercy of God remains an inexplicable surd shrouded in our finite freedom.[52]

Exploring the Multiple Shapes and Faces of Sin

The Bible and church traditions are rich and variegated but in basic consensus about the many shapes and faces of human sin. My purpose in this section is to explore some of these shapes and see where we can find a consensus.

The Augustinian Tradition

The Augustinian tradition has been formidable in history in shaping the church's understanding of sin. Among many others, Paul Tillich and Reinhold Niebuhr are prominent exponents of this tradition.[53] The three basic shapes of sin are unbelief, pride, and concupiscence. *Unbelief* is the most elemental face of sin and is the turning away from God and the creation of idols. It is the refusal to be the creature God has intended in creating humanity. Rather than trusting in God, human unbelief turns away and trusts—invests in—that which is not God and which cannot finally confer blessing and flourishing. *Pride [hubris]* is that turning toward oneself that becomes self-centeredness and selfishness, excluding God and the human other. In pride we engage in the Promethean effort to have life on our own terms and under our own control. This unmitigated primacy of self-interest—as the controlling passion of one's whole life—subordinates other persons to being no more than instruments of one's own interests and desires and their satisfactions. As Niebuhr convincingly shows, hubris is also reflected in group pride or the pride of those who regard themselves as *alike* over against and in self-righteous superiority over others. *Concupiscence* is the face of inordinate and distorted desire or erosic attraction that does not desire the goods that can confer life and flourishing. While it includes lust and compulsive sexual desire, it is not simply these alone. In concupiscence human desire searches urgently for that satisfaction and happiness that can bring en-

[52] See Kierkegaard's *The Concept of Anxiety*, ed. and trans. Reidar Thomte, in collaboration with Albert B. Anderson, *Kierkegaard's Writings*, vol. 8 (Princeton, N.J.: Princeton University Press, 1980) and *The Sickness unto Death*.
[53] See Tillich, *Systematic Theology*, vol. 2, especially 44–55; Niebuhr, *Nature and Destiny*, vol. 1, especially 178–264.

during satiation. But such enduring satiation is forever elusive—human desiring seems unable to find that object that will finally bring peace and satisfaction. Since God is the only object that can provide enduring happiness and ultimately satisfy human desire, the restless heart is driven to search desperately for that next satisfaction that will quench the appetite, misunderstanding how transient the satisfaction is from any finite object. Such distorted eros is rooted in and expressive of a corrupted heart.

Paul, Luther, and Early Barth

In Paul, Luther, and the early Barth, the primary face of sin is *works righteousness*. It is the multifaceted attempt to secure and justify one's life, but now justified in such wise that one can control and determine the justification. It is manifest as idolatry in the creation of gods who will serve one's justification and give one meaning on one's own terms. This sin is especially evident in *human religiousness*—even in 'Christianity'—as the prideful attempt to make oneself righteous, religiously fit, morally upright, in order thereby to be justified and deserving of a positive reward and destiny. We might characterize this face of sin as the search for the religious *'determiners-of-destiny'* so that one can secure one's destiny in the face of uncertainty. When this sin gets a grip on us, we cannot face the radical judgment of sin and radical conferral of grace by the free and loving God revealed in Christ Jesus. This is the quest for a righteousness and justification to which one has a *right because one deserves it*. We should firmly note here that sin as works righteousness always expresses and results in an erroneous understanding of God.

The Later Barth

The later Barth—with my taking some liberties of interpretation—puts some interesting twists on the traditional faces of sin. There are three faces of sin: pride, sloth, and falsehood.[54] *Pride* is that willing to be lord over one's own life and the lives of others and the whole creation. It is the inclination to control, to dominate, and to be served. Such pride is rooted fundamentally in *ingratitude*: we refuse to accept gladly our human creatureliness. And we continue to refuse the grace of God in

---

[54] *Church Dogmatics*, IV/1, 358–513 [Pride]; IV/2, 378–498 [Sloth]; IV/3, First Half, 368–480 [Falsehood].

Jesus Christ. It is to be noted that in using the term 'lord' in describing this sin, Barth is also dismantling the various worldly understandings of lord in contrast to the way in which Jesus Christ is Lord of the world as the one who serves God and others. *Sloth*—a concept available in the Middle Ages but much neglected in Protestant theology with its preoccupation with pride—is the downward fall of the *refusal to be free*, to be and become a spirit lovingly constituted by God's Spirit. In sloth the self relinquishes the summons-to-be-a-spirit to the powers of others, to the powers of the social order, or to the power of 'fate.' It is to allow powers other than God to fundamentally name us and tell us who we are and what our value is. It is the uncanny refusal to be a particular, responsible self before God who has commitments and projects of personal integrity and virtue. Kierkegaard also referred to this face of sin as the *despair in the unwillingness to be a self*.[55] *Falsehood* is that shape of sin in which we will the lie about ourselves and the neighbor. It is the perpetual human inclination to *self-deception*, of refusing to face the truth about oneself, including that one is a forgiven sinner. It is especially the refusal to acknowledge grace and the confession of sin and the refusal to acknowledge the human other as graced and forgiven. We prefer to *misrepresent* our situation before God and in the world. This face and power of sin is evident in the discourses and practices of human social worlds.

A Medieval List of Sins

Christopher Morse has an insightful updated medieval list of sins and their social consequences:[56]
   a. the primary sins are *superbia* [pride] and *acedia* [despair] which afflict individual persons and prompt their affliction of others by violating their good;
   b. *avaritia* [greed] as the crippling of the neighbor through selfish and inordinate acquisition;
   c. *invidia* [envy] as begrudging and willing to confiscate the neighbor's good;
   d. *gula* [gluttony] as overconsumption in neglect of others' good;
   e. *luxuria* [lust] as the violation of the integrity of another;
   f. *ira* [fury or anger] as ill-will directed against another.

---

[55] See Kierkegaard, *The Sickness unto Death*, 49–67.

[56] See Christopher Morse, *Not Every Spirit: A Dogmatics of Christian Disbelief* (Valley Forge, Pa.: Trinity, 1994), 242.

Liberation Theology and Systemic Sin

While some of the previously mentioned shapes of sin were not without their implications for the social analysis of sin, it is to the various brands of liberation theologies that we owe a debt for retrieving the genuinely biblical dimensions of societal sin. So far as the common theme of liberation theologies has been the liberation from oppression largely understood as social oppression, they have emphasized *sin as the systemic domination of a less powerful group by another more powerful group.*[57] The prominent faces of systemic sin are 'sexism'—domination of women by men; 'racism'—domination of one race or ethnic group by another; 'classism'—domination of one economic class by another, especially the domination of the poor and impoverished by the wealthier powers. We could easily add to this list 'militarism,' 'nationalism,' 'ecological anthropocentrism,' and 'heterosexism.' Liberation theologies have brought to clarity the multiple ways in which sin infects systemically the social worlds and through these worlds infects individuals. Such sin affects individuals as *victims* of the dominating social powers; it infects the individual's self-understanding and *identity* by virtue of her internalizing the oppressive identity which the dominating powers communicate [our dialogical being]; it infects individuals as they become themselves actual *agents* of oppression.

Liberation theologies thus offer helpful and insightful ways of recovering the biblical language about 'principalities and powers' and 'elemental spirits of the world' that transcend simple individual, human decisions and yet exercise massive destructive influence on human life.[58] I proposed earlier that we think of these transpersonal powers as *force fields of evil* that seduce and oppress persons into situations of conflict, violence, enmity, and misery. These force fields of evil are the demonic powers of the kingdom of death that demean and destroy human life and hope. Think of the force fields of patriarchy, of ethnic enmity, of racial prejudice, of national pride and rivalry, of practices of scapegoating the frightful Others [*them*] as the cause of our misery and fear, and of the swirling and spiraling of violence enacted for a 'justified cause.'

---

[57] For the many ways in which liberation engages in praxis-oriented, social theological analyses of sin, see *Mysterium Liberationis: Fundamental Concepts of Liberation Theology*, ed. Ignacio Ellacuría and Jon Sobrino (Maryknoll, N.Y.: Orbis, 1993).

[58] See Gal 4.3, 9; Rom 8.38; Eph 3.10; 6.12; Col 1.16; 2.8, 15, 20.

Some Feminist Concerns

In addition to providing insightful analyses of systemic sin, some feminist theologians have raised some appropriate questions about how some major Protestant theologians have described sin.[59] They question the adequacy of thinking of sin primarily in terms of human pride. Isn't this only a particular problem for Western males who are bedeviled by aggression and the urge to dominate? Pride is a problem for them. But what about women and other oppressed and marginalized people who have had any sense of self squelched and diminished by the social powers? Is it adequate to see their situation in terms of *pride*? Don't those in these situations really need a greater sense of self, a sense of *pride and self-esteem*? And hasn't *self-denial*—as the opposite of pride—been the preached instrument of ruling classes and males to control women and other powerless persons?

These are compelling insights and show that 'sin' and 'pride' are *terms* that are used in a wide variety of ways and can easily obscure or distort the proper Christian use. It is indeed a supreme but painful irony that the excoriation of pride—in the name of Christian faith—has been used by the powerful as a way of controlling others. But however apt might be the critique of these sinful practices of control, we do not want to fall into the trap of exempting the oppressed of embodying any of the faces of sin. Maybe the concept of *sin as sloth* can be helpful here. Given the historical oppression of women, they may be more subject to the sin of sloth—the sin of refusing to become the free persons they are in Christ and allowing oppressive social powers to place, identify, and determine them and their possibilities—than to the sin of pride—selfishly willing to dominate others for one's own ends. These persons need to have that sense of self as one summoned to life and loved by God and therefore persons who know they have a value that the oppressive systems can neither give nor take away. But the church must be wary in its teachings about *self-esteem*—and there is a powerful teaching about self-esteem before God—that it not appear to build on an esteem that is controlled by

---

[59] Valerie Saiving is generally credited with first raising concerns about the way in which the concept of sin was focused around pride; see her essay from *The Journal of Religion* (April 1960) in *Womanspirit Rising*, ed. Carol P. Christ and Judith Plaskow (San Francisco: Harper, 1979), 25–42. For a more sustained treatment of these issues, see Judith Plaskow, *Sex, Sin, and Grace: Women's Experience and the Theologies of Reinhold Niebuhr and Paul Tillich* (Washington, D.C.: University Press of America, 1980).

the world or that purchases the esteem at the expense of other persons.[60]

But this feminist critique does show us how the language of faith can be corrupted. Simply on the basis of the analyses of sin that we have been considering, we should remind Christians in positions of social power to forswear speaking of pride and self-denial without first applying such concepts to themselves and their social power.

A Grammatical Synopsis

Let me attempt a grammatical synopsis of the shapes and faces of sin. I affirm that *the primal form of sin is unbelief*: the refusal to acknowledge God's creative summons to be spirit in relationship to God; the refusal to believe in God, to trust in God; the repudiation of belief that God exists; the investment of one's heart in that which is not-God. It is ingratitude in not gladly being and becoming a creaturely spirit created in the image of God. Unbelief is not primarily an intellectual dissent from belief—it is basically the practical refusal to acknowledge the triune God in one's actual living. It is *practical and passionate atheism*. With the true God practically out of the picture, unbelief issues into the other forms of sin as *pride, concupiscence, sloth, and falsehood*. It is the practical unbeliever who is consumed by prideful self-centeredness and illicit self-love, by distorted and unruly desire, by slothful self-forgetfulness as one created for fellowship with God, and by the falsehoods of self-deception and lies.

These faces of sin grind themselves into human existence, becoming the habituated condition of human life, from which the continual acts and patterns of action emerge that devastate human life and society. These faces of sin are the roots of the systemic sins that afflict humans as doers of sin and victims of sin. And these sins are transmitted by traditions of our social worlds, thus perpetuating sin as *the way things simply are*.

---

[60] See Kathryn Tanner, *The Politics of God: Christian Theologies and Social Justice* (Minneapolis: Fortress, 1992), 228ff, for an insightful distinction between '*idolatrous self-esteem*' and '*non-idolatrous self-esteem*.'

The Consequences of Sin and Jesus Christ

Sin is the disruption and corruption of the creation, of the God-intended human world and its impingement on the world of other creatures. Sin corrupts human persons and human social worlds. In this corruption we see how the disintegrating and destructive consequences of sin are inherent in the very structure of sin's enactment. Hence, it is appropriate to say that *sin corrupts human nature*—the human essence. It does not *destroy* the nature, but it diminishes and thwarts the great potencies with which God endowed human beings.

Sin corrupts, distorts, and fractures the being-in-act of human being—humans enact a life that is *alienated* from its own creaturely, personal, and spiritual essence, that is alienated from the enactments of other humans, and alienated from the enactments of God's living actuality. Sin profoundly brings forth conflict among the enactments of persons and the enactments of God's life.

Sin corrupts the human heart and her personal linguistic, epistemic, emotive, and agential life, rendering her vulnerable to hardness of heart and passions and desires at the expense of her own true good. Such corruption of the heart—as the alienation of the person from her own true good—leads in the direction of destruction of the personal self and death. Despair arises about the possibilities of life and destiny. Persons become thwarted by their own self-deception, illicit self-love, and inappropriate self-forgetfulness. Such corruption of the heart issues into entrenched habits that diminish and subvert human flourishing.

Sin corrupts human social worlds and institutionalizes human fear, discord, enmity, and injustice. The great potencies and structures of human spiritual being are corrupted into instruments of pride, concupiscence, sloth, and falsehood, resulting in and perpetuating fear, mistrust, misery, oppression, rivalry, conflict, and violence. These social worlds and their systems and subsystems of relations and relationships become occupied by force fields of sin that produce and induce mean-spiritedness and hard-heartedness among persons. The pervasive presence of violence, both among persons and within social institutions, and both in its random occurrences and its institutionalized social rationalizations and justifications, is a salient sign of the power of sin. Hierarchies of power arise and the distributions of goods are controlled by the powerful at the expense of the less powerful. Thus sin fills human historical life with despair, rivalry, strife, conflict, violence, enmity, fear, and hate in such a way that humans are *both agents of sin and victims of sin*. Sin perpetuates and transmits sin.

Sin fuels the great power of the fear of death. Thereby death is given a presumed finality and consummating judgment. Death—and the threat of death—instill fear and enmity, which confer on death the power to determine human identity and destiny. Death becomes the final determination of human life—that destined end, the avoidance of which becomes the supreme and urgent goal of life. Pride, sloth, and falsehood are inflamed and provoked by the stalking fact of death that confronts every human person and is present in every human social world.

Sin most drastically alienates persons and societies from the reality of the triune God. In their refusal to be God's valuable creatures made in God's image, human spirits intend the eradication and death of God. God becomes the Enemy, the Stranger, or the Absent and Silent One. Sin aims to cut off humans from the creative power of God. *This is sin in its primal reality as unbelief.* Precisely because the spiritual being of humanity has not been destroyed, there are still signals of longing for God. But this longing—ironically—can intensify the desperate creation of idols.

In all these consequences of sin it is manifest that sin is not a shallow situation from which humans can extricate themselves if they just try harder—if they just will to be good. In the depths of these consequences, *the human will is profoundly encumbered and enslaved by and in sin, and therefore without the power to overcome the past of sin and the future threat of sin. Left to their own devices—in sinning and being sinned against—human destiny is alienation, conflict and death.*

Jesus Christ Affects the Consequences of Sin

But from the perspective of the self-communicating life of God in Jesus Christ it is possible to understand that *sin seeks to enact what is finally impossible*—that human decisions, institutions, and social arrangements are the final arbiters of the meaning of human life and the ultimate conferers of human identity and destiny. *Sin wills to be the ultimate determiner-of-destiny.* That this is finally impossible is what the triune God has been trying to communicate in salvific interactions with the world.

Sin is what is already defeated and overcome in the death and resurrection of Jesus Christ. Sin wills to have a life separate from the free love of the triune God, which is to will only death and which is finally impossible. Sin falls under the radical judgment and wrath of God: God says 'no' to human sin and refuses to grant sin the power to determine ultimate destiny. In Jesus Christ God acts to defeat the power of sin as the final real power in human life. In Jesus' death, God dies a human death at the hands of the principalities and powers of sin and therewith disarms them of their presumed power to crush, control, and determine human life before God. *God takes the sins of the world upon God's own Life.* Jesus Christ—in his life, death, and resurrection—reveals and enacts the love of God as that supreme and final power that will not allow sin to triumph ultimately. *In his resurrection, Jesus Christ is established as the Lord of the world and its creational history. Sin is defeated as that imperious lord and presumptuous determiner of human life and destiny.*

Sin—in its massive particularities of power and scope—may continue to dominate the individual and corporate *historic destinies* of persons, but even its power in history is limited and doomed: nothing of whatever magnitude of sin and evil will be able to separate persons in their historical becoming and destiny from the ultimately triumphant love of God. Precisely in human historical becoming and destiny, sin is what is under sustained and sovereign assault by the triune life of God in her liberating and redeeming work as the Holy Spirit. The Holy Spirit—the Spirit of the Father and the Spirit of Jesus Christ—moves within the world, empowering movements of the human spirit to bring good out of evil—empowering liberation and redemption. Sin can historically be overcome and redeemed by God's triune action and the response of persons who are forgiven, know they are forgiven, become new creatures, and live in freedom and love for God and others.

Sin is shown to be that which has no real future in God's ultimate redemption of the world. The resurrection of Jesus Christ is the definitive signal that the powers of sin are eschatologically doomed.

These are the decisive reasons why sin is not yet understood if it is not understood through Jesus Christ. Hence, Christians are precisely the persons who come to know themselves as sinners because they know their sin and the sins of the whole world as having been dealt with and defeated in Jesus Christ. In knowing this, they are empowered by the Holy Spirit to faithful lives—performing liberating works of love for the neighbor and conveying hope in the ultimate triumph of God's grace. The Christian witness to the reality of God is the witness to the triune God's defeat of sin and promise of ultimate salvation.